FROM YAHWEH TO YAHOO!

THE HISTORY OF COMMUNICATION

Robert W. McChesney and John C. Nerone, editors

A list of books in the series appears at the end of this book.

From Yahweh to Yahoo!

The Religious Roots
of the Secular Press

DOUG UNDERWOOD

UNIVERSITY OF ILLINOIS PRESS

URBANA AND CHICAGO

© 2002 by the Board of Trustees
of the University of Illinois
All rights reserved
Manufactured in the United States of America
C 5 4 3 2 1

∞ This book is printed on acid-free paper.

Library of Congress Cataloging-in-Publication Data
Underwood, Doug.
From Yahweh to Yahoo! : the religious roots of the secular press /
Doug Underwood.
p.   cm. — (The history of communication)
Includes bibliographical references (p.) and index.
ISBN 0-252-02706-X
1. Religion and the press—United States—History.
I. Title. II. Series.
PN4888.R44U53   2002
070.9—dc21   2001003514

For Susanne and Marika and Alida

CONTENTS

PREFACE

A few years ago, my former editor at the *Seattle Times*, Mike Fancher, issued a directive to his newsroom subordinates: pick a church, go to church activities, interview church members, and find out what is going on out there among churches and the people who attend. However, writing in his Sunday column in the *Times*, Fancher said he hoped to dispel a rumor that the *Times* was requiring its journalists to become churchgoers. The exercise had nothing to do with the newspaper's concern about its employees' spiritual lives, he explained. The purpose was to help the newspaper get a better handle on how churches in the community work, how they involve themselves in politics, and how to do a better job of covering the religious lives of readers.[1]

As I read Fancher's column, I found myself struck by a number of ironies that might occur to anyone who has had a career in the daily newspaper business. American journalists can seem most awkward when they face news stories that take them far outside their professional culture and their normal frame of reference. Somehow I just could not keep from smiling at the odd prospect of a group of wary, reluctant journalists, notebooks in hand, fanning out around the community to attend church, like anthropologists heading off to visit the natives.

Beyond this image of journalists as modern-day Margaret Meads and the churches as some sort of primitive culture to be studied and probed, I found myself asking the broader, philosophical questions that come up whenever critics examine the press's attitude toward religion. How can organizations devoted to clear-eyed pragmatism and hard-nosed fact gathering cover the ineffable, the unknowable, essentially the collective life of the soul of their audience? How can a news business whose professional values grew out of the Enlightenment ideas of Voltaire and Thomas Paine, with their rational skepticism and their undisguised hatred of religious dogma and Christian orthodoxy, report in a balanced fashion on a religious community that in many quarters still harbors the most traditional of religious beliefs? Besides, who is to say that the *Times* journalists weren't already going to church on their own? What does it say about the culture of the newsroom when editors simply assume their journalists have no contact with church-going people?

I also found myself wondering if this newfound interest in religion among the *Times* management sprang from the agenda that has become the hallmark of modern-day, market-oriented journalism—how to stay in better touch with readers. Religion has seen an upsurge of interest among Americans, particularly aging baby boomers, and U.S. media organizations everywhere have been wrestling with how to better cover an issue that has long been relegated to the Saturday religion page.[2]

I have written extensively about the impact of "market-driven" or "reader-driven" journalism on today's media organizations and the new generation of newsroom managers who let audience research guide their news judgment.[3] Religion plays a powerful role in the lives of Americans and to a much greater extent than the news media generally recognize, but I also found myself asking: is it possible that all this hoopla over religion coverage—by the *Times* and other media organizations—amounts to little more than a marketing ploy? If that is so, how can religion reporting become better if the motives are thoroughly commercial at the core and, at some fundamental level, at odds with the true meaning of religion?

At this point, I must acknowledge that, in the nearly fifteen years since I left the daily newspaper business, the subject of religion has come to hold more than passing interest for me. When I read Fancher's column, I was set to embark on an unlikely odyssey for a veteran of the daily newspaper reporting business: a year of study at a Quaker seminary, the Earlham School of Religion in Richmond, Indiana, where I hoped to learn more about the faith in which I had been raised but with which I had lost touch during long stretches of my adult life. My growing interest in religion coincided with my exit from journalism and my entry into the academic world—and I suspect that the two events were not unrelated. In one respect, I was happy to leave a business that I felt had lost sight of its public service obligations amid the push for higher profits and the fixation on marketing strategies to gain readers. But since I left the *Times,* I had come to realize that my differences with the new breed of media managers were about something more than just professional philosophy. For me, journalism had been a higher calling—a place for me to "speak truth to power," as the well-known Quaker maxim puts it—and I now recognized that my disillusionment with the profession was tied to my perception that major elements of the media business were no longer maintaining the faith.

While I spent much of that sabbatical year at the Earlham School of Religion exploring personal issues, I also had time to reflect on what it meant to my former colleagues to be left behind in a profession where the idealism that attracted many of them to journalism was being undermined by severe economic, technological, and sociodemographic pressures. Journalism, as so many of my old newsroom friends were discovering, is now viewed at many news organizations as just another commodity in the world of commerce. Although journalists would likely be loath to put it this way, I found myself wondering if there was not a "crisis of faith," as I have come to see it, in the newsrooms where my former colleagues still toiled away.

As I reflected on the meaning of the journalistic mission in spiritual terms, I found myself ruminating about other ironies, too. Journalists in the United States have long been highly attuned to the moral void at the core of our commercialized culture, but, sadly, this often manifests itself in cynical, negative, self-righteous ways. Mainstream reporters and columnists rail in high moral pitch against the corruption of special interest money in politics, the hypocrisies of high officialdom, the lack of personal morality of public figures, the inequities inherent in astronomical salaries in business and sports, and the damaging effects of the consumer culture on youth. But the American public seems thoroughly unimpressed by journalists who hold themselves up as the moral guardians of the age.

Why is it, people seem to be saying, that journalists are so quick to criticize a society increasingly devoted to prosperity and the pursuit of material goods, all the while promoting those values through a news media system that seems to be so much like what they are criticizing? Why is it that journalists—moralists, on the one hand, yet wedded to coverage of sexual peccadilloes, celebrity gossip, and salacious crime, on the other—seem much better at writing about the substitutes for religion in our society (such as big-time sports, the stock market, or the Internet) than about religion itself? Why is it that journalists take a worshipful approach to the coverage of science, psychology, business, and new technology yet have only recently awakened to the importance that so many Americans place on traditional forms of religion? And why is that journalists want to serve as champions of civic values and as critics of others' self-seeking behavior but turn into rationalizers and apologists when it comes to their own organization's business practices?

In recent years, communications academics and research scholars—like the journalists they study—have grown more interested in the subject of religion. There have been a number of new books on the topic of media and religion, new media and religion divisions set up within academic organizations, and a burst of new academic papers on the topic. Despite this, there is considerable disagreement in the few studies that purport to examine the religious beliefs of American journalists and how those beliefs might apply to their professional activities. Members of the religious Right cite data (some of it dated) they contend demonstrate that journalists are irreligious, non-church-going people who are indifferent, if not downright hostile, to religious, particularly Christian, culture. More recent studies, which indicate that a large proportion of journalists do, in fact, identify religion as important in their lives, have called those conclusions into question. However, none of these studies has examined the nature of journalistic belief in much depth, and none has done justice to the complex role religion appears to play in the value system of modern journalists.

This dearth of authoritative data about journalists' religious orientation raised a large question for me: how exactly should one describe the religious views of journalists? Perhaps of even greater importance, what does it matter what journalists believe, and should we care whether those beliefs influence the practice of journalism and the product of the journalistic endeavor? Should the religious values of American journalists, for example, be seen only in the context of how much they may or may not subscribe to the views of religion that are identified with the traditional church establishment and the orthodox interpretations that have grown out of the Judeo-Christian tradition? Or is it possible that journalists' religious beliefs might be better measured in terms of the values that they put into practice rather than their espoused theology? What does it matter what the ethical and moral underpinnings of journalists' belief systems are? Is it important to ponder the religious origins of journalists' moral beliefs if those moral beliefs have become thoroughly secularized and can be seen as expressions of universal ethical standards that can be found in cultures throughout the world? What of the demands of their profession that they be tolerant and open to the views of people of many faiths, particularly in a society that is becoming more religiously diverse and more aware of the world's religious movements? Conversely, does it make any difference if American journalists are unaware that their nation's religious heritage might play a role in the often unacknowledged assumptions that are made when they cover, say, the activities of Islamic fundamentalists or the Dalai Lama?

The more I looked into the matter, the more convinced I became that simply asking journalists about their religious views—as so many studies have done—was not enough to comprehend fully the way religious values play a role in journalists' operating principles and the way the news is portrayed in the American media. Conservative critics of the press tend to judge journalists' religiosity, or lack thereof, by their church attendance or denominational affiliation, and they blame this for everything they do not like about what they perceive as the media's bias against their religious views. Other analysts have come to different conclusions by noting that in surveys journalists demonstrate a favorable view of religion, although one expressed in tolerant and pluralistic terms. This, they imply, means that journalists' antireligious bias has been overstated and that press coverage of religion is not as unsympathetic as critics claim. But is it possible, I found myself wondering, that the conclusions of those researchers who found journalists to be antireligious and those who found them to be favorable toward religion and religious pluralism might, in some fundamental sense, both be correct? Is it possible that journalists could be skeptical about and even hostile toward certain notions of religion while still operating at a religious level in their values, their ethics, and their professional principles? Could a clearer picture of the relationship between religion and journalism emerge if a research method could be developed that went beyond simply asking journalists questions about their church attendance, their denominational affiliation, or the importance of religion in their lives?

As I began to do the research for this book, I found myself delving into the fascinating but largely unexamined parallels between religious and journalistic developments since the time of Jesus, as well as the myriad writings of well-known journalists on the topic of religion, to understand better why the relationship is so misunderstood, even among journalists themselves. Not only has there been no thorough study of the role that religion plays in modern American journalists' moral and ethical outlook, but there has not been a comprehensive examination of the historical relationship between the religious tradition and the evolution of mass media in Western society. In trying to do both here, I hope to illuminate—both through social science research and historical analysis—the debt that journalism owes to the culture's religious heritage, as well as the complex attitudes that religious organizations hold toward a mass media system that their members often loathe and criticize but are willing to exploit to shape cultural attitudes toward religion. In particular, I hope that by examining the religious impulses at work in the typical newsroom and by shedding light on the way those impulses have been transformed as well as disguised in the course of the historical development of journalism, I might help to explain some of the tension that exists in journalism today on the topic of religion and to dispel some of the confusion and suspicion the public feels when it tries to fathom where journalists are coming from when they deal with religion matters.

A comment on the title of the book, too. When I first came up with *From Yahweh to Yahoo!* I thought I had found a catchy phrase to capture the transformation of the media from a religious to a secular purpose. Since then, I have discovered there is a lively discussion among academics and on the Internet about the linguistic source of the word *Yahoo* and the fact that the spelling of *Yahoo* is sometimes used as one of dozens of Hebrew variations on the sacred name Yahweh and that a Hebrew variation of Yahweh, when used on the end of a name (such as Netanyahu), means "gift of God" or something similar. Scholars have noted that the eighteenth-century satirist Jonathan Swift—whose term *yahoo* for a race of brutes in *Gulliver's Travels* is credited with introducing the word into the English vocabulary—attended school where Hebrew was taught, and they have speculated that he may have chosen the word as a satiric reminder that humans, created in the image of Yahweh, are capable of degenerating into great depravity. Another commentator has expanded on this connection by discussing other Hebrew equivalents of computer terms (such as the Hebrew pronunciation of "www") in terms of their implications for scriptural prophecy and even identifying the search engine Yahoo! with the Antichrist. However, one can only wonder how this discussion would sound to Swift, who saw the folly in so much pointless human activity, or to David Filo and Jerry Yang, the youthful founders of Yahoo! who say the name stands for "Yet Another Hierarchical Officious Oracle."[4]

* * *

I have a number of special people to whom I wish to express my gratitude. First and foremost, I thank my wife, Susanne Kromberg, who has given me much encouragement and loving support, and our young daughters, Marika and Alida, who have provided the inspiration for me to carry on with this task despite the many exciting and demanding changes in our life. Susanne and I met during my year at the Earlham School of Religion, and I am grateful that I was able to convince her not to return to her beloved Norway but to settle with me in Seattle. Susanne's strong Quaker belief and the spiritual gifts she has brought into my world have added immeasurably to my understanding of what love grounded in faith can mean in one's life. Her fine editing skills also were instrumental in bringing the book into its present shape, and I am thankful she found the time—among many other pressing tasks—to apply her keen sense of writing and organization to improve the manuscript immensely.

I also want to give a word of appreciation to my family—my parents, Ray and Mary Betty Underwood; my brother, Jeff Underwood; my sister, Barbara Underwood Scharff; and my niece and nephews, Elana, Jesse, and Thomas Scharff—whose love and support through all things have been a great comfort to me. The Quakerism in which my parents raised me—and which I rediscovered a few years ago at a crucial time in my life—has provided me with a sense of grounding that carried me well through my career as a journalist, as it has through my academic life. The addition to the family of my brother-in-law, Gary Scharff, with his intense Catholic sense of justice, in combination with my sister's deep commitment to social causes, has only strengthened my sense of the importance that religion can still serve in the world.

Mickey Edgerton has been a spiritual mentor, a godmother to Marika, a wonderful friend, and an example of what Quaker values in action can mean to the many people whose lives she touches.

I have many folks to thank at the Earlham School of Religion—in particular, John Punshon, whose Quaker studies courses were critical in illuminating the themes I examine here, and Tom Mullen, whose religious writing class played a key role in helping me formulate the outline of the book. Tracy Peterson kept telling me that I needed to be writing, writing, writing. Tony Stapleton, Chris Buice, Noël Carey, Chris Jorgenson, Tom Gates, Samuel Johnson, Manuel Guzman, Denora Uvalle Vasquez, Melanie Watson, Derek Watson, and so many more provided the spiritual community that helped support me through that important year of my life.

I thank Keith Stamm, who provided me with patient counsel and generous help in finding my way through the thicket of social science research methodology and analysis. I have also received advice, support, and emergency help from other people at the University of Washington, including Richard Kielbowicz, David Domke, Nancy Rivenburgh, Jerry Baldasty, Kevin Kawamoto, April

Peterson, Jan Maxson, and the late and much-missed Pat Dinning. I greatly appreciate John Nerone's thoughtful critiques, which were key to bringing the manuscript into its final form, as well as the editorial support I received from Richard Martin and the careful and attentive editing of the text from Jane Mohraz. I also thank the William Test Fund at the University of Washington School of Communications, which provided the funding for my survey research.

My friend John Jamison took the time in a busy life to read the science material and to chew over historical and theological themes. As always, old and good friends, such as Steve Gettinger, Henry Breithaupt, Lee Moriwaki, and David Jay, gave me plenty of encouragement, as did new ones, such as Sarah Kretzmann and Nathan Montover. Many of my colleagues and friends were not quite sure what I was up to when I headed off to seminary in 1994. I was not sure myself at times, but I hope this manuscript will show to what degree it was a transforming experience.

FROM YAHWEH TO YAHOO!

Introduction:
Journalism Facing Faith

The columnist Richard Reeves describes the modern media as being like the weather—always there, always surrounding us, and always a major factor in our lives, whether we like it or not.[1] Yet as we begin the twenty-first century, it seems that virtually everyone—from philosophers to media critics to ministers to academics—identifies the media as a powerful, alienating force that must bear a large share of the responsibility for human beings' feeling resentful and angst-ridden about modern circumstances. The existentialist philosopher José Ortega y Gasset lamented the "low spiritual plane" upon which the press operates,[2] and the media analyst Jacques Ellul complained that the widespread loss of religious belief leaves many helpless in the face of media that foment anxiety by emphasizing catastrophe, danger, and troubles.[3]

How have the media led us into this bind? Perhaps we should begin with a religious concept, the Hebrew prohibition against the worship of the graven image. For the ancient Jews, this prohibition dealt with a practical concern. They were in tough competition with other religions in the Mediterranean Near East. The faith allegiance of the Jews was in such constant dispute because they owed their loyalty not only to a monotheistic deity but also to an invisible god. That meant that, unlike their tribal neighbors, they did not worship the image of something humans knew directly—animals, emperors, or forces of nature. Instead, their allegiance was to something transcendent and ineffable that had come to their forebears in the form of divine revelation and was passed on in the teachings and the sacred texts of temple life.

It is true there were many concrete manifestations of God's special relationship with the Israelites, such as the temple, the Torah, and the appearances in the form of a burning bush, thunderstorms, and a pillar of fire. But the ancient Jews also understood that God, or Yahweh, was infinitely grander and more magnificent than even words could convey and that devotion to anything less than a power beyond all symbolic representation ran the risk of being turned into the worship of human likenesses or idols dreamed up in the human imagination.

It does not take much insight to apply these lessons to our own "mediated" age. On television, we are watching images of ourselves. Just as the Hebrews might have predicted, we have become transfixed by new gods that compete for our souls' attention. Public opinion guides the direction of mass media and has grown into something bigger and more powerful than any human being can control—an irrepressible and monolithic force that is all of us and none of us at the same time. Television viewers live in a mirrorlike world where they are continuously exposed to reflections of their fantasies and pictures of themselves as they would like to be, constantly seduced by the allure of a world where images rule and fulfillment comes in the form of material possessions. The Internet has refined this condition of electronic idolatry, offering individuals their every wish and desire in tailor-made, customized, interactive exchanges with e-commerce marketers, pornographic Web studios, and anonymous chat rooms. Daily newspaper journalists, like the scribes and rabbis who kept alive Jewish identity by putting into print the Torah and the culture's sacred stories, work to maintain community and civic consciousness by maintaining the written tradition. But inexorably, the battle seems lost as people—especially the young—grow ever more wedded to the beguilements of electronic gratification.

From this, scholars have made the obvious connection. In particular, television, with its richness in imagery and its success in transmitting the new, media-generated myths of the culture, has replaced traditional religion in fulfilling the sacramental needs of modern life. Gregor Goethals, in *The TV Ritual: Worship at the Video Altar,* saw an almost direct displacement effect: TV commercials have become the most distinctive icon in our secular culture, jingles are visual and musical catechisms, the news and programming formulas provide comforting ritual. In Goethals's analysis, modern secularity and the banishment of mystery and myth have left a vacuum to be filled by electronic images. Television programming has become the medium to fill our spiritual emptiness, with advertising offering the promise of material redemption. "By buying a product, everybody has a chance to become members incorporate in the mystical body of those who have been redeemed from obesity, ring-around-the-collar, bad breath, or simple human loneliness," Goethals wrote.[4]

Goethals's analysis may work better at a metaphorical level than it does in describing the way Americans live out their faith. Despite the impression to the contrary, religion in its traditional form not only survives in the United States but thrives. Ninety-five percent of Americans believe in God or a higher power, and almost seven in ten Americans are members of a church or synagogue, with 40 percent regularly attending religious services, according to George Gallup Jr. and D. Michael Lindsay.[5] With the exception of the Irish Republic, the

United States is the most religious of the modern developed Western nations. Gallup's religious index (measuring weekly church attendance, belief in God, importance of God in daily life, etc.) was more than three times as high in the United States as in Denmark, for example, and nearly twice as high as in Great Britain and Norway in 1989.[6]

In effect, a curious phenomenon is occurring in American culture. Americans show every indication of retaining a strong religious identity and, with it, a deep suspicion of the mass media, which they see as eroding the culture's moral and spiritual values. At the same time, they are embracing enthusiastically the wonders of the world of electronic media in their personal values and their personal and professional lives. In many cases, they appear to be perfectly comfortable when their own religious organizations use the mass media to evangelize, fundraise, and reach out to followers. A measure of how these seemingly contradictory attitudes are playing out is in the proliferation of religious television and radio networks, congregations advertising on commercial local television, and religious groups migrating to the Internet—all part of a landscape that has come to reflect the image of the United States as a place where everything from the sacred to the profane is packaged, promoted, and marketed in great abundance.

This ambivalence about the role of mass media has opened up elements of the religious community to charges that they have become too accommodating to the popular culture. There is much irony, for example, in seeing Christian conservatives—whose movement is historically rooted in the protest against the use of outward symbols of belief—so enthusiastically utilizing electronic image-making to promote their cause, all the while speaking out vehemently against the lack of morality in much mass media content. Anyone who has watched the lavish sets and the well-coiffed guests on Pat Robertson's 700 Club, read about the theme parks and time-share units at Jim Bakker's PTL resort, or cast an eye over the affluent southern California backdrop of Robert Schuller's *Hour of Power* performances senses an intellectual disconnect in people who can speak so bitterly about the modern media while so willingly embracing the consumerism and the material lifestyle that modern media help promote.

Liberal religious people (when they are not taking issue with religious conservatives) like to take their shots at the media industry, too. While they may spurn the "family values" language of their conservative cohorts, members of mainline and liberal Christian congregations often talk about the dubious values of the mass media—the single-minded commitment to making money, the devotion to treating individuals as rating points, the readiness to shift with the winds of popular opinion—which they see as anathema to the religious spirit. William Fore, a Methodist minister and network religious consultant, offered the classic, liberal Christian critique: "The media promote luxuries, encourage waste, and praise the life of things. . . . Technology—'what works'—has become our god, expressed in all the most powerful myths of the most powerful media, while the God of justice and love is relegated to the sidelines of life."[7]

Criticism of the mass media's contribution to the depletion of the national spirit comes not just from religious quarters. It is not uncommon for members of the public who are secular in orientation to voice concerns that the mass media are contributing to a sense of demoralization and a hollowness in our cultural life. One does not have to look far to find people, whether religiously oriented or not, who express a deep disenchantment with the way the world is presented through the prism of the modern media and an anxiety that much that is conveyed through the media is damaging individual psyches and undermining the national spirit. The criticism that members of the public level against the modern media is often vague and visceral, and it invariably reflects the personal biases and the political perspectives of the individual faultfinder. But beneath the critical commentary, whether it is coming from the Left or the Right, from the religious or the nonreligious, is a hunger among members of the public to understand why they are experiencing a spiritual emptiness, a feeling that something fundamental to the culture has been lost, whenever they encounter mass media content.

Journalists themselves are not immune to disenchantment with the media. There has been a proliferation of articles in professional journals recounting the anger, frustration, and despair among journalists working in newsrooms where marketing and bottom-line management schemes are in ascendancy. Journalism's higher "mission" seems thwarted in today's media climate. The pain to the journalistic "spirit" is evident when Tom Rosenstiel, a former *Newsweek* and *Los Angeles Times* correspondent and director of the Pew Charitable Trust's Project for Excellence in Journalism, wrote:

> What is going on in the so-called serious press is a crisis of conviction, a philosophical collapse in the belief in the purpose of journalism and the meaning of news. . . . Amid all the recent changes, we journalists have been traumatized because we were never really very clear about what we were doing in the first place. We even gloried in avoiding a kind of serious or rigorous discussion about what journalism was, what our responsibilities were. We talked about journalism in mystical terms. . . . When we again believe in the meaning and the power of news, we can figure a way out of the crisis.[8]

My thinking in seminary and my research during the following five years have coalesced into the key arguments of this book. First, I have come to realize that the angst many of my former journalist colleagues feel in watching their professional lives turn from a vocation in service to a higher calling into one in hock to the marketing ethic has all the dimensions of a spiritual dilemma. I recognize that journalists, who can be very suspicious of religious dogma and organized religion in general, seldom think of themselves as operating in a religious context. But by closely examining the way the history of religion in the United States has been inextricably intertwined with the growth of what today we call the media, I think the case can be made that journalists are solidly connected to the nation's moral and religious heritage and operate, in certain important ways, as personifications of the old religious virtues. Odd as it may sound, I am talking about faith in the context of the newsroom and the journalists who work there, and I am arguing that, whether recognized or not, the professional predicament that faces today's journalists is linked to the crisis of faith throughout society. Although I discuss why religion has been so badly covered by the media—a common criticism that has been tossed at journalists—my main purpose is to unearth the way that religious values, hidden though they may be, guide journalists in their thinking and their daily tasks and how those values have been shaped by the historical developments of Western religion. I argue that journalists draw much of their professional inspiration from the Bible's prophetic complaints about moral corruption, as well as the calls for reform that grew out of the Protestant Reformation, the Progressive and Populist movements, and the muckraker and Social Gospel campaigns in the United States during the late nineteenth century and early twentieth. By better understanding this history and the largely unexamined role that religion has played in the development of journalists' professional standards, journalists will, I believe, be better able to help renew their own faith, as well as the public's, in the journalistic enterprise.

Second, I expand this argument by asking how much better media coverage of many topics would be if journalists better understood the role religion plays as a motivating force in so many areas of society. Throughout the book, I argue that journalists would be better served if they perceived the religious undercurrents of the stories they write about politics, science, psychology, and technology, as well as the way religion works in their own value system. Journalists, as I have noted, have become more aware (for marketing reasons, if nothing else) of the importance that religion, traditional and otherwise, plays in the life of many Americans. But by not being more broadly sensitive to the underlying role of faith in the culture, journalists miss out on a fuller understanding of the wellsprings of human motivation in a wide variety of issue areas, and their coverage suffers for it. I am not pretending that every story is about religion—far from it. But I do argue that journalists are missing good and important stories by not being better attuned to the religious dimensions of American culture and by not better connecting with that part of their audience that does recognize faith at work in broad aspects of American life. We all would be better served, I believe, if the coverage of religion were deeper, more perceptive, and more nuanced in its grasp of the spiritual impulse in people. This way we might be less threatened by religion and instead recognize how much it influences the way the world works—and how much less we understand about the world when we ignore it.

Third, I argue that, in their often unrecognized role as the covert promoters of a religious perspective, journalists have taken a reverential approach to a whole ranges of topics where—secularists as they believe they are—they can more comfortably express the religious side of their personality. Any reader of modern journalists' coverage of such areas as science, psychology, technology, sports, or business does not have to look far to find the quasi-religious themes that are imputed to so many aspects of modern life. It may be going too far to say that journalists often look for religious meaning everywhere except in traditional religion, but there is much evidence to this effect. That journalists tend to see themselves as followers of the skeptical and irreverent Enlightenment tradition and as firm believers in empiricism and a scientific approach to fact gathering only further blinds them to the ways their devotional needs become unconsciously fixed on seemingly nonreligious subjects. Devout nonbelievers that many believe themselves to be, journalists only muddle matters when they pretend they are immune to the search for spiritual meaning in life.

Although I speak of religion in its broadest meaning throughout the book, I focus largely on the country's heritage as a Christian culture, the Judeo-Christian ethical concepts that permeate our institutions (including our secular ones), and the impact of Protestantism on the national outlook. Although it is now the trend to expand the teaching of American history beyond the study of Western (i.e., Christian) civilization, any analysis of the relationship between religion and media in the United States has to rely on historical patterns as they were—and there can be no question that the development of journalism here was influenced primarily by the moral outlook and values of Christianity, particularly Protestantism. However, it is important to recognize that, even though the Protestant ethic, as it has come to be known, plays an important role in my analysis, I discuss it in the broader, almost metaphorical context of its influence on the journalistic psyche without tying it specifically to Protestant theology. As American society has grown more pluralistic and the ethnic and the religious landscape of the United States has changed during the last three centuries, Christianity's—and Protestantism's—explicit hold on the culture has diminished, and many of the moral and religious assumptions that used to be taken for granted have come in for extensive reevaluation. Still, journalism in the United States grew out of the soil of the English Reformation, and it is necessary to examine it through the prism of its religious heritage, whether one likes that heritage or not.

This does not in any way mean I do not fully recognize the impact of other religious movements on American journalism. The Catholic influence, in the church's political and social role in cities and regions with large Irish and southern European immigrant populations and through the acquisitions of French and Spanish landholdings, has played an important role in the development of American press history, as have the many diverse religious movements that settled on American soil and, for practical reasons if nothing else, led to an American constitutional system that recognizes freedom of religious conscience and the right of the population to worship free of government influence. The Jewish contribution to American press history has also been important, and Jewish journalistic figures—ranging from Joseph Pulitzer to Ben Hecht to Walter Lippmann to A. J. Leibling to I. F. Stone—have made a mark on American journalism in numbers far larger than the proportion of Jews in the population.[9] But evaluating the impact of Judaism on the American press is complicated by the difficulty of separating the ethnic identity of a Jewish person from Judaism as a religion (one can be a Jew and have no interest in the Jewish religion), as well as the complex way that the New Testament of Christians is greatly dependent on the Hebrew scriptures (or the Old Testament, as it is called, in the first portion of the Christian Bible) but in a fashion that has caused great division between the two groups.[10] Throughout this book, I refer to the Judeo-Christian tradition or Judeo-Christian values, but I do it in a way that refers to a general cultural outlook that can be traced to the shared moral values of the Hebrew scriptures and the New Testament of the Bible.[11] These moral values are not unique to Judeo-Christian teachings (Islam, for example, was greatly influenced by the tenets of both Judaism and Christianity), but they are the ones that American journalism has tended to reflect as it evolved in a nation that has been, and continues to be, profoundly shaped by religious attitudes.

What this means is that when I talk about religion I am not parochial or exclusive in my approach. I discuss, for example, the problematic manner in which the American media cover other global religions, as well as recently imported and nontraditional religions that have proliferated in the United States. Cultural and demographic diversity has become a reality in the United States, and the global reach of television has expanded Americans' awareness of the religions of the world. It is ironic that even as the American media have moved in secular directions and away from explicit identification with their Christian heritage, they are accused by overseas critics (particularly those in Muslim countries) of framing the news in the historical context of colonization, imperialism, and Christendom's rivalry with other world religions. It may be small comfort to foreign readers and viewers of Western-generated news accounts that American media workers do not believe they are making cultural assumptions or demonstrating any overt bias toward anybody. In the places in the world where religion is seen as a threat to American diplomatic or overseas business interests, few believe that those cherished Western journalistic values—objectivity, freedom from government dictate, a commitment to tolerance and diversity— amount to much more than platitudes; for them, the news as it is presented in the Western model is little more than a guise for a cultural imperialism that sees non-Christian religions as exotic and strange at best and frightening and sinister at worst.

Although I still think of myself as a journalist, nearly fifteen years in the academic world have turned me into something of a scholar in outlook. I owe much in this book to the intellectuals and communications researchers whose critical analyses of mass media have framed the debate in academia. I am particularly indebted to the seminal thinking of Harold Innis and the work of his intellectual heirs—Marshall McLuhan, Walter Ong, and Joshua Meyrowitz—who have convinced me that understanding the prevailing forms of communication in a culture goes a long way in determining what that culture is and how the members of it think, feel, and act. Historians have long noted how the invention of the printing press facilitated the Protestant Reformation and made it possible for such figures as Martin Luther, John Calvin, and George Fox to challenge the authority of the established church and to see their messages spread in ways that would have been impossible when church authorities controlled the production and distribution of writing. Innis broadened such insights into a sweeping analysis of the history of civilizations as the history of their media systems, and he illustrated his thesis by examining such key epochs in communications history as the shift of ancient cultures from oral to written forms of communication, the transformation of medieval manuscript culture to technologized print culture, and the implications for nineteenth- and twentieth-century society in the rapidly developing forms of electronic means of communication.[12] During my seminary studies and with Innis's concepts in the back of my mind, I began to notice how often important religious figures—such as Moses, Paul, Augustine, Martin Luther, and, most important, Jesus himself—lived in those transitional periods when a culture was shifting from one dominant form of communication system to another. Although Innis showed some interest in religion and its interplay with media systems, he stopped short of developing a full-fledged theory about the importance of the prevailing communications systems on faith and religious belief within a culture.

It is interesting to note how Innis and McLuhan, both of whom expected to leave their mark among historians, economists, and communications theorists, are beginning to become as important to cultural and religious scholars as they are to modern communications researchers. In the decades since their deaths, quantitatively oriented social scientists have criticized the two for taking a "mystical" view of the role of communications in culture. Their critics maintain that their thinking was governed more by inspiration and flashes of philosophical insight than by sound methodological analysis. For McLuhan, in particular, the tag of "mystic" makes a good deal of sense. He was a devout Catholic who believed that the new electronic video technologies were leading to a more fluid and dynamic "re-tribalization" of society, where hierarchical institutions would be transformed by television's power to break down the barriers of education, class, and the rational categories of knowledge upheld by the old print culture. McLuhan's theory "rests on a new version of the Christian myth," as the media historian Daniel Czitrom put it. "For Eden, the Fall, and paradise regained, McLuhan substituted tribalism (oral culture), detribalization (phonetic alphabet and print), and retribalization (electronic media)."[13]

Among Innis's followers in religious studies, I have been particularly intrigued by those who use his theories to speculate about the impact of media development on the message and legacy of Jesus in the Christian world and on Paul's role in spreading that message. Thomas Boomershine, for example, borrowed from Innis's thinking to argue that Jesus' role must be reexamined in the light of the struggle of Judaism within literate Hellenistic culture and that Jesus' mode of thought within a largely oral ministry accounts for much of its distinctive influence in shaping later literary history.[14] Joanna Dewey followed a similar line of thinking by contending that Paul's use of letter writing in a world of criers and storytellers served to propel Christians into the mainstream of a growing text-based culture. How Jesus—clearly a "heroic" character based on the mythological standards common to oral-based cultures—was transposed into the cosmic and theological figure of the early church, she said, probably had as much to do with this shift from an oral to a print-based culture as anything else did.[15] Ong, a Jesuit priest and a disciple of Innis, moved the discussion in an explicitly Christian direction by arguing that Innis's view of history as driven by media development can be seen in the context of the Christian "word" and that the "word" can be viewed as the moving force of history and an entry point for the divine.[16]

I also found myself veering away from Innis, though. I have never put much stock in the criticism that Innis failed to develop a social science methodology to test his theories. We can not administer a social science survey to the people of antiquity, and we will never be able to know how behavioral research might be applied to the attitudes of the ancient Egyptians or Babylonians. But modern journalists can be surveyed, and I thought it was vital to test the various hypotheses I posit in this book against the responses of journalists. Beyond the considerable historical research that has gone into this book, much of what I say reflects the findings of a survey my University of Washington colleague Keith Stamm and I administered in 1998 that examined the religious attitudes of newspaper journalists across the United States and Canada. The results, like other recent research probing journalists' views of religion, indicated that journalists are much less irreligious than their critics have made them out to be and are motivated by both conscious and unconscious religious impulses in their moral and ethical value systems. We also found that journalists hold complex, varied, and multidimensional views about religion and the role of religion in their professional lives and that past efforts by researchers that tend to put journalists into narrow categories—religious or irreligious, believers or nonbelievers, reverent or irreverent—are far too limited in their conclusions.

In looking to Innis's work as the beginning point for my own examination of the relationship between journalism and religion, I find myself outside another camp that often divides communications departments: the cultural studies proponents and critical theory analysts who look to cultural forms and qualitative rather than quantitative analysis of human interactions and institutional activities to explain mass media behavior and audience response. Even Innis, with his nonquantitative approach, does not have a particularly strong following among advocates of critical theory or cultural studies. They tend to favor the concepts of someone such as Jürgen Habermas, the German social theorist, who has become something of a cult figure in certain academic circles. Habermas's notion of a "public sphere," where the press once played a role in high-minded, public-spirited discussion among civic-minded elites, is viewed in near romantic terms by academics who long to find a meaningful place in the social order for their critique of the failings of the mass media. Habermas's contention that the public sphere has been eroded since the eighteenth century by the commercial and technological reshaping of modern mass media (Habermas's ideal of the fully functioning public sphere were coffeehouses, salons, and other forums for public discussion in eighteenth-century Europe, where intellectuals gathered to discuss democratic ideas in opposition to traditional forms of hierarchical and feudal political authority) is elitist and bourgeois in orientation, even though Habermas emerged as a figure from the leftist student movement of the 1960s.[17]

Habermas's views, with their Hegelian, German romantic flavor and their systematic, all-encompassing critique of social and historical developments, have never been as convincing to me as they are to some of my colleagues. But others have pointed out parallels in Habermas's and Innis's thinking, and that led me to reexamine Habermas in the context of my own discussion of media and religion in this book. For example, James Carey (a prominent advocate for a cultural approach to the study of communications and one of the communications academics who admires Innis) implied that Innis's objections to electronic mass media and his enthusiasm for oral culture amount to a "public sphere" argument reminiscent of Habermas's.[18] I think Carey's analysis is an interesting one, and, even though I find Innis's critique more convincing in its historical analysis than Habermas's focus on eighteenth-century salon life, I treat this connection seriously in the upcoming discussion.[19]

It is important, though, to stress here the dangers of seeing religion as a function of everything that happens in society and overstating its importance in the historical development of the media. Just as Innis and McLuhan have been accused of reductionism in their fixation on the impact of media systems on history, one can fall into the trap of reducing all historical and sociological questions to their religious dimensions. I hope to avoid this pitfall, while at the same time confessing to my fascination with how religion and the religious impulse in our more secular age can take forms that might not always be readily apparent.

There is also a risk of presenting religion as only a good or a bad thing, which seems too often the case in our society wracked by the "culture wars" between religious conservatives and liberal groups. I operate from the assumption that it is not possible to avoid the issue of one's religious beliefs in a book about religion and journalism, and my faith perspective informs my thesis in important ways. However, I am acutely aware of the damage religion has done to individuals and to people throughout history, and I hope no one takes from my arguments that I believe everything that can be identified as "religious" about the history of journalism is good. Like many things, religion plays a complex role in the world, and my chief goal is to elucidate the ways religion has shaped media development and vice versa, not to hold up religion as a panacea or as a curse.

As someone with only a nominal interest in religious matters during my years as a political and government reporter, I can understand why journalists would not see or would not care about the connection between their work and the world of faith. During my years as a reporter, I, like many of my colleagues, saw religion through largely unexamined stereotypes: as a subject that held little interest unless it involved the controversial or the bizarre, as a system of thought made anachronistic by the discoveries of modern science, as a place where people masked their self-seeking and political motives behind a veil of high-sounding moral rhetoric. However, my reconnection with Quakerism has helped give me another perspective on the religious dimension of American life and its subterranean role in the newsroom. It has been an eye-opening exercise for me to realize that I needed to look to the values of my faith as much as the values of journalism to understand why I, like so many journalists before me, was so drawn to the profession as a place to make a difference in the world.

During my time in seminary, I experienced the revival of a long dormant interest in the historical-critical method of biblical scholarship, which I had studied as an undergraduate more than thirty years ago. In seminary, I rediscovered why Rudolph Bultmann, the German theologian whose efforts to "demythologize" Christianity by separating issues of faith from the questions surrounding the factual accuracy of the biblical accounts, has both intrigued and scandalized Christians. During my undergraduate years, Bultmann liberated me from many of the doubts and the disbelief that sometimes alienate young people from Christianity and helped me discover a basis to believe that it might be possible to call myself a Christian, even if my interpretation of it fell outside the bounds of what is commonly called the orthodox viewpoint. I also found I was attracted to Bultmann's writings for the same reasons that I believe I was drawn to journalism and later to scholarship. Bultmann was rigorous in his methods, tough-minded in his conclusions, and courageous in finally acknowledging that one could never know much of anything about the historical Jesus—certainly never enough to gain a true picture of him because of the tenets of orthodoxy that color the texts of the early church. Still, Bultmann never let his commitment to the historical method undermine his own Christian faith. What I have come to realize is that, in separating faith from the search for historical truth, Bultmann pointed the way to a methodology that allowed me to be a person of faith and to be a journalist and a scholar in the most skeptical, aggressive, enterprising tradition.[20]

In part 1 of the book, I attempt to lay out the historical and theoretical foundation for my hypothesis that the moral and ethical roots of American journalism and the foundations of the modern journalist's professional value system can be found in the religious history of the past. In chapter 1, I focus on the crucible period that has so influenced both American journalism and religious culture—the seventeenth century in England, when the religious civil war was fought and when the earliest newspapers appeared. In the earliest practice of what scholars would identify as modern journalism, the writers were often people of strong religious faith who used the "newsbooks" of the time to carry on religious disputes. Many of these figures were inspired by the prophetic messages of the Bible, and I contend that prophetic impulse still guides journalism, even if it has been diluted by many of the commercial forces that now drive modern journalism.

In chapter 2, I explore a theme I have written about elsewhere: how economics and commercialism have come to supplant the traditional "spirit" of the journalistic mission and have undermined what is often, at heart, an almost religious commitment by journalism professionals to the higher journalistic values. My analysis focuses on the invention of the printing press and its impact on the transformation of writing from a spiritual endeavor into the money-making form it takes today, as well as the growth of modern marketing concepts that have led to a resurgence of interest in covering religion—but in ways that, in their marketing focus, can miss the whole point of religious experience.

The Enlightenment was a redefining period not only for the intellectual world in general but for the evolving field of journalism as well, and this is what I examine in chapter 3. Journalism as we identify it today largely came into existence simultaneously with the infusion of rational and empirical ideas into Western culture, and journalistic values are shot through with many of the notions and assumptions first expressed by the "philosophes" of the eighteenth century. Enlightenment rationality is often seen at odds with religious orthodoxy. However, there are many contradictions in the attitudes of Enlightenment thinkers about religion, as well as an unconscious debt in Enlightenment philosophy to the Christian tradition, and I ask whether journalists' "faith" in Enlightenment skepticism sometimes keeps them from better recognizing the role that religion plays in their own value system.

In a similar vein, I examine in chapter 4 the impact of the nineteenth-century romantic movement on journalism, and how the great romantic poets and philosophers—who rose up in revolt against both Enlightenment rationalism and religious orthodoxy—came to infuse such a strong element of romantic thought into nineteenth-century journalism that it lingers there today. This spirit of romantic idealism, which became an alternative religion for many of the period's most famous artists and writers, as well as journalists, can still be found in most modern newsrooms.

The most vivid illustration of the connection between the biblical prophetic tradition and journalistic values can be seen in the journalistic muckrakers of the early twentieth century and in the Social Gospel movement, in which the muckrakers (either implicitly or explicitly) participated. Again, as I argue in chapter 5, the spirit of the Social Gospel movement still animates American journalism, although with less zeal, courage, and commitment to radical social reform.

In chapter 6, I discuss the forces in modern life—and modern journalism—that have pushed today's journalists away from identifying themselves with religion as it has been expressed throughout much of American history. Here I focus on the heterodox American journalistic figures of the eighteenth, nineteenth, and twentieth centuries, particularly the notable journalists who went on to distinguished careers in literature and fiction. Many of these figures protested against religion perhaps too much, such that their campaigns to debunk religious cant became almost religious in obsession, particularly in their obsession with the void left after the abandonment of faith.

I conclude my discussion of the historical connections between journalism and religion with an examination of a turn-of-the-twentieth-century intellectual movement that has been called the most "American" of philosophies—and which, I believe, offers important insights into the state of the relationship today between religion and the modern mass media. William James's philosophy of pragmatism, which is the subject of chapter 7, has been very influential in American journalism and offers a bridge for the open-minded journalist to cover the intangibles of religion and yet maintain a faithfulness to journalism's empirical heritage.

Part 2 includes the results of the survey of journalists in which Keith Stamm and I tested my hypothesis that journalists' morals and ethics are rooted in Judeo-Christian values, even though many members of the media do not always recognize them as such. I open this discussion in chapter 8 by examining the complex role that Judeo-Christian ethical concepts have played historically in the professional value system of journalists, and I discuss my contention that even the most irreverent, agnostic, and contrarian journalists still reflect those fundamental values in their outlook and conduct.

In chapters 9 and 10, I test my hypothesis empirically by presenting our data summarizing the survey of 432 American and Canadian newspaper journalists who responded to our questionnaire about their religious beliefs and the source of their ethical values. The study, which we conducted in 1998–99, showed that journalists are strongly motivated by religious values, particularly in the way they put their values into action. We found that journalists are anything but irreligious in their avowed beliefs and in the ethical impulses that guide their professional activities. However, journalists' religious views are highly complex, and few journalists are one-dimensional in their religious outlook. While offering some caveats and cautions, I conclude from the results of the survey that my hypothesis—that religious values are embedded deeply in the professional values of many of today's journalists—was largely supported. Despite the secular directions of society and the skeptical and irreverent traditions of their profession, journalists seem solidly connected to the nation's moral and religious heritage, even though they may not always be aware they are.

The data from Canadian journalists are included in our study; however, in developing my thesis and my historical overview, I have focused on the United States. While there were no dramatic differences in the way that Canadian and American journalists responded to the questions, I am sure that questions designed to uncover differences would have found them.[21] One only has to recognize how Innis's and McLuhan's Canadian consciousness influenced the development of their theories to realize that it is always a great mistake not to see Canadian culture as distinct from American culture. I know enough about Canadian journalism and Canadian religious history to recognize that there are important similarities to what happened south of their border, but I also recognize that there are significant differences, too. I hope that Canadians who read this work take from it what seems relevant but do not assume that my conclusions apply to them.

In part 3, I examine why modern mass media organizations are seen as a force that undermines religious values, while, in important respects, they still operate as powerful voices for moral and ethical values in the culture. I argue that journalists' seeming alienation from religion is an important factor in understanding the modern media but that, beneath the superficial antagonism, journalists continue to search for ways to express their religious feelings. I pay particular attention to the substitutes for traditional religion to which many modern, secularly oriented journalists have come to attach their religious longing. Whether it is in their awestruck attitude toward science (chapter 11), their near religious faith in the principles of modern psychology (chapter 12), their tendency to reduce religious questions to political questions while at the same time paying little attention to the deeper dimensions of religion in their political reporting (chapter 13), or their near mystical celebration of the Internet and new media developments (chapter 14), journalists operate, I contend, with a faith in their own rationality and objectivity and with an unconsciousness of the debt they owe to their religious heritage. This leads to a journalism that is shallower than it would be if the broader role of religion in the culture were better understood and examined. Even the movement founded on the acknowledgment of journalism's contribution to the erosion of civic culture, known as public journalism, has been embraced by journalists without a full recognition of its connection to the nation's religious heritage, as I discuss in chapter 15.

In part 4, I examine why the modern news media have such difficulties covering spiritual experience and how a profession that prides itself on its skepticism and its empirical approach can produce coverage that is so uncritical, formulaic, and unhelpful in better understanding religious phenomena and the diversity of the world's religions. In chapter 16, I look at the role communications technology played in shaping our image of Jesus and the early Christian message. In Jesus' case, I contend the mystery, awe, and reverence that grew up around him had much to do with the fact that he was an oral preacher in a largely preliterate era but that his memory was perpetuated as it was because of the way the "media" of his time (in this case, letter writing and early handwritten manuscripts) served as a tool for preserving the accounts of his life for posterity. In this chapter, I speculate what it would mean to imagine the search for the "real" Jesus in journalistic terms or at least in ways that would be familiar to a journalist using the tools of modern reporting analysis, and I ponder the likelihood that even if the methodologies used by modern journalists were available in Jesus' time, we still might know as little about him as we do today.

In chapter 17, I analyze how today's media cover one of the most persistent examples of modern mystical experience: people's claims that they have "communicated" with the Virgin Mary or seen a "likeness" of her projected into the world. The Mary visions story offers the modern news media one of the greatest challenges to their epistemological assumptions about the nature of the world, and it offers interesting insights into how today's secular media handle the coverage of matters that fall outside the boundaries of verifiable fact.

In chapter 18, I examine the one religion story that seems to captivate the mainstream press: the political activities of religious conservatives and their role in the phenomenon known as televangelism. In examining the growth of religious broadcasting, I ask how the press can cover the religious Right so critically and yet with so little context and perspective. I also explore how the establishment media, while appearing to scorn electronic evangelism, have played a major part in allowing Christian conservatives to capture the airwaves.

Finally, I turn my attention to the ironic situation in which the American press—viewed by its domestic critics as hostile to Christian culture—is criticized in other countries as a vital element of Western cultural imperialism that frames world developments in the context of the historical outlook of Christianity. Key focal points of chapter 19 include the media's coverage of Islam and the press's tendency to cover global religions and nontraditional domestic religions in negative terms if they are perceived to threaten American business and political interests.

Electronically transmitted news and entertainment have grown into a ubiquitous presence in our media-saturated age—almost to the extent that religion once permeated all elements of life in an earlier era. However, to describe the activities of the modern mass media in the context of religious history may seem baffling to some—the content of the mass media, in many religious followers' view, has become the opposite of what religion is about. But, as I argue throughout this book, to understand the origins of our modern concept of communications, we need to look back to an age when this division was not so clear and to recognize how much the spirit of religion still persists, even in the modern newsroom. For many readers, it may seem strange to imagine today's media as rooted in the history and traditions of religious faith. The hostility toward Christianity that grew out of Enlightenment thought, the forces of secularity that were let loose by the Industrial Revolution and the triumph of the capitalist ethic, the impact of Newton, Darwin, and Einstein, and the advances of modern science—combined with the conviction in many quarters that the separation clause in the U.S. Constitution means religion should be kept out of the realm of public life—have served to create a press that is now viewed as one of the most avowedly secular forces in today's society. Yet to see the modern American media in the broadest and the deepest context, we need to become familiar with a time when the act of communication could not be separated from people's fixation with the source of all communication, when the news was, in the richest sense of the phrase, something that was about communion with a power that transcended the human ego.

In our media-saturated world, where politicians rail at Hollywood for its paucity of moral values and where the critics rail at politicians for buying the airwaves at election time, everyone is a media critic. With the omnipresence of media in our environment and the growing awareness of how electronic images shape everything from our buying impulses to our voting decisions, everybody is eager to critique the messages in which we are immersed. Whether it comes from the Left or the Right, there is endless handwringing that media organizations are turning the population into glazed-eyed channel surfers, video-numbed consumers of soap operas and big-time sports events, and balkanized species of on-line prestidigitators. Deep within a culture where television ads trumpet that "image is everything" there lies a lurking sense that maybe the Hebrews were right in prohibiting the worship of the graven image. When we become mesmerized with our own reflections pulsating on the video screen, we may find we have lost touch with those sacred principles that have animated humankind from time immemorial: the world is mysterious, things in it reflect the imponderable and the divine, and a power higher than ourselves may be in charge.

But this book also includes much that draws its inspiration from the optimistic and the hopeful elements of the journalistic tradition in the United States. I take my cue from Walter Ong, the Jesuit priest and media theorist, who is very upbeat about the impact of media systems—particularly electronic media—on the spiritual enlightenment of the world. Ong believes that television has furthered the cause of religious progress by bringing us closer together as a world community, making it easier to understand our many different cultures and advancing peace through open channels of communication. I believe this, too—although not quite as wholeheartedly as Ong does. My own view is that the spirit does its work buried deeply in the sinews of journalistic and media activity—whether journalists or media executives know it or not. If journalists continue to operate at the highest levels of professional principle—to do the kind of journalism that challenges injustice, demands of others the highest of ethical standards, and yet is sensitive to the human consequences of their work—they will be fulfilling the moral imperative that, I believe, lies at the heart of the journalistic mission.

PART 1

The Religious Roots
of the Mass Media

CHAPTER 1

Prophetic Journalism:
Moral Outrage and the News

When the Protestant-dominated Long Parliament in England faced an upsurge in polemical religious literature in 1643, it did the accustomed thing: it passed an ordinance that attempted to control the content of printed material through licensing and censorship laws. At the time, a young man was wandering the English countryside, preparing for a ministry that would challenge religious and governmental authority, thereby playing an important role in ending censorship of the press in England and laying the foundations for today's press freedoms.

George Fox is best remembered as the founder of the Quaker movement, but the spirit embodied in his radical campaign cannot be separated from the communications mission that we now identify with modern journalism. In his biblically based, prophetic writing and speaking, Fox called for political reform, defended the sanctity of individual conscience, and advocated freedom of expression—all precursors to the vital principles that make up today's journalistic credo. While Fox is not as widely recognized as a pioneer in carving out new press freedoms as, say, John Milton is, Fox's motivation for demanding the right to express his conscience without restriction draws on religion as its source as much as did the Puritan poet-scholar Milton. Although modern media historians tend to see Milton's classical defense of press freedoms in largely secular terms, the religious partisans of the seventeenth century would not have missed the religious overtones in Milton's message.

It is almost forgotten in our more secular times that many of the early advocates of freedom of the press were preachers and proselytizers whose religious zeal—and the writings that poured forth from their pens—placed them solidly in the tradition of the world's first "journalists." While the values of free expression put forth by these religious reformers have been transformed into secular principles that we now identify as constitutional (as in the protections of free speech and press freedom in the U.S. Constitution) or professional in nature (as in journalists' defense of the "public's right to know"), the origins of these bedrock principles of a free press can be found in the passionate religious disputes of a time when religion was interwoven with virtually all controversies of public life. Few journalists would recognize that when Milton talked about truth in his famous maxim—if truth and falsehood are pitted in an equal contest, truth is sure to prevail—he capitalized *Truth,* meaning that he was confident that God's truth would be revealed to people who were receptive to it. Journalists today seldom recognize that the prophetic impulse to protest injustice and to root out corruption—which Fox found spelled out in key passages of the Bible—still rests, admittedly in diluted and secularized form, in the modern journalistic commitment to social justice and reform.

Back in the 1600s, in the period of the English civil war, most of what embroiled England had to do with religion, and that counted for the news, too. The religious cauldron that was England at that time—where Protestants took full power of the English government in 1649, beheaded the Catholic-sympathizing Charles I, and established a theocratic government that unsuccessfully tried to unite a nation teeming with dissident religious groups—was also the breeding ground of the modern newspaper. The first printed newssheets hawked by booksellers and circulated in the marketplaces contained a form of journalism we would recognize today—news of murders, speeches, military victories, executions. But these "newsbooks," as they have come to be called, were also packed with thundering theological broadsides and partisan religious attacks that reflected the passions of the English Reformation.[1]

A powerful element in Fox's crusade was the tract, or the pamphlet—printed on the newly invented printing presses (many of them mobile, so that they could be moved quickly to avoid discovery by the authorities). Fox and his followers' determined use of the printing press has led one of his biographers to speculate that Fox may have come across the 1644 tract *Areopagitica,* written by Milton, during Fox's first visit to London that same year.[2] Even if Fox did not see the essay by Milton—whose ringing defense of free expression and unlicensed printing is viewed as the foundational statement of modern press liberty—it likely would have appealed to him. After all, wrote Cecil Sharman, "as events turned out, for forty years it was Fox, his fellow Quaker writers, and their printers, who most persistently defied all censorship."[3]

The Quaker movement provides an important illustration of the way that what today we would call press freedoms were intertwined historically with religious dissent. Quakers were both the recipients and the producers of the bombast and the vitriol characterizing much of the printed material that circulated throughout England in the 1600s. Many Quaker pamphlets were printed to rebut the claims made in the newsbooks of the time (some produced by rival clerics who detested the Quaker cause), and Fox complained of being the victim of "newsmongers."[4] Quakers were accused of regularly spewing forth blasphemies and heresies, spurning marriage, believing in free love, and being papists in disguise.[5] Fox himself was said to wear ribbons to attract and seduce women.[6] Fox—and the other defenders of Quakerism—answered in kind. The later image of Quakers as a humble, soft-spoken people was hardly reflected in such bitter denunciations as the 1659 pamphlet in which Fox defended Quakerism against "the great mystery of the great whore unfolded: and antichrists kingdom revealed unto destruction."[7]

To understand fully the elements making up modern journalism, it is important to realize that Fox—despite a life devoted exclusively to religious matters—stands squarely in a tradition of writing that reaches back to the Hebrew prophets of the Bible and forward to today's most outspoken columnists, investigative reporters, and editorial champions of social causes. Although now almost fully secular in outlook, journalistic advocates are heirs to the reform spirit that inspired Fox to resist paying tithes to support the state church, to plead the cause of the poor and the persecuted, and to rail against what he saw as the hypocrisy and incompetence of the Anglican clergy. Fox clearly saw his life modeled on the Hebrew prophets, who were outraged at the religious corruption of their own time and called for a revitalized Judaism. Fox also followed in the footsteps of early Christian prophetic figures, such as the apostle Paul, whose revelatory experience of the indwelling Christ and whose belief that he was taught the truth of scripture directly from God deeply influenced Fox's own theology.[8] As it was for Paul and the Hebrew prophets, whose written texts were used to help maintain Jewish and early Christian community solidarity in times of exile and political oppression, writing was a central element of Fox's missionary activity and his efforts to bolster Quaker resistance to persecution. Fox produced more than five thousand letters and circulated more than two hundred published pamphlets; it takes an eight-volume publication to encompass his writings.[9]

To call Fox's writing journalism may seem a stretch for the modern imagination, but in the most basic sense it represents an important strain in journalism during its formative period. Fox's writings are representative of a raw and inspired expression that I call "prophetic journalism"—a journalism of passion, polemic, and moral opinion that has come to exist alongside the modern ethic of objectivity and the commercial elements of profit making that dictate so much of what journalism constitutes today. To be sure, the impulse that drove Fox is now found largely on the editorial page, in opinion publications, or (in its most direct form) in religious broadcasting and pamphlets handed out on the street corner by religious groups. However, in Fox's day, the idea of truth as something to be discovered by testable, observable experimentation and the subjectivist notion of the importance of each individual's perception of the truth as he or she sees it were just developing. In one respect, Fox was influenced by these emerging forces of modern science and individualism, and he put a high

premium on the individual's personal experience of God and religious truth—
what he calls knowing something "experimentally"—in discerning the validity
of spiritual experience.[10] But Fox also was still medieval in outlook, and he, like
most of his contemporaries, tended to treat fact, just as it been done since ancient times, as something inseparable from what we would call opinion and to
use bombast and polemic as a method to assert the truth.

To understand Fox—as well as the spiritual impetus behind the tradition of
prophetic journalism—it is valuable to see the way the prophets of the Bible
loom behind the writing that today we would call advocacy or adversarial journalism. In his written broadsides, as well as the way he led his life, Fox gained
much spiritual inspiration from the prophets, particularly Jeremiah, who spoke
of God's making a "new covenant" with people by touching "their hearts."[11] In
the Hebrew prophetic tradition, the prophets tell the Israelites the hard truths
about the condition of their society and warn of the consequences if they do
not follow the ways of God. Hebrew prophecy falls into two broad categories.
When the Israelites are oppressed or in captivity, the prophets speak a message
of hope and promise a restoration of their independence as a sign that God has
not forgotten them: "When the poor and needy seek water, and there is none . . .
I the Lord will answer them, I the God of Israel will not forsake them" (Isaiah
41:17–18). But when the Israelites are a successful nation, the prophets hold them
accountable to standards of equality, justice, and compassion for the weak and
downtrodden and excoriate in fearless ways those who fall short of God's demands: "Cease to do evil, learn to do good; seek justice, correct oppression;
defend the fatherless, plead for the widow" (Isaiah 1:16–17). Although the religious overtones may not always be evident in today's journalism, one can recognize the prophecy of hope in the journalistic tradition. "It is a great thing to
be truly a Reformer, even one misinterpreted and scorned through life," said
the nineteenth-century editor Horace Greeley, adding, "To speak firmly the word
destined ultimately to heal Man's deadliest maladies . . . this is a heroism where-
of no other forlorn hope than that of Humanity is capable."[12] The prophecy of
moral indignation rings loudly in the modern press champions of reform, too.
"Every government is run by liars," declared I. F. Stone, one of the preeminent
Washington, D.C., investigative reporter from the 1950s to the early 1970s. "That
is a prima facie assumption until proven wrong."[13]

The elements of Jewish prophetic expression are most clearly evident in the
"journalism of outrage," as modern investigative journalism has been described.[14] Lincoln Steffens acknowledged as much in his *Autobiography* when
he placed "muckraking" investigative reporters in the direct lineage of the Hebrew prophets.[15] One only has to look at an adage of that period—the journalist Finley Peter Dunne's celebrated phrase that the proper role of journalists is
to "comfort the afflicted" and to "afflict the comfortable"[16]—to see the biblical
parallels between the muckraking movement and the progressive political period of the late nineteenth century and early twentieth that muckraking so in-

fluenced. Compare Dunne's comment with, for example, Ezekiel 34:16: "The Lord said: 'I will seek the lost, and I will bring back the strayed, and I will bind up the injured, and I will strengthen the weak, but the fat and the strong I will destroy; I will feed them with justice.'"

Many elements of the prophetic tradition—the spirit of righteousness, the indignant moralism, the effort to maintain purity of values, the call for spiritual and ethical renewal, the fierce sense of corruption abounding everywhere—are as typically found in today's best investigative reporters or crusading editors as they were in the prophetic voices who tried to keep alive Jewish faith and morality during the Israelite empire and the Jewish exile in Babylon. The image of the investigative reporter as the heir of the prophetic tradition is exemplified by I. F. Stone, the son of Russian Jewish immigrants, who spent almost twenty years mining federal government documents for examples of waste and duplicity that he published in his widely circulated newsletter. Described as a "cheerfully angry man," Stone impressed people with his "permanent sense of outrage," as the *Washington Post* reporter Peter Osnos put it. "He sees black and whites where others are willing to see gray. A scandal or an injustice is not to be excused. Compromise when it is a sell-out is not to be excused."[17]

The prophetic message was incorporated into the news formulas from the earliest days of the large commercial newspapers in the United States. James Gordon Bennett—one of the first and most powerful voices in the establishment of the nineteenth-century "penny press"—used religious language, closely covered developments in the religious community, and recognized the appeal of calls for reform as part of the free-wheeling formula he developed in the 1830s that set the tone for the modern-day, big-city, commercial newspaper. Trained to be a priest and intimately familiar with scripture, Bennett regularly displayed the unabashedly righteous tone of biblical prophecy, such as he did when he jabbed in ironic ways at his fellow editors who helped launch the famous "Moral War" against the sensationalistic tactics of Bennett's newspaper. "They can only find room for the lies and slander of politicians—but not for the truths and facts of religion and morals," Bennett editorialized. "The immoral, indecent, irreligious, obscene *Morning Herald,* however, finds time and room to report all these valuable doings."[18] Bennett, never known for his lack of hubris, lambasted the religious establishment for its hypocrisy and its phony moralizing, and he even went so far as to proclaim journalism to be the higher religious calling when he declared that "the temple of religion has had its day" and that now the newspaper must take the lead in reforming society.[19]

Bennett's form of acerbic, no-holds-barred commentary has largely disappeared from the discourse of today's more restrained mainstream, commercial press. But, even without Bennett's self-promoting, self-congratulatory tone, the thrust of much modern-day journalism—ranging from editorial calls for civic reform to investigative reporting of fraud and corruption—is in the tradition of the prophetic call for righteousness and renewal. The media sociologist Herbert Gans, in pointing to the reform-oriented values of modern journalists, maintained this is no coincidence. The late-nineteenth-century Progressive movement came into being at just about the time the mass market magazine and large circulation newspapers, where such muckrakers as Steffens did their work, had become the dominant form of media in the United States. Many of the beliefs that Gans identified as part of the "enduring" values of journalists— they are against waste and environmental degradation, violations of legal and political rights, and bigness and monopoly in business and government and are in favor of democratic ideals, individual freedom, grass-roots citizen activity, and the maintenance of a just social order—can be seen, in much modernized ways, as parallels to the social protests launched by the prophets of the Hebrew scriptures.[20] As the historian Richard Hofstadter put it in describing journalism's contribution to the investigative and reform mood of the time, "The fundamental critical achievement of American Progressivism was the business of exposure, and journalism was the chief occupational source of its creative writers. It is hardly an exaggeration to say that the Progressive mind was characteristically a journalistic mind, and that its characteristic contribution was that of the socially responsible reporter-reformer."[21]

As with the Hebrew prophets, who preached hope to people in desperate straits, so too did the muckrakers. The prophetic books of the Bible oscillate between denunciations of the corrupt ways of the Israelites at the height of their empire and expectations that, after initially punishing his people, God would rescue Israel from captivity. What has sometimes been characterized as the relentlessly negative tone of modern reform journalism (a tone that led President Theodore Roosevelt to dub the turn-of-the-twentieth-century reform journalists "muckrakers," in honor of the figure in John Bunyan's *Pilgrim's Progress* who would not look up from raking the muck even when a crown was offered to him) can mask an idealistic, optimistic countenance.[22] Jack Anderson's description of his mentor, Drew Pearson, the much-feared 1950s Washington, D.C., exposé artist, captured what Anderson claimed was this spirit. "'It is the job of the newspaperman to spur the lazy, watch the weak, expose the corrupt,'" Anderson reported Pearson, a Quaker who helped organize food collection drives for the World War II–ravaged populations of France and Italy, would insist. "'He must be the eyes, ears and nose of the American people.'" Anderson (himself a devout Mormon) said it was Pearson's general optimism and his lack of cynicism that always impressed him. "His preoccupation with scandal never seemed to shake his belief in the basic foundations of the American system," Anderson observed. "All that was needed for its indefinite improvability, he felt, was exposure of the bad and inculcation of the good."[23]

Interestingly, many of the prophetic, reform-oriented figures in American journalism history—including Bennett, the peripatetic journalist-turned-poet Walt Whitman, and the journalist and novelist Mark Twain—are identified as critics of traditional religion. It is easy to get the idea—as many have done with

Twain's debunking of organized religion, for example—that the prophetic personality in journalism has been so alienated from conventional expressions of American Christianity that he or she has come to oppose religion in all forms. But it is important to look closely at what Twain (who was obsessed in his own way with religion) was saying. The nature of prophecy in the biblical tradition is that it calls people back to a purer form of religious worship that has been lost in the pursuit of worldly affairs. Like the Hebrew prophets, who urged the Israelites to return to their ancestral faith and blamed their sufferings on their faithlessness, prophetic reformers—in both religion and journalism—advocate a restoration of values that they feel have been lost in the self-seeking ways of the culture. Whitman, with his pantheism and his search for the one true universal truth behind all religions, and even Twain (who in his many pages written about religion, once wrote, "This is indeed a God! He is not jealous, trivial, ignorant, revengeful—it is impossible. He has personal dignity—dignity answerable to his grandeur, his greatness, his might, his sublimity") clearly believed that their vision of spirituality was more authentic than the corrupted practices of the religionists of their time.[24] Bennett also fits this mold. He saw himself as the bearer of true Christian virtues in his battles with the civic, religious, and business establishment—"an enthusiast" in matters of the "delicious and charming mysteries" of faith, as he described himself, compared with his clerical opponents, "infidel[s] to the holy petticoat, and all that it contains."[25]

The prophets, of course, felt they were not honored in their own land, and this fits the mold of the journalist-prophet, too. The legendary editor Joseph Pulitzer—who, because of his endowment of the Pulitzer Prize, is often thought of synonymously with the most noble aspects of reform and investigative journalism—saw himself as taking a prophetic stance on many issues, and he believed he suffered for it, too. Pulitzer, a German immigrant born of Jewish and Catholic parents, married to an Episcopalian woman, and nominally a member of the Episcopalian church (which he seldom attended), was a religious skeptic. Yet Pulitzer's heterodoxy, as well as his Jewishness, became the subject of attacks and vilification—which (not unusual for editors who are better at dishing out criticism than taking it) was quite painful to him. For example, the editorials in the *Evening Sun* by Charles Dana, another of the legendary editors of the time, called Pulitzer "Judas Pulitzer," "a renegade Jew who has denied his breed," and contained these epithets: "His face is repulsive, not because the physiognomy is Hebraic, but because it is Pulitzeresque. . . . The Wandering Jew! . . . Move on, Pulitzer, move on!"[26]

In recent times, scholars have speculated about the mental health of some of the Jewish prophetic writers (read the opening passages of Ezekiel, for example) and raised questions about the relationship between the prophetic personality and the eruption of material from the subconscious mind.[27] This analysis can certainly be applied to the world of journalism—or at least, to Pulitzer's *New York World*—as it has been by the novelist Theodore Dreiser, who worked briefly

under Pulitzer as a reporter. Pulitzer, Dreiser noted admiringly, had turned journalism in New York upside down and had "attacked, attacked, attacked." Yet,
Pulitzer, who suffered severely from mood swings, had made working conditions at the *World* a journalistic hell, Dreiser claimed, where editors ever fear-
ful of dismissal tried to please the owner—"undoubtedly semi-neurasthenic, a
disease-demonized soul, who could scarcely control himself in anything, a man
who was fighting an almost insane battle with life itself, trying to be omnipotent and what not else, and never to die." Life at the *World,* concluded Dreiser,
a man with his own history of breakdowns who understood what it meant to
try to live life on a mythic scale, was "immense, just the same—terrific."[28]

Three modern conservative media researchers have extended this critique by
calling for a psychological evaluation of the entire media profession. S. Robert
Lichter, Stanley Rothman, and Linda S. Lichter reached conclusions that fit
comfortably with the model of the journalist as prophetic personality—albeit
an unbalanced one. The Lichters and Rothman probed the psyche of the profession (based on a personality test given to a group of journalists, as well as
journalism graduate students at Columbia University), and they concluded that
journalists want power but are repelled by it, that they struggle with narcissism
and grandiose self-images, and that they tend to project their inner struggles
onto the outside world. This leads to a range of characteristics in the profession
that can be connected to the prophetic impulse: an addiction to new stimulation and heightened experience, the projection of negative inner feelings onto
outer figures of authority, the impulse to seek social reform as a way to allevi-
ate psychic tension, and a desire to lead an insider's life while holding onto an
outsider's self-image.[29]

In reading the analysis of the Lichters and Rothman, one can not help recognizing a journalistic personality type in particular—that of the reform-oriented investigative reporter. It is intriguing that—at least metaphorically—the
biographer of Lincoln Steffens, author of *Shame of the Cities* and the most celebrated of the muckraking American journalists, implied that powerful psychic
tension was at work in Steffens (who, like Whitman, Dreiser, and Twain, suffered from "black moods" of "hopelessness and nightmare"). Justin Kaplan saw
Steffens's passion for reform and his investigative zealotry as a reflection of his
inner turmoil. For example, in describing Steffens's lifetime difficulties with
women and his painful honesty in dealing with failed relationships, Kaplan
wrote that Steffens believed he "had finally succeeded in muckraking himself.
He had laid his shame more bare than the shame of the cities. . . . But, like
muckraking as he had practiced it, exposure of this sort led to no structural
changes" and did not alter in the least "the laws of his personality but merely
showed how they worked."[30]

Anytime anyone steps into the world of psychological analysis, the terrain gets
tricky and controversial, certainly for anyone who tries to psychoanalyze modern journalists or the prophetic impulse within journalistic personalities of an

earlier era. Not every journalist—in fact, probably very few of them—could be categorized as a moral crusader or messianic reformer. But there is an aspect of the prophetic tradition that is reflected in the progressive, social reform tradition of certain newspapers and in the personality of certain journalists. Investigative reporters, in particular, are often driven, obsessed personalities, and they probably need to be, given the obstacles to unearthing stories that they face. Seymour Hersh, the former *New York Times* reporter best known for exposing the My Lai massacre during the Vietnam War, is often held up as the prototype of the implacable, unrelenting journalistic investigator who lets nothing deter him from a story. Hersh was described by Leonard Downie, for example, as a renegade radical journalist fueled by outrage and a craving for ego-feeding attention, a boat-rocking, rumpled-looking opportunist who would go to extraordinary lengths to get his stories into the newspaper so that they could "sear the conscience of America," as Hersh once put it.[31]

There is a tendency to view the professional ethic of twentieth-century journalism—with its emphasis on objectivity, fairness, and the telling of both sides of any controversy—as the outgrowth of Enlightenment rationalism and the adoption of the empirical ethic in modern journalism. Yet the moderation of tone and the tempering of the prophetic impulse that we see in today's "balanced" journalism had less to do with the Enlightenment than with commerce. Initially, prophetic expressions resided comfortably with the profit impulse that emerged through the distribution of newly liberated forms of thinking expressed by those who were challenging the prevailing social and political order. Grand prophetic claims were made at the time for the power of the printing press to dispense new ideas about Christianity, the gospel, and the rights of humankind. Religious and political dissenters, advocates of Protestantism in England and the European continent, and radical social thinkers all enthusiastically embraced the products of the printing press. For nearly three hundred years after the invention of the printing press in the mid-1400s, it was common to hear such exuberant comments as that made by Daniel Defoe, the journalist, dissenter, and early novelist, "The preaching of sermons is speaking to a few of mankind [but] printing books is talking to the whole world," or by John Foxe, the English Protestant who wrote in the *Book of Martyrs*, "The Lord began to work for His Church not with sword and target to subdue His exalted adversary, but with printing, writing and reading."[32]

But prophetic claims—like much else that was transformed by the invention of the printing press—were soon captured by and intertwined with the capitalist system that was establishing itself during the early modern era. Censorship—once exercised rigidly by the medieval church and the feudal monarchies—was relaxed, and, by the end of the eighteenth century, it was commercial pressures and public opinion that dictated many of the restraints on the prophetic voice. Although by then the concept of press freedom was embedded in the U.S. Constitution and press freedoms expanded during England's Glorious

Revolution and the French Revolution, printers, publishers, and newspaper editors were learning that—even with expanded freedom of speech—they must pay careful attention to what their readers and the marketplace wanted to hear. For every Thomas Paine, whose best-selling, incendiary essays and prophetic propagandizing for political freedom fueled the cause of revolution in America and Europe, there was a Benjamin Franklin, whose advanced ideas and skepticism about Christian orthodoxy always were couched so they would not harm the economic prospects of his publications. Editors perhaps took note that Paine, who once declared that "my country is the world; to do good my religion" and who refused royalties for much of his writing, died broke and ostracized and was denied burial in a Quaker cemetery;[33] Franklin, the cautious editor whose publications printed all sides of a dispute and avoided "printing such Things as usually give Offence either to Church or State," died prosperous and celebrated by his contemporaries.[34]

By the nineteenth century, the voice of prophecy had been fully absorbed into the commercial dictates of a journalism industry that, in most parts of Europe and America, had become a force in the capitalistic establishment. With the coming of the penny press in the 1830s, American newspapers increasingly adopted the model of the circulation- and advertiser-supported publication, and strategies to maximize readership and revenue became the first priority of the businessmen-journalists who ran them. With newspapers setting the tone of the *New York Times* (with its motto "All the news that's fit to print"), newspapers were separated into news and editorial opinion pages, and newspapers increasingly jettisoned the vitriolic and partisan approach of the press of the early American republic. Celebrated nineteenth- and early-twentieth-century editors—such as Bennett, Greeley, Whitman, Dana, Pulitzer, and William Allen White—still used their newspapers as forums to promote causes and as vehicles to wield power and influence. Some were even willing to pay an economic and a personal price for their outspokenness—but not many. Increasingly the monetary motivations of ever more entrenched journalistic organizations, like the other expanding enterprises of the Industrial Revolution, came to the forefront, and the financial calculus could not be separated out from even the most noble of crusades. Much ink has been spent trying to analyze how much of the big-city newspaper crusade—pioneered by Bennett and brought to full flower by such entrepreneurs as Pulitzer, William Randolph Hearst, and E. W. Scripps—was sincere in its motivation and how much was about the promotion of the newspaper's financial interests. Still, no matter how much the early captains of the newspaper industry focused on competition, self-aggrandizement, and the maximization of circulation, the spirit of public service did become embedded in the philosophy of their news and editorial pages.

The newspaper historian Michael Schudson argued that many editors, despite adopting the pose of the crusader, were not really that interested in exercising a role of community leadership. Such editors as Pulitzer, Greeley, and White cared deeply about their editorial page and their influence in the community, but others (such as Hearst, who viewed the editorial page with contempt, and the *New York Times*'s Adolph Ochs, who considered eliminating it altogether) thought of themselves as businessmen rather than essayists or political thinkers.[35] Ochs was particularly successful in molding the *Times* into a formal, even-handed publication that would not offend the wealthier, upper-middle-class readership he sought—a model that became widely imitated as the example of the respectable newspaper. The *Times* traditionally has done some investigative reporting but not much (its exposés of the Tweed Ring in the early 1870s notwithstanding, even today the *Times* is remarkably free of investigative reporting).[36] The tone of the *Times,* described by some as the "voice of God" in its weightiness and seriousness, appears to find its inspiration from something other than the outraged voice of the Hebrew prophets.

Despite the transformation of the media environment, the prophetic voice did not die. The most celebrated form of American prophetic journalism—the muckraking movement of the late nineteenth century and early twentieth—emerged in a highly capitalistic environment. While the names of Steffens, Dunne, Ida Tarbell, Upton Sinclair, Ray Stannard Baker, and Will Irwin are most associated with the muckrakers, it was S. S. McClure, the founder of *McClure's* magazine in 1894, who helped make muckraking possible. McClure—a businessman more than a social visionary—recognized early on that there was a market for probing investigations of the abuses of big-city political bosses and the huge industrial trusts of the time. Muckraking, McClure thought, "was the result of merely taking up in the magazine some of the problems that were beginning to interest people."[37] An ebullient, charming, and charismatic personality ("a supernova in the journalistic firmament," as he was once called), McClure was also a buccaneer capitalist who aimed his publication at an audience that, influenced by the Populist and Progressive movements of the era, was perceived as having a strong interest in social and political reform.[38]

Throughout the twentieth century, there was a tension between profit and the prophetic voice in journalism. Many times commercialism looked as if it had won out completely, but then the spirit of prophetic journalism surfaced again. One has to remember that the greatest mystery that surrounds muckraking—why did it die out so quickly?—must be understood in terms of the marketplace. In many respects, the muckraking phenomenon was an aberration—a rare and unusual outbreak of reform journalism that, with its high moral and ethical purpose, exposed more in the way of wickedness than a capitalistic social order was willing to fix. Justin Kaplan, Steffens's biographer, put the muckraker firmly in the prophetic tradition (the muckrakers, he contended, identified with "the Prophets and the Apostles" and saw themselves standing "at Armageddon, battling for the Lord").[39] Yet analysts have pondered what led to the muckraking movement's demise in the early nineteenth century after less than twenty years of life. Was it the advent of World War I or the economic prosper-

ity of the 1920s? Was there less public disenchantment with the economic and
government system? Or did people simply grow weary of the crusades that always seemed to be so negative in tone? Reform movements, by their nature, tend
to come in cycles and burn out when the first generation of reformers discov-
ers that social change does not come easy. Whatever the answer, the economic
explanation is fairly well accepted; many other magazines crowded into the
marketplace and drove off most of the publications devoted exclusively to
muckraking. Since then, the prophetic voice in journalism has only sporadically
appealed to the masses, and today's heirs to the muckraking publications (which
include such magazines as *Mother Jones,* the *Nation,* the *Progressive,* and the
Washington Monthly) have only tiny followings.

Technological and scientific advances also contributed much to the continued erosion of the prophetic voice. The development of the telegraph in the mid-
nineteenth century spurred the creation of the Associated Press, a consortium
of newspapers that banded together to pool the production of wire news and
spawned a form of safe, unthreatening, homogenized news coverage that still
dominates modern media. The AP's need for simple, fact-oriented writing that
would be acceptable to all its clients, no matter what their political orientation,
reinforced the belief, which emerged so strongly in the late nineteenth century
and early twentieth, that there was an objective way to cover and present the
news. This view—buttressed by the growing empirical and scientific outlook
of the era—further solidified the split between news and opinion pages that is
still the model for most American daily newspapers (but which is much less
established in Europe, where many publications are still purchased because of
their political outlook). Yet it is the faith of American editors that the news can
be distilled to a neutral essence that has done so much to submerge the prophetic
voice in the economic, organizational, and technological calculus of modern
news organizations.

For much of the twentieth century, this view of the news organization as a
bastion of truth and objectivity led to a placid form of mainstream commercial journalism that contained little that was upsetting to readers or challenged
established institutions. Much has been made of the upsurge of radical and
muckraking journalism that accompanied the Vietnam War and Watergate, but
little remains today of those prophetic voices of the left or advocacy journalism in general. The underground or alternative press largely disappeared in the
complacent, self-absorbed mood of American culture in the 1980s and 1990s,
with many of these "alternative" papers transforming themselves into yuppie-
throw-away-sheets stuffed with personal ads, entertainment and restaurant
guides, and stories on the latest lifestyle trends. Small publications on both the
left and the right carried on the tradition of polemics and rhetorical rabble-
rousing. But the prophetic voice in the mainstream press has grown muted as
corporate ownership has expanded its hold on the media industry and left its
stamp of scientific management, cautious journalism, and homogenized news

content as a way to ensure that the audience it caters to will not get riled up against the corporate product.

Perhaps the strongest and most continuous litany of media criticism in the late twentieth century was directed against commercial television and its effects on modern society. Among Marshall McLuhan's other theories about the electronic media, he maintained that television is a more effective vehicle for the "cool" personality (relaxed, low-key, comfortable body language that puts viewers at ease) than it is for the forceful and intense, or "hot," personality (which, almost by definition, would include the prophetic personality).[40] Given this dynamic, it is not surprising to find that the occasional commentary on television seldom veers from mainstream opinions and press-corps group think. Since the advent of television, few "hot" personalities have become television media celebrities.[41] Considering what the prophetic personality on television might look like—for example, the mentally deteriorating, wildly visionary news broadcaster played by Peter Finch in the movie *Network*—we may be thankful. But it still tells us a great deal about how influential the nature of media can be on the prevailing form of social dialogue within a culture.

Joshua Meyrowitz, a McLuhan protégé, argued in his book *No Sense of Place* that the nature of television—with its capacity for bringing us live, close-up encounters with public figures in our living rooms and for probing into the once private realms of their lives—has lessened the distance between us and our leaders and has reduced the awe and respect we once felt for figures of authority. By allowing us a sense of intimate connection with people on the screen, television is a "de-mystifying" force in the culture and, by implication, a place where only those people who make us comfortable are likely to thrive.[42] The prophetic personality has never sought to make people feel at ease about themselves or their society, and the television screen, with its capacity for intimate close-ups and easily shared emotions, has not proved to be a place for delivering a message that makes viewers feel bad about themselves or the television industry (a business that, with its fixation on ratings and programming fare with as wide an appeal as possible, hardly seeks to promote ideas that are not widely embraced in the culture).

Perhaps the grandest hopes for liberating journalism and providing an outlet for prophetic voices has been the Internet and the development of interactive electronic communication environments. Media scholars have waxed enthusiastic about the possibilities for a communications system that meets the deeply felt human need for direct interaction with others and allows users to circumvent the traditional gatekeeping role of the press with unmediated, person-to-person interaction. The World Wide Web has been used by protesters—such as the activists who oppose the World Trade Organization—as a tool for organizing and communicating among like-minded individuals. Anyone who uses the Internet, however, also has to be amazed at the chaos of content and the anarchy inherent in the unleashing of millions of individual voices in contact with one another. Some believe that the advent of the Internet—with its opportunities for individual "flaming," its rumor-spreading, its undocument- ed "facts," and its potential for every sort of crack-pot group imaginable to es- tablish a Web page—has led to a upsurge of what might be called a form of prophetic journalism. But if this is the vision of prophecy at the dawning of the twenty-first century—millions of voices "expressing themselves" to one another in chat rooms and on Web pages and Internet bulletin boards—we may decide that media advancements tell us as much about the fragmented and cacopho- nous nature of modern life as about the possibilities for the emergence of true prophetic personalities.

Of course, many modern people will find it difficult to endorse the very no- tion of the prophetic personality—of anyone who might arrive with a claim to a convincing truth or with a critique of the social order that could force people to consider changing their lives or changing their ways. Too often a prophet presents us with a series of uncomfortable choices—to make sacrifices, to aban- don our complacency, to consider a painful truth. It is too easy to chalk it up as just another claim of another false prophet, which many feel they have witnessed all too often in modern life. Today we have a host of reasons to be skeptical of prophetic claims: our awareness of the effects of mental illness, our recognition of the dangers of demagoguery, our suspicion of the excessively righteous and those who believe they have a revelation that the world should embrace. We have too much sophistication to believe that anyone has a monopoly on truth. But it is important to recognize how much the media culture that surrounds us has contributed to these attitudes—and how much our sophistication is based on the often unrecognized influence of the media on our lives.

Marshall McLuhan was not fully a determinist in his belief in the power of elec- tronic media over us, and he recognized that there were a few visionaries (he saw them as the "artists" among us serving in a "prophetic" role) who could pick up "the message of cultural and technological challenge decades before its trans- forming impact occurs." But McLuhan did not hold out much hope that this prophet figure would have much impact given "the endless power" of people to "hypnotize themselves into unawareness in the presence of" the media's in- fluence. If people "were able to be convinced that art is precise advance knowl- edge of how to cope with the psychic and social consequences of the next tech- nology, would they all become artists?" he asked. "But the counter-irritant usually proves a greater plague than the initial irritant, like a drug habit. . . . So it is in our social lives when a new technology strikes . . . and the censor acts at once to numb us from the blow and to ready the faculties to assimilate the intruder."[43]

CHAPTER 2

The Profits of Reform: Printers, Capitalists, and the Priesthood of Believers

Soon after Martin Luther posted his ninety-five treatises on the church door in Wittenberg, Germany, in 1517, he was surprised to discover that he had become, in modern parlance, a best-selling writer. In a matter of days, his message had been translated and reprinted on the newly invented printing press in such towns as Nuremberg, Leipzig, and Basel, and it had circulated so widely that, in the words of the media historian Elizabeth Eisenstein, it had "won top billing throughout central Europe—competing for space with news of the Turkish threat in print shop, bookstall, and country fair."[1]

Luther was the first—but certainly not the last—to experience a deep historical irony inherent in the invention of the printing press. The printing press could serve as an instrument of the highest religious purposes; in his case, it helped spread the potent ideas that fomented the Protestant Reformation. But it could just as easily be exploited as an instrument of commercial gain—as the printers of his time were quick to capitalize on. Luther expressed his own consternation at this phenomenon: "It is a mystery to me how my theses, more so than my other writings . . . were spread to so many places. They were meant exclusively for our academic circle here. . . . They were written in such a language that the common people could hardly understand them."[2]

As happened during the time of Jesus and Paul, when writing transformed the oral cultures of Europe and the Mediterranean, the invention of the printing press in the mid-fifteenth century was a pivotal historical event that helped reshape the religious landscape of the Western world. The connection between printing and Protestantism made Luther, the one-time priest whose belief in salvation through faith and the supremacy of the Bible as the guide to faith rocked the Catholic world, and Johann Gutenberg, the German businessman who is credited as inventor of the printing press in Europe, cultural heroes of their time and two of the most significant figures in Western history. But it also put Luther in the awkward position of complaining about the corruption of Catholic practices and accusing the church of becoming too focused on wealth and property, while his own supporters were making money off the sale of his writings.

A large body of historical literature has grown up that links the invention of printing, the rise of Protestantism, and the emergence of the capitalist spirit as the driving elements in the creation of our modern commercial culture. Even more so than Luther's writings, the doctrines of John Calvin, the Swiss theocrat who exercised great influence on Protestants in England and Scotland, are identified with what has come to be called the Protestant ethic and its intertwining of piety and spiritual zeal with the elevation of material success as the surest possible sign of salvation.

Enlightenment skepticism, the rise of science, and the substitution of colloquial languages for Latin contributed to the weakening of the religious role that once monopolized the uses of writing. But the commercial pressures that were unleashed with the invention of printing were enormous, and they did much to undermine the original religious purpose of the employment of the printed word and to turn the venture toward commercialism and profit making. Today, the religious aspect of writing and mass communications remains, but it is submerged beneath deep currents of commercialism and layered below material goals and values. From St. Thomas Aquinas, who used writing to try to reconcile reason with the ways of God, to Luther, whose writings inspired widespread religious revolt, to Benjamin Franklin, who blended Calvinistic notions of thrift with great business success in the early American journalism industry, to James Gordon Bennett, who saw journalism as a superior moral mission that nonetheless should never stand in the way of making lots of money, to Gannett's Al Neuharth, the wealthy modern media mogul whose interest in religion has been largely to mock it, the transformation of the role of writing and communications from a religious to a commercial one has been profound. Yet, for anyone who looks deeply enough, the religious origins of writing and mass communications still can be found resonating powerfully within the commercial impulses of the media industry, particularly among journalism professionals.

To understand fully the tension between commercialism and religious purpose that coexists in the modern media, it is necessary to examine the peculiar way that early American editors and journalists infused the attitudes of religion—particularly the Puritan and Protestant mind-set, which was in ascendance when America was colonized—into their business and professional practices. The themes that have been so fruitfully explored by Max Weber, R. H. Tawney, and Ernst Troeltsch, who linked the emergence of Protestantism with the unleashing of the capitalist spirit, can be applied to the early American editors and publishers who, in a variation of what has come to be called the Weber thesis, believed that it was possible to incorporate a meaningful religious purpose into a higher commercial goal.

Weber held up Franklin, the printer, editor, and pioneering figure of colonial American journalism, as a prime example of the modern capitalist who worships industry and prosperity and sees making money as the equivalent of a religious "calling." In recounting Franklin's circulation of his commonsense advice—"Remember that time is money"; "He who wastes five shillings murders all that might have been produced by it"—Weber described Franklin as typical of a Calvinist age in which businesspeople treated money making as a religious obligation that conferred a special blessing on the successful.[3]

We can utilize Weber's thesis if we think of Franklin as a personification of two strains in journalism that developed in the centuries following the invention of the printing press. First, Franklin epitomized the free-thinking colonial journalist who used the printed word in service to idealistic causes (exemplified by Franklin's blunt but witty advocacy of liberal, reformist ideas; his irreverent critiques of current affairs and social convention; and his defense of freedom of the press in drafting the U.S. Constitution). At the same time, Franklin was a businessman and an entrepreneur who saw journalism as a vehicle for commercial success (witnessed by the wealth he amassed as a publisher, editor, and investor in a "chain" of print shops that enabled him to retire early and devote himself to science, politics, and diplomacy).[4]

It is worth noting that the printing press Franklin used was not much more technologically advanced than the one Gutenberg invented almost three hundred years earlier—even if the entrepreneurial spirit had intensified considerably over the years. Still, it is fascinating to realize how quickly writing was transformed into a profit-making venture in the hands of booksellers and the operators of the first printing presses. As Elizabeth Eisenstein noted, no sooner had Gutenberg finished printing "the last sheet" of his "monumental Bible" than John Fust, the financier of the firm, "set out with a dozen copies or so to see for himself how he could best reap the harvest of his patient investments," thus forever connecting "spiritual aspirations to an expanding capitalistic enterprise." Throughout Europe, a growing number of printers, translators, distributors, and book peddlers recognized the profit potential in the religious agitation created by the writings of Luther and his Protestant allies. "The linking of concern about salvation with shrewd business tactics . . . seems to have been no less pronounced in the early sixteenth century than among Bible salesmen today," Eisenstein pointed out.[5]

We are so accustomed in our time to associating the world of printing and writing with the world of commerce that is hard to imagine what an unsettling development it was for religious people, including Luther, to find the most sanctified of disputes hashed out in an environment where businesspeople were waiting to exploit the controversy for commercial gain. It is in Luther's written protests that we get a beginning glimpse of the tensions between the religious impulse and the profit-making schemes of the early mass media. Luther once described printing as "God's highest and extremist act of grace, whereby the business of the Gospel is driven forward," and it is clear that (despite some initial uncertainty about the value of publicity) he made no real effort to keep his friends from disseminating his views.[6] By emphasizing Bible reading as a way of achieving true faith and yet looking askance at the profits being reaped by booksellers and printers, Luther was a figure with one foot planted in the new capitalistic economy and the other in the moral and ethical world of the Middle Ages. Luther, for example, shared the medieval view that religious principle should serve as a restraint on the unfettered operation of the marketplace. This meant Luther did not just rail against the corruption of the church; he also was deeply troubled by the rampant economic individualism of the emerging financial class.[7] This is reflected in his description of the printers who made hasty reprints of the Bible for quick profit: "They look only to their greed."[8]

To understand Luther's ambivalent feelings about the consequences of the printing revolution, we have to understand the old attitudes that he reflected, as well as the new attitudes that ushered in the Protestant Reformation. Luther's disgust with the spiritual laxity of his day, it must be remembered, was spurred by such things as the Catholic church's practice of selling indulgences, the extravagance of church wealth and priestly lifestyles, and the general exploitation of the Germany peasantry by the papacy. But the moral outrage that Luther targeted with equal passion at the capitalistic practices of the bankers, financiers, and merchants of his era was based on traditional church teachings about usury and moral law applied to economics. One of the interesting developments of the period that followed the invention of the printing press is that it led to a burst of new popularity for older writers, such as Thomas Aquinas, who in the thirteenth century had laid down many of the ecclesiastical rules to govern the marketplace and scotch the predatory practices of speculators and middlemen. The view of Aquinas and the medieval church—which Luther shared, in spirit anyway—was that economic interests always must be subordinated to the business of gaining salvation.[9]

Yet, in breaking the monopoly of the Catholic church, Luther—in most respects inadvertently—also broke the hold of the medieval church over economic matters and, in essence, helped convert the marketplace to the realm of the secular. Luther, for example, found himself torn when it came to usury, which in our deregulated, free-market times, we have largely abandoned by doing away with most government limits on interest rates for borrowing money. Luther recognized the moral and spiritual advantages to both individuals and society in putting restraints on economic exploitation; however, repulsed at the church's history of externalizing religion in rules and regulations, he was reluctant to advocate the church's involvement in the regulation of the economy. As R. H. Tawney noted, Luther, despite denouncing covetousness and economic excess, said of borrowing and loan rates, "The preacher shall preach only the Gospel rule, and leave it to each man to follow his own conscience. Let him who receive it, receive it; he cannot be compelled thereto further than the Gospel leads willing hearts whom the spirit of God urges forward."[10]

The capitalistic forces affecting printing were only part of the larger growth of the secular arena in the Europe of Luther's time. In following Christ's precept to "render unto Caesar what is Caesar's," Luther was, in one sense, simply facing economic reality. The newly released energy of capitalism that had been building throughout the Middle Ages helped let loose the new ideas that led to the Renaissance, the Enlightenment, and the Reformation. From the late fifteenth century through the late seventeenth century, the economies of northern Europe and Great Britain saw a slow but steady expansion of trade, financial markets, networks of merchants, and low-level industry. The importance of canon law, the regulation of prices and interest, the authority of the church courts in economic matters, and the appeal to asceticism and worldly renunciation—in essence, all the elements that created the medieval synthesis of the economic order and the spiritual one—shrank in importance before the advance of mercantilism. Even in the areas of Europe that remained Catholic, the church was increasingly less successful in controlling the growing powers of medieval guilds and financial markets, and the appearance of Protestantism, with its calls for a greater individualism in matters of faith and conscience, only further weakened the church's say in matters of the marketplace.

Tawney noted how strange it is that Protestantism—which was intended to bring about a purification of the corruption of Christian doctrine and a greater attention to morality in all matters of life—has come to be identified with the release of economic forces from religious restraint. As with Luther, Calvin preached against the accumulation of wealth for purposes of ostentation or self-gratification, and in the theocracy he established in Geneva, he instituted a thoroughly medieval program that censured harsh creditors, punished merchants who cheated, and guarded against extortionate prices. However, Calvin's doctrines appealed to an urbane community of traders and merchants who had accommodated themselves to the new capitalistic spirit of the age. In advocating an activist creed that called for the purification of the individual and the spiritualization of every aspect of life, Calvin saw its manifestation in a community dedicated to Christian duty, character building, industry, hard work—in short, a virtual blending of the Christian virtues with the economic values that had come to be associated with worldly success. Calvin also argued for relaxed attitudes about capital and interest as practical necessities in the development of commerce, and he celebrated the example of the thriving trader as a benefit to the Christian order—thus setting in motion a religious movement that would embrace wealth as furthering God's purpose and as a sign of spiritual salvation and being one of God's elect.

In our age, when it is so easy to see how the Calvinistic ethic has served as a justification for the crass and unrestrained pursuit of wealth and success, it is

tempting to write off Calvinism as a system of thought that only serves to justify the prevailing economic order and, except by metaphor, cannot be described
as Christian—as R. H. Tawney did.[11] However, in the context of the growing
commercialization of the journalistic world, the religious impulse often has
tended to go underground, only to resurface in the form of a strong belief in
social justice, institutional reform, and democratic values—even among those
who have been busy making their fortunes by distributing news and information. The idea that one can pursue wealth and still do good in the world has
become a guiding principle of many much admired Americans—and none more
so than American publishers and editors. The journalism field is one of the top
places to look for examples of that odd mix that Puritanism contributed to the
world of commerce and industry: the business leader who demonstrates a strong
strain of moral character, self-reliance, and civic conscience, all the while engaging in aggressive financial self-seeking. The Puritan ethic, it should be noted, while identified with Protestantism, has come to have little connection to
any particular theology and has tended to spread throughout the business world,
where it has been adapted to a generalized philosophy that success is the blessing of hard work and a favored relationship with the forces of the universe but
carries with it certain social obligations.

James Gordon Bennett, the Scots immigrant who is credited with establishing the formula for the modern, commercial newspaper, stands as perhaps the
best example of the early American editor who saw the money-making potential in serving the public good. A Catholic by background, Bennett showed how
much both the Catholic and Scots Calvinist culture in which he grew up had
adapted to the mercantile ethic of the time when he proclaimed journalism, in
his characteristically flip and provocative manner, to be a potentially greater
moral force than organized religion: "A newspaper can send more souls to
Heaven, and save more from Hell, than all the churches or chapels in New York—
besides making money at the same time."[12] This led the journalism historian
Frank Luther Mott to note mordantly that, while we do not know if Bennett
saved any souls by his stories, "he certainly made money by them."[13] Joseph
Pulitzer, although also not a Protestant by background (his father was Jewish,
his mother Catholic), expressed his philosophy of journalism and business in a
way that certainly fit with the Calvinist attitudes toward money, charity, and
public service found in typical circles of the progressive American business elite.
"We respect wealth when it is made the instrument of good," Pulitzer editorialized in the *New York World*. "We despise wealth when it . . . is prostituted to
shoddy display and to the gratification of coarse and vulgar tastes."[14] Similar
sentiments were expressed by such moralistic rogues and buccaneer capitalist-
publishers as E. W. Scripps, S. S. McClure, and William Randolph Hearst. Even
Horace Greeley, widely admired for his moral stances and his disinterest in
money (he allowed much of his stock in the *New York Tribune* to pass into others' hands, and he took little more than a salary throughout his career), was

nettled by criticism of his advertising business practices and occasionally yie. to business office pressure.[15]

American editors have always been quick to criticize the subjects of their news stories for hypocrisy, but the accusation has also been hurled back at them, particularly when it comes to issues of profiteering and the bottom line. The Calvinistic notion that one can make a profit without sacrificing moral principles has been tested sorely throughout American journalistic history, and few publishers and editors, at least in the minds of their critics, have passed the test. Theodore Dreiser, who worked on Pulitzer's *World* early in his career, complained in his memoirs of Pulitzer's exploitation of his underpaid reporters and the terror he inspired in the newsroom that made "a veritable hell of his paper and the lives of those who worked for him." Dreiser greatly admired Pulitzer for his "vital, aggressive, restless, working mood, and his vaulting ambition to be all there was to be of journalistic force in America." But Dreiser contrasted that image with one of Pulitzer issuing orders from his yacht while sailing around the world or from a villa on the Riviera, or from Bar Harbor, or from his townhouses in London and New York. "All the time in this very paper, I could read the noblest and most elevating discourses about duty, character, the need of a higher sense of citizenship, and what not," Dreiser observed. "I used to frown at the shabby pecksniffery of it, the cheap buncombe that would allow a great publisher to bleed and drive his employees at one end of his house and deliver exordiums as to virtue, duty, industry, thrift, honesty at the other."[16]

Journalism historians—who largely admire Pulitzer for developing the newspaper crusade and credit his reformist principles as genuine—have reserved their harshest portrayal for the celebrated yet widely scorned media mogul William Randolph Hearst, Pulitzer's competitor in the newspaper wars that engulfed New York City at the turn of the twentieth century. Hearst has come to symbolize the capitalist excess associated with the swashbuckling practices of a newspaper industry that played a prominent role in the era of trusts, monopolies, and profligate profiteering (which was eviscerated in "muckraker" Will Irwin's fifteen-part series in *Collier's* magazine in 1911).[17] Hearst, a largely a-religious person who evinced no interest in the worship of anything but himself and his ambitions, epitomizes what can happen in journalism when the religious force is gone. Despite his efforts to portray himself as a reformer and a defender of the little guy, Hearst is largely remembered as the editor who would do anything to sell newspapers—a master self-promoter who used his chain of newspapers to advance his political hopes and "to gratify his overwhelming passions for wealth, power, and position," as the biographer W. A. Swanberg put it. "While he spoke piously of ideals in journalism, he left no gutter unexplored."[18]

The nineteenth century probably represents the most extreme period of America's dual passion for money making and moralizing, and that was true in journalism, too. On the one hand, the editor-poet Walt Whitman's "religion of America," with its notions about America's manifest destiny in the world, is portrayed as an optimistic time of upbeat Calvinistic and individualistic attitudes, masking an era of rapid industrialization, aggressive nationalism, relentless economic expansion, and ruthless fortune seeking. On the other hand, a critic of the culture, the journalist and satirist Mark Twain dubbed this period the "Gilded Age" and mocked the pious sermonizing and the unctuous moral tone of an era when the Industrial Revolution was wrenching the country through cycles of prosperity and depression.[19] In this environment, newspapers not only made money for their owners but also encouraged the population to do the same. Newspapers and magazines served as important vehicles of upward mobility—for both readers, who relied on newspapers to help them make their way in the economic jungle of city life, and owners, who became some of the country's richest capitalists. The big, mass-circulation newspaper became the model of nineteenth-century industrial efficiency, with its strict deadlines, its hierarchical chain of command, its formulas for news gathering and reporting, and its tightly coordinated production and delivery schedules. In this environment, the meaning of the word *soul* lost its connection to the old religious traditions, and the loss of soul came to symbolize what it meant to work for large, bureaucratic, industrial organizations and to live in the harsh and impersonal environment of commercial city life.

In American journalism, we can think of the nineteenth century as the period when the voice of morality was appropriated from the church to the editorial page but also when the owners of those newspapers were growing ever richer through the expansion of advertising, accelerating circulation, and burgeoning urban populations caused by factory growth, job losses in agriculture, and immigration. In the early part of the nineteenth century, Thomas Jefferson's pastoral vision of American life as a rural, community-oriented network of yeoman farmers, craftspeople, and merchants still applied to the American press, which, as Alexis de Tocqueville pointed out, was highly parochial and reflective of a wide range of viewpoints.[20] During this period, religious journalism still flourished in the United States and reflected religion's powerful influence on the grass roots of the population. Virtually every denomination had major periodicals or newspapers (often in each city or region); such publications as the *Dial*, the literary journal for New England transcendentalism, were widely read; and newspapers covered the succession of religious revivals that swept the country in the early nineteenth century. After the Civil War, the press began to reflect what we see today, and the news organization emerged as a major industrial force with its own (sometimes dubious) codes of professional conduct, its moralizing editorial pages, and its enlightened (and sometimes not very enlightened) self-interest in business practices. In this environment, coverage of religion was pushed to the margins; what coverage there was tended to be skeptical or to concentrate on the fantastic and the sensational; and denominational periodicals abandoned general news to focus on internal matters of the faith community or religious opinion.[21]

Most important, from the standpoint of the change in religious outlook, the new communications field became an integral part of the market economy that rose up in the United States in the nineteenth century—a place where economics was rationalized into every aspect of life, where the culture of the marketplace became incorporated into the human imagination, and where religious values were refashioned so that they blended seamlessly with financial self-seeking. Shortly after Tocqueville's visit to the United States, Benjamin Day used the new steam-powered printing press to launch what is recognized as the first "penny" paper, the *New York Sun,* in 1833, and the large, cheap, industrialized, mass circulation urban newspaper was on the way to supplanting the more expensive commercial and partisan newspapers of the postcolonial era. By 1846, when the *Baltimore Sun* published the first news transmitted by telegraph (President James Polk's announcement of the Mexican War), the penny press newspapers of such famed editors as James Gordon Bennett and Horace Greeley—with their emphasis on independent news and analysis—had largely replaced the shrill, partisan, party- and politician-controlled press as the dominant news voice in America.[22] The telegraph, and later such inventions as the telephone, the typewriter, and the wire machine, soon led to the creation of a nationwide communications system, where news could be sent and received instantaneously and where information was increasingly treated as a commodity designed to draw an audience to the newspaper and to stimulate the sale of advertising.

By the end of the twentieth century, the capitalistic ethic had tightened its hold on American news organizations, particularly in the 1980s and 1990s when technological advancements combined with growing corporatization and profit pressures to revamp the ethos of the news profession. Today, even the faint echoes of the demands of moral integrity and community responsibility inherent in Calvinism have disappeared from many corporate media boardrooms, and modern media moguls often feel free to espouse a philosophy of unfettered capitalism without even pretending they are making money in service to anything but Wall Street and their own careers. Al Neuharth, the retired chief executive of the Gannett Company, symbolizes this image of the modern publisher as someone operating free of moral restraint and unworried about how his actions reflect on the moral code of journalism. With his sharkskin suits, his corporate jets, and his futurist Florida beachfront palace, Neuharth spent much of his career promoting himself in iconoclastic, attention-seeking ways, such as writing an autobiography called *Confessions of an S.O.B.* and telling journalists that it is okay to backstab and deceive if it advances their own or their company's goals.[23] Many of Neuharth's press contemporaries found his aspirations to celebrity ridiculous. But the deeper significance of Neuharth's garish public posturing has been the way it brazenly challenges the tradition of modest publishers who tended to operate in a noblesse-oblige manner consistent with the Calvinistic principle of putting wealth to work for good causes. Neuharth has gone out of his way to offend religious sensibilities (such as the time he sponsored a company "Last Supper" and dressed up, complete with cross and crown of thorns, as the "crucified" top executive during the difficult start-up period of *USA Today*), and the huge bust of himself that he had installed in the lobby of Gannett's twin-tower offices near Washington, D.C., smacks of a media-age version of pagan-emperor worship.[24]

There is one place where the historical evolution of the media from a religious to a commercial purpose appears, at least at a superficial glance, to have reversed course: the press's newfound interest in the coverage of religion beyond what has traditionally appeared on the Saturday religion page. Religion, news executives have found through their marketing data, appears to be very much on the public's mind. Editors and publishers, who are terribly eager to please an audience that is not watching their networks or reading their newspapers in sufficient numbers anymore, have turned to religion as one of the trendy, "relevant" topics (along with health, sports, environment, women's issues, and personal finance, among others) that are increasingly the focus of today's market-driven news coverage. "Religion reporting is hot, and for a good reason," the *American Journalism Review* gushed in a 1995 cover story, "The Media Get Religion." "More and more people are searching for a spiritual element in their lives, whether it's inside a Muslim mosque, Catholic cathedral or through a New Age shaman leading a wilderness vision quest." Or as Ralph Langer, the executive editor of the *Dallas Morning News,* told the magazine, "For us not to adequately cover religion is tantamount to not covering the Cowboys in the Dallas market."[25]

Langer's comment, offered up as the "good news" about the press's rediscovery of religion, in reality illuminated something troubling about the American media's outlook on religious life in a time of hyper-consumerism, global corporate expansion, and the popular embrace of the marketing ethic. In drawing an analogy between sports and religion, Langer elevated big-time sports to the level of religion. This, cultural critics say, is exactly the problem in a society saturated with money and celebrity values. By treating religion as simply another item to attend to as the result of a marketing survey, religious life is implicitly denigrated to a secondary purpose, behind the "higher" purpose of modern media corporations: catering to their audience and making bigger profits. One cannot expect news organizations to operate as anything other than businesses, of course, but one always needs to be suspicious of claims of having "found religion," when what that really means is having found religion as a way to make more money.

Even more problematic is the way that marketing-oriented media firms choose to define religion in their coverage. Like other personalized, "reader friendly" subjects that are now the focus of media coverage, religion often is defined in terms of self-actualization, self-discovery, and self-fulfillment. Religion as part of the self-seeking that goes with a prosperous American life sets the tone for much media coverage, and the moral message or the personal sacrifice involved in religious activity gets mentioned scarcely, if at all. Religion is viewed in much of the press as a private activity, and, as a private activity, it is seen as something that one chooses to "consume" along with other options for smoothing out the rough edges of life. Religion is increasingly framed by news organizations as just another lifestyle topic, and seldom do they cover the aspects of religious life having to do with death, illness, emotional struggle, personal loss, or service to the poor or the disabled.

It is almost irresistible to draw a parallel between the way modern news executives evangelize for reader-driven journalism and the turbulent religious periods of the past, when religion and other forces blended into a vast polyglot of spiritual influences. The neo-Hellenistic atmosphere of American religious life at the turn of the twenty-first century—complete with cults, New Age groups, self-proclaimed gurus, and self-help, self-fulfillment books and programs to bring spirituality into the boardroom—fits perfectly into the marketing schemes of today's corporate news organizations bent on finding the formula for capturing audience attention. The problem is that this media mix of consumerism, commercialism, market research, self-fulfillment, and self-absorption can take journalists away from what might be recognized as true faith. In too many cases, what passes for religion in today's society is a vaguely spiritualized version of the culture's "worldly" ways. It is sometimes hard not to see journalism's newfound interest in religion as just another measure of a society saturated in surface values embracing religion and then holding it out for commercial gain.

Historians and cultural observers have long worried about the state of the national spirit in a culture when marketing forces—and none more so than those working in the media industry—are forever measuring public opinion to determine how to engineer content and to package a product to entice an audience. The feedback loop created by the consumer-driven, market research approach to journalism can be seen as the antithesis of what religion teaches about the importance of principle and conscience and self-denial. From Tocqueville to Daniel Boorstin, social critics have questioned Americans' fixation with public opinion and their tendency to tie all decision making to perceptions about majority views and consumer choices. "By whatever political laws men are governed in the age of equality," Tocqueville wrote about the America he visited in the early 1800s, "it may be foreseen that faith in public opinion will become for them a species of religion, and the majority its ministering prophet."[26] As Boorstin pointed out, the definition of "opinion" three hundred years ago was that it implied error and that multiplying it many times over and calling it public opinion do not add to its veracity.[27] In the modern commercial world, however, the nature of public opinion and the judgment of the marketplace have become monolithic. The specter of media executives, bowing down to what they perceive as the indomitable force of the marketplace, is hardly a comforting substitute for the traditional examples of religious humility.

In this regard, the trend toward market-oriented journalism can be seen as little more than the triumph of a corporatized form of Calvinism. The notion that business success is fundamental to the achievement of social and community improvement goals is an old and time-honored tradition in the American business community. But the corporate program—by formalizing, institution-alizing, and depersonalizing everything in service to the company's corporate goals—has removed even the human face that old-style Calvinist capitalists (what the press critic George Seldes called "the Lords of the Press") brought to the business.[28] The widely acknowledged "great" editors—William Allen White of the *Emporia (Kansas) Gazette,* Ralph McGill of the *Atlanta Constitution,* Thomas Winship of the *Boston Globe,* and Ben Bradlee of the *Washington Post*— are much missed in an era of chain editors, as is the concept of the principled and independent editor operating "free and outspoken on the frontier," as Herbert Altschull described White.[29]

Perhaps the most charitable critique of Calvinism has been that it was a sys-tem of theology to celebrate the good that could come from the established economic order. But in a highly secular age such as ours, many ideas have been disconnected from their religious roots and incorporated into societal norms, and this is certainly the case with journalism. Eisenstein pointed out how in our times, where "communion with the Sunday paper has replaced church-going," the church has proved to be no match for the forward-marching power of the media—in first colonial newspapers, then the penny press and the big urban newspapers, then radio and television, and now the Internet—to capture the public's attention. "Pitted against 'the furious itch of novelty' and the 'general thirst after news,' efforts by Catholic moralists and Protestant evangelicals, even Sunday schools and other Sabbatarian measures proved of little avail," she wrote. "By the [nineteenth] century, gossiping churchgoers could often learn about local affairs by scanning columns of newsprint in silence at home."[30] This does not mean that the press has truly displaced the pulpit—far from it, as we know from the polls about Americans' religious commitment. But that is the rub. The press does carry on many roles today that connect it to the broader religious spirit and heritage of the country, but in its obliviousness or its indifference to this tradition, the press does not always serve the public well, and journalism itself is impoverished.

The sociologist Herbert Gans, in his classic work defining American journal-istic values, pointed to a variety of beliefs, often held unconsciously, that moti-vate modern journalists. The value system of journalists, Gans claimed, includes a belief in "responsible capitalism"—what, in essence, can be seen as the Calvin-istic ethic transposed to journalism. Capitalism, Gans argued, appears to be the system most journalists embrace for the freedom it offers individuals, but *respon-sible* means that, while applauding business's capacity for bringing prosperity and economic growth, journalists want business to refrain from unreasonable profits and gross exploitation of workers. Of course, Gans wrote more than twenty years ago—just as media chains began swallowing up independent news outlets at record rates and the intense profit expectations of publicly owned corporations began having their impact on the management of newsrooms. Although Gans did not talk about the role of religion in any direct manner, I find myself wondering how well the progressive and populist attitudes of journalists that he did identify will fare in a future of even tighter corporate control of the journalistic endeavor. After all, as Gans prophesied and a generation of journalists is learning, "News organizations are overseen by corporate executives who are paid to show a profit. News judgment is resistant to change, and journalists will fight hard to preserve their autonomy; but if corporate economic well-being is threatened, executives may insist that their news organizations adapt."[31]

William Fore, a United Methodist church minister, laid out one of the most far-reaching critiques of the threat that excess commercialization and the triumph of the marketplace present to the religious culture of a nation, and he placed much of the blame squarely on the media. Fore noted that since the conversion of the Roman Emperor Constantine to Christianity in 312 A.D., when spiritual and temporal power were united, secular forces—particularly economic forces—have been at work eroding the Christian values of community, self-giving love, and compassion for others. Today, he contended, the media represent the most potent—yet one of the most subtle—tools of the commercial order for molding people into obedient servants of the commercial economic system and encouraging them to embrace the economic status quo. The mass media worldview, he claimed, teaches people that happiness is the chief goal of life, that happiness consists in obtaining material goods, and that narcissism, the yearning for creature comforts, and the goal of immediate gratification are good things. "It is possible, of course, to find ways to use mass media to sensitize people to moral and spiritual values," Fore wrote. "But the dangers of people being taken in by the media are so subtle and so powerful that religious communicators need to approach all programming in television and radio with the greatest caution and theological sensitivity."[32]

In certain journalistic periods, most notably the abolitionist period prior to the Civil War, the muckraking and Populist era of the early twentieth century, and the anti-Vietnam War activist era of the 1960s and 1970s, there has been an upsurge of commitment, including among journalists, to many key religious ideals—support for good works and social equality; denunciation of the greedy and the power seekers; concern about moral decline and corruption in government and business. But these outbreaks of idealism have occurred in tandem with the relentless push by the commercial interests that control the media to expand their consolidation of the communications industry, to increase profits and satisfy investors, and to keep news workers in line when they threaten business goals. In the last twenty years, journalists have even seen the once sacrosanct barrier between the news and business departments—symbolically termed the "church-state" wall—knocked down in favor of the notion of the news organization as a place where all the operations, including the newsroom, are coordinated around the company's commercial and marketing goals.[33] In truth, the separation of the journalistically sacred from the profane—as represented by the promise that business interests would not intrude on journalist's professional integrity—often has been honored more in principle than in reality. But the maintenance of the myth of journalistic independence always has been significant in its own right, and it has provided news workers with important notions of integrity in a business that faces the danger of being overwhelmed by the commercial imperative.

To see the dilemma facing many journalists working in these circumstances in spiritual terms may, in their minds, be stretching the matter. But the journalistic calling is facing serious pressures in a profession that is experiencing greater incursions of the marketplace ethic. The struggle for the soul of journalism, the fate of journalism as a higher calling, the future of the journalistic mission—all these terms with all their religious connotations have been used to describe the condition of the news profession in a time of traumatic change. It has become commonplace to hear media executives who have bought into the marketing ethic say that there is no reason why journalistic quality and a marketplace orientation need to be mutually exclusive.[34] But the pharisaic aspect of many modern media managers' jobs—mouthing all the right words while undermining the "spirit" of the journalistic enterprise—is something that the world has seen before.

Marketing itself—whether it is the marketing of religion, the marketing of journalism, or the marketing of journalism claiming to cover religion—always runs the risk of overwhelming the substance of what is being marketed. The constellation of factors that motivate today's market-oriented news executives— a fixation on what the customer will purchase, a willingness to tailor the product to that perceived demand, a commitment to commercial imperatives above all else—have come together to form a powerful ideology within the free-market culture of the United States. Never before has there been so much pressure to submit every product, every transaction, every service—no matter how sacred to the culture—to the goals of the great American sellathon.

No place is this demand to please the audience greater than on television, which, as one critic once put it, is the greatest device ever invented to deliver people to advertisers.[35] The extent of the media's willingness to market religion is captured in *TV Guide*'s 1997 special report, "God and Television: Who's Caring for Prime Time's Soul?" In a world of television networks eager to do whatever it takes to draw an audience, one can only be ruefully fascinated by the shrewdness of the network executives who have discovered, as writer Jack Miles put it, that there is a potentially huge, spiritually hungry audience for new television shows (such as *Touched by an Angel*) that go beyond TV's traditional formula in which God plays only a peripheral role, if any, in the lives of television characters. "If and when God finds the writer-producer team He is looking for, He may go from guest star to superstar overnight," Miles prophesied.[36] Can the triumph of media marketing over the cause of true religion be far behind?

CHAPTER 3

Skeptics of Faith or Faith in Skepticism? Enlightening the Journalistic Mind

Samuel Johnson was once asked what he thought of the philosophy of Bishop George Berkeley, who, as a "subjective idealist," believed that reality was lodged only in the mind of God and that matter did not exist apart from its being perceived in the God-given human imagination. Johnson, in a demonstration of disdain, kicked a nearby stone and declared, "I refute it thus."[1] In this famous gesture, Johnson, the eighteenth-century journalist and lexicographer, conveyed exactly what we recognize today as the journalist's pragmatic, commonsensical stance toward the great questions of life. We can argue about "reality" forever as the world passes by, Johnson believed, but the sensation in his foot was proof enough for him that objects exist independent of our perceptions of them and that to engage in metaphysical reasoning beyond that was a waste of time.[2]

The eighteenth century is best noted for the triumph of the Enlightenment, a philosophical movement characterized by rationalism, an emphasis on practical learning, and a spirit of skepticism and empiricism in intellectual thought. But the eighteenth century is also the period when the business of commercial newspapering and the profession of "journalism" first flowered in England and the United States. The influence of the Enlightenment, or the Age of Reason as it has been called, on the development of journalism has been considerable. Journalists today see themselves as connected in virtually a straight line of philosophical kinship with the Enlightenment rationalists who hoped to banish forever the arcane metaphysical reasoning of church theologians and postmedievalists such as Berkeley and to hold up scientific accomplishment and inductive analysis as the way to human progress. The deductive reasoning of the medieval church scholars—done by applying first principles dictated by church doctrine to the world's phenomena—was anathema to the Enlightenment mind-set, as it has become to journalists who have come to value facts over philosoph-ical or theological ideas and who believe they operate by a methodology that is empirical at the core. But, as we shall see, the Enlightenment philosophes' com-mitment to reason is really still very much about faith, particularly if one sees faith in skepticism as almost a faith in itself and the Enlightenment as not just a movement to banish religion but as something of a substitute religion.

Although Johnson is best known as a great essayist and literary critic, he also was immersed in the life of the early commercial newspaper. Johnson published three broad sheets of periodical essays, *The Rambler, The Adventurer,* and *The Idler,* all of which can be seen as precursors to today's newspaper commentary; he spent much of his time in coffeehouses and Fleet Street taverns, where these early newspapers circulated and from which they extracted their mix of gossip, satiric prose, and social commentary; and he was an early version of the celeb-rity figure the mass media have thrust on the human scene. "I believe there is hardly a day in which there is not something about me in the newspapers," Johnson once remarked to his equally renowned biographer, James Boswell.[3]

In certain respects, Johnson can be seen as the quintessential figure symbol-izing the influence that the Enlightenment had on practical people of learning and letters who were breaking away from the hold that church dogma and spec-ulative philosophy had exercised over intellectual life throughout Europe. Johnson grandly conveys the spirit of this era of new freedoms and a new hu-manism. In this respect, he can be seen as the English counterpart of Voltaire, the wit, bon vivant, and great Enlightenment-era journalist, whose utilitarian-ism and gibes at dogmatic thinking characterize both the Enlightenment and the mood of modern journalism. (Historians have referred to the eighteenth centu-ry as both the "Age of Voltaire" and the "Age of Johnson.")[4] Johnson's gesture toward the stone appears, in this context, perfectly in the spirit of Voltaire; it embodies all the frustration, the contempt, and the liberating experience of the eighteenth-century mind breaking free from the chains of an obscure form of theological thinking that had cramped the human spirit for far too long.

But Johnson, in reality, was very different from Voltaire, particularly in his attitudes toward religion. Johnson's brand of Enlightenment humanism proved quite distinct from that of the irreverent Voltaire. While advocating tolerance, the rule of law, and freedom of opinion, Voltaire held a very low opinion of the role of traditional religion in life, especially the role of the clerical establishment. Voltaire's brilliant, scornful mind and his jabs at the church—mocking the cor-rupt clergy, ridiculing what he felt were Christianity's superstitions, applying wit and reason in the places where religion offered fixed beliefs and moralizing piety—have made him a favorite among modern thinkers who dislike dogma-tism, absolutism, and authoritarianism in the application of religious doctrine.

In contrast, Johnson was a defender of the status quo when it came to religion, and he did not like Voltaire or his irreverent views. Johnson saw Voltaire as a dyedin-the-wool contrarian, an irresponsible heckler from the galleries who took more delight in challenging institutional authority and poking holes in others' world-views than in promoting a life philosophy of his own. To Johnson, Voltaire not only was a skeptic of religion but had made a religion of skepticism as well.

A loyal Anglican, Johnson was particularly offended by the views of the Deists, such as Voltaire, who substituted for Christian doctrine their own view of "natural" religion, with its reasonable but detached creator who expected humans to rely on God-given scientific law and their God-given human reason to comprehend the divine plan that lay behind empirical discovery. The Deists, who were deeply impressed by the theories of Isaac Newton and the emerging discoveries of science, did not reject belief in God, but their scorn for Christian explanations was part of a process that ultimately led to the emergence of modern atheism for those who took it to a further extreme. Johnson in temperament was closer to a second strain of Enlightenment thinkers, who also viewed Newtonian physics as perfectly compatible with a belief in God but thought it was nonsense to discard the truths of Christian doctrine, church authority, and revealed religion simply because one relied on reason, empirical experimentation, and skeptical analysis in determining what made the universe work.

Johnson, it is fair to say, is not a particularly sympathetic historical figure. Smug and high-handed, he tended to dismiss those who expressed skepticism about Christian teachings by arguing that Christian doctrine must be correct because it has been accepted by so many wise and respected people throughout history.[5] This kind of reasoning—to accept conventional wisdom largely because it is conventional—is very much a reflection of the eighteenth-century mind, and it holds little appeal today for people who are less willing to believe anything based on received authority. It is tempting to dismiss Johnson as simply another stuffy thinker defending a fading worldview. This is particularly so when one considers that modern journalists—in their position as detached critics of everything and everyone—think of themselves as following in the path of Voltaire, who was comfortable in the gadfly role and did not believe it was his responsibility to construct a comprehensive philosophy on the rubble of the intellectual systems he was challenging.

Before we declare the iconoclastic Voltaire to be the model for the modern journalist, however, we need to look more closely at Johnson's blend of Enlightenment reasoning and conventional thinking and the residue of this thinking in the modern newsroom. It is common for scholars to point to the Enlightenment as the major philosophical influence on today's journalists in the development of their professional attitudes and value system.[6] Usually this is celebrated; journalists, as well as journalism historians, are proud of journalism's roots in the independent and free-thinking tradition of the seventeenth- and eighteenth-century rationalists we have come to view as the embodiment of "enlightened" individuals. But there are critics of the press who view this in suspect terms: Clifford Christians, John P. Ferré, and P. Mark Fackler, for example, complain that the residue of Enlightenment philosophy has left today's journalists with an excessive focus on individual autonomy and an unbalanced belief in individual rights at the expense of the common good.[7] Although Christians and his cohorts see the solution to this in journalism's taking a more community-oriented approach to news coverage, one can easily follow the logic of their analysis into the realm of media and religion. In doing so, one would expect to find journalists' attitude toward religion explained by an extreme individualism and an antipathy toward doctrinal systems inherited from early journalistic forebears, such as Voltaire or his American counterpart, the zealous democrat Thomas Paine, who was as vehement as Voltaire in his attacks on the irrationality of orthodox Christian tenets.

Yet it would be misleading to characterize Voltaire or Paine as the true journalistic personality and not to recognize the pragmatic—and I would argue ultimately journalistic—spin that Johnson put on his ruminations about religion. Johnson's defense of religion and his acceptance of Christian teachings are more in line with what many journalists today believe than the critics of journalism would have us believe. (Research findings on the religious beliefs of modern American journalism in subsequent chapters make this point more clearly.) Johnson's blending of Enlightenment practicality with support for religious tradition is very much more in the mainstream of modern journalistic thinking— particularly as it is reflected on the editorial page or in the public positions of media institutions—than is Voltaire's loathing of conventional religion.

I am not arguing here that a modern journalist could—or should—be expected to embrace Johnson's views as he expounded them. The self-satisfied eighteenth-century mentality of an upper-class intellectual like Johnson—with his supercilious outlook and his disdain for those who would question prevailing attitudes—does not fit with the image of modern journalists as independent thinkers and challengers of the establishment. But the image of journalists (and certainly their self-image) does not fully correspond to reality, either. In Johnson, modern journalists can find clues about how the Enlightenment values operate at the practical level in today's commercial media organizations, particularly how they operate within a residue of religious values that were absorbed, often unknowingly, by important Enlightenment thinkers, just as they have been by their philosophical heirs working as journalists today.

The tensions that have driven the religious influence in the modern newsroom underground have led journalists to believe, falsely I contend, that as heirs to Enlightenment individuality and rationalism, they operate free from the impulses of religion. It is true that the Enlightenment was the philosophical force that pushed modern society, and with it journalism, in a secular direction. But historians tend to overemphasize the influence of the Enlightenment personalities who wanted to have no truck with religious tradition and to underestimate the way Enlightenment values were absorbed into journalism and blended with a current of religious thinking that continues in the newsroom to this day. Textbooks on the philosophers and historical figures influential in journalism have lengthy sections on such heterodox thinkers as Voltaire, Paine, Benjamin Franklin, and Thomas Jefferson but nothing about eighteenth-century editors who embraced traditional religion in one form or another, such as Johnson, Daniel Defoe, Jonathan Swift, or even Joseph Addison and Richard Steele, the publishers of the *Tatler* and the *Spectator,* the most famous of the eighteenth-century newspapers, who balanced the irreverent and witty repartee of their newspaper columns with the writing of religious hymns (in Addison's case) and a book advising people how to live the pious and religious life (in Steele's).[8]

Take Defoe as a case in point. Now credited as a pioneer in the development of the modern novel, he was most prominent in the eighteenth century as an editor of a newspaper that was perpetually embroiled in the religious discussion of the time. Defoe was a passionate dissenting Protestant who supported William of Orange of "Glorious Revolution" fame and twice was jailed for satirical writings that mocked and nettled high church Tories. Or go back a bit further in history to the English poet John Milton, whose 1644 tract *Areopagitica* is held up as the first and most passionate call for freedom of the press in Western history.[9] Historians often do not point out that it was religious idealism as much as an Enlightenment commitment to free speech that led Milton to call for an end to government licensing and censorship of the press and to reassure his readers that they had nothing to fear from an unfettered contest of ideas. Milton's notion has been so thoroughly absorbed into the ideology of journalists that few would recognize it as a concept grounded in a blend of Christian, Enlightenment, and classical faith. From the time of Plato, who believed that if people know the good, they will do the good; to Isaac Newton, whose scientific discoveries in the seventeenth and eighteenth centuries provided the basis for believing that the human mind could penetrate the divine design of the universe; to John Locke, whose deeply religious views on the virtuousness of humankind and the rationality of the universe ignited political reform movements from the seventeenth century onward, this optimism about God's plan for the universe as the foundation of correct action provided the historical basis for journalists' faith in a free press as the proper institution to protect God-given human liberties.

It is fascinating to see how the underlying religious faith in Milton's credo is used interchangeably with the rational tolerance of someone like Voltaire. *Truth,* for Milton, had a capital *T,* with all the religious connotations that went with it, and when he wrote, "Let [Truth] and Falsehood grapple; whoever knew Truth put to the worse in a free and open encounter?" he was speaking as a Puritan confident that God would guide people through their religious conscience to a clear understanding of the truth if they openly debated matters in good faith.[10] (As in his famous poem, *Paradise Lost,* free will is a critical aspect of God's plan, and without the opportunity to wrestle with sin or false opinion, Milton believed, truth and salvation cannot be achieved.) Journalists may be more comfortable with Voltaire's pithier phrasing of a similar sentiment ("I disapprove of what you say but I will defend to the death your right to say it").[11] But the religious idealism that underlies Milton's ringing phrase is still very much alive in newsrooms today, as will be seen in future chapters, even if its source is not always recognized.

Religion was such an all-pervasive subject in the seventeenth and eighteenth centuries that few journalists of the time could have imagined how it would not be both the topic of journalism and its guiding influence. The notion that religion should not be a motivating force for those involved in government would have been an alien one to many of the journalists of the Enlightenment.[12] Even more curious to them would have been the modern idea that journalists—with their secular responsibilities and their notions of a free and independent press—should operate completely free of religious purpose. The belief in the importance of keeping religion out of journalism at some fundamental professional level has come to be viewed as a logical extension of the Enlightenment mind-set—even though there is ample evidence that journalists did not operate by that principle in the seventeenth or eighteenth century, nor, if one probes very deeply into their professional value system, do they do so today. Resisting government interference in journalism is another matter; journalists after Milton were ever more vehement in their insistence that government, including government operating in concert with religious authorities, not try to control the press.

It is important to recognize, of course, that journalism as we define it today was only in its infancy in seventeenth- and eighteenth-century England and America and that the modern commercial newspaper had not fully come onto the scene. Newspapers in the England of the Enlightenment circulated on a much smaller scale than they do today, and they were, like Johnson's, largely extensions of their editors. What we would call the newspapers of the era were actually a mix of journalism and literature: essays and social commentary, satire and facetious items, light verse, political commentary, letters from readers that were often invented or editorially inspired, gossip and dialogue between fictitious characters, often written under pseudonyms or disguised personalities and aimed at a relatively elite audience of intellectuals, merchants, artists, and government officials. One only has to encounter Johnson's journalistic philosophy—as a lexicographer who compiled one of the early dictionaries, Johnson liked to educate his readers by including words in his newspaper articles that were purposefully difficult and obscure—to recognize that the operating principles of the eighteenth-century newspaper were very different from those today.

Although Johnson and his peers may only vaguely resemble modern journalists, academics—particularly the followers of the German sociologist Jürgen Habermas—have become fond of looking back to this period as the pinnacle of the operation of the "public sphere" in civic life. According to Habermas, this was the era when newspapers and the people who published them were at the apex of their influence over public opinion and the world of politics. In Habermas's presentation of the coffeehouse life of that period, such figures as Defoe, Swift, Addison, and Steele (he does not mention Johnson) were at the center of a robust civic culture in which intellectuals and people of letters rubbed elbows with the political elite and played important roles in political debate.[13] In Habermas's view, the "public sphere" has been in a state of constant erosion ever since, with the modern, commercialized mass media, the large-scale organs of public relations and public-opinion monitoring, and an impersonal, bureaucratized government replacing the select and intimate civic-minded associations that once drove democratic life.[14]

Habermas's critique has been challenged by those who think he presented an idealized picture of political life in England and France and too readily embraced a model for public debate based on the influence of a bourgeois elite. Whether that is the case, it is clear that Habermas—a one-time leftist who rose to prominence during the student revolts in Germany in the 1960s—had a narrow vision of what the debate in the eighteenth-century "public sphere" was all about, and religion was not much included in that view. Habermas rather blithely dismissed the role of religion as something that became a "private matter" after the Protestant Reformation, and he seldom alluded to religion without characterizing it as largely unimportant to public debate. If one looks closely at the intrigue and the scheming by "coffeehouse" insiders to influence government policy in eighteenth-century England, however, religion is time and again at the center of the controversy. Much of Defoe's editorial life, for example, was spent resisting efforts to bar religious dissenters from academic life and government jobs, and his jailings all had to do with writings about religion. While editing his newspaper, Defoe also was on the payroll of a series of parliamentary leaders; he worked as a spy and a member of what today is known as the British Secret Service, and he was engaged in bitter debates with other, equally passionate and politically and religiously motivated editors. One of those was Swift, an Anglican clergyman and another pioneering novelist, whose newspaper and courtship of top-level British politicians competed with Defoe's.[15]

In Johnson, I would argue that journalists—particularly those who are serious about better covering religion—can find a practical attitude toward religion, an openness to the value of religious experience, and a respect for the role that faith can play in human life, all the while still holding firm to the Enlightenment values of skepticism and rationality that provide modern journalism's professional foundation. Johnson, like most journalists today, was a thoroughly commonsensical individual who throughout his life defended Christian faith as an effective way to deal with life's difficulties. Not one to be drawn into abstruse discussion, Johnson repeatedly argued that it is the practical value of religious faith that sustains the human spirit and provides a useful basis for making one's way in the world. For Johnson, religion contains the utilitarian solutions to the imponderables of human existence, and he saw nothing in it that offended the pursuit of a life of reason and good sense.

Johnson's humanity was much on display in Boswell's biography of him, and his openness and honesty in acknowledging the suffering underlying his religious views are difficult to scoff at. When he endorsed Christian attitudes, Johnson was always modest in his claims, and he always looked to the pragmatic, real-life value of religious belief, particularly the role that religion plays in assuaging human pain. Johnson's candidness about the difficulties in his own life—his "horror" at the prospect of his own death, his "constitutional gloom," his "unsettled and perplexed" mind, his struggles with depression and anxiety, his painful experiences of loss at the death of friends and relatives, his loneliness at the end of his life—was mixed in amid the pithy commentary and witty maxims. Johnson's anxiety about his salvation (good Calvinist that he was), combined with his frail physical and emotional condition, gave him an acute sensitivity to human suffering—and what he believed was the necessity of religious faith to assuage it. Johnson's response to his mother's death tells much about his human heart, and what he viewed as the only possible consolation for his misery: "The dead cannot return, and nothing is left us here but languishment and grief. [Surely then] there is no man who, thus afflicted, does not seek succour in the Gospel, which has brought 'life and immortality to light.'"[16]

While Johnson was scandalized by the irreverence of Voltaire, it was his "debate" with the Scottish philosopher David Hume, which occupies an important portion of Boswell's autobiography of Johnson, that has some of the greatest relevance for journalists today. Modern journalism has drawn much inspiration from Hume, whom the media historian Herbert Altschull has called the "relativist supreme" and whose philosophy is of "special importance" in the ideology of journalists.[17] Unlike Voltaire, Hume—with his philosopher's bent—raised skeptical analysis to the level of a comprehensive philosophical system. For the skeptic Hume, nothing could be known for sure through humankind's limited capacities of comprehension—not God, not the physical world, not our perceptions of how that world works. In Hume's philosophy, everything we experience is derived from our impressions about the world and the ideas we maintain in our minds about the way life operates. In this hazy realm of cognition, the best we can do is to draw probable conclusions based on the limited facts we can perceive. Hume applied this thinking to all facets of life—but particularly to religion—in his claim that humankind operates largely by conventions, customs, natural passions, and illusions that can never be proved in any rational or fully empirical sense. Hume hammered hard on the notion that "we are not justified in attributing to the author of nature omnipotence, wisdom, or goodness" and that "we can form no rational conclusion for assigning to this cause the attributes of a Christian God."[18]

On one level, Johnson was speaking with the voice of his age and against an emerging religious skepticism, which was already beginning to influence the value system of Johnson's fellow journalists, when he complained of Hume's "infidelity" and attacked Hume for questioning the truths of Christian doctrine, which had a widespread impact on the intellectual community of Johnson's time.[19] Johnson was troubled by what he thought were Hume's challenges to the role of religion in society, which, despite our view of the eighteenth century as the Age of Enlightenment, still was a fact of life for virtually everyone in Johnson's time. To Johnson, Christianity was about truths that have been "taught to our infancy; they have mingled with our solitary thoughts and familiar conversation, and are habitually interwoven with the whole texture of life," and he viewed (as did many of Johnson's contemporaries) Hume's critique as an assault on the fundamental underpinnings of society.[20] In point of fact, Hume was relatively circumspect in articulating his own religious belief system, but he was still demonized in his time as a Deist (which was often a pejorative term attached to anyone who questioned Christian orthodoxy), an atheist, and an agnostic.[21]

Yet Johnson was not just a knee-jerk defender of the orthodox faith, and it would be a mistake not to see his dispute with Hume as a preview of a debate—between those who fundamentally are hostile to religious notions and those who believe that religion should be taken seriously and treated with respect—that is still held in newsrooms today. In his fascination with Hume's arguments, Johnson shared with Hume a skepticism about the role of reason in human deliberations. Like Hume, Johnson was forever questioning the certainty of knowledge (Johnson, Boswell says, was always inclined to talk about "the force of testimony, and the little we could know of final causes"), and he was no less convinced than Hume that we can trust only the testimony of individuals, not dogma or authoritative systems, to give us our picture of truth, no matter how flawed and limited that individual picture may be.[22] Also like Hume and the modern journalists he came to influence, Johnson was mistrustful of those who claimed to know anything for sure, and he took great pleasure in puncturing what he felt was the unwarranted certainty of the other side, even to the point of taking a position simply because it would nettle an intellectual opponent.

Hume, like Johnson, stood against many of the Deists and the great thinkers of the Enlightenment who believed they could comprehend the divine plan of the universe through the use of their God-given reasoning faculty and the exercise of their senses alone. Johnson, too, was a critic of those who tried to found religion on reason, and he often commented sarcastically about the Deists of his time who did so. The difference between Johnson and Hume is that Johnson maintained his faith without necessarily pretending it was grounded in reason, while Hume used his reason to become convinced that faith made no sense, all the while neglecting to emphasize the elements of his own philosophy that told him to be wary of asserting his position with too much certainty. Hume, despite believing that nothing can be proved beyond doubt, thought it was patently ridiculous to argue that God could suspend the laws of nature to perform miracles; Johnson believed it was no less reasonable to accept the testimony of individuals and historical personages in favor of revelation and miraculous events.[23] It is evident that Johnson was very much influenced by what Hume would have termed a reliance on "convention" or "custom" and that Johnson often justified the truth of Christian premises by what he called the self-evident benefits for humanity and the testimonies of important personages to its validity. But both men were far from intellectually consistent in pushing their positions (Johnson sometimes used a specious form of reasoning to defend a faith that was ultimately not rational, and Hume advanced reasonable arguments to undermine a position that he knew could not be ascertained through reason alone).

Hume, of course, aroused so much controversy because he was one of the first great philosophers to articulate an openly (albeit extremely cautious) anti-Christian view of philosophy. Hume was taken so seriously because his arguments touched a deep chord of doubt that ran through the eighteenth century and was to split into dispute and division in the centuries ahead. Johnson himself noted that nothing Hume said in questioning religion had not occurred to Johnson himself ("Every thing which Hume has advanced against Christianity had passed through my mind long before he wrote," Johnson told Boswell).[24] Johnson was aware that Christian certainties were under serious intellectual assault in his time, and, as someone not unfamiliar to doubt, Johnson, one senses, was deeply pained by it. Like many before and after him, Johnson needed religion to keep hopeful, to keep healthy-minded, to keep balanced, to keep going. Johnson's certainty in defending the true faith was, at heart, a sign of how profoundly he worried that the religion that meant so much to him was slipping in public esteem. Johnson was a creature of society first and foremost, and he could not bear the idea that anyone might think less of him because he needed to believe something that might not be broadly accepted as true. In this way, Johnson was no different from Hume—his need to believe (or, in Hume's case, not to believe) outweighed his determination to be consistent on every point.

Despite Johnson's worries, the intellectual challenge to religion presented by Enlightenment skepticism only slowly made its way into the attitudes of the profession of journalism, and even today one is not likely to find much Voltaire-like mocking of religion in journalistic quarters. The journalism of eighteenth-century England—which was becoming increasingly market-oriented and yet found its appeal in its irreverence and its intellectual sophistication—reflected the careful manner in which religious heterodoxy was approached. In the *Tatler* and the *Spectator,* Addison expressed a contempt for the irrationalities of Catholicism and the dourness of Puritanism, condemned both religious enthusiasm and superstition, and, when he wished to praise the Creator, "praised Him as the maker of the universe revealed by the microscope and the telescope."[25] Yet Addison, not unlike Johnson, could not conceive of a world in which religion did not play a powerful socializing role. For Addison, who insisted that it was possible to "serve God and be cheerful," the notion of disbelief in a deity was "manifestly absurd," and he ridiculed atheists at every opportunity.[26]

The growing commercial structure and the economic interests of the press, if nothing else, led journalists in the eighteenth century—as is the case today—to be wary of offending the religiously minded. The eighteenth-century balancing act between irreverence and the fear of the consequences of irreligion was carried out across the ocean by Benjamin Franklin, who, as an editor of his own colonial newspapers and magazines, was deeply influenced by the writings of Addison and Steele. Franklin first became embroiled in religious controversy as a young man working as an apprentice in his brother James's printing shop in Boston in the early 1720s. As the editor of the *New England Courant,* James Franklin was an acerbic critic of the theocratic Puritan rulers of Massachusetts. Increase Mather, one of the colony's prominent religious leaders, once stopped the brash young printer on the street and warned him he was inviting the judgment of God for "bantering and abusing" the ministry. James Franklin's newspaper was described by Cotton Mather as a "Scandalous Paper" filled with "Nonsense, Unmannerliness, Railery, Prophaneness, Immorality, Arrogancy, Calumnies, Lyes, Contradictions," and items intended to "Debauch and Corrupt the Minds and Manners" of New England. "The Town is become almost a Hell upon Earth, a City full of Lies," wrote Cotton Mather in complaining of the *Courant*'s criticisms.[27]

Unlike his brother, Benjamin was never willing to stray too far from the acceptable viewpoints of society (this impulse, Franklin explained in his *Autobiography,* was spurred by his experience on the *Courant,* which he left partly for fear his "indiscrete Disputations about Religion began to make me pointed at with Horror by good People").[28] Known for his shrewd business sense, Franklin went on to purchase his own newspaper, the *Pennsylvania Gazette,* founded the first monthly magazine in America, invested in a series of printshops and newspapers throughout the colonies, and promoted the notion of the newspaper as an organ of profit and commercial success. While amusing his audience with a mixture of humor, satire, and jaunty moralizing, he regularly poked fun at evangelism and what he viewed as religious sophistry and superstition, although he was always careful to soften his commentary so that it did not threaten the business interests of his publications. Franklin's circumspect strategy—to espouse the values of free expression, all the while carefully guarding that expression for fear of offending one's audience and potentially eroding profits—is one that has come to serve modern media editors well.

This tension in American press ideology between the expression of truth and the price of telling the truth is captured particularly well in the discreet manner in which Franklin advanced his Deist views, all the while making sure that he did not overstep the bounds of propriety and risk his good reputation or the financial success of his publications.[29] Like other eighteenth-century intellectuals, Franklin was a believer in applying the laws of reason to religious myth and a utilitarian who valued religion primarily for its moral benefits to society, but the symbols of Christianity also were ingrained in Franklin's mental process. During the course of his lifetime, he wrote a new version of the Lord's Prayer, advocated translating the Bible into modern idiom, and worked hard, if ultimately unsuccessfully, to reconcile his private views of religion with orthodox systems of worship. As Alfred Aldridge put it, "The paradox in Franklin's religious life is that he completely disbelieved Christianity; yet he was attracted by its system of worship. . . . Intellectually he had little more faith in orthodox doctrine than in witchcraft or astrology; yet he sympathized with the church as a social institution and supported it so loyally that many sectarians identified him with their causes."[30]

In the end, Franklin, like Johnson, felt that he needed religious faith to find inner tranquillity, and he came to believe that society needed religious people to maintain a properly functioning social order. Franklin's loathing of Puritan rigor—which caused him such difficulties early in his life—was matched by his rejection of supernatural revelation in the Bible and his embrace of Deism. But Franklin's celebration of American technical know-how—or his view that gadgets can save us, as one of his critics put it—gradually mellowed during his lifetime as he sought to express his religious beliefs in ways that would be acceptable to both Deists and orthodox Christians. Franklin ultimately expressed these beliefs in the highly optimistic manner so characteristic of the eighteenth century: "Whatever an infinitely good God hath wise Ends in suffering to be, must be good, is thereby made good, and cannot be otherwise." Franklin—who editorialized for rational religion for more than thirty years—finally turned his irreverence on its head in a way that would make great sense to many editors and journalists, who for decades have managed to produce highly reverent and morally responsible editorials despite the iconoclastic and antireligious impulses in the newsroom.[31]

While Franklin thought better of inflaming public opinion on the basis of his religious views, the revolutionary essayist Thomas Paine, Franklin's friend and fellow Deist, was an example of that rarest of journalists—a truly outspoken personality who was willing to suffer considerably for his passionately irreverent views. In his *The Age of Reason,* a slashing denunciation of Christian orthodoxy, Paine described his mission as going "through the Bible as a man would go through a wood with an axe on his shoulder and fell trees."[32] Paine had turned his back on the Quakerism in which he was raised as too pious and pacifistic for him, but his passionate activism—and the animating principles of his thunderous calls for revolution and the triumph of the rights of man—can be found in the social reform principles of his native religion. Still, Paine's reputation sank greatly after the Revolutionary War days, largely because of his broadsides against religion (Franklin once wrote to Paine warning him against taking an extremist position in religion, but to no avail).[33] Paine suffered the ultimate indignity when, after escaping sedition charges in England and imprisonment in France, he died ostracized and impoverished in New York in 1809; he was refused burial in a Quaker cemetery for his unwillingness to forswear his deistic beliefs; and, ten years later, after his bones were dug up and returned to England, they were lost.[34]

It is worth pointing out that Voltaire, like Franklin and unlike Paine, suffered little personally for his cynic's sniping at religion. That may be because while Voltaire shocked his contemporaries with his seeming irreverence, the body of his beliefs would hardly be seen today as antireligious. By defining himself so often in terms of what he was against and then using satire, mockery, wit, and, most important, his reason to advance his views, Voltaire left the impression that he was a more unorthodox thinker than he actually was.[35] Carl Becker, in his *Heavenly City of the Eighteenth-Century Philosophers,* argued that modern historians make too much of the Enlightenment rationalists' break with the Western religious tradition. Becker called their shift in thinking only a "subtle" one and said it led to a situation where the "philosophes" simply substituted humanism and faith in the laws of nature for a traditional God. Deists scoffed at the Christian view of God but, as Becker observed, paid homage to the Deity; they mocked the idea that the world was created in six days but retained their belief in the universe as a smooth-running instrument that reflected the rationality of a divine plan; they rejected the authority of the church and yet were true believers in the authority of nature and reason as gifts of God.[36]

It is no stretch to apply Becker's insights to the world of modern journalism. Today's journalists—forged in the cauldron of Enlightenment values—carry on in a tradition that only looks as if it is disconnected from religious tradition. To analogize from Becker: journalistic skepticism masks a deep idealism and an irrepressible faith in the potential for human community to solve its problems; the reform instinct of journalists grows out of a persistent belief that sin is at work everywhere but that humankind can be redeemed; journalists' faith in facts and experience is grounded in the deepest respect for the rationality of the universe; and the journalistic elevation of the average person to a revered subject of coverage reflects the most basic Christian views about the equality of all in the eyes of God. Optimism about human progress, an abiding faith in public opinion, a deep belief in democracy, a commitment to open and honest exchange—all these journalistic credos reflect a religious worldview that, while much transformed from the outlook of early Christian and medieval times, lives richly and intensively within the best traditions of journalism. It is no coincidence that Voltaire—the very essence of the Enlightenment skeptic, wit, and intellectual provocateur—is seen as the patron saint of journalism.[37] Yet Voltaire's cynicism, in Becker's words, "was all on the surface, signifying nothing but the play of a supple and irrepressible mind, or the sharp impatience of an exasperated idealist. . . . Voltaire, skeptic—strange misconception! On the contrary, a man of faith, an apostle who fought the good fight, tireless to the end, writing seventy volumes to convey the truth that was to make us free."[38]

This tension inherent in Voltaire's philosophy—in which a belief in reason and skepticism overlays a deeper, if somewhat unconscious, obligation to fundamental religious thinking—still makes up the dynamic in many modern news organizations, both within the individual journalists who work there and in the newsroom's struggle in deciding how to cover many matters, including religion. News professionals can be seen as operating like modern-day Voltaires—saucy, irreverent, and deeply skeptical on the surface, yet animated by a passionate idealism, a strong commitment to social activism, and a deep faith in humanity. Within this modern journalistic mind-set lurks not only the inherited attitudes of Voltaire, Paine, and Franklin but also the religious idealism of Milton, Johnson, and Defoe. Even today, it would be a mistake to see faith in skepticism—which many see as the credo of many modern journalists—treated as something synonymous with skepticism about faith, as too many of journalism's critics mistakenly have done.

The eighteenth century was a transitional period between an intensely religious age and a time when secularism was making its way into American and English life. It is true that many of the journalistic figures of the eighteenth century were pioneers in the rebellion against doctrinaire religion, but religion still preoccupied them. While the Enlightenment emerged as an intellectual movement to oppose Christian dogma and authoritarianism, it was a cause that was defined as much by religious idealism as any that came before it. In this way, it is difficult to see the values of the Enlightenment—faith in reason, confidence in a harmonious universe, certainty that a benevolent creator guided humankind through the laws of nature—as separate from the religious culture from which they sprang. By extension, the same can be said about journalism's connection to the religious past via the bridge of Enlightenment thought that has so strongly left its mark on the profession.

CHAPTER 4

Mystics, Idealists, and Utopians: Journalism and the Romantic Tradition

Journalism has always been considered a romantic profession, at least by journalists themselves. The greatest journalistic figure to span the romantic age was Horace Greeley, whose famous statement, "Go West, young man, go West and grow up with the country," encompasses the yearning, the hopefulness, and the grand ambitions associated with the pursuit of the American dream.[1]

Greeley imbibed fully the nineteenth-century atmosphere of romantic idealism and packaged it into what we consider even today as the prototype of the public-spirited American editor. Beneath the Greeley ethic—as beneath the whole romantic movement in America—lay religion, transformed and suffused into the culture in new ways that profoundly reflected the optimistic mood of the time and the journalism of the era.

Not only did Greeley know literature and advance its cause in his newspaper, but also he was surrounded by journalistic colleagues, including William Cullen Bryant, John Greenleaf Whittier, and Walt Whitman, who spent long years in editorial or reporting careers while refining their skills as poets. These journalist-poets developed an artistic vision that, in its commitment to moral and political reform, its doctrine of absolute egalitarianism, and its fusion of a deep faith in the individual with the idea of democracy, reflected important aspects of American journalism while contributing to the full flowering of the romantic movement on American soil.[2]

The literary output of these journalists-turned-poets—along with their prose writings that, like Greeley's, exhibited interest in matters ranging from art, politics, and history to religion and philosophy—can only be called a metamorphosed expression of the old religious impulse. As leading figures in the American romantic movement, which blossomed before the Civil War and spanned much of the nineteenth century, Bryant, Whitman, and Whittier produced poetry that blended traditional theological concepts with a worship of nature; substituted a faith in American destiny for notions of Christian progress; invested utopian hopes in the settlers' movement west and the opening of the frontier; and raised the common person to an altar of high reverence. The humanitarianism, the deep belief in reform, the elevation of nature to a pantheistic creed, and the mystical embrace of populist themes reflect both a profound faith in and a reaction against the expansion of the American economy and the Industrial Revolution as it spread west. In all this, these literary journalists tapped into a romantic vein that lay within the American journalistic tradition and is still with us today.

Modern journalists like to see themselves as romantics, at least in the Humphrey Bogart, Hollywood-style meaning of the word (witness all the novels and screen plays written by journalists with hard-bitten dreamers, big-hearted cynics, or lonely, crushed idealists as the journalistic protagonists). But journalists seldom tie this big-screen variation of the term to the nineteenth-century romantic movement itself or, beyond that, to romanticism's ties to Christian idealism. Probably few journalists realize that their image of the journalist as hero—the idealist battling the forces of greed and corruption, the teller of truth committed to the cause of the public good, the story spinner celebrating the human spirit in feature articles and human interest stories—connects them to a romantic tradition that, in its various permutations through the centuries, is deeply embedded in the history of Christianity.

It is in Greeley—perhaps the greatest of the romantic journalistic personalities in America yet one who never penned his own literature—that the measure of the mark that romanticism has left on American journalism can best be seen. Greeley was the quintessential editor for the romantic myth that animated nineteenth-century American individualism: the up-by-the-bootstraps product of a poor farming family who migrated to the city and apprenticed himself in printing offices; a self-educated businessman who read voraciously and became a powerful advocate for the doctrine of self-reliance after he founded the *New York Tribune* in 1841; and a reformer and a civic activist who used his newspaper to champion women's rights, the antislavery cause, and good-government practices. As a self-made man, Greeley has come to embody the virtues and the character traits that epitomize our image of the progressive and principled editor. He was a supporter of Fourierism and the collectivist experiment at Brook Farm, he flirted with socialism and backed the free soil movement for liberal land distribution for settlers, and he held Ralph Waldo Emerson and his self-help philosophy in near reverential regard. Idealist and reformer that he was, Greeley was so crushed by his unsuccessful run for the presidency in 1872 against Ulysses S. Grant that he suffered a mental and physical breakdown and died a few weeks later.[3]

Yet it was Greeley's deep love of literature and his involvement with the transcendentalists of his day that distinguished him from the other early penny press editors of the nineteenth century. Transcendentalism, as preached by Emerson and his followers, was a form of romantic idealism imported from Europe that emphasized living close to nature, surrounding oneself with intellectual companionship, and relying on conscience and intuition in making moral decisions. The movement, centered largely in New England, placed great importance on spiritual living and maintained that a person's relationship with God was a personal matter and beyond the mediation of the organized church. In reacting against the prevailing Puritan Calvinism of New England, with its focus on original sin and humankind's struggle to escape damnation, transcendentalists believed strongly in the inherent goodness of the individual and the essential brotherhood of humankind. As Emerson put it in his 1838 Harvard Divinity School address, in what many considered a scandalous lecture, Christ should be worshipped not as the unique Son of God but as merely an example of the divinity attainable to all men and women.[4]

Greeley's own theology, like that of many transcendentalists, was not aligned with any denomination. Yet, influenced as he was by his avid Bible reading as a youth and the powerful model that Christ served in his life, Greeley's philosophy was still decidedly Christian in tone. Greeley noted in his autobiography that he took his religious philosophy directly from the Bible, that he believed in the universal application of the Golden Rule, and that he acknowledged the supremacy of God and the Lord Jesus Christ (although he declared himself no trinitarian). The distilled form of Christian idealism and optimism evident in so many nineteenth-century romantics shines through in Greeley's expression of his faith that the "dark problem of evil" can be solved by embracing the Christian concept of perfection through suffering. "Once conceive that an Omniscient Beneficence presides over and directs the entire course of human affairs, leading ever onward and upward to universal purity and bliss, and all evil becomes phenomenal and preparative—a mere curtain or passing cloud, which hides for a moment the light of the celestial and eternal day," he wrote.[5]

Such inspired language was not unusual for an era when journalistic prose—which was only just coming under the staccato influence of the telegraph, the typewriter, and the spare wire service writing style—was still lush, florid, and exuberant. Greeley's willingness to let his language soar with his overbrimming emotions is, in itself, a sign of the influence of romanticism on nineteenth-century journalism. Before journalists felt the need to adopt tough-guy poses and worldly wise and cynical ways, romanticism in journalism meant letting one's idealism and one's embrace of life's transcendent values have full vent. The loss of hope that left Greeley a broken and crushed spirit after his presidential defeat is only one more sign that Greeley—with his grand dream of national greatness and human equality (his "New Dawn" and "New Departure," as he called it in the campaign, "the dream that had haunted him all his life," as one biog-

rapher put it) buried under "a deluge of abuse and defamation rarely seen before or since in American politics"—was a tragic romantic personality in the
nineteenth-century meaning of the term.[6] At the unveiling of his grave-side
statute, one of his former reporters said, in true nineteenth-century romantic
fashion, "Only those who stood nearest to Greeley can truly know how his life
was glorified by self-denial and self-sacrifice. . . . A life like his cannot be lost;
something of him has been absorbed in other lives."[7]

Greeley's romantic view of America, with its grand-scale, panoramic vision
of an American destiny, still animates the journalistic imagination and sets the
tone for the civic consciousness of today's editors. With his intense pride in
American institutions and his desire for national harmony, Greeley absorbed
romantic notions about human perfectibility and the nineteenth-century faith
in progress, and he put out a publication that was "redolent of patriotism and
morality," as Glyndon Van Deusen put it.[8] Greeley's *Tribune,* which was read
throughout America and attracted readers with its high-principled editorial
page, its leadership role against slavery, and its support of progressive reform,
was held in near religious esteem by many of its readers. "The *Tribune* comes
next to the Bible all through the West," said Bayard Taylor on a lecture tour.[9]

Today's version of the Greeleyesque editor is much less expansive in outlook
(hemmed in by the demands of corporate ownership and economic performance), but the vision is the same of America as the land of unbounded opportunity, a place of justice and equality, a beacon to the world (romanticism
and nationalism, it should be noted, often go hand in hand in the United States).
"It was Greeley who repeated the message again and again, sounding the trumpet call to one and all to head into the undeveloped western lands, to build up
fortunes . . . to fulfil the dream of a bountiful and just America," wrote Herbert
Altschull. "America, in this image, would be the new Eden."[10]

Greeley, with his exalted imagination and his impassioned admiration for the
transcendentalists, was the model of the ideal editor for the young Walt Whitman when he began his newspaper editing career in the 1840s. Whitman fashioned his first editing job at the *Brooklyn Eagle* in Greeley's image of the ideal
editor, as someone with progressive values who saw the newspaper as an open
university for the masses that combined human interest stories, current events,
and a strongly moral editorial stance. Much has been made of Whitman's role
as one of the most influential poets in America history and his impact on the
development of the romantic tradition in American literature. But much less has
been made of the manner in which Whitman's early journalistic experiences were
critical to the development of his poetic career and the way in which that vision
still reflects the romantic tendencies found in the typical newsroom. Critics have
long marveled at how Whitman—a rather ordinary journalist who showed no
early signs of literary genius—could suddenly come forth with a brilliant book
of poetry, *Leaves of Grass,* which would leave such an indelible impression on
American literary life. But in his journalism career, Whitman had been imbib-

ing both the experiences and the values that were to become memorialized in his verse. Suffused throughout Whitman's poetry, as it was in his journalistic credo, were the democratic ideals of Paine, Voltaire, and Jefferson mixed with the transcendental vision of Emerson, who believed that the poet should be the prophet of democracy (along with, it should be added, a streak of jingoistic nationalism, as witnessed by Whitman's aggressive advocacy of the Mexican-American War). "*Leaves of Grass* began life with a mission, to provide a bible for the new democratic man," wrote Whitman's biographer, Philip Callow. "A man was to look to his own soul. God was there in his own heart. The real life of the senses and flesh transcended what had gone before. 'Oneself I sing.'"[11]

It is no coincidence that, as journalists and poets, most of these romantic figures were involved with or at least loosely connected to nonconformist religious movements—individualistic, reform-oriented faiths, such as Quakerism (Whitman and Whittier) or Unitarianism (Bryant), or a generalized, personal univeralism (Greeley). In both Whittier (an active, lifelong Quaker) and Whitman (whose exposure to Quakerism in his early family life greatly influenced his poetic worldview), the Quaker themes resonated in barely disguised fashion (as Whitman put it so often in his poetry, God is in every person, individually, and within the nation, collectively, acting with divine force; or as Whittier phrased it in his simple Quaker terms, "To one fixed trust my spirit clings; I know that God is Good!").[12] Bryant's Unitarianism (like that of Emerson) was the product of a heterodox theology and a faith in a rationalistic humanism. Bryant was "the poet who found that the groves were God's first temples" and someone who ultimately discovered that "the doctrines of no church . . . could fully satisfy him," as one biographer described him.[13]

Whitman, in his odyssey from the angry young journalist who raged at the antiwar faction that resisted involvement in the Mexican-American War (Quakerism's influence on him did not extend to an embrace of pacifism) to the mellow, white-bearded artist of advanced years who had achieved the stature of poet-prophet, has come to symbolize the romantic optimism that fueled nineteenth-century American economic expansion and the democratic fusion of the individual into the social fabric of the country. Whitman, the poet, the populist, and the mystic, elevated his vision into a "gospel of America," as it has been called, by offering up the founding fathers' Enlightenment ideals and his faith in the innate value of the average American as a combination to be worshipped.

This underlying ideology—a blend of Judaic notions of a chosen people with New Testament concepts of God's love for all humans and God's truth unfolding in the world—has come to infuse many aspects of the journalism business, if not in the same poetically inspired ways that it does with Whitman. While the mystic may not lie in the soul of most journalists, the romantic surely does. Although identifying themselves as rationalists, journalists are generally anti-intellectual in orientation; although viewing themselves as dispassionate, journalists are often motivated by strong emotions; although they may maintain a gruff, hard-bitten exterior, journalists are often hopeless idealists; no lovers of abstraction, journalists are moved by the concrete, the specific, the real-life elements of daily existence. "Logic and sermons never convince," wrote Whitman, in conveying the creed of the romantic poet-journalist. There is more truth, he said, in "the damp of the night."[14]

Like Greeley, who spent his journalistic career advocating for the laboring classes, the antislavery movement, and social utopianism and collectivism, the poet-journalists of the romantic movement were devoted to reform causes. Whittier was a passionate abolitionist and a cohort of William Lloyd Garrison, whose editorial offices were once burned by an anti-abolitionist mob; Bryant, as the longtime editor of the *New York Post,* crusaded for such liberal causes as abolitionism, collective bargaining, and freedom of speech and religion; and Whitman, in his role as an itinerant editor, championed various nationalistic and expansionary causes and served in the northern army.

Whittier—the most overtly and traditionally religious of the romantic poet-journalists—was, in true Quaker tradition, a deeply involved social activist. Whittier's powerful commitment to the abolitionist movement was rooted in the traditional Quaker commitment to causes that aided the helpless and the downtrodden. Like Greeley, Whittier blended the romanticism of the nineteenth century, which was quintessentially reflected in his mystic and poetic expressions, with a fervent championing of the antislavery cause, which he carried on in the pages of the weekly newspapers, the *Haverhill Gazette,* the *New England Weekly Review,* the *Pennsylvania Freeman,* and the *Middlesex Standard,* which he edited during the 1830s and 1840s. Whittier's abolitionist prose breathed with a "Hebraic fire," and (despite his Quaker detestation of war and his naturally shy and gentle nature) he propagandized with a zeal matched only by Garrison and other leading lights of the movement. Whittier also was a forceful advocate of a free press and an opponent of censorship of any kind. Shortly after the anti-abolitionist mob burned the office of the *Pennsylvania Freeman,* Whittier was back at work putting out the newspaper and publishing an editorial, "The Work Going On." Whittier even went so far as to put Milton's defense of free speech in *Areopagitica* to verse: "To brave Opinion's settled frown / From ermined robe and saintly gown / While wrestling reverenced Error down."[15]

Bryant, too, reflected this same amalgamation of the romantic impulse, the reformer's passion, and the poet's vision, all blended into the role of the newspaper editor. Like his fellow American artist-editors of the nineteenth century, Bryant believed in the notion of the newspaper as a democratic medium that educated and raised the cultural level of its readership.[16] Bryant's *New York Post* was known for its fairness, its independence, and the excellence and literary quality of its writing. Although Bryant became an editor mostly because he could not support himself as a poet ("Politics and a bellyful are better than poetry and starvation," he commented in 1829 soon after assuming the editorship of the *Post*), he always recognized journalism as a higher calling and carried it out in a sober, serious, and responsible manner in the half-century he ran the newspaper. Bryant straddled two strains in nineteenth-century letters that tugged at him all his career: the call of his fellow artists who believed he was wasting his talent on journalism (Bryant once complained that he was "harnessed to a daily drag . . . too much exhausted to use my wings") and the demands of trying to survive amidst the big circulation, penny press publications in New York (Bryant's *Post,* in appealing to a smaller, literate readership, remained at six cents) that threatened the *Post*'s business prospects with their flamboyant formulas to build readership.[17] In the end, Bryant's journalism—tempered, restrained, dignified, resistant to the sensationalism so prevalent in nineteenth-century New York journalism—remained much like his somber-toned poetry, which celebrated the quietude of nature without demonstrating Whitman's unrestrained emotionality.[18]

To understand the fascinating phenomenon of the nineteenth-century literary newspaper editor, it is instructive to be reminded of the stature of Greeley and Bryant in their time and their impact on the romantics and the progressives who increasingly found their way into the American newsroom. It has been said that most of what Whitman did as editor of the *Brooklyn Eagle* from 1846 to 1848 followed the lead of Greeley's *Tribune* and Bryant's *Post,* with a succession of editorials on health, morals, and humanitarianism; campaigns for civic improvement in matters of sanitation, lighting, and parks; reviews of operas, plays, books, and lectures; and a fundamental championing of democracy, America's manifest destiny, and antislavery.[19] It was an honor and a pride to have a personage such as Bryant, "who, to our mind, stands among the first in the world," serve as editor of one of the city's illustrious newspapers, Whitman told his Brooklyn readers; he was a "beautiful poet" and a "prophet" without enough fame in his own time who would someday rank far higher than many more honored artists.[20] Whittier, a friend and staunch defender of Greeley, even during the 1872 campaign when ridicule and calumny was heaped on him, wrote after Greeley's death, "I have known him as the educator of a people in liberty, temperance, integrity, economy, and industry, vigorously taking the side of the poor, enslaved, or suffering of every color and nationality."[21] Greeley, in V. L. Parrington's words, the "incorrigible idealist" who vexed "his soul with all the problems of society,"[22] and Bryant, described by the poet Edmund Clarence Stedman as the "beautiful, serene, majestic ideal of a good and venerable man,"[23] exercised a profound hold over a generation's attitude toward journalism, social reform, and the arts, in a way that has never been repeated but has left its legacy even in the commercialized newsrooms of today.

The affection in journalistic circles for these two flinty New Englanders may seem quaint in a journalistic profession that, more than a hundred years later, has come to be characterized by skepticism, secularism, and the deepest discomfort surrounding exclamations of open emotion. But the legacy of the romantic movement lives on in the modern news organization, albeit in ways that are not as redolent of mysticism, utopianism, or the expression of grand passions as in Greeley's time. For many of today's clear-eyed journalists, as with the culture at large, the word *romantic* has come to symbolize sentimentalism and is seen as synonymous with a fanciful (and largely foolish) idealism about the nature of the world. But romantic idealism can be seen in the profession's myth and its lore—its love of the accounts of fearless reporting or the tales of intrepid reporters from days-gone-by or the notion that the role of journalists is to help make the world a better place. For the modern newsroom aspirant, the glories of the journalism profession—that come, for example, in serving as a foreign correspondent or as an investigative reporter working to right social or institutional wrongs—are still suffused with a rich, romantic glow, even if most journalists recognize that their professional lives are mostly about the things of the mundane, routine, work-a-day world. (It is probably no coincidence that one of the most memorable short stories about the heroic but pathetic dreams of a grandiose fantasizer, "The Secret Life of Walter Mitty," was written by the humorist James Thurber, who also was a journalist).[24]

The idealized image of the journalist, it is true, came to flower in the same romantic atmosphere of the nineteenth century that nourished Greeley, Bryant, Whitman, and Whittier. The acknowledged first superstar of the news reporting business, Richard Harding Davis, has been memorialized for the self-conscious manner in which he created, and then spent his life living up to, the romantic typecast of the reporter-superhero—the American journalistic version of the poet Lord Byron, whose narcissism, bravado, and libertine ways made him the epitome of the romantic hero. Like Byron, Davis became a virtual overnight celebrity, with the glamour of his reputation built on his overseas exploits covering the Spanish-American War, among other famous assignments, and the manner in which he blended the code of the Tennysonian Sir Galahad into the "beau ideal" of the news correspondent, as Booth Tarkington put it. Although a dandy and a prig, whose gloves, cane, and fashionable dress made him something of a self-caricature, Davis cast a spell over a generation of readers and young people who found his life to symbolize "the hero of our dreams," in the words of one of Sinclair Lewis's characters.[25]

Yet, to fully understand the incorporation of the romantic myth into the world-view of modern journalism, it is vital to distinguish between the mood of hero worship and nostalgia for the past that characterized much nineteenth-century romantic literature and the more subtle strain of romantic idealism that remains in journalism today. Even in the nineteenth century, there were those who mocked what they considered the sentimentality and the silliness of the popular variety of romantic literature. Led by Mark Twain, many of the nineteenth- and early-twentieth-century journalists who turned so successfully to literature expressed their contempt for what they considered the falsely sentimental mood of their times, as represented in the medieval romances of Sir Walter Scott, the frontier adventure tales of James Fenimore Cooper, or the gothic romances popular throughout Europe. Twain—who wrote repeatedly of his disdain for Scott (a man who did "measureless harm" with his "sham grandeurs, sham gauds, and sham chivalries of a brainless and worthless long-vanished society")[26] and Cooper (in Cooper's *Deerslayer,* Twain said, the "humor is pathetic; its pathos is funny; its conversations are—oh! indescribable; its love-scenes odious; its English a crime against the language")[27]—was a pioneer in the development of American literary realism. There, along with other journalists-turned-fiction writers, such as William Dean Howells, Theodore Dreiser, Frank Norris, and Stephen Crane, Twain developed a new and forthright form of fiction, emphasizing common speech and characters of humble background, truthfulness, and a pragmatic outlook on life, which has come to be seen as the antithesis of the sentimental literature of the romantic era and the fulsome language, flattering sentiments, and an insincerely affected tone that characterized it.[28]

But Twain did not escape the mood of his day, no matter how much he may have mocked it. Twain's own strain of romanticism was more subtle, but it was there. Anyone who has read Twain's *Huckleberry Finn* can see that, despite the injection of the earthy realism and the lampooning of bathos and mawkish sentimentalism, the romantic idealism of the age still permeates almost everything in the book, from the fundamental nobility of the central characters, Huck and Jim, to the central myth (we can escape civilization's grip if we can just break free to float down a river) that has given the book its memorable appeal.[29] Twain's romanticism in *Huckleberry Finn* parallels that of Jean-Jacques Rousseau, the French romantic philosopher, and William Wordsworth, the English romantic poet: that, in Wordsworth's terms, the child (Huck) is father to the man (Jim); or that, as Rousseau believed, it is civilization that corrupts the fundamental goodness of the individual.[30] It is true that, as with many journalists, Twain's romantic outlook was undercut by his disillusionment with the world, fluctuating from a deep cynicism about human nature to the expression of the highest Christian ideals (although always camouflaged, as they were with Huck, in humor, irony, and self-deprecation). Twain's dual-mindedness—the romantic idealist one moment, the world-weary cynic the next—is still reflected today among romanticism's journalistic progeny, who can summon up the most elevated ideals to justify their actions and explain their values and then turn around and damn the entire human race. If one examines the journalistic ethic at all closely, one is forced to acknowledge that the romantic vision—with its emphasis on the pursuit of real-life experience, the honest expression of emotion and feeling, the commitment to life's highest ideals, the embrace of a heroic individualism, and the celebration of the common person—is still deeply woven into newsroom life, despite the hard-bitten undertone of much of its modern expression.

The way in which the optimistic and spiritualized romanticism of the nineteenth century carried into the skeptical world of twentieth-century journalism can be seen in the life of Carl Sandburg, who, like many journalist-literary figures both before and after him, toiled as a newspaper reporter before his lit-

erary career took off. In good romantic fashion, Sandburg as a young man set
off to experience the world firsthand, leaving the home of his Swedish immigrant parents in Galesburg, Illinois, to vagabond through the West by rail and
work a variety of manual and sales jobs before turning to journalism. Committed to reform causes from an early age, Sandburg worked from 1909 to 1932 as a
reporter and writer for socialist newspapers in Milwaukee and Chicago, as well
as for major dailies in those cities, all the while composing poetry on the side.
Moving with a coterie of important Chicago writers of the period, many of
whom started in journalism or copywriting jobs, such as Ben Hecht, Edna Fer-
ber, Sherwood Anderson, Charles MacArthur, and John Gunther,[31] Sandburg
perfected the free verse cadence and the prairie populism of his literary philosophy while working at his journalism job, in Hecht's characterization, as the
nemesis of his news editors, "a dreamer in the hardheaded world of news gathering, trudging into the city room . . . with a faraway look in his eye that baffled"
his supervisors. The poet-journalist had secured his job at the *Chicago Daily
News,* according to Hecht, because of a managing editor with a soft-spot for
literary types. Amazingly, Sandburg was hired even though he had once stood
up in the press room of the County Building in Chicago and read his poetry to
a group of big-city reporters—most of whom, Hecht recounts, were not much
impressed.[32]

Although deeply influenced by his Swedish Lutheran background, Sandburg,
like other romantic poet-journalists, never embraced the cause of formal religion, even though many find in his poetry a nativist mysticism and an unmis-
takable, "gently pervading spiritual essence," as his biographer Hazel Durnell
put it. Sandburg's Bible-reading comes through in his many biblical references,
a "religious understanding of faith and hope supporting his poetry," Durnell
added. The biblical mood of his poems, the biblical flavor of his social reform
themes, and the debt he owed to the Bible's free verse lyricism (which Sandburg
readily acknowledged) moved Norman Vincent Peale to characterize Sandburg
as having the "'quality of New Testament patience and Old Testament faith,'"
Durnell said. According to Durnell, "The spiritual values of Sandburg's writing may perhaps be characterized not as mighty carillons from magnificent
cathedrals, but as the humble, quietly pervading tones from Religion's Cottage.
These qualities have deservedly won him recognition among the churches of
America. I personally know of sermons based upon Sandburg writings—even
upon a single Sandburg poem."[33] With his fascination with folklore and the
American dream, his love of the land, his belief in the heroism of the common
person, and his support of socialism and progressive causes, Sandburg the poet
is presaged by Sandburg the journalist, who was once described at his desk by a
colleague at the *Chicago Daily News* as "The Poet at his window, lounging deep
in his chair, his powerful hands knotted, his dark, rugged face locked in a sol-
emn dream. . . . Who is he, after all? A great man, or only one of us?"[34]

Still, it is not the shambling, distracted, head-in-the-clouds, poetic person-

ality that sets the tone for our modern-day conception of the romantic journalist as much as it is the hard-boiled character with the deeply sensitive heart.
During the twentieth century, Ernest Hemingway occupied the central place in
the gallery of the romantic figures of the profession—courageous, adventure-
some, hard-drinking, passionate, idealistic, stoical, a writer who forged a celebrated literature out of the basics of clipped and succinct journalistic prose style.
The Hemingway myth—along with the intensive self-mythologizing he engaged
in all his life—comes as close as there is to a twentieth-century literary hero of
Byronic stature. Hemingway infused his literature with all the heroic elements
of his life as a military volunteer, journalist, foreign correspondent, and itinerant fiction writer that took him from the front in World War I to expatriate café
life in Paris to the Spanish Civil War to big-game hunting in Africa to marlin
fishing in Cuba.

In his novel *The Sun Also Rises,* the protagonist, journalist Jake Barnes, symbolizes the mystique of the Hemingway philosophy that has so appealed to the
romantic streak in modern Americans: tragically wounded in World War I; unable to consummate his relationship with Lady Brett Ashley, the love of his life;
bravely carrying on the demands of his profession; chasing his dead dreams in
expatriate travel and drowning them in endless bouts of drinking. This prototype for the Humphrey Bogart–style romantic movie hero—tough and caustic
on the outside but crying on the inside—has been duplicated by Hollywood in
films ever since. Yet, beneath the macho exterior of his characters and the disillusionment expressed in their philosophy of life, Hemingway exhibited a longing to find a substitute for the loss of traditional religious feeling that is characteristic of many later romantic writers. Infused throughout *The Sun Also Rises* is
Hemingway's belief that the spiritual meaning found in such manly pursuits as
bullfighting, trout fishing, and fiesta celebrating can serve as a form of compen-
sation for the withdrawal of old-fashioned religious consolation. At one point,
Jake, clinging to his Catholicism, tries to find some relief by praying in a Spanish
cathedral, but it does nothing for him. Still, Jake clearly suffers from his lack of
religious emotion. "You know it makes one feel rather good deciding not to be a
bitch," says Lady Brett at one point in the novel. "It's sort of what we have instead of God," she adds. "Some people have God," Jake responds. "Quite a few."[35]

The 1920s, of course, are viewed as the great romantic period in modern
American literature, and journalists or ex-journalists pop up everywhere in the
midst of the celebrated writers of this time. Besides those like Hemingway who
were living the "Lost Generation" life of Paris and Europe, such ex-journalists
as Sherwood Anderson, Ring Lardner, Willa Cather, Sinclair Lewis, and John Dos
Passos were beginning or in the middle of literary careers; the famed *New Yorker*
magazine of the period included in its stable of writers such journalist-literary
figures as Thurber, E. B. White, and Robert Benchley; and the legendary Algon-
quin Hotel in New York City gathered around its roundtable such journalistic
and literary luminaries as Harold Ross, H. L. Mencken, and Dorothy Parker. The

image of journalists-turned-literary-celebrities at the center of this circle has captured the imagination of many a reporter pining for loftier literary success, even to the point of creating an almost reverential quality to the way journalists, historians, and literary critics have come to celebrate literature as an alternative to the religious life.

Yet, even in the twentieth century, one could find at least one journalist-romantic whose vision of literature was fashioned directly out of traditional religious beliefs. James Agee, screenwriter, social activist, and longtime journalist for Henry Luce's *Time* and *Fortune* magazines, was religious in his attitudes, even though he, too, shared much of the romantic's distaste for organized religion. Agee's writings—with their richly textured, lyrical treatment of nonfiction subjects that grew out of his journalistic assignments— were a forerunner of what became known as the new journalism of the 1960s and 1970s. Agee, a tortured figure who drowned his troubles in alcohol and self-destructive behavior, has been treated as a James Dean of the journalistic world, a brilliant but out-of-control personality who died young and never fully reached his potential. Agee's difficult life can be framed in terms of his religious upbringing, swinging from a zealous piety and fixation on Christian self-sacrifice when he was a schoolboy to his dissolute later years when he struggled to maintain a weakened faith worn down by disappointments and self-indulgence. In *A Death in the Family*, his moving account of his father's death in an automobile accident when Agee was a young boy, he tried mightily to recapture the feeling that his mother's Anglo-Catholic faith held for him, and he came to realize that he did not truly understand his father's death, as one of his biographers put it, until he understood the meaning of the death of Christ. The religious battleground of Agee's early years—focusing on his mother's puritanism and devotion to prayer, his father's unbelief and commitment to a life of freedom and pleasure-seeking, and Agee's own pervading sense of sin and powerful experience of loss—became the cauldron of both the book and his own life, as he balanced an unstable personality and a fevered romantic imagination with the desire for some form of spiritual epiphany (as symbolized by the butterfly that landed on his father's coffin just before he was interred) that would give coherence to his otherwise chaotic existence.[36]

The romantic spirit of the nineteenth century went through a great deal of change in the twentieth century, and the remnants of romanticism in journalism today are quite different from the explicitly spiritual beliefs that animated such editors as Bryant, Whitman, and Greeley. Even in the nineteenth century, journalists imbued with the romantic spirit began to express their spirituality in very different ways than did Whittier, an avowed Christian who stood apart from the mainstream of the romantic movement by complaining about pagan elements of British romanticism and calling Byron and Shelley infidels.[37] Unlike Whittier, Whitman, Bryant, and Greeley all repudiated organized Christianity or at least kept themselves at arms length from it. For them, the values of

the romantic movement—the cult of nature, the passion for liberty, the celebration of democracy, the support for civic reform, the faith in common people, the belief in the universality of God's presence in all things and all people—
amounted to what can only be called a new religion, something they saw as a
worthy substitute for formal Christianity. Yet their values, subsumed as they may
have been by a vision of romantic pantheism, are closely linked with Christian
idealism, Christian mysticism, and the activist traditions of Christians who have
labored to put the gospel message to work in the world.

Today, the secularizing elements of modern life have transformed the religious
impulse in journalism into something even less recognizably religious, but, in
its transformed form, it still retains aspects of the religious worldview. While
transcendentalism became a substitute for Christianity for many of the romantic
journalists, secularized romanticism has been passed on to today's journalists
in forms that still contain a faint but important outline of their religious heritage. The moral outrage and passion for the truth that motivated Bob Woodward and Carl Bernstein in their Watergate investigation contained powerful
elements of the romantic worldview and helped make them romantic heroes
to the profession. That romantic stance—the young do-gooders battling the evil
establishment, the incorruptible reformers rooting out knavery and injustice—
resonates with the same inspiring themes that flavor the religious messages of
the Bible with romantic overtones (David versus Goliath, Daniel in the lion's
den). The romantic image of the outsider hero found in the Moses story or Joseph's rescue and rise to riches and power still retains a deep hold on the journalistic imagination ("Gunga Dan" Rather, dressed in his khaki fatigues, dropping in to cover the Afghan-Russian War; CNN's Peter Arnett staying on in
Baghdad during the U.S. bombing in the Gulf War), even if carried out in ways
that few journalists would recognize as religious at root. Romantic stories and
romantic images often have been used to further religious purposes (some might
even argue that the story of Jesus' heroic sacrifice and his ultimate triumph came
to mean what it has when it was presented as a romantic story). The romance
of the news business is still a great lure to would-be journalists, and its professional lore and professional ideals are still closely connected to the Judeo-Christian ethic as it metamorphosed during the romantic period. The journalist as
good guy fighting evil is celebrated in hundreds of books written by journalists
(catalogued by Steve Weinberg at the University of Missouri), and countless
movies and television shows have been based on the journalistic pursuit of justice. That the inspiration for this can be found in the historical links between
romanticism and Christianity and Judaism—and even further back in the
themes of pagan mythology—only highlights the enduring nature of the romantic story in the human imagination.

It is revealing to see how many of the modern American journalistic values
identified by the sociologist Herbert Gans as "enduring" are romantic in nature
and implicitly religious in their underlying idealism. Gans described a number

of these values—most notably, the pastoral values that imbue the news—as explicitly romantic and idealized versions of the small-town democratic ideal that trace back to the nineteenth century. Gans saw a number of characteristics of the news flowing from the small-town pastoralism that still illuminate journalistic beliefs: the bias toward preservation of nature and the environment, the fear of bigness and impersonal corporations or government agencies, the suspicion of the dehumanizing elements of new technology, and the importance of tradition (except when it involves discrimination of any kind). Gans also listed a whole range of other journalistic values—a deep faith in American destiny and the United States as the upholder of the democratic ideal, a belief in altruistic democracy and the importance of political reform, a sympathy toward citizen participation and grass-roots activity—that can be seen as directly linked to the American romantic tradition and the Christian idealism out of which romanticism grew. Most important, journalists see themselves as the protectors of the individual's freedom against the encroachments of society and as opponents of forces that rob people of their initiative—a reflection of an almost pure Rousseauian vision of a society where pure-hearted and free-thinking people living without restraint can be counted on to do the right thing.[38]

At the same time, it is important to distinguish the ways in which the romanticism of American journalists differs from the literary and philosophical variety studied in the university. While journalists retain their version of the Byronic hero myth, they are also practical, pragmatic folk who do not celebrate lost causes or quixotic efforts to change society. Journalists' passion for reform extends largely to improving established institutions, and journalists are strong believers in social stability, the capitalist order, and the preservation of social mores and important customs. Journalists' belief in the possibility of a better world falls far short of the revolution envisioned by such radical romantics as Rousseau or Karl Marx, and their faith in the common person is balanced by a healthy skepticism about the dark side of human nature and a keen awareness of how power corrupts. Unlike Byron and Shelley, journalists are wary of celebrating the emotions or the senses too excessively, particularly at the expense of reason or science. As moderates, journalists tend to eschew extreme solutions; they dislike excess sentimentality or naive idealism; and they temper their passions with what they believe is a realistic outlook about what life holds. Even Greeley, who dabbled with socialism, championed transcendentalism, and was attracted to utopian experiments, called Byron a "cynical, irreverent, law-deriding libertine" and labeled Wordsworth's protests against the intensity of the Byronic school "needed and wholesome."[39]

Yet, since Greeley's time, when transcendental and romantic themes could be woven unselfconsciously and unapologetically into a journalistic ethic that was still closely tied to the nation's religious tradition, the newsroom of today has moved relentlessly in the secular direction. As with other influences that have diluted the hold of orthodox Christianity on the culture—science, Enlightenment thought, psychology—the romantic movement grew up as both a product of and a reaction against traditional Christian attitudes, first making its way into the American newsroom as a liberalizing alternative to the dogmas and the rigidities of the prevailing Puritan value system and then receding into a background presence as twentieth-century journalists increasingly identified with institutional norms and professional standards as the basis of their working values.

Still, in case modern journalists forget the exalted heritage of their profession, they should recall the romantic-religious language in which Greeley defended the reform tradition in journalism: "Let us cherish the Reformer! . . . The earnest, unselfish Reformer,—born into a state of darkness, evil, and suffering, and honestly striving to replace these by light, and purity, and happiness,—he may fall and die, as so many have done before him, but he cannot fail. His vindication shall gleam from the walls of his hovel, his dungeon, his tomb. . . . As the untimely death of the good is our strongest moral assurance of the Resurrection, so the life wearily worn out in doubtful and perilous conflict with Wrong and Woe is our most conclusive evidence that Wrong and Woe shall yet vanish forever."[40]

Today's journalist might put it more bluntly. As Les Whitten, a colleague of the renowned modern muckraker Jack Anderson, once said, "You really do feel that there is a sort of missionary quality about laying low the people most journalists don't have the guts to go after. I felt reborn when I came to work for Jack."[41] Clearly the sentiments—at some core level—are the same.

CHAPTER 5

Muckraking the Nation's Conscience: Journalists and the Social Gospel

The humor magazine *Puck* published a satiric cartoon in 1906, depicting American muckraking journalists as Christian crusaders—with S. S. McClure carrying a crossbow in the lead and Lincoln Steffens helmeted and sitting astride a war horse—heading off to do battle with the forces of evil.[1] The muckrakers proudly accepted the idea that their reform movement was being carried out in the spirit of Jesus' call for social and religious renewal. When criticized for his "Jesus complex," Upton Sinclair responded, "The world needs a Jesus more than it needs anything else."[2] At one point, Steffens planned to write a biography of Jesus, and, in his later writings, he "preached the Golden Rule . . . and declared himself something more dangerous than an anarchist—'a Christian,'" wrote Justin Kaplan, Steffens's biographer.[3]

Many modern journalists admire the muckrakers and, to this day, talk about the investigative reporters' mission in terms of the muckraking tradition. However, few of today's journalists are aware of how directly the muckrakers were influenced by the social ethics of Christianity and how—explicitly and implicitly—they incorporated Judeo-Christian principles into their journalistic crusades. The reform tradition in American journalism—where journalists are allowed to step outside the methodology of objective news reporting and openly advocate cleaning up corruption and doing away with injustice—owes much to the message of community responsibility and social equity found in the Bible.

In claiming Jesus as their greatest antecedent, the muckrakers preached a fiery brand of reform politics that was known then as the social gospel. Drawing largely from the Sermon on the Mount (Matthew 5–7) and the radical social elements in Jesus' teachings, the muckrakers distilled the Christian message into a reform agenda that denounced moral corruption, worldly excess, social inequality, exploitation of the poor, and inhumane treatment of any kind. Inspired by the Hebrew prophets, the muckrakers held up the prophetic strain in Christianity as the proper model for dealing with the failings of the social order.[4]

But the muckrakers' inflammatory and forceful brand of advocacy seemed anything but patient and loving at times. Both Steffens and Sinclair saw in Jesus a reflection of their own ideals and most passionate beliefs, and they did not hesitate to define Jesus' message in more socially radical terms than can be gleaned from any explicit reading of the gospels. Sinclair believed that many of the quotations from the apostles and the saints proved that Jesus and his followers were really social revolutionaries; he once rewrote the twenty-third chapter of Matthew as socialist doctrine; and he promoted his vision of social revolution like a new religion.[5] When Steffens, frustrated at the pace of social reform, turned to communism late in his career, he found there, too, a model in Jesus, who he said "saw what we see; he understood, as his disciples don't, the evils, their causes; and he had a cure."[6] In his autobiography, Steffens argued that the economic changes and communal practices Jesus and the apostles taught "showed them [to be] practicing communists!"[7]

Steffens, who gained widespread fame for his exposure of municipal corruption in *McClure's* magazine and his 1904 publication *Shame of the Cities,* was particularly explicit in articulating the Christian and biblical underpinnings of his reform philosophy. The answer to corruption, Steffens came to believe, was a change of heart among society's leaders, a philosophy of "applied Christianity" that would lead to a transformed world.[8] In his autobiography, Steffens described how he became curious about the vision that motivated the few "honest fanatics" who devoted themselves to social reform, and "suddenly it occurred to me that Christianity conveyed such a faith, hope, and—vision." It was then that Steffens experienced what can only be called a journalist's version of a conversion. "The experience was an adventure so startling that I wanted everybody else to have it," he wrote. "I still recommend people to re-read the New Testament as I read it, without reverence, with feet up on a desk and a pipe in the mouth, as news. It is news. It made the stuff I was writing in the magazine, old stuff. All my stories of all the cities and States were one story . . . and these were all in that old story of Christ in the New Testament."[9]

Yet, as passionately as they advocated the social gospel, the muckrakers were no friends of the organized Christian establishment—nor was their image of Jesus one that was even close to being accepted by orthodox Christians. Throughout their careers, Steffens and Sinclair issued one scathing indictment after another of doctrinal and institutional Christianity.[10] In praising the great progressive and reform leaders of his age, Steffens complained of the Christian churches that would not "recognize Christianity if they saw it," and he excoriated the Christian denominations for ignoring the real story of Jesus, the social reformer and prophet of peace. "I have never heard Christianity, as Jesus taught it in the New Testament, preached to Christians," Steffens wrote.[11]

   The most scorching broadside against the Christian establishment came from
Sinclair in *Profits of Religion,* one of many Sinclair exposés of the American institutions he believed had been corrupted by capitalism (including the meat-
packing industry, the press, the arts, and the schools). Sinclair described how,
growing up an Episcopalian, he came to see his "beautiful church for what it
was and is: a great capitalist interest, an integral and essential part of a gigantic
predatory system." In language clearly designed to shock the believers of his day,
Sinclair lambasted the Christian churches for their hypocrisy, their greed, and
their transformation of the message of Jesus into false prophecy. Sinclair was
particularly harsh in denouncing Christianity's adaptation to the inequities of
the capitalist system and its turning away from Jesus' more radical pronouncements. "All church members go through this same performance," he wrote. "The
oldest and most venerable of them steal potatoes and throw mud all week—and
then take a hot bath of repentance and put on the clean clothing of piety. In this
same way their ministers of religion are occupied to scrub and clean and dress
up their disreputable Founder—to turn him from a proletarian rebel into a
stained-glass-window divinity."[12]
   Most of the muckrakers turned so strongly against Christian orthodoxy because they had had such a strong dose of it in their youth. Steffens was exposed
to the gospel by his militant Methodist grandfather, which led to his own youthful soul-searching and conversion;[13] Sinclair described himself as a "devout little Episcopalian" in his boyhood, teaching Sunday school at the age of fifteen;[14]
the Irish-born McClure was raised in an evangelical sect known as the Brethren, a stern and joyless group that condemned lighthearted pleasures and believed that nonbelievers would suffer eternal damnation;[15] Ray Stannard Baker
was brought up among strict Presbyterians;[16] William Allen White sang gospel
hymns and attended revival camp meetings during his Kansas boyhood;[17] and
Ida Tarbell knelt at the Methodist mourners' bench as a young girl growing up
in the Pennsylvania oil country. Tarbell's description of her conversion captured
the experience of many young people reared in small towns and frontier churches in the late 1800s: "In my tenth or eleventh year I 'went forward' not from a
sense of guilt but because everybody was doing it. My sense of sin came after it
was all over and I was tucked away in bed at night. I had been keenly conscious
as I knelt at the Mourners' bench that the long crimson ribbons which hung
from my hat must look beautiful on my cream-colored coat. The realization of
that hypocrisy cut me to the heart. I knew myself a sinner then, and the relief I
sought in prayer was genuine."[18]
   Tarbell's matter-of-fact recollection of her childhood religious experiences—
and the fact that religion seldom shows up explicitly in her biography—is the
exception rather than the rule with the muckrakers. For such muckrakers as
Steffens, Sinclair, and Baker, religion always hovered close by when they framed
their view of their journalistic mission. While the muckrakers may have abandoned the doctrinal rigidity of their upbringing, they never escaped the "mor-

alistic, evangelical, millennial" spirit of the Christianity in which they had been reared, as Justin Kaplan put it.[19] It was that spirit of militant righteousness—along with their fervent desire to root out the evils of the world—that was retained in their journalistic crusades. "For some muckrakers the higher criticism of Bible commentators had shaken the certainty of the old-time religion," wrote the media historian Bruce Evensen. "Their challenge then became finding an absolute to substitute for a belief in the Bible as the inspired Word of God, something that could arouse a generation to right thinking and conduct."[20]

The remnants of religious conscience that churned inside the muckrakers cannot be separated from the evangelical cross-currents in the United States in the late nineteenth century and early twentieth. The muckrakers burst onto the scene during one of the most zealously religious periods in American history—a time when the Christian "revival" movements that swept through the American heartland were accompanied by the equally fervent Populist and Progressive calls for municipal and governmental reform, a greater voice for the "common" person in political affairs, and a political system with ethics and equity as the animating principles. In this hothouse of political and religious renewal, the social activism we associate now with the liberal political agenda quite often was carried out in the name of activating Christian values and applying the gospel message to social, economic, and political circumstances. This is quite different from today's political alignments, where the most vocal of the Christian evangelicals identify themselves with the conservative political agenda. Then many evangelical Christians could be found as supporters of social reform, allies of government intervention, and activists in their view of responding to the economic problems of the underprivileged.[21]

Muckraking must be seen in the context of a nation that throughout the late eighteenth century and nineteenth century had been transformed by industrialization, urbanization, and immigration into a land filled with a displaced and unchurched population disconnected from the religious underpinnings of early colonial life. The succession of evangelical revival movements, which had such an influence on the muckrakers, emerged, in essence, as a way to renew the moral standards and spiritual life of this population. The various Christian renewal campaigns—coming wave upon wave, beginning in the mid-1700s with what is known as the first Great Awakening and reaching peaks with the Baptist and Methodist revivals of the late eighteenth century and the Second Great Awakening in the early 1800s—have been so persistent and so tumultuous that some historians see the history of religion in America as one of continuous religious revivalism, right up to the present day.[22]

The muckrakers, despite being called radicals and atheists by their critics, were clearly secular preachers in this movement. Coming at the end of a particularly zealous period of evangelical revivalism, virtually everything in the muckrakers' tone and style fit with the pattern of Christian proselytizing and moral denunciation of worldly corruption that had become woven into the fabric of

late-nineteenth-century America. The forces that converged to create this unique
historical movement—the evangelical revival movements, the excesses of the
Industrial Revolution, the creation of unprecedented empires of wealth and
power, the corruption of municipal political machines, and a succession of
boom times followed by jolting recessions—have never come again in exactly
such a dramatic fashion, although similar moods in the body politic have flared
up during times of economic troubles and social upheaval (such as during the
Great Depression of the 1930s and the civil rights and Vietnam War protests of
the 1960s and 1970s). The muckrakers and their progressive cohorts were crusading against the "degradation of Christian citizenship," in a *McClure's* magazine catch phrase,[23] or as William Allen White described the movement in his
autobiography, "It was not religious—at least not pious—this progressive movement," but it was "profoundly spiritual," with the "insurgents" sharing the "crusader's ardor" and "crusader's fellowship. . . . . It was an evangelical uprising
without an accredited Messiah."[24]

The journalistic emphasis within this evangelical crusade varied considerably,
but it seldom abandoned the broader Christian purpose of the movement. Tarbell, for example, reflected the Protestant, Puritan strain of Christianity, and her
early years in a small Pennsylvania oil town where she attended prayer meetings and imbibed her parents' frontier values about the self-sufficiency of wom-
en and hatred of privilege resulted in her aiming her "Davidian slingshot" at
the Goliath Standard Oil Company years later. The Protestant righteousness that
emanated from Tarbell's compelling critique of the Rockefeller oil trust—which
grew out of the experiences of Tarbell's father, an independent oil producer, in
resisting Standard Oil's efforts to establish control over the region's oil production—led her to be called "the Joan of Arc of the Oil Regions" and one of her
biographers to describe the "Puritan fist beneath the glove" in her meticulous-
ly documented account of the rise of the Rockefeller oil cartel.[25]

Steffens's revolutionary interpretation of Christianity and his embrace of
communism brought him into conflict with Tarbell, who did not share his conversion to the necessity for violent social change. When Steffens's frustration
at the pace of reforms led him to turn to Marxism, he found a biblical basis for
his change in philosophy not only in the New Testament but also in the lessons
and the stories of the Hebrew scriptures and the Hebrew prophets. This ultimately led Steffens to reject reform and advocate revolution—something he
dramatized in his book *Moses in Red* by presenting Moses as a forerunner and
justifier of Lenin.[26] In noting how Steffens returned from a post–1917 revolution visit to Russia "like a man who had seen a long hoped-for vision," Tarbell
declared that Steffens had become what she could not abide—a dogmatic person and a propagandist.[27]

Most of the muckrakers, however, were believers in the capitalist order who
wanted to reform it, not overthrow it, and few saw Jesus as the political radical
that Steffens and Sinclair did. White, as a muckraker for *McClure's* magazine but

even more so as the much-celebrated editor of the *Emporia (Kansas) Gazette,* where he served as prototype of the progressive and outspoken small-town editor, found inspiration for his moral renewal themes in Jesus, but not in the same social revolutionary fashion that Steffens and Sinclair did. White traced his conversion to a conversation with a stranger on the street who convinced the youth that Jesus was the "greatest hero in history" and someone who demonstrated the "futility of force and the ultimate triumph of reason in human affairs." White developed from this an incremental reform philosophy that focused on how Jesus' teachings had slowly improved, even if only slightly, the practices of human institutions. White's moderate progressivism—while every bit as religiously motivated as Sinclair's or Steffens's (White refers to this conversation as "the night of the Great Light" that set him "on the road to Damascus")—is reflected in his admission that many middle-class people like him supported reform "not primarily because the have-nots were loyal, humble, worthy, and oppressed—Heaven knows we knew that the underdog had fleas, mange, and a bad disposition—but rather because we felt that to bathe and feed the underdog would release the burden of injustice on our own conscience."[28]

Another of the "moderate" muckrakers, Ray Stannard Baker, found it annoying that the advocates of the social gospel could be so "hopelessly confused" in mixing Jesus into their views of radical reform. For example, Baker, who rose to fame on the basis of his articles in *McClure's* exposing big business collusion that grew out of the economic panic of 1893, described his strong disagreement with William T. Stead, an English journalist and reformer, who wrote the book *If Christ Came to Chicago.* Stead had argued that Jesus would have been radicalized at the sight of the poverty and inequality of wealth in the city. Even though Baker repeated throughout his life his belief that the world's moral redemption depended on people imitating Christ's life, he felt Stead's argument was a naive view of a religious figure who Baker believed was interested mostly in humankind's spiritual condition and hardly had offered a blueprint for social reform.[29]

However, with Baker, there was a persistent anger, as there was with virtually all of the muckrakers, at the failure of the political establishment to develop a program to improve the economic and social circumstances of humankind. The most vilified of the muckrakers was the political radical Sinclair, who came the closest to real political power. Sinclair ran for California governor in 1934 as an avowed socialist and was narrowly defeated only because of a vitriolic counter-campaign by the state's business establishment. Sinclair understood the promotional value of exaggeration and overstatement in excoriating the established order, and he believed that the best way to make a point was to attack society's class and economic inequities and the churches' moral hypocrisies in ways he hoped would shame Christians into action. That may help explain why he later described his differences with the church establishment as "teasing." "My quarrel with the churches is a lover's quarrel," Sinclair once said. "I do not want to

destroy them, but to put them on a rational basis, and especially to drive out
the money changers from the front pews."[30]

Sinclair was a highly spiritual person who might best be described as a mystic whose religious experiences do not fit into traditional categories. He dabbled in telepathy, clairvoyance, spiritualism, and psychic research. Sinclair described how, walking in a Baltimore park while he was a youth, he was
overwhelmed by a feeling "startling and wonderful beyond any power of words
to tell; the opening of gates in the soul, the pouring in of music, of light, of joy
which was unlike anything else" that left him seized with "a happiness so intense that the distinction between pleasure and pain was lost." Sinclair concluded that "if I had been a religious person at this time, no doubt I would have had
visions of saints and holy martyrs, and perhaps have developed stigmata on
hands and feet. But I had no sort of superstition."[31]

It is somewhat ironic, of course, to find a man of such profound religious
experience defending himself against charges of atheism all his life, but Sinclair
did it with a great equanimity (and some would say great pleasure). Sinclair once
asserted that he was not an atheist since he found atheists to be "as dogmatic as
a Christian." But his descriptions of his beliefs—the striking conviction that
"you are in the hands of a force outside of yourself" or his certainty "that there
must be a creative energy animating and directing the universe [that] I suspect . . . knows more than I do"—were not enough to keep him from being
excoriated by the more orthodox.[32]

The muckraker era was a time when a host of social, psychological, technological, and theological controversies were shaking up the old religious order,
and the muckrakers were fully immersed in them. The traditional Christian
worldview was challenged on a number of fronts, most notably by Darwin's
theories and discoveries, which called into question the origins of humankind
and the earth presented in the Book of Genesis, and by a host of new religions
that were reminiscent of what we call the New Age movement today. The muckrakers, like many religious progressives of their time, hoped to find a faith that
did not fly in the face of what they thought reason and science were telling them.
Steffens was deeply influenced by his exposure to the ideas of Darwin and Herbert Spencer,[33] as was Tarbell (leading to a religious crisis that spurred her to
reject formal religion and her belief in immortality—although "she still believed
in God and always would," according to Mary Tomkins);[34] Darwin's theories
of evolution disturbed Baker and left him "much at sea" about his faith;[35] White
was "stirred up" by the works of Spencer but was finally able to reconcile Darwinian evolution with his religious beliefs;[36] and Spencer's thinking influenced
Sinclair's theories of socialism (although, like many reformers, Sinclair rejected Spencer's concept of social Darwinism as a "cruel canon" that had been
corrupted into a "secular confirmation of the Calvinist rock upon which the
Republic was built").[37] As a result, Sinclair and Baker were attracted to exotic

religious movements that satisfied their spiritual needs but allowed them to stay at arm's length from Christian orthodoxy.

The inner tug between old religious certainties and the advanced thinking of the time was poignantly reflected in Baker's autobiography, *American Chronicle*. A product of a conservative religious upbringing, Baker grew critical of church attitudes, particularly toward social problems, but "deep down," he wrote, he continued to feel "the essential truth of the teachings of Christianity." Soon after his marriage, Baker was invited to rejoin the Presbyterian church of his youth, and he admitted he was greatly tempted "by the safe harbor of the old church." However, when presented with a copy of the church's creeds (something that, in an interesting reversal of traditional Christian views, he described as an "insidious temptation" from a "serpent" in the guise of the minister), Baker fled, certain that he was "not then ready to unite with any church."[38]

At the deepest theological level, the muckrakers were disturbed by a rift that had begun to appear in Christian circles—and has grown into a chasm today. Although it might be disputed by some conservative scholars, most biblical critics view the New Testament as a collection of themes and dicta woven into one document by many Christian writers throughout the years. The problem is that many of the New Testament's messages appear on the surface to be contradictory—including passages that conflict with the exhortations so dearly held by the muckrakers. Perhaps the best illustration of this is the issue of faith versus works—a dispute that has wracked the church and led, in part, to the Protestant Reformation. In a New Testament book such as James—with its philosophy so consistent with the social activism of the muckrakers—Christians are repeatedly instructed to perform good works and told that "faith by itself, if it has no works, is dead." But James's claim runs counter to Paul's powerful message in Romans 3:28 that "we hold that a person is justified by faith apart from works prescribed by the law," which ultimately became the basis for Martin Luther's breakaway from the Catholic church.[39]

As Christians in spirit, if not in creed, the muckrakers tended to take the Bible seriously and not just dismiss it as a mass of outmoded and conflicting moral data. But with the exception of Steffens, they were adamant about their dislike of the cruel accounts of Israelite conquest and the unforgiving moral codes of the Hebrew scriptures, as well as what Sinclair called the "fairy tale" aspect of the New Testament cosmology and theology. Sinclair described himself as "turned into an agnostic by reading the official defenses of Christianity."[40]

Today, we would identify the muckrakers as humanist, social activist Christians, meaning that they focused on the moral teachings and the social message of Jesus, particularly in the Sermon on the Mount, rather than on the mystical, ethereal figure of Christian devotion portrayed in the Book of John, the epistles of Paul, and the other pastoral letters. While the traditional formula of orthodox Christianity emphasizes the divine element of Christ, the muckrakers saw Jesus as a deeply human person whose life and ministry provided a model for the social activist causes that were so important to them. Like other Christians who have tried to reconcile Christian teachings with science, the muckrakers tended to be skeptical of the stories and the traditions that grew up around Jesus and became enshrined in the creeds, gospel accounts, and accepted canon of the church. This mixture of respect for Jesus but irreverence for the way his message was lost once Christianity was institutionalized is illustrated in a story that Steffens told to his fellow muckraker Will Irwin. "The other day, I walked up Fifth Avenue with the Devil," Steffens reportedly told Irwin. "We came to a crowd on a street corner. There stood Christ on a soapbox, speaking to the multitude. He seemed to be making a great impression. I nudged the devil and said: 'Aren't you afraid?' 'Afraid of what?' said the Devil. 'Of Him!' I said. 'Oh, no!' said the Devil. 'Just as soon as He gets it going, I'll join it and organize it!' "[41]

The muckrakers raised an important question that continues to divide Christians: was Jesus a figure of spiritual salvation or was he an activist seeking a just society? An important strand of modern journalism in America has followed the muckraker tradition of embracing Christian ethics and social ideals but spurning much of the rest of Christian theology. (This is made clearer in the research that is presented later.) Still, few journalists have taken the next step, as Steffens and Sinclair did, in presuming that Jesus was calling for a major restructuring of the economic and social order.

One cannot blame journalists for not achieving clarity on this—not the least because it is not all that clear that this is what Jesus was advocating. Clearly, Jesus' message was a radical one, in the context of both his and our time. No society in history—least of all, modern American society—has lived up to such exhortations as "If you wish to be perfect, go, sell your possessions, and give the money to the poor" (Matthew 19:21); "Whoever wants to be first must be last of all and servant of all" (Mark 9:35); or "When you give a banquet, invite the poor, the crippled, the lame, and the blind" (Luke 14:13). But it also appears clear (despite the muckrakers' reading of the New Testament) that Jesus resisted projecting himself as a political figure or into social causes; as threatening as his ministry may have been to the civil authorities, his message was aimed at the spiritual condition of his fellow citizens more than at their economic or political circumstances. When Jesus talked of rendering unto Caesar what is Caesar's (Matthew 22:21, Luke 20:25), when he talked of how the poor will always be with us (Mark 14:7, John 12:8), when he recounted the parable of the talents (where the nobleman rebukes his slave for not putting the nobleman's money into the bank and earning interest—Luke 19:12–27), one can find in Jesus' message an acceptance of the social and economic order and a conviction that social transformation grows out of spiritual transformation, not vice versa.

The muckrakers were prone to indulge in what today would be called "proof texting," or reading the scriptures selectively and paying attention to only that which reinforces what one already holds to be true. Few on either the liberal or the conservative spectrum of Christianity would dispute that Jesus was attempting to lead people into a new and transformed relationship with God. But deciding exactly how to establish that relationship has led to rivalries and even warfare among Christian factions throughout the centuries. The muckrakers' picture of Jesus (at least that of Steffens and Sinclair) closely parallels the Jesus portrayed by the proponents of today's "liberation theology," a movement that preaches that spiritual freedom cannot be achieved without political liberation. Typical modern journalists would more likely put themselves in the conscientious reformer camp of Tarbell or White rather than in the social revolutionary cadres of Steffens or Sinclair. Journalists, even activist ones, tend to think of journalism as a spur to reform within the prevailing social and political order rather than a catalyst for revolutionary change. The standard working journalist tends to be a moderate, to avoid both extremes of the political spectrum, and, particularly, to shy away from those who are convinced that God is on their side when it comes to revamping the social order.

In the open articulation of the clearly religious underpinning of their worldview, the muckrakers already were an anachronism in journalism by the time they arrived on the scene. The scientific and philosophical developments of the nineteenth century had transformed the intellectual climate of the news business and—combined with the rise of the highly industrialized, mass circulation, commercial newspaper—had turned the typical newsroom of the late nineteenth century and early twentieth into a place where religion increasingly was treated with skepticism, detachment, or disinterest. The new breed of American in the news business had become the big-city reporter, typically a scoffing, irreverent, hard-boiled prototype for the many Hollywood movies that came out in the 1920s, 1930s, and 1940s glorifying the breed. Newspaper owners had become more interested in money and profits and had lost interest in much having to do with religion. By the early twentieth century, news of religion had been relegated to the back pages or the church pages in most metropolitan dailies, and religion was not an openly motivating factor in the way most journalists went about their business. This situation is aptly illustrated in a story Ray Stannard Baker related about William Stead's efforts to convert the turn-of-the-twentieth-century media mogul William Randolph Hearst to the teachings of Jesus. Stead, Baker wrote, emphasized to Hearst the opportunities for a man like him to enrich American life. "He impressed on Mr. Hearst when he met him . . . the importance of giving a 'soul' to 'sensational journalism,'" Baker recounted. "By a soul, he meant a 'moral purpose in some social movement or political reform.' He [Stead] did not stop to ask whether the young man he was arguing with had any 'soul.'"[42]

In point of fact, there was no better candidate than religion for banishment to the back pages in an industry that increasingly believed in balancing opinion and shied away from taking controversial stands lest it risk advertising, circulation, or profit. While the financial incentives always had been there in American journalism, the growth in the size of news organizations and their institutionalization around standards of professionalism, economic efficiency, and the satisfaction of market demands made it increasingly tricky to deal with issues that so hotly divided their audience. Besides the economic and marketing factors, the Christian revival movements that so influenced the press of the nineteenth century also ran up against the wider public acceptance of the theories of Darwin; the spread of the ideas of such "pessimistic" Continental philosophers as Nietzsche, Schopenhauer, and Kierkegaard; and the advancement of an atheistically based philosophy of social reform among Marxist urban and industrial revolutionaries. This tension, which we have come to know so well, helped contribute to a growing split between a liberal intelligentsia that accepted a tolerant and secular outlook on life and orthodox Christians who often felt their faith was being ridiculed, threatened, and undermined. Newsrooms in the late nineteenth century and early twentieth became more populated with educated people who had come into contact with these urbane ideas and who, like the muckrakers, found in them a basis to rebel against Christian upbringings that they came to identify with moral rigidity, closed-mindedness, and judgmentalism. At the same time, Christian positivism and the optimism about America as a land of democracy and equity, which the muckrakers also stood for and which characterized the national mood throughout much of the nineteenth century, were on the wane.

Baker, perhaps better than anyone else, captures the ennui and the pessimism that began to creep into the national consciousness at the time of World War I. The gloom, the resignation, and the apprehension about the future in Baker's autobiography—taken from his notes of a time that was supposed to be a high-water point of American optimism—may help explain why muckraking as a social and political movement, for all intents and purposes, disappeared with the advent of World War I. Baker, who idolized Woodrow Wilson, nonetheless found himself musing about the dark possibilities ahead as Wilson traveled to Paris in 1918 for the signing of the armistice ending World War I. Already, Baker noted, the political enemies of Wilson were attacking his plans for establishing a peaceful international order. "I have curiously a feeling of doom in the coming to Europe of Wilson," Baker wrote. "He occupies a pinnacle too high; the earth forces are too strong. . . . For all people are cruel with their heroes. . . . They become impatient with his justness, fret at his idealism, chafe under his discipline, and, finally, the last test having been passed, they will turn upon him and rend him."[43]

This mood of disenchantment that settled over the muckrakers after World War I can be found throughout their writings. Tarbell described her "melancholy" days after visiting the war-ravaged parts of Europe and the sadness and the fall of great hopes at America's refusal to join the League of Nations.[44] Sinclair, who briefly resigned from the Socialist party because of its opposition to the American war effort, wrote of "confronting the ruins of my beautiful hopes" after the events of the war.[45] After the war, White wrote to Baker, "What a God-damned world this is! . . . If anyone had told me ten years ago that our country would be what it is today. . . . I should have questioned his reason."[46]

Even though many of the muckrakers carried on with their careers in their own individual fashions, the end of World War I saw the end of Steffens- and Sinclair-style muckraking with its spiritualized approach to reform journalism. This was captured by the mood at the Paris Peace Conference, where in attendance was another journalist who eyed this new world "sourly" from the assembled press corps, as his biographer put it.[47] Humbled, broke, having lost his magazine, discredited and dismissed in publishing circles, S. S. McClure glumly watched the proceedings.

"I must either get a magazine," he wrote to his wife from Paris, "or withdraw from mingling with real newspapermen. I really am nobody here." In the end, McClure—despite a brief renaissance and the recovery of his magazine—faded from the scene by 1925. Bizarrely, his last appearance on the world stage was as a seventy-year-old man visiting Mussolini in 1926. "Bowled over" by fascism as a "new and dawning civilization" and a solution to "the problem of democracy," he embarked on a campaign to promote the duce.[48]

At that point, to say the hey-day of idealistic, spiritualized journalism in the United States was over and done with is an understatement, to put it mildly.

CHAPTER 6

Mencken, Monkeys, and Modernity:
A New Metaphysic for the Newsroom

When the young Theodore Dreiser, ambitious, impressionable, and at the beginning of a lifelong rebellion against conventional religion, went to work as a reporter for the *Chicago Daily Globe* in 1892, he discovered among his professional cohorts an exciting new guiding philosophy—a metaphysic for the newsroom that probably exists in as many of today's big-city newsrooms as it did in Dreiser's time. Among the cynical and irreverent journalists of the *Globe*—"hard, gallant adventurers," as Dreiser described them—Dreiser said he was "finally liberated" from the "moralistic and religionistic qualms" that he had inherited from a rigid and orthodox German Catholic father, who had dragged his family through a succession of small Indiana towns eking out a living as a woolen mill worker and laborer. His coworkers, Dreiser wrote in his memoirs, were free from the notions of conventional thinking, suspicious of the motives of all people, and confused by the passive American acceptance of the Sermon on the Mount and the Beatitudes. His colleagues "did not believe, as I still did, that there was a fixed moral order in the world which one contravened at his peril," Dreiser said. "Most of these young men looked upon life as a fierce, grim struggle in which no quarter was either given or taken, and in which all men laid traps, lied, squandered, erred through illusion: a conclusion with which I now most heartily agree."[1]

Dreiser's easy adoption of what he called the "pagan or unmoral" outlook of the newsroom came to infuse the fiction that led him to be called the great American practitioner of "naturalism," a literary genre known for its gritty realism, its grim fatalism, and its tragic characters whose lives were shaped by internal and external forces largely beyond their control. The naturalists were particularly influenced by the theories of Charles Darwin and adapted his biological teachings into a social philosophy that put the imperative of personal survival above other moral considerations. Dreiser's philosophy, as reflected in *Sister Carrie,* his first novel about a wayward young woman who rose to success in the big city, was considered scandalous by many of his contemporaries but, in its indifference toward Victorian social mores, is now viewed as a pioneering work that ushered in modern attitudes toward sex and morality.[2]

Like many journalists both before and after him, Dreiser was not particularly well read in philosophy or theology. But he knew enough to be deeply impressed by the writings of Herbert Spencer, whose theory of social Darwinism held out the notion of "survival of the fittest" as justification for the inequities in the social and economic order, and Julian Huxley, the scientist brother of Aldous Huxley and one of Darwin's strongest public advocates. Although his understanding was incomplete, Dreiser felt the "lingering filaments" of his Catholicism severed as he read Huxley, who treated Christian dogma as superstition, and Spencer, whose philosophy of evolution portrayed every person as insignificantly and helplessly adrift in a universe of Darwinian forces. "[Spencer] nearly killed me," Dreiser wrote, "took every shred of belief away from me; showed me that I was a chemical atom in a whirl of unknown forces."[3]

For Dreiser, like many of his generation, this virtual "warfare" between science and theology was a defining issue, profoundly unsettling him and making orthodox Christian belief virtually impossible. It was during this era that modern journalism took many of its attitudes, and many journalists, like Dreiser, began to drift in secular directions. This did not happen without wrenching social and psychological changes that saw not only the rise of science and the triumph of the Industrial Revolution in the United States but also a religious struggle that sometimes took place within individuals deeply pained at the loss of the old religious certainties. Dreiser's era can be seen as a watershed period that climaxed three hundred years of conflict in America between orthodox Christians and Enlightenment skeptics. The repeated revival movements and upsurges of Christian enthusiasm were in part a response to the steady growth of a population alienated from Christian life and contributed to the schisms, divisions, and sectarian rivalries within the Christian community itself. Ironically, as these religious currents pulled along news organizations in their wake, journalists—increasingly scornful of Christian pieties—became ever less aware of how deeply rooted their own professional values were in religious history and how profoundly Judeo-Christian principles had been absorbed into the ethos of the newsroom.

Still, Dreiser's memoirs, published when he was fifty-one, did not complete the story. When Dreiser was in his seventies, he took up work on the novel *The Bulwark,* which told the story of a Quaker businessman whose belief in universal love was tested by the cutthroat environment of nineteenth-century capitalism and a series of personal tragedies. Influenced by the writings of such Quaker mystics as Rufus Jones and John Woolman and the simplicity and nonceremonialism of Quakerism, *The Bulwark* reflected Dreiser's own growing mysticism and his "vast hunger," as one of his biographers described it, for some kind of direct communion with the divine.[4] By the end of his life, Dreiser had come full circle from the religious rebellion of his early years and was reading oriental philosophy, forcefully defending the existence of God, and pursuing his theories about how individuals communicated with their creator and the creative force that inhabited all living things.[5]

Dreiser, of course, is not the first person to replace his youthful agnosticism with a growing interest in the eternal in his older years. Throughout his life, Dreiser felt his modernist outlook forced him to reject the traditional Christian explanations of the universe and human nature. But Dreiser also suffered, particularly in his later years, from the loss of the comfort of Christianity and the troubling sense that humankind had become disconnected from the hope and the optimism that religion once provided. "He was on a religious quest," the biographer W. A. Swanberg said of Dreiser in his later life, "though he called it a quest for understanding and peace." Dreiser's interest in religion and spirituality grew so great that his good friend, fellow journalist, and celebrated cynic H. L. Mencken once wrote him, "I laid a bet that you will enter Holy Orders before you leave this earth."[6]

Many of today's journalists would identify with the youthful Dreiser—with his proud skepticism and his disdain for religious tradition. Perhaps it is unfair to accuse the journalism profession of harboring immature attitudes toward religious questions, as Dreiser himself came to feel that he had done. But in many ways journalists tend to see themselves as heirs to those cocksure journalists of the late nineteenth century and early twentieth who, like the young Dreiser, came to identify with the scientific spirit of the age and to grow ever more distant from, if not openly hostile to, the world of traditional religion. Pragmatism, clear-eyed realism, and a resistance to moralism and romantic sentimentality all became key elements in an emerging ethic that sought to reshape the journalism profession around the belief that events could be reported on "objectively" and that practical life experience and an openness to empirical discovery were better paths to truth than was religious doctrine. In the growing split between a secular intelligentsia and the Christian community that was increasingly defensive about what it considered attacks on the eternal verities of Christian faith, journalists—at least many who became our best-known journalistic figures from that period—often sided with the forces of secularism and modern science. Yet, as happened with Dreiser, the search for a greater meaning to life and a yearning for spiritual experience quite frequently did not disappear from the writings of these great journalists; they simply were transformed in ways that would no longer be called traditionally religious in form.

Reporters in the work-a-day world have few opportunities to muse publicly about their religious beliefs or religious struggles. As a result, some of the most telling tales about journalists' abandonment of conventional religion and their search for a substitute come from the accounts of the impressive number of American literary figures who, like Dreiser, began their careers as journalists but came to express themselves most intimately in fiction. These writers shared a remarkable kinship in their skeptical attitude toward organized religion, particularly Christian explanations, but, like Dreiser, many retained a strong interest in spiritual matters and gave to the world a literary vision that included deep religious dimensions, if not necessarily conventionally Christian ones.

A number of the important figures associated with the nineteenth-century literary movement known as American realism, which preceded and deeply influenced "naturalism"—Mark Twain, William Dean Howells, Bret Harte, and Ambrose Bierce—were former journalists whose differences with Christian orthodoxy helped set the stage for their even more agnostic literary colleagues in the twentieth century. In their literature, the American realists emphasized values that they had put into practice in their early careers in journalism: experiencing life directly and honestly, writing simply and colloquially, and celebrating common sense at the expense of false sentimentality and Christian sanctimony. In their antipathy toward traditional religion, all identified the moral outlook of their day with an oppressive Christian piety, excessively puritanical attitudes, and a hypocrisy that masked the harsher realities of American life. Harte, Twain's friend and fellow journalist, grew up in a religiously "haunted" family—his father was a Catholic and his mother an Episcopalian—whose faith "didn't take" with him.[7] Bierce (whom some have called an "impressionist" rather than a realist) was described as someone whose disbelief went even further than Twain's; he was the most "thorough-going cynic" he had ever met, remarked Mencken.[8]

However, in a good many cases—particularly in the cases of Twain and Howells—one would be hard pressed not to recognize a fixation on religious matters and a tendency to "protest too much," as the Shakespearean line goes, when it came to attacking Christianity's hold on the culture. Twain abandoned a brief ambition to be a preacher—he lacked "the necessary stock in trade, i.e. religion," he once wrote his brother—and tried for a time to conform to the Christian beliefs of his wife and her family, but to no avail. In 1867, at the start of his writing career, Twain accompanied a pilgrimage to the Holy Land organized by the Reverend Henry Ward Beecher, which Twain described in a mildly dyspeptic article in James Gordon Bennett's *New York Herald* and later in a caustic public lecture that earned him a denunciation as the "son of the devil" from one minister. If his contemporaries had known Twain's true thoughts, they would have been even more shocked. In private notebooks, never published in his lifetime, Twain derided what he saw in the Holy Land, called the Arabs there "ignorant, depraved, superstitious, dirty, lousy, thieving vagabonds," and complained that Palestine needed a coat of paint. The high price of the boat trip across the Sea of Galilee led him to write, "Do you wonder now that Christ walked [on water]?" All the while he scrawled notes for a never-published fantasy about the boyhood of Christ, in which he planned to describe the pranks of the young Jesus—"striking boys dead, withering their hands"—and to end on this note, "No Second Advent—Christ been here once, will never come again." Twain died longing to "tell the truth" about what he felt about God and religion but demurred because he was afraid it might get his heirs "burned at the stake." For more than fifty years after his death, his daughter succeeded in suppressing the publication of "Noah's Ark Book," which Twain worked on in his last years, because, as one biographer put it, of its "hilarious unbelief."[9]

Yet Twain, despiser of Christian pieties that he was, cannot escape the impression that his works show an almost obsessive interest in matters of religion and, despite his cleverness at turning Christian hypocrisy on its ear, a personal vision of Judeo-Christian morality and spirituality. In the same way that Twain scoffed at romanticism while writing one of the great romantic adventures in American literature, Twain's humorous jibes at religion in *Huckleberry Finn,* for example, cannot disguise the fundamental moral core that gives the novel its great appeal or the essential spiritual message that gives the river trip its allure. On the surface, Twain told the reader religion had gone wrong by reinforcing society's distorted moral values. Twain pointed to Huck's primal ethical goodness (which Twain presented with such effective irony in Huck's laments at his fundamental "badness" and lack of proper Christian upbringing) as the appropriate barometer for moral conduct. But in his use of irony, Twain was also saying that fundamental moral and religious values should be guiding us: love (some would call it Christian love) in the relationship between Huck and Jim; self-sacrifice (it could be called Christian self-sacrifice) in Huck's acts of charity and kindness; simplicity (it could also be termed Christian simplicity) in Huck's suspicion of money and his spurning of material things. In presenting Huck as a figure of primitive goodness, Twain seemed to be saying that it is not the essence of the Judeo-Christian moral vision that is wrong but society's corruption of that vision that is responsible for many of the culture's ills.[10]

Howells, too, revolted against all forms of "supernatural" religion and, as the genteel patron of nineteenth-century American letters, remained a quiet agnostic all his life. Influenced by the biblical historical-critical method and a growing commitment to cultural and religious pluralism, Howells even abandoned the "soft" Darwinism, as one of Howells's biographers put it (meaning the theology created by those Christians who had managed to transform Darwin's theories into a reconstituted form of Christian evolutionary positivism), and simply exercised the private right to disbelieve. But Howells also was strongly influenced by the religious values of his father, a Quaker who became a follower of the Swedish mystic Emmanuel Swedenborg, and he never pushed his skepticism with the enthusiasm of Twain. "There are many things that I doubt, but few that I deny; where I cannot believe, there I often trust," was as far as Howells would go in expressing religious disbelief.[11]

Twain and Howells were, however, transitional figures whose distaste for conventional religion paled compared with their literary heirs' nonbelief. The turn of the twentieth century was noted for the bitterness in which many in the American intelligentsia—including many of the period's best-known journalists and journalist-literary figures—turned against the religion in which they had been reared. This rebellion against orthodox Christianity took on a new force among a generation of American journalists-turned-fiction-writers who found a home for the nurturing of their talents, as well as fame, income, and adventure, as correspondents for the burgeoning mass-market publications of the era. The "naturalists"—Dreiser, Stephen Crane, Frank Norris, and Jack London—took the realism of Twain and Howells a step further and created a literature imbued with pessimism and a mechanistic determinism that found little place for religious credos. London, like Dreiser, was greatly impressed by Spencer and his portrayal of humans as locked in a brutal struggle for survival, as well as the philosophy of Friedrich Nietzsche, who believed that the true "superman" should have the courage to reject the Christian concept of salvation and live life by individual rules alone.[12] Norris, a nominal Episcopalian, was largely disinterested in Christianity and, as a disciple of the French naturalist Emile Zola, produced fiction distinguished by themes of social realism and a self-consciously pagan, Homeric symbolism.[13] Crane, the son of a pious Methodist preacher, led a bohemian and dissipated life in conscious defiance of the moralistic values taught to him in his youth. However, Crane's writing, as the poet Amy Lowell pointed out, resonated with his troubled reaction to his religious background. "He disbelieved it and hated it, but he could not free himself from it," she wrote. "Crane's soul was heaped with bitterness and this bitterness he flung back at the theory of life which had betrayed him."[14]

This grim outlook of a world stripped of religious meaning was reflected in Crane's "Open Boat," a much praised short story built around Crane's experience in a shipwreck while a newspaper correspondent heading to Cuba in 1897 to cover the preliminaries to the Spanish-American War. In its starkly realistic journalistic prose style, Crane's account of the four men in a lifeboat rowing against the elements reflects the modernist attitudes about human life locked in a grim struggle with a universe that is not "cruel" or "beneficent" or "treacherous" or "wise" but "indifferent, flatly indifferent." "When it occurs to a man," Crane wrote, "that nature does not regard him as important, and that she feels she would not maim the universe by disposing of him, he at first wishes to throw bricks at any temple."[15]

The growing rift between a secular press, in which most all of these literary figures developed their writing personality, and the community of traditional Christian believers came dramatically to the surface during the coverage of the Scopes "Monkey" trial in Dayton, Tennessee, in 1925. There much of the press— led by the master debunker, Mencken—belittled the claims of Christian fundamentalists about the inerrancy of Scripture and helped discredit William Jennings Bryan, the onetime populist Democratic presidential candidate and

defender of the biblical account of creation. The trial of a Tennessee schoolteach-
er who broke a state law forbidding the teaching of evolution in biology classes
was one of the first true media events of modern journalism, with radio lines
brought into the courtroom, crowds of reporters, and press conferences held
regularly on the courtroom lawn. Mencken closely consulted with Scopes's at-
torney, Clarence Darrow, made famous in the 1950s movie *Inherit the Wind,* and
helped mastermind a strategy that consciously attempted to deliver "the final
mortal blow" to Puritanism in America. "Modern evangelists are usually being
paranoid when they say that the media are out to destroy them," the journalist
and historian Garry Wills wrote of the Scopes trial. "But that would have been
an accurate description of Mencken's work behind the scenes at Dayton."[16]

Mencken was a caustic critic of traditional Christian theology, which, he said,
was "shot so full of holes that it is no wonder it has had to be abandoned."[17]
Mencken's and Darrow's efforts to ridicule Bryan's biblical literalism have ob-
scured the fact that Bryan held deep, legitimate concerns about the moral implications of evolutionary theory and the philosophy of social Darwinism that
grew out of it. While Mencken was a firm believer in Spencer and his application of Darwin's theories to the human order, Bryan worried that this could lead
to a might-is-right superman philosophy. As Wills pointed out, Bryan, like many
nineteenth-century Christians, was a humanitarian and a progressive in matters of politics, despite his fundamentalist biblical beliefs. Mencken, it should
be added, was an admirer of Nietzsche and his notions of the "superman" philosophy, and the implicit elitism in Mencken's view of humankind—he felt most
common people were "boobs" and deluded idiots—had a disturbingly antidem-
ocratic tone to it.[18]

This fundamental rivalry between Bryan and Mencken—reflective of what
today we call the "culture wars"—was in its early stages at the opening of the
twentieth century. But the origins of this vast chasm of antagonisms, mistrust,
and hostility can be found in the Enlightenment thought that has so influenced
the development of modern journalism and ultimately thrust journalists, in the
minds of many Christians, into the camp of the infidels. Christian progressives
worked throughout the nineteenth and twentieth centuries to reconcile Christianity with the findings and theories of Darwin, and many Christians have found
in Darwinian evolutionary thought a positivist picture of a universe that exists
quite comfortably alongside Christian notions of progress, moral improvement,
and spiritual destiny. For those Christians who do not view the Bible as the final
word on such matters as the creation of the universe and the origin of humankind, Darwinian science has come to offer no threat to the retention of a Christian belief system. But for conservative Christians who look to the Bible as the
source of cosmological proofs and literal historical truths, their more accommodating fellow Christians—the liberals, the modernists, and the compromisers
with the secular moral order—are only a cut above the press in their responsibility for the "secular humanism" that has spread through society.

The commercial press that evolved throughout the nineteenth and twentieth centuries came to thrive on controversy and conflict, and this growing clash between religion and science easily found its way onto the news pages. The news values that emerged in this period encouraged journalists to frame the debate in the stark, simplistic terms that led to cartoons of Darwin and ape men and caricatures of Christian fundamentalists but also led Walter Lippmann to accuse the press of relying too heavily on stereotypes and glib categories of analysis.[19] In bringing long-festering cultural and theological divisions into the spotlight of a newly emergent electronic media of national reach, the Scopes affair was a spectacular conclusion to a period that saw big-city journalists, better educated, more conscious of their professionalism, and ever more urbanite in outlook, increasingly open about their skepticism of the evangelical Christianity community.

By 1925, the press had largely settled on which side of the religion versus science debate it fell; even in Tennessee, only one major paper, the *Memphis Commercial Appeal,* consistently supported the prosecution of Scopes. Others expressed chagrin at the image the trial was presenting of Tennessee. The "seriocomedy" of the trial, commented the *Chattanooga Times,* was a "humiliating proceeding" that left every lawyer in the state "holding his head in shame." Around the rest of the country, most major American newspapers favored the defense team (one study of the news coverage of the Scopes trial concluded that the press was biased in favor of Darrow and Scopes but mostly because of its insensitivity to faith-based arguments rather than intentional advocacy). Reporters tended to pay more attention to the controversy and the spectacle of the first real "media event" of the electronic age than to the underlying theological issues. That and the influence of the pro-Darrow movie *Inherit the Wind* led *Life* magazine in the early 1960s to look back at the time when the Darwin debate "erupted in a glorious explosion in the tiny burg of Dayton, Tenn., where in 1925, as every student of American humor knows, Spencer Tracy gave Frederic March the verbal thrashing of his life."[20]

Too often critics of journalism identify religious teachings as the basis of journalists' skepticism about religion instead of looking at the culture of the newsroom and the temperamental outlook of the journalists for clues about journalists' uneasiness over religious questions. Class, education, economic status, and, most important, life experience often come into play when journalists deal with their stereotypical picture of religious believers. Few journalists would put it quite so bluntly (or as publicly) as Mencken when he expressed his dislike of Christianity in the Bible Belt, but his viewpoint is far from unknown in the newsrooms of today: "All I can detect is a rapid descent to mere barbaric devil-chasing. In all those parts of the Republic where Beelzebub is still real . . . the evangelical sects plunge into an abyss of malignant imbecility, and declare a holy war upon every decency that civilized men cherish."[21] In his less acerbic moods, Mencken more accurately captured the discomfort of the modern, cosmopolitan journalist, trained in the no-nonsense, pragmatic tools of news gathering, when confronting religious matters. "My essential trouble, I sometimes suspect, is that I am quite devoid of what are called spiritual gifts," Mencken wrote. "That is to say, I am incapable of religious experience, in any true sense. Religious ceremonials often interest me esthetically, and not infrequently they amuse me otherwise, but I get absolutely no stimulation out of them, no sense of exalta-tion, no mystical katharsis. . . . Thus the generality of religious persons remain mysteries to me, and vaguely offensive, as I am unquestionably offensive to them. . . . This lack of understanding is a cause of enmities, and I believe that they are sound ones. I dislike any man who is pious, and all such men that I know dislike me."[22]

It is this now entrenched clash of cultures—journalists, trained to be skep-tics, often unschooled in matters of religion, and always on the lookout for a good story, trying to make sense of the religious community—that lies at the heart of the dilemma for those who believe journalists are missing out by not better appreciating the role of religion in American life. The theologian Luke Timothy Johnson—in a viewpoint often advanced in traditional Christian cir-cles—has argued that today's media tend to be interested in religion only if it can be attached to scandal, celebrity, sexual misconduct, politics, cults, or oth-er controversy. Although Johnson probably slighted the growing movement toward better coverage of religion in certain journalistic quarters, he did cap-ture the atmosphere at many news organizations when he wrote, "Religion is, generally, the chronically non-news area of culture. . . . There is not much in the liturgical year to raise eyebrows or sell papers. Religion does not lend itself to front-page or top-of-broadcast coverage. . . . Being religion editor of the daily paper is like being the Maytag repairman in the TV commercials. You mainly watch the store and reprint the bulletins."[23]

Compounding Johnson's complaints is the image that modern journalists tend to have of themselves as lonely individualists, unfettered by authority, con-ventional rules of conduct, or traditional belief, whose sole commitment is to the story and the pursuit of truth. This view is, of course, a romanticized one in the context of the cautious and conforming corporate culture of most news organizations, but it retains a powerful hold on the journalistic imagination. John Merrill, in his writings about the philosophical heritage of modern jour-nalism, concluded that today's journalists should take their cue from twenti-eth-century existentialists, such as Albert Camus and Jean-Paul Sarte, who be-lieve that things have no true meaning except for what humans attach to them. In the philosophical void left by the retreat of religious belief, existentialists see humans as finding sustenance in an unflinching individual integrity, a brave facing up to the absurdity of the human dilemma, and courage in overcoming hopelessness through individual acts of creativity, defiance, and human solidar-ity. It is this model, Merrill said, that journalists, pressured by the demands of corporate life and the anomie of living in a mass society, should emulate.[24]

Science and philosophy have contributed to the modern journalistic mind-set and—at least in an indirect fashion—have helped nudge journalists away from an appreciation of (or much understanding about) the religious moorings of their own profession. In this respect, existentialism is the modern philosophy that serves as the natural inheritor of the naturalism of Dreiser, Crane, and London and the skeptical realism of Twain and Howells. The pose of the modern journalist, Merrill observed, is a detached one and implicitly secular. Journalists, to borrow from the message of a Camus novel, should accept the indifference of the universe, cease speculating about what cannot be known, and live life as if it is all we have. The emptiness of life without illusions is not a comforting one, Camus acknowledged in *The Plague,* but it is preferable to embracing the unconvincing explanations for human suffering that religion offers.[25] For the central characters in the writings of Camus (himself a leftist journalist in Algiers and Paris and an editor of a celebrated World War II resistance newspaper, who was known for "his resemblance, in his rumpled beige raincoat with cigarette dangling from his lips, to Humphrey Bogart"), the meaning of life is found not in religious consolation or incomprehensible theological claptrap about suffering fulfilling some divine and mysterious plan but in the brave embrace of life's human moments—moments of love, compassion, and human sharing.[26] "Knowing meant that: a living warmth, and a picture of death," Camus said of his hero, Tarrou, after he died in the plague.[27]

Existentialism, with its stoical approach to life's mysteries and life's sufferings, had a profound impact during the era when journalism developed many of its modern professional attitudes. The shattering events of the twentieth century—World War I, the Great Depression, World War II, the Holocaust, the explosion of the atomic bomb, the cold war, the Korean and Vietnam wars, and Watergate—have deeply influenced modern journalists, who shared in those events, often in firsthand ways, and many have found much appeal in Merrill's attitude, even if they would not necessarily put a philosophical label on it. Ernest Hemingway, the writing hero to many a modern journalist, typified the way journalists have absorbed the ethos of existentialism and the existential hero into their life philosophy (although Hemingway also personified the epicurean strain in journalistic attitude, which, as much as the stoical, has animated journalists' image of their profession). The Hemingway biographer Carlos Baker described how Hemingway's religious views evolved from that of a young ambulance driver on the Italian front in World War I, frightened after being wounded and clinging to the rituals and beliefs of his Christian upbringing, to that of the veteran journalist-writer who became hardened, agnostic, and unable to pray after years of writing, drinking, and adventuring. Hemingway, Baker said, once told his fourth wife, Mary, that they had to come up with a sentimental, hedonistic substitute for the traditional religious faith that he could no longer accept. "Deprived of the ghostly comforts of the Church, yet unable to accept as gospel the secular substitutes which Marxism offered, he had abandoned his simplistic faith in the benefits of personal petition and turned . . . to embrace a doctrine of 'life, liberty, and the pursuit of happiness,'" Baker wrote.[28]

It may make perfect sense that journalists of the nineteenth century and early twentieth—many of whom grew up under the strictures of Puritanism and became journalists to escape the stifling atmosphere of provincial, church-dominated, small-town life—rebelled against the rigidity of their religious upbringing and embraced a carpe diem philosophy. But in their time, when encounters with the church and Christian tradition were inescapable for anyone growing up in American culture, journalists, even if they had turned away from traditional religion, usually displayed a keen understanding of the role of religion in American society and in the lives of individuals. If there is one theme that dominates the writings of these famous American literary journalists beyond their contempt for organized religion, it is their poignant sense of what they may have lost by abandoning it.

No one typified this better than Hemingway, whose literature at its deepest level can be seen as resonating with religious themes or at least religious longing. In his first serious novel, *The Sun Also Rises*, Hemingway dropped in references to religion everywhere: in the title, taken from the passage in the biblical book Ecclesiastes; in Jake Barnes, the hard-bitten, war-wounded protagonist, who clings to his Catholicism but finds little comfort in it; in Lady Brett Ashley, who is fascinated with Jake's Christianity but inspired by it to do little more than quip about the emptiness of her own life; and in the presentation of bullfighting as a pagan, spiritual rite that provides a temporary place of refuge for the expatriates.[29] Other Hemingway works—*The Old Man and the Sea* (again with its pagan ritual of the old fisherman battling the huge fish that takes on noble, almost divine attributes), *For Whom the Bell Tolls* (with its themes of love and heroic self-sacrifice raised to spiritual dimensions)—also demonstrate Hemingway's propensity for giving certain elevated human activities a spiritual meaning that has been lost for those who can no longer accept the traditional Christian worldview.[30]

Mystical themes and spiritual yearnings showed up in the work of other celebrated journalists-turned-fiction-writers who, like Hemingway, ceased calling themselves religious in the traditional sense but demonstrated a profound literary understanding of the importance of religion to the human condition. Jack London's interest in spiritualism and the mythical unconscious of Jung became the basis for his interpretation of his own literature late in his life.[31] The religious broodings of James Agee forcefully appeared in his autobiographical *Death in the Family*, as he wrestled with the fanatical Anglo-Catholicism of his mother and his own spiritual interpretation of his father's death.[32] Willa Cather's mystical sense of the land suffused her writings, and the protagonist of her first novel, *O Pioneers*, written shortly after she ended an extensive journalism career in Lincoln, Nebraska, and Pittsburgh, Pennsylvania, and with *McClure's* magazine, was regularly visited by a powerful, spiritual presence.[33] Graham

Greene—another former journalist who explored multifaceted religious themes in his many novels—captured the dilemma of how a person struggling with issues of faith deals with the emptiness of modern life in such novels as *The Power and the Glory, The Heart of the Matter,* and *The End of the Affair.* A Catholic convert, Graham enjoyed playing the role of the "doubting convert," and his critics have accused him of being more "interested in religion" than in "being religious."[34] In his explorations of religion, however, Greene showed how much a journalist with literary skills could illuminate the spiritual struggles in the human heart and how much attention to the religious impulse can tell us about the depth of human experience.

Cather also served as a wonderful example of what a journalist-turned-novelist could do with religious themes, even though her own religious interests were negligible until relatively late in life. Cather's early works have been called realistic, and the authenticity of her settings and characters reflect the straightforward writing style that she learned in her journalism jobs. Cather, however, also demonstrated a strongly romantic streak, and her prose is redolent with sonorous, evocative lánguage. "Every natural fact is a symbol of some spiritual fact," as Cather's biographer, quoting Emerson, put it. Like other writers of her era, Cather demonstrated contempt for institutionalized religion and in her youth reportedly professed she did not believe in God. Art served as a more than satisfactory substitute for religion, and she often equated the two. After World War I, Cather, disenchanted with the world situation and having come out of a period of harsh criticism of her works, appeared to have suffered something of a midlife crisis and in 1922, at the age of forty-nine, joined the Episcopal church in her hometown of Red Cloud, Nebraska. From that time forward, Cather put aside the free-thinking skepticism of her youth and began to express an overt religious sympathy in her novels, particularly in her most celebrated work, *Death Comes for the Archbishop,* published in 1927.[35]

Yet, if anything characterized twentieth-century journalists' attitudes toward religion, it was probably not a rebellion against religious tradition or even a longing left in the wake of its demise but simply indifference. Although such journalist-turned-literary figures as Crane, Twain, and Mencken were widely recognized for contributing to the antireligious attitudes of much nineteenth- and twentieth-century literature, their antagonism toward Christian orthodoxy probably characterizes far less the mood toward religion in the typical newsroom today than does apathy, disinterest, or entrenched secularism. Throughout the twentieth century, a variety of forces contributed to journalists' growing more distant from the nation's religious roots: more children (particularly those of the intelligentsia) grew up in homes that were not explicitly Christian in worship; public schooling and education at state universities provided a secular environment as young people came of age; migration from farms and small towns to the big industrial cities severed many people from their rural, church-going backgrounds; and war and depression contributed to a mood of cynicism and disillusionment with optimistic American assumptions about faith and progress.

Walter Lippmann, the most famous columnist of the twentieth century, conveyed in his personal outlook the a-religious attitude that has come to be identified with the modern journalist. Described by one biographer as someone who "bore the weight of the world with intellect and stoicism rather than with emotion and religious faith," Lippmann served as the journalistic model of the calm, sophisticated modernist who simply never needed religion in the course of a busy, accomplished life.[36] In fact, Lippmann was quite interested in religion—or to be more precise, he was interested in the growing role of nonbelief in modern life. In *A Preface to Morals,* Lippmann laid out a basis for morality and ethics for those intellectuals and educated people who found the maintenance of traditional faith intellectually unsustainable. Lippmann felt himself to be one of those who had experienced the "acids of modernity" dissolving the old religious order, leaving him and other educated people "choked with the debris of dead notions in which men are unable to believe and unwilling to disbelieve." Yet Lippmann felt that "the irreligion of the modern world is radical to a degree" that there was no going back and that liberal Christians had been creating empty rationalizations for a religion that no longer meant much to the cosmopolitan personality. For Lippmann, a new and inspired humanism had to replace the old beliefs. "In such a world simple customs are unsuitable and authoritative commandments incredible," Lippmann wrote. "No prescription can now be written which men can naively and obediently follow." Since this means people "are unable to find a principle of order in the authority of a will outside themselves, there is no place they can find it except in an ideal of the human personality."[37]

As the twentieth century wound to a close, one could debate journalists' prevailing attitude toward religion, as well as the degree to which Lippmann's liberal elitism is embraced throughout the newsroom. But it is clear that, at least in the professional sense, many journalists operate from Lippmann's assumption that "the central truth" of Christianity "no longer appeals to the best brains," that the fundamentalist movement "is recruited largely from the isolated, the inexperienced, and the uneducated," and that fundamentalism has become "entangled with all sorts of bizarre and barbarous agitations."[38] The so-called culture wars, which have pitted religious conservatives against what they call the "secular humanists" over issues of race, ethnicity, sexual orientation, abortion, affirmative action, prayer in school, and the like, have had a deep impact on the relationship between journalism and religion and have sharply divided journalists from the most aggressive advocates of a religious viewpoint. At the beginning of the twenty-first century, modern American journalists have a lot of reasons to be wary of the "hot button" issues that are now identified with traditional Christian belief; the polarization of the culture has forced many journalists and journalistic organizations to look with suspicion at true believers and to retreat into a posture of detachment when it comes to dealing with religious matters. Whether this has made journalists more indifferent toward religion, more cynical, or more reluctant to acknowledge that they may hold personal religious views is an open question, but it certainly has forced journalists to become much more careful in how they position themselves on religious issues that have vocal adherents on both sides. Religion still may be an undercurrent in the way journalists make moral and ethical decisions (as I attempt to demonstrate in the pages ahead), but it is certainly nowhere nearly as powerful a force as the standards of balance and objectivity and detachment that dictate journalists' professional activities.

Perhaps it comes as no surprise then that the newsroom may not be the easiest place to measure the religious values of journalists, at least if one acknowledges that the depth and the subtleties of spiritual life have limited outlets in a black-and-white environment where stories are driven by conventional news judgments, the search for controversy, stereotypes, and audience-grabbing formulas. Journalists can easily recognize why many of the celebrated journalists-turned-novelists exited a profession that could not satisfy their desire to express their visions of the larger truth of things. But we should not forget that these visions sometimes included wrestling with something else that rarely gains open expression in the typical newsroom: the search for spiritual meaning in life. Most of the famous journalists who left the newsroom to seek a literary career did not do it—at least consciously—because they were looking to express the religious side of their personality, but it is interesting how often they used the greater latitude granted in the conventions of literature to probe spiritual and religious themes. Even when their books touched on the absence of religious belief and the impact it had on the inner life of their literary characters, it was those themes that can be seen as key elements in what distinguishes their literature from their journalism. It is enough to make one wonder what might happen in journalism if those same themes—more personal, more profound, more penetrating than those of conventional reporting—were explored regularly and intelligently by the mass media.

Pragmatism and the "Facts" of Religious Experience: The Model for a Synthesis

One fall morning in 1908, the nineteen-year-old Harvard under-graduate Walter Lippmann answered a knock at his dormitory door. To Lippmann's astonishment, standing outside was a white-bearded Harvard professor, perhaps the most famous writer and thinker of his generation, who told Lippmann that he had come to congratulate him for an article that Lippmann had written for a student magazine. In the article, Lippmann had attacked cultural elitism and defended the values of working people, and it had clearly impressed the social justice–loving William James, the philosopher, psychologist, and author of *The Varieties of Religious Experience,* which laid out James's pragmatic and empirical reasons for embracing religion and personal spiritual experience.

After taking a walk through Harvard Yard—where they chatted about socialism, faculty politics, and the latest lectures James was preparing—the young national-columnist-to-be and the philosopher-psychologist decided to make the walks a weekly ritual on their way to tea at James's home. Lippmann, according to the biographer Ronald Steel, responded eagerly to James's passion for social reform, commitment to experimentation, abhorrence of dogma, and deep sense of personal morality. When James died in the summer of 1910, he was the subject of Lippmann's first signed article of journalism out of college. Lippmann eulogized James as "perhaps the most tolerant man of our generation," who "listened for truth from anybody, and from anywhere, and in any form."[1]

Journalists are a decidedly nonintrospective, unphilosophical lot. But if one were going to identify a philosopher whose worldview captured the spirit of modern, American journalism, it would have to be James, the "father" of American pragmatism and the figure who refashioned the weighty and abstract philosophical doctrines of the nineteenth-century European "Filosofs" into a practical, optimistic, can-do process of analyzing life choices uniquely suited to the American way of thinking.

This also makes James—who did so much to synthesize the philosophy, psychology, and the emerging social sciences of his time—the ideal thinker to formulate an intellectual basis for today's journalists who might hope to reconcile the skeptical and practical demands of their profession with the seemingly ineffable aspects of individual religious experience. Although James's conclusion—that the "truth" of religious experience has a basis in fact and that God's impact on human lives can be empirically verified—is hardly beyond dispute, his determination to ground his reasoning in the language of common human experience and the practicalities of everyday life makes him accessible to journalists who follow a methodology, like James's, that frames subjective experience in the language of objective "fact" and portrays the expressions of human emotion as an important measure of reality.

It always is a risk to suggest to modern journalists, who tend to be ahistorical, that they might find a model in history that could help them resolve some of the problems in today's journalism. But James, despite living almost a hundred years ago, was as modernist in his thinking as any journalist living today and can be credited with articulating the intellectual and philosophical mindset that journalists still draw on to interpret the world. The ideas in *The Varieties of Religious Experience* (recently listed by the Modern Library near the top of the most important books of the twentieth century) seem as fresh and original—despite James's somewhat Victorian way of expressing himself—as they did when he delivered them as a series of lectures at University of Edinburgh between 1899 and 1901.

I also must confess to my own satisfaction while writing a book about the connection between journalism and religion in discovering the symmetry between James's pragmatic philosophy, with its great appeal for journalists, and James's advocacy for the place of religion in a pragmatic worldview. On the one hand, James reflected many of the attitudes of the most skeptical of modern journalists: he shunned the organized church; he scorned credal and absolutist attitudes about religion; he respected personal experience that put a premium on real world learning; he was suspicious of moralism and self-righteousness; and he had little use for what he called "second hand" philosophies based on superrationalistic or highly theoretical thinking. On the other hand, James applied this respect he held for firsthand experience to the realm of the spiritual, which he insisted must be gauged with the same scientific open-mindedness and the same respect for individual experience as any other human phenomenon. "Mystical experiences are as direct perceptions of fact for those who have them as any sensations," he declared.[2]

To better understand how James's philosophy relates to journalism—and to the link between journalism and religion—it is useful to see why his theories about "pragmatism" are so engaging to the American journalistic imagination.

The press historian Herbert Altschull has claimed that, of all the philosophies introduced in the Western world, James's system is the one in which journalists have most comfortably operated.[3] Altschull acknowledged that most journalists have not studied philosophy and are deeply suspicious of formal thought systems based on dogma or rigid guiding principles. So, of course, was James. This shared suspicion of philosophical abstractions and structured intellectual worldviews shows the congruence between James's thinking and the value system of the journalistic profession.

The pragmatic method, in James's view, rested on the importance of human experience and was guided by the discovery of what works for people.[4] Less a fully formed philosophical system than a process for arriving at useful truths, it was based on the notion that all human beliefs—including religious belief— must be judged by the consequences of implementing those beliefs in the world and the practical value of the exercise for human beings. James's approach to philosophy was, in essence, psychological—how, in the end, did the belief meet the needs of individuals for inner harmony and personal well-being. James was (and still is) accused of being a moral relativist. But he argued that the most important of humankind's cherished values—freedom, justice, democracy, morality—were best maintained in a system where belief was continually tested and retested for its practical validity and then applied in the activities of individuals. James saw himself as a scientist first and foremost, and his dedication to the scientific method was firm. But he believed that his devotion to scientific analysis was in no way inconsistent with his conclusions about the practical value of religious experience. For James, religious impulses and expressions, like other psychological events, were capable of being analyzed as "facts" in the pragmatic sense of the word, and the ultimate test of God's meaning for humankind was in the consequences of belief as it was manifested in concrete human activities.

Although the list of journalist-writers and thinkers about journalism who knew or were influenced by reading James is a long one (the list includes William Dean Howells, Mark Twain, Lincoln Steffens, Upton Sinclair, Ray Stannard Baker, John Dewey, Robert Park, H. L. Mencken, Ernest Hemingway, as well as Lippmann), most journalists today probably have only the vaguest recollection of who James was. But they most assuredly would identify themselves as pragmatists—the term James used to describe the followers of his philosophy—and they certainly would embrace James's belief that a philosophical principle is worthwhile only if it leads to active involvement in the world, promotes a willingness to take risks for the sake of a cause, and can be validated by experience.

R. W. B. Lewis, one of James's biographers, argued that James—despite never practicing journalism or producing literature (as his equally famous brother, the novelist Henry James, did)—has had an enormous influence on poets and novelists, as well as scientists, psychologists, and philosophers. Hemingway, in particular, came to embody in action, as Lewis put it, the Jamesian philosophy that the heroic personality can "stand this Universe" and deal with the unwelcome things of the world by courageously facing up to inner fears by living on the edge of risk and danger.[5] The muckraker journalist Ray Stannard Baker cited the "clear-sighted observer, Professor James" to back up his claim that a new religious idealism interesting itself in "the wonders of the human mind, the attribute we call consciousness, the self, the relation of mind to mind, telepathy, the strange phenomenon of double or multiple consciousness, hypnotism, and all the related marvels" was winning intellectual respectability even in an age of empiricism and faith in science.[6] Sinclair, a spiritualist as well as a dedicated social reform journalist, was deeply impressed by James's open-minded attitude about religious experience.[7] Even Lippmann, who evinced little interest in religion throughout his life, was persuaded as a student by James's argument that religion could be reconciled with science by the standards of empiricism.[8]

For James—a troubled man who suffered from bouts of deep depression, chronic psychosomatic illnesses, and an intensely anxious disposition—life's journey included looking to religion as a solace for human suffering and as a source for finding the inner resources to live the heroic life. A member of one of the great intellectual and aristocratic families of his age, James was educated at Harvard to be a medical doctor, but he soon turned his attention to philosophy and the emerging field of psychology, where he is widely known for his pioneering work. Despite his genteel background (he grew up attending schools in Europe and America, dabbled in art studies, and then was appointed a Harvard lecturer in 1872), James was a restless spirit who grew disenchanted with both the narrow specialization of the sciences and the obtuse nature of philosophical expression. James's broad reading, his generalist interests, and his unbounded curiosity led him—like so many journalists—to discard philosophical abstractions and esoteric speculation that seemed disconnected from real life and to discount explanations for human behavior that did not take into account the rich spiritual depths of the human personality.

James decided on the basis of his own emotional struggles and the mystical writings of many of the world's great religious figures he cites in *The Varieties of Religious Experience* that human beings cannot do without religion and remain psychologically healthy. James's assertion was fostered by his own battles with morbid anxiety and profound depression (he once said that he could not have survived if he had not clung to biblical scriptures and repeated them to himself in his deepest moments of despair). A universalist in his sympathy for the religious impulse in all major faiths, James was interested in the "New Thought" movement of his time (something akin to our New Age movement) and various forms of parapsychology and spiritualism, which certainly put him on the fringe of conventional religious thinking.[9]

James's method for examining the importance of religion in individual human existence—in conjunction with his commitment to empiricism, his medical research, and his early study of psychology—encouraged him to seek a "sci-

ence of religion" that would convince the many religious skeptics of his generation that religion could play a vital role in the construction of a healthy, integrated personality. James himself admitted to having mystical experiences, but
the measure of their value, in his view, was always the good they did in healing
the troubled spirit and restoring a person to the capacity to accomplish good
things in the world.

Although James determinedly called himself a scientist, his real interest was
in the realm of human feelings, emotions, and intuitions. James's definition of
what is scientifically grounded was that which the average person would feel was
embedded in the practical experiences of life. James was also a passionate humanist, and he scorned the scientific determinists and philosophical material-
ists of his era, on the one hand, and the dogmatists of conventional religion and
believers in absolute, ideal truths, on the other. In his forays into religious studies,
James hoped to steer a middle ground where, using his credentials as a scientist, a psychologist, and a philosopher, he could present his case for the validity
of spiritual experience and the importance of religious belief to the psychological well-being of humankind in a way that would be convincing to a society
that had come to believe wholeheartedly in the scientific method.

James's book *The Varieties of Religious Experience* provides any journalist
with a clear road map for articulating the way religious insight can illuminate
life experience in the practical realm of human existence. James focused on
the personal testimonies of some of the world's great religious figures—chosen for their forceful, moving expressions—that are apt to leave even the most
skeptical reader convinced of the powerful manner in which religion can shake
up a person's life. One does not have to believe in the ultimate "truth" of these
testimonies to religious faith—many of which focus on the conversion experience—to recognize the meaningful nature of religious experience and the
examples of how faith can be taken out into the world and can change the
world. James also made the measurement of the value of religious belief—a
view with which many journalists could concur—the good that a person of
faith does in the world.

James's viewpoint was, in essence, a variation of the biblical precept that the
fruits of the spirit are the measure of God's work in the world (see Romans 8:23,
Ephesians 5:9) and the Bible's admonition that faith without action is dead
(James 2:17–18). James, ever practical, ever the positivist, ever scornful of absolutist thinking, merged his pragmatic philosophy with these expressions of
Christian faith, even though he was only vaguely a Christian and highly pluralistic in his religious outlook. His personal experiences had taught him of the
power of religious faith to rejuvenate life, and, in his lectures, he used the quotations from these great religious figures, as well as his own thinly veiled personal testimony, to buttress his contention that spiritual experiences can be the
catalyst for real life change and that God's work in the world is capable of being measured. "Persistence in leaning on the Almighty for support and guid-

ance will . . . bring with it proofs, palpable but much more subtle, of his presence and active influence," James wrote.[10]

James also was a product of the highly optimistic era of the late nineteenth century and early twentieth in which progressive and reform values were being tested by new—and, in the minds of some, discouraging—theories emerging from science, economics, and psychology. Although a Darwinist and a believer in the importance of scientific experimentation, James detested the scientifically mechanistic approach to examining the world's phenomena, such as that advocated by Herbert Spencer, and he insisted that human experience must be the key criterion for deciding if events and stimuli from the outside world had any worth. A passionate believer in free will and free choice, James nonetheless was not unlike others of his generation who were reluctant to let go of religious certainties as a way to keep up their spirits and maintain emotional equilibrium. James has been linked with the Victorian poet Matthew Arnold (James most certainly would have concurred with Arnold's statement that the problem with Christian religion is that "men cannot do without it . . . [but] they cannot do with it as it is"), as well as the psychologist C. G. Jung, who also believed that religious faith could be a key element in a well-integrated psyche.[11]

Still, what makes James such a suitable catalyst for any discussion of the synthesis of journalism and religion is the tough-minded way that he insisted on defending religion on the most practical, pragmatic grounds and his persistent assertion that religious experience was real experience, grounded in the deepest realms of human psychology and emotion. James felt that the palpable nature of the divine spirit at work in the universe could be verified by even the most skeptical, doubting person—as long as that person was open to hearing the testimony of those who had witnessed religious experience firsthand. James's method for supporting his claim was one that most journalists would be familiar with—he relied on the personal accounts of such figures as Saint Teresa of Avila, Martin Luther, John Bunyan, George Fox, Jonathan Edwards, and John Wesley, as well as a host of lesser-known mystics and religious writers, to try to convince his listeners that communion with the divine is something real and tangible and has real effects in the world. Like most journalists, James used the writings and quotations of his subjects to convey the "proof" of their beliefs and relied on the power of their eloquence and the force of their emotion to capture the "meaning" of experience.

Although journalists, like James, prefer to think of themselves as empiricists who demand hard evidence of every assertion they transmit, in reality, much journalistic "truth" relies, as it did for James, on what individuals say is their perception of the world's ways and their perspective on their own experiences. James put a great premium on feeling, as do journalists who (while thinking of themselves as rationalists) greatly value the "punchy" quote that conveys strong sentiment. Journalists, too, should relate to James's phrase—"the way in which it works on the whole"—as the ultimate test of a belief and its usefulness for

the world.[12] James applied this notion time and again to his measurement of
the impact that individual contact with the divine can have on life's events; again
journalists (skeptical idealists that they are) should be very familiar with the
notion that beliefs and opinions do not count for much if they are not matched
by beneficial activities and tangible accomplishments in the world. Or, as the
great nineteenth-century journalist James Gordon Bennett once expressed it,
"Religion—true religion—consists not . . . in presuming to judge the opinions
of others beyond what their acts will justify."[13]

I would argue that James's pragmatic philosophy provides the ideal framework for journalists—and the journalism profession as a whole—to establish a
basis for reporting on religion without abandoning the tenets of skepticism,
open-minded scrutiny, or the demands for hard evidence on which the profession is based. Although James never linked the conclusions he reaches in *The
Varieties of Religious Experience* to journalism explicitly, many of them can be
most helpful to journalists faced with the dilemma of determining how to deal
with faith issues in a professional environment where solid evidence and sound
facts are held up as the coinage of verification. James's definition of empirical
proof is, for example, much the same one that journalists—as practically minded
realists—would apply to their work in a world where nothing can be known for
certain and where the demands of a day's work in getting the news do not allow for the luxury of grand-scale philosophical speculation. Beliefs, James contended, are in essence simply rules for action, and the guiding element of philosophy must be that every belief must make a difference and that the best
method of discussing a point of theory is to ascertain what practical outcome
would result from its being true.

It is hard to imagine the generations of journalists—from the stone-kicking
Samuel Johnson to Bennett, the gadfly antagonist of the churches, to the great
debunker Mencken—disagreeing with this. Even as James applied his pragmatic
philosophy to the world of religion, one can imagine journalists—Bennett, for
example, with his great interest in religion and his sense of the importance of
religion to his reading public—moving comfortably along with him. In the end,
most journalists, although they might not express it in the explicitly religious
language of James, would probably agree with his statement, "The roots of a
man's virtue are inaccessible to us. No appearances whatever are infallible proofs
of grace. Our practice is the only sure evidence, even to ourselves, that we are
genuinely Christians."[14]

In our survey of journalists' religious attitudes, most journalists endorsed the
biblical passage that the measure of faith should be one's works in the world.[15]
It is not difficult to translate this belief into a basis for improved religion coverage, particularly in helping journalists recognize the religious impulse as it plays
out in the world. One does not have to endorse any particular theology to be
sensitive to the faith dimension that lies behind much of what happens in the
community and the religious motivation of those who perform those deeds.

Journalists can be expected to perform their job in a deeper, richer fashion—and, incidentally, connect more effectively with many of their readers, viewers, and listeners—if they are attuned to the way faith is lived out even in secular settings. This does not mean that journalists should go around writing feature stories about all the faithful do-gooders of the world. But, in good Jamesian fashion, it does mean staying alert to the stories showing faith in action that may bubble up or that may add important context and perspective to what might otherwise seem to be no more than ordinary news accounts.

Journalists can also find in James's pragmatic criteria a guide for uncovering the sham and the hypocrisy they so despise—particularly among the avowedly religious—as well as help distinguishing between genuine religious insight and the fantasies of the mentally unbalanced. James, like Hemingway, whom he so influenced, put an absolute premium on finding those examples in life that reflect what is authentic, genuine, and sincere about a person's life philosophy and its symmetry with how one's life is lived out in the world. As a relativist, James did not pretend to know what that life philosophy should be. But his pragmatic process for evaluating how consistent one's belief is with one's actions is something that most journalists can heartily endorse—and often do in the judgments that befall those religious figures who fail to live up to the principles their faith demands.

In reaching out to his skeptical academic colleagues, James spent a good deal of time trying to establish the basis whereby one can distinguish between authentic spiritual experience and delusion, hallucination, or mental illness. (This, of course, would be of great importance to journalists who, at the top of their list of professional embarrassments, do not want to be seen as naive, gullible, or impressionable.) James acknowledged that many great religious thinkers and leaders have shown "symptoms of nervous instability" and have been subject to "abnormal psychical visitations" that led up to their conversions and the development of their religious philosophies. But James offered a list of categories to distinguish between these "great souled persons" whose religious perceptions are to be trusted and those who are simply emotionally troubled. He maintained that—regardless of whether the religious vision of these people originates in the realm of the psychological or the divine—it is the "veracity" of their message rooted in spiritual inwardness and their ability to connect with the inner life of their fellow beings that gives them their influence and their authority.

James's critics have noted that, despite his pretensions to a science of religion, he did not succeed in offering a methodological model that satisfactorily distinguished between "legitimate" religious experience and the illusions of the emotionally disturbed. But the important point here is that—like the typical journalist—James built his case in *The Varieties of Religious Experience* by using multiple examples of personal testimony, taken from the writings, the sermons, or other forms of powerful witnessing, of the experiences of such individuals as John Bunyan, Leo Tolstoy, and Saint Teresa of Avila as evidence of the mental agony and emotional melancholy that can lead to a profound conversion experience. James combined his own verbal mastery with the impassioned accounts of his subjects to share with his readers and his listeners the experience of the power of the moment of conversion, the peace that comes afterward to the transformed person, and the change it can bring in that person's activities.

Unquestionably, James's methodology—despite the accumulated weight of the personal testimonials—was only loosely that of the empirical researcher, and he made no claims about the universality of religious experience or the extent of belief within the population (in fact, he acknowledged that many people simply do not have such experiences). But with an eloquence that would be envied by any journalist, James came back again and again to his contention that so-called scientific conclusions must be based on what works—what he called "the facts of personal experience"—rather than on abstract expressions of belief or the conclusions of researchers (whose studies often rely on some form of compilation of individuals' descriptions of their attitudes or experiences). Trying to be objective by overlooking the subjective elements inherent in humans' ways of knowing the world is a vain goal, James said, particularly when in the dimension of religion. "If definite perceptions of fact like this cannot stand upon their own feet, surely abstract reasoning cannot give them the support they are in need of," he observed, adding, "In the religious sphere, in particular, belief that formulas are true can never wholly take the place of personal experience."[16]

As one of the pioneers of the field of psychology, James also brought a sophistication to his study of religion that should appeal to journalists who have become highly sympathetic to the methods of psychological theory and research. James believed that the source of religious tension resided in the psychology of the believer, but (in somewhat the same way that Jung did) he felt that, in surrendering one's will to a higher power, emotional healing could occur. Again, James looked to the practical experience of individuals to test his hypothesis, and, as he had discovered in his own bouts with melancholy and despair, he found much evidence for it. For James, as with Jung, religious need and the spiritual impulse were basic, tangible aspects of the human personality, and religious belief was what kept certain people sane, balanced, and fulfilled.

Journalists, sympathetic with the idea of relative truth, should have no difficulty accepting James's idea that the search for what is real is always approximate and that the quest for truth—including religious truth—is always circumscribed by the limitations of human understanding. Admittedly, religious skeptics, including the doubting journalist, might resist the next leap that James took from this contention—that if faith in God or encounters with the divine have such beneficial effects in the world and in the individual, then the existence of the divine must be acknowledged and treated as if it were fact. But one always must keep in mind what James meant by fact, and how it was always circumscribed by his theories of the pragmatic method of knowing. James's dismissal of absolutist belief systems was, in itself, absolute, and the act of human knowing, for him, was always relative and subjective—a subjectivity that is "obliquely cognitive, a blurry apprehension of objective realities," as another of his biographers, Gerald Myers, put it.[17] Journalists, despite their sometimes less than modest epistemology, still tend to measure truth by their own experience of it, but they are also taught to respect the claims of others' experiences. James himself made no claim to certainty about the nature of religious truth, but his statements about religious tolerance most certainly would resonate with many of today's pluralistically oriented journalists.

On the other side of the coin, James also did not hesitate to reject the notion that there must be some form of universally acknowledged, fully rational, scientific proof of God's existence to assert the validity of the spiritual realm. James took some of his greatest intellectual risks here, and he did not stop by claiming that pragmatic analysis alone points to the possibility of a divine influence in life. James went so far as to maintain that "that which produces effects within another reality must be termed a reality itself," and, as one who had witnessed this influence in his life and that of others, he had "no philosophic excuse for calling the unseen or mystical world unreal." By this pragmatic and subjective definition of religion, James claimed, the experience of union with a power beyond us—even if it was experienced only by people of certain religious sensibilities—should be treated as if it were literally, rather than just apparently, true.[18]

This is the point at which James veered from the argument of an empiricist into the realm of a person of faith, and the skeptic has every right to balk at this leap of logic. But there are indications that James had not arrived at complete consistency on this point in his own mind. While this may not be of concern to the journalist, it is to the theologian. James, the empiricist and the pragmatist, put it this way: "God is real since he produces real effects." But for James, the humanist, the pluralist, and the cautious skeptic, he hedged a bit, taking refuge in verbal flight. "Does God really exist? How does he exist? What is he? are so many irrelevant questions. Not God, but life, more life, a larger richer, more satisfying life, is, in the last analysis, the end of religion." Finally he concluded on a fully subjective yet tentative note: "What the more characteristically divine facts are, apart from the actual inflow of energy in the faith-state and the prayer-state, I know not. But the [belief] on which I am ready to make my personal venture is that they exist."[19]

Historians have observed that James was part of a transitional generation that—liberal in matters of faith, confident about human progress, yet troubled by the secular direction of society—simply could not let go of the support and the strength provided by religious belief, despite rejecting traditional Christianity and refining religious terminology to what believers would call agnostic levels. In this context, many of today's journalists might be inclined to look at James not as the inspiration for a renewed commitment to covering matters of faith but as an anachronism from an era when people had not fully faced up to the consequences of scientific discovery and the modern mood of doubt and pes-

simism. James, it is true, was an optimist and a progressive, whose determined
efforts at trying to reconcile the empirical outlook of his age with his own need
for religious faith sometimes seemed strained and unconvincing—at least to
those of thoroughly rationalistic temperament. Viewed by some of his intellectual contemporaries as an apologist for an outdated Christian worldview who
was overly anxious to prove to a skeptical intelligentsia that it was mistaken in
disowning religion, James has continued to be treated by commentators in the
twentieth century as an early apostle of personal religion who believed deeply
that regenerative experiences could come from a faith life, but whose need for
religious belief and desire to launch a religious revival of sorts among the doubting classes were rooted in the peculiarities of the nineteenth-century intellectual conflicts between religion, science, and psychology.

James's "will to believe" can certainly seem quaint to the modern mind, which
has had a century more than James had to reconcile itself to the loss of religion
as the explicit guiding force in the operation of the social order. James's position
that the need to believe is tantamount to having faith can seem almost like wishful
thinking and certainly less than satisfying to those with atheistic beliefs or a more
rocklike faith. James once answered "emphatically, no" to a questionnaire asking whether he believed in God because of some argument; to the question of
whether he believed because he experienced God's presence, he replied, "No, but
rather because I need it to be so that it 'must' be true."[20] Some might find this
answer unconvincing; Nietzsche, who felt that the truly courageous person was
one who had the fearlessness to embrace his or her nonbeliefs no matter the consequences, surely would have. Such an answer to life's mysteries can make James's
talk of a science of religion seem little more than a gesture to the scientific establishment—a rationalization for religious belief rather than a rational method
for documenting its validity. There are even those who have questioned whether James—in asserting that the experience of God must mean that God exists—
actually followed his own pragmatic reasoning process in arriving at his views
about the divine. (In his critics' minds, James's pragmatic view should have been
that we can know only the "consequences" of the belief in God and leave it at
that, rather than infer anything about God's existence.)

Be that as it may, there is still much in James's philosophy that can be useful
to journalists, especially those who hope to treat the faith world seriously. James's
most fundamental principle—that it is irrational to reject what we cannot know
for sure—is the basis for true open-mindedness and can be a valuable starting
point for any journalist who covers religion. James's views that we must show
respect for mystical experiences; that there are tangible, pragmatic consequences
of faith's activity in the world; that while we cannot explain the experiences of
religious people, neither can we explain them away—these should be able to be
comfortably absorbed into journalistic methodology without compromising its
skeptical tradition. One can always choose to see religious experience in psychological, physiological, or even pathological terms (in many respects, James felt

this himself—he believed the susceptibility to religious experience was rooted in one's physiological and psychological nature). But even if that serves as an explanation for the experience, as James might say, it does not substitute for the quality of the experience itself. If truth is still to be found through each individual's subjective encounters with the world—and journalists very definitely operate from this principle—then individual religious experience cannot be excluded from the equation. Myers tended to see James as close to a nonbeliever at heart, despite his powerful protestations about his need to believe. As Myers put it, "He did not really believe; he merely believed in the right of believing that you might be right if you believed."[21] This, it seems to me, is an excellent stance for journalists, no matter how skeptical their fundamental theological views. Who, least of all journalists, can argue with the notion that someone might have important experiences that the world would profit from knowing about?

Journalists are, in Jamesian fashion, practical people who believe themselves to be empirical in outlook but largely record what people say and witness as the truth. Subjectivity and emotion are at the heart of the feature story; the personal conveyance of opinion and life outlook are the stuff of the interview; attribution (what people say or put their name to) can be the test of whether a statement or a viewpoint makes it into a story in the framework of newsroom decision making. Journalists put great store in scientific opinion, but usually more as the testimony of scientists and experts to the validity of their experiments and discoveries than as independent verification of the data by journalists themselves. The journalistic method has pretenses to being scientific and empirical, but, in fact, it usually is not, at least in any definition that goes beyond James's. Journalists do very little of their own testing or analysis of primary material or data, and they certainly do not participate in scientific experiments. Journalists seldom have the patience or the expertise to wade through the data in the scientific studies that do come to them. The attitude of most journalists is simply this: just give me a summary and a few quotes from the scientists or the researchers, and that's enough for a story. Social scientists scorn this imprecision and the lack of scientific methodology in what they often refer to as "journalistic inquiry"; hard scientists are usually just plain scared about how their studies will be simplified and sensationalized when journalists get hold of them and frame them in a journalistic context. If the truth be told, most journalists see themselves as rational empirical practitioners, but—not unlike James—they really put the greatest store in strong feeling and subjectivity, in personal witnessing and emotion-laden quotes, and in their own firsthand experiences.

James, not unlike a good journalist, is, in the end, most convincing not because of his scientific attitude or his empirical methodology but because of the eloquence of his language, the moving nature of his tributes to human experience, and his sympathy for the pain and the passions of others. In his Gifford lectures, James said, "I believe the pragmatic way of taking religion to be the deeper way. It gives it body as well as soul, it makes it claim, as everything real must claim, some characteristic realm of fact as its very own."[22] Time and again, James demonstrated his argument by pointing to the record of the divine spirit at work in the human heart, and the only real proof that James needed was the same proof that is so often offered by journalists—the witnessing of experience, the testimony to the reality of the individual's encounter with the world, and the example of the life transformed by embracing meaning beyond one's self. In the final analysis, James's accounts of those who have discovered profound visions and life-altering energy in their experiences of suffering and healing serve to speak for themselves. "Many readers have felt the powerful effect produced by confession upon confession," Myers said of *The Variety of Religious Experience,* "such that even the most staunch atheist may begin to wonder whether a religious dimension might exist whose threshold he has never crossed."[23]

Myers described James as a person who "relied on the testimony of mystics and upon his own experiences which resembled mystical ones."[24] James was generally hesitant to go beyond that. He despised religion when those individual experiences were relied on to create a foundation of secondhand worship, when they were extrapolated for the basis of churches or organized religion, when they were refashioned and hardened into creeds, or when they were asserted as answers to the great universal questions. James had great problems with religious belief that had become rigid, institutional, and dogmatic, that was offered to others or imposed on them, or that was held up as indisputable truth.

In this respect, his thinking was completely in line with the pluralistic and tolerant spirit of modern American journalism. But James's message, delivered with an eye toward the religious skeptics of his day, is equally relevant to the dubious, the disillusioned, and the debunkers of our time. Much of the resistance to religion—based on the modern suspicion of absolute certainties and the distaste for those who do not hesitate to say that they have the answer—overlooks the fact that the origins of faith always grow out of individual experience. And usually it is in language—in the expressions of those human passions, visions, and insights—that the spirit of those experiences is transmitted from one individual to the next. James would never have asked anyone—certainly not the modern journalist—to take away from his book anything more than that. But if that could happen, James will have provided the foundation for a method of respectful, even sympathetic, coverage of the importance of religion in the human experience. That, as James might say, would be a most happy outcome for seeing improvement in the media's reporting on the world of the unseen.

PART 2

Research, Religious Beliefs, and the Ethics of the Press

CHAPTER 8

Trusting Their Guts:
The Moral Compass of a
Doubters' Profession

 E. W. Scripps was a quarrelsome old cuss, a hard-drinking, will-ful, dominating personality who said what was on his mind and the world be damned. While Scripps may be best known as one of the earliest developers of the newspaper chain, in his memoirs he spent a good bit of time musing about journalistic morals and philosophizing about the conflicting feelings he had about religion's impact on his professional outlook. "I cannot recall the time when I was not what is commonly called an atheist," Scripps wrote. "I do not believe in God, or any being equal to or similar to the Christian's God. . . . Yet when I called upon myself to classify myself as to what school of philosophy or religion I belong to, I have had no doubt but that I should be classified as a Christian. My morals, or my moral convictions, are those common to members of the Christian religion."[1]

Scripps's ambivalent feelings about the relationship between religion and morals go a long way in explaining the complex role that Judeo-Christian eth-ics plays in the professional practice of journalists, particularly in carrying out a newspaper crusade, to which Scripps heartily subscribed. Scripps believed that biblical values made for good journalism, and he was much more open in rec-ognizing this than the modern journalist, who may subscribe to Scripps's eth-ics but no longer has the knowledge of or the interest in religion to put it into historical perspective.

Scripps, like many of his fellow journalists, did not put much stock in what he considered the mythological and legendary explanations of many biblical stories or in the orthodox theology that grew up around Jesus' life and teach-ings and was adapted by the church as a measure of belief that determined ev-erything from church membership to the potential for a believer's salvation in the afterlife. Scripps did, however, place great store in the wisdom of the Ten Commandments, and, when he retired in 1908, he included them as part of his guidelines for editors to follow. All his writings and correspondence were sprinkled with quotations from the Bible, and he once referred to the newspaper's editorials as "the teaching department, the statesmanship department, the spiritual department." Although Scripps had no use for the organized church ("All that Christ taught is good," Scripps once said. "Most, perhaps all, of the interpretations of Christ's teachings by the theologians, have been untrue, unscientific, un-Christian, unnatural, wicked"), he believed that all reformers—including those in journalism—were forever trying to improve social conditions by applying the first principles of Christianity. "It is noteworthy that the most radical, the most determined, reformers are . . . outside the pale of the Christian church," Scripps wrote. "These men may long have lost all faith in the church . . . but nevertheless, having been born into a world which had no other ethical point of view than the Christian, they have been so formed by their environment as to have no other than a Christian point of view."[2]

Scripps's views fit neatly into the idea of a "civil religion," advanced by the sociologist Robert N. Bellah, who contended that a secularized version of Judeo-Christian morals and ethics has become absorbed into the operation of our system of politics, governmental life, arts, and sciences.[3] It is no great leap to see Bellah's concept applied to journalistic institutions. In this view, journalistic values of virtuous conduct, dislike of intolerance, and belief in fundamental moral and ethical precepts may have been moved out of their explicitly religious application and into the secular, public sphere, but they still have their roots in basic religious concepts—in this country, largely Judeo-Christian. The media ethicist Ed Lambeth assumed this viewpoint when he argued that journalism ethics reflect Judeo-Christian values, not for religious reasons but because they have become the core cultural values of the larger society in which journalistic principles are an integral part.[4]

Other observers of the journalistic scene have noted this phenomenon at work. Jay Newman has argued that while few journalists are prepared "to devote their careers to working for a great religious awakening," the historic connection between religion and the ideals of civilization promoted by journalistic organizations cannot be ignored. "The Christian religion can be presumed to exercise still an indirect but pervasive influence on all major Western social institutions, so that however religiously neutral modern Western journalists strive to be, they carry on their work in a society guided by a vaguely Christian world view," Newman wrote in *The Journalist in Plato's Cave*. "An observer unsympathetic to Christian doctrine and practice, such as a Nietzsche or Marx, would not have much difficulty in showing how even the most secularized Western newspaper takes certain aspects of the Christian world view to be matters simply of natural or intuitive morality."[5]

The modern journalism profession's ethical condition is less than comprehensible if it is taken out of historical context. A hundred to 150 years ago, during the penny press era or the yellow journalism period, journalists' ethics were considered quite low—even though Judeo-Christian teachings still provided the dominant ethical framework for the culture and Christianity was the defining belief system for most Americans. Today, American society has grown more secular, and the prevailing Judeo-Christian outlook has been diluted by pluralistic and heterodox influences in the culture. Yet it is widely believed that the professional ethics of journalists have improved considerably since the nineteenth century, with newsroom codes of conduct in force, articulated ethical standards propagated in the course of journalism training, and media reviews, ombudspeople's columns, and professional associations serving as a check against journalistic miscreancy. This state of affairs—where journalism appears to have become a more ethical profession while the hold of traditional religion has faded in the culture at large—might appear, on the surface, to challenge the notion that Judeo-Christian teachings continue to serve as a guiding force, even an indirect one, for ethical and moral decision making in journalism. If we look more closely at the historical circumstances of American journalism, however, we can see that the situation is not as contradictory as it might seem.

To understand the evolution of the press's ethical standards, it is important to follow two strands in the development of journalistic ethics in America: that of the publishers in their role as civic-minded members of the business establishment and that of editors and reporters in their professional roles as employees of news organizations. A key reason media owners embrace ethical values is to avoid offending the sensibilities of their audience and to ensure that, by maintaining an image of respectability for their publication, they will maximize success in the marketplace. Publishers from Benjamin Franklin to Joseph Pulitzer to Adolph Ochs emphasized the moral virtues of the culture on their editorial pages and in their calls for civic action, but they also recognized the money-making potential in producing a publication that appealed to readers who valued a high-minded approach to social and political issues. Reporters have usually had less overt economic motives for embracing ethical standards. But, as the media sociologist Warren Breed has pointed out, journalists learn their professional values largely through osmosis while working in the newsroom environment, and reporters, particularly as ethical standards have improved throughout the twentieth century, have found it advantageous to their careers, regardless of their own personal value systems, to follow the ethical dictates their bosses have come to believe constitute good business.[6]

It is important to remember that one of the reasons for the adoption of the free press clause in the Bill of Rights was the founders' perception that newspapers, in ideal form, should serve as important organs of education, civility, morality, and democratic nation building. Franklin is often held up as the example of the colonial publisher who epitomized the virtues of the progressive and enlightened editor and, although a Deist and a skeptic of Christian orthodoxy, still believed deeply that religion forms the basis of a moral culture and that religious belief among the citizenry was necessary to maintaining a civilized society. When he became the owner of his own publications, Franklin elevated fairness, balance, civic-mindedness, and a decent respect for the opinions of humankind to the level of a professional standard. Franklin was kin to Scripps in his disbelief in traditional Christian theology but strong embrace of the morals and ethics in the Christian value system. It is true that, unlike Franklin, the partisan press of the postcolonial era could be scurrilous in its willingness to ruin reputations and to publish all sorts of tawdry details and defamatory political attacks, as Franklin's friend Thomas Jefferson often experienced. Even so, Jefferson, like Franklin, never gave up his hope for the potential of the press as a lofty organ of civic virtue that would advance the cause of ethics, democracy, and justice in American society.

The advent of the penny press and the rise of the cheap, mass-market, commercialized newspapers of the large urban areas in the 1830s added a new dimension to the development of journalistic ethics. Such publishers as James Gordon Bennett produced newspapers that, while eager to maximize circulation and use the liveliest storytelling means to gain audience, defined themselves as nonpartisan champions of the interests of the common person. Like Franklin, Bennett was no believer in Christian orthodoxy, and, during the famous "Moral War" against his newspaper, he was roundly attacked by the clergy of New York and other members of the business and political establishment. But Bennett was already evolving a no-holds-barred moral and ethical credo for newspaper publishers that combined the use of audience-building news and money-making advertising techniques with the advocacy of reform values that he believed most truly served the democratic interests of his readership. Bennett liked to argue he was the truly moral figure with his attacks on hypocrisy and false piety in society (including religious society). He, like Joseph Pulitzer and other nineteenth-century editors who followed him, combined sensationalistic, tabloid techniques with a highly responsible and civic-minded editorial page and a strong belief that a newspaper should be a moral force in the community and a willing crusader for the average person's rights.

Bennett also was one of the first editors to define the modern beat system and to employ reporters to find the stories that would fascinate his readers. Reporters, however, were slow to embrace high moral values, largely because reporters in those times were so poorly paid and so exploited by editors seeking audience-grabbing news. The newspaper historian Ted Curtis Smythe described the "not fully developed" ethical standards of nineteenth-century newspaper reporters—as well as their general employment circumstances—in fairly bleak terms. Reporters, whose pay was based on the column inches they produced, sometimes fell prey to dubious practices: some took payola from politicians and public relations people looking for good coverage; some were simultaneously on the payroll of government organizations; others wrote advertisements on the side or dropped names into stories for pay; many padded expenses to compensate for low salaries. Beyond that, reporters often had little moral guidance except their own consciences in how to get news stories: bribery, misrepresentation, false reporting, the stealing of criminal evidence, and the squirreling away of witnesses in big stories were not unheard of, particularly in the intensively competitive and sensationalistic news environment of the time. "Editors praised or censured reporters on the basis of whether they had a story and how good it was, not on their own good deeds," Smythe concluded.[7]

The late nineteenth century and early twentieth certainly saw plenty of "moral" journalism practiced with high ethical standards—the muckraking movement comes to mind, for example (including Will Irwin's famous fifteen-part series revealing the business practices of the newspaper industry, which called to public attention some of its greater abuses). But journalism also became a haven for ambitious, opportunistic young people, often minimally educated and from working-class backgrounds, who were using the newly emergent profession of the reporter as a way to begin the climb up the ladder of economic and career success in a society that was deeply imbued with the laissez-faire values of industrial capitalism and the Horatio Alger model of personal advancement. Utilitarian attitudes toward morality and social issues, combined with the emerging philosophy of pragmatism as the basis of journalistic practices, were reinforced by a cultural climate in which Darwinism and the rise of science undermined traditional religious attitudes and left many people feeling at sea when it came to morals and values. Scripps's capacity to separate skepticism about Christian theology from his embrace of Judeo-Christian moral values was a sophisticated act, and many less thoughtful journalists had not achieved his level of ethical insight.

The moral philosophy in the typical newsroom of the period may explain, at least in part, why questionable ethical practices were tolerated. Theodore Dreiser's portrayal of the journalists with whom he worked in Chicago indicated that, by the time news reporting had become a full-fledged profession, the ethic of the newsroom was something less than the Judeo-Christian ideal. "'People make laws for other people to live up to, and in order to protect themselves in what they have,'" Dreiser quoted his first city editor telling him. "'They never intend those laws to apply to themselves or to prevent them from doing anything they wish to do.'"[8] Even Scripps's philosophy reflected something of the hard-bitten cynicism that journalists had come to feel for the moralists and expounders of pieties in a world where ruthless business practices and crass financial self-seeking seemed to rule the day. "Men do not believe what they say they believe," Scripps wrote. "There is no 'peace on earth and goodwill toward men.' Such a condition is in direct conflict with every known and suspected natural law."[9]

The rather abysmal state of journalistic ethics in the nineteenth century was not the focus of most of the complaints about press corruption at the time, however. In the still moralistic tone of the Victorian era and in a century when America had been swept by a series of great Protestant awakenings, most press criticism concentrated on the tactical habits of the press—its sensationalism, its invasion of privacy in pursuing stories, its emphasis on crime, sex, and gossip, and its insatiable profitability.[10] Hazel Dicken-Garcia noted that this kind of criticism—often coming from church and religious quarters[11]—did not much concern itself, at least in the early years of the penny press, with the ethics of individual journalists. Not until 1850 were there any charges about journalists accepting "freebies" or "junkets"; the first call for ethics training and a code of conduct for journalists did not appear until 1856; and it was not until 1869 that the first college journalism course in America was offered at Washington College.[12]

In studying criticism of the press and formulas for press reform in the nineteenth century, Dicken-Garcia found the word *ethics* appeared only rarely in discussions through the 1880s.[13] Nineteenth-century critics' focus on the broadscale evils of the press as an institution meant they did not concern themselves much with the everyday conduct of individual journalists. That fixation was left largely to the twentieth century—a time when even though individual journalists were prodded to raise their moral standards, the rest of America was shedding the optimistic and moralistic attitudes of the nineteenth century and moving toward a more pessimistic worldview bred by global scale warfare, economic depression, and the arms race. America's position as a monolithically Christian country, cultural historians will say, was on the wane throughout the twentieth century, undermined by the rise of science and growing secularism in many quarters of society, immigration from non-Western and non-Christian countries, and the competition of psychology and other faiths. While journalists spent much of the twentieth century debating the adoption of new and tougher ethical codes within media organizations and wringing their hands over ethical lapses within the profession, the members of the American public—themselves less Christian in outlook as a group—seemed to grow increasingly disgusted with what they considered excesses in media behavior.

So what would explain this increased attention to individual journalistic ethics just when traditional religious patterns in the broader society were in decline and public impatience with media performance on the rise? On one level, the growing pressure for ethical standards appears to have occurred exactly because there were fewer universally embraced moral norms in the society at large. Although by the late nineteenth century the newsroom, particularly the big-city newsroom, had become a hotbed for the skeptical, hard-boiled, worldly-wise young opportunists in revolt against Puritan pieties and Victorian morality, newspapers as organizations still largely reflected the conventional moral outlook of the broader culture. Despite the criticism they received for their sensation-seeking news formulas and the amorality of their business practices, most news organizations in the late nineteenth century and early twentieth—including some of the most notorious—subscribed to the normative Christian values of their day and reflected these views on their editorial pages and in the way they framed news stories. The news practices of the early tabloid newspapers encouraged some employees to abandon ethical standards on occasion, but the media organizations' overall presentation of the news and employees' explicitly stated expectations in gathering and presenting it were in conformance with the moral platitudes of American commerce, widely held Christian cultural norms, and the general values of institutionalized Christianity. The growing commercial and competitive environment in which news organizations operated may have encouraged, in reality, a more free-and-easy attitude toward personal morality and tolerance of dubious professional practices, but the typical nineteenth-century news organization still tended to present its public face as a champion of public morality and civic respectability.

In this environment, news executives began to worry more about the ethical standards of their employees, if for no other reason than because they were concerned with public reaction to ethically shoddy news-gathering practices. Throughout the nineteenth century and early twentieth, news organizations became fewer, larger, and more entrenched bureaucracies, and there was a growing emphasis on the newsroom employee as a functioning member of a highly regulated organization subject to institutionalized rules and professional standards. Slowly the image of the newspaper reporter as a flamboyant, free-wheeling, story-hustling, morally dubious character underwent a revamping. Christianity may have lost some of its hold on society during this period, but a new set of institutional forces grew up to place ethical restraints on journalists. Two-fisted newspaper competition, which encouraged anything-goes reporting practices, began to diminish as the ranks of big-city daily newspapers grew thinner throughout the twentieth century. Such newspapers as the *New York Times,* with its motto of printing "All the News That's Fit to Print" and its targeted audience of respectable citizens and members of the business community, became the model for the typical twentieth-century American daily newspaper more than the tabloid-style publications of Hearst or Pulitzer. As the more professionalized, respect-seeking publications set the tone in American daily journalism, the constraints on journalistic misconduct grew and ethical corner-cutting found fewer rewards.

The ethical consciousness of reporters and newsroom employees also was on the rise during this period. The Populist and Progressive political movements—which rose up to combat corruption in municipal government and business during the late nineteenth century—had their influence in newsrooms, as did the expanded educational opportunities for people who increasingly saw the practice of journalism as a profession. In 1908, the University of Missouri founded the nation's first college of journalism; by 1912, Pulitzer's school of journalism had been established at Columbia University.[14] By 1925, journalism courses, departments, and schools had proliferated around the country; many newspapers had adopted codes of ethics; and press associations had formed that exercised at least some form of ethical control over their members.[15] Although some of their rhetoric was still couched in religious terms, these early journalism educators were more likely to be influenced by the morality expressed in the progressive and municipal reform movements and even more so by the notion that journalists should operate as guardians of the public good and see their role as serving as a check on abuses in government and business.[16]

As the broad-based Christian moral consensus in American society began to wane in the years following the two world wars, the issue of journalistic ethics was discussed more in secular, professional terms and less in religious ones. After World War I, the debate about journalistic ethics focused on such issues as the licensing of reporters and the establishment of accuracy bureaus and ethics tribunals (which were rejected as incompatible with the press's First Amendment standing), as well as Walter Lippmann's call for a cadre of government information specialists who could compensate for the bias and the superficiality of press coverage.[17] Secular institutional voices—both inside and outside the press—began to exercise gentle pressures for reform. Journalism schools were accredited, professional organizations multiplied and promulgated codes of conduct, and academic critiques of press performance became commonplace. In 1947, the Hutchins Commission—proposed by Henry Luce, publisher of *Time* magazine, and established under the guidance of Robert M. Hutchins, chancellor of the University of Chicago—issued a report that suggested ways journalism could be less unfair, less slanted, and less sensational and urged journalists to become more "objective" and "responsible" in pursuing and presenting the truth.[18] Meanwhile, press critics, such as George Seldes, Oswald Villard, and A. J. Liebling, carried on the prophetic tradition by writing scathingly about the growing impact of chain newspapers' and newspaper executives' selling out to advertisers and big-money interests. Although openly ignored in mainstream journalistic circles, the critics made it increasingly clear to media owners that they were being watched.[19]

By the 1960s and 1970s, explicit references to religion had largely disappeared from the debate over newsroom ethics, and few journalists were much aware of—or much interested in—how the press's value system related to the religious past. Ethical issues, within both the press and the larger society, were framed against the social and political unrest of the era, and religion and religious controversy took a backseat to the civil disputes dominating the national scene. While religious values were interwoven with these events, particularly the civil rights movement that grew out of the black churches of the South, few journalists saw the religious community as a place to find exciting stories. The Vietnam War and Watergate spawned heroes of investigative reporting—such as Bob Woodward and Carl Bernstein, who have been widely credited with bringing down President Richard Nixon, and Seymour Hersh, who revealed the atrocities at My Lai— and any explicit mention of a religious mission had vanished from the discussion. The colorful, subjective, highly textured, point-of-view prose of "new" journalists, such as Tom Wolfe, Hunter Thompson, and Norman Mailer, pushed the traditional boundaries of the profession and made celebrities of the iconoclastic, antiestablishment journalist. Underground newspapers touting countercultural values and contemptuous of traditional "objective" or "professional" journalistic standards thrived, and religion, if it was mentioned, included Zen Buddhism, Indian swamis, or the other meditative religions embraced by the readers of alternative media as a sign of their rejection of mainstream Christian mores. The politics of the youth culture, the appearance of hippies and love children, the sexual and women's liberation movements, and the "credibility gap" between what politicians said and did in carrying out the Vietnam War and Watergate all proved to be much more fascinating stories for the mainstream press than anything to do with religion. All the while, much of the public—continuing to attend church and faced with what seemed like a loss of standards in every direction they looked—did not hesitate to vote for such conservative candidates as Richard Nixon and Spiro Agnew, who scored points with their attacks on a press that they claimed had become out of touch with the values of the "silent majority" of Americans. This, however, only served to help polarize the thinking in newsrooms and to encourage the press—its numbers swelled with idealistic young people attracted to the business because of its image as a place to help clean up a corrupt establishment—to identify Christianity with conservative causes and reactionary politics.

Beneath the national protests and countercultural politics influencing journalism, however, there was a quiet struggle to restore order and traditional lines of authority in newsrooms by editors worried that the professional and even ethical standards of the news business had suffered during the moral confusion of the time. Although not necessarily any more openly religious in belief than their reporters, many of these editors had been strongly influenced by the growth of professionalism taking place in the media business in the 1960s and 1970s. During that period, news organizations, once the domain of autocratic publishers, saw the reins turned over to newsroom professionals, a stronger barrier put up between the news and advertising departments, and the adoption of professional standards that were perceived as more in tune with the corporate values of the conglomerates that increasingly owned American media organizations. Although the new generation of antiestablishment, "do-your-own-thing" journalists was welcomed into the business, it was not long before editors and publishers were trying to find ways to subdue them and reassert control over their newsrooms.

The lore attached to Woodward and Bernstein—so romanticized as the heroes of the *Washington Post*'s Watergate investigation— illustrates the phenomenon. Bernstein has been portrayed as the rebel of the pair, the Peck's Bad Boy who wore his hair long, identified with the counterculture, and challenged or manipulated editors to get his way whenever possible. But at the core of the *Post* management's concerns about Bernstein (he was reportedly on the verge of being fired before the Watergate story) were the tactics he used to secure a story. Bernstein was known for manipulating sources, evading direct disclosure of his purposes if necessary to secure information, and asking sources to provide him with illegally obtained information (all of which he reportedly did during the course of the Watergate investigation). These techniques have been treated in Woodward and Bernstein's behind-the-scenes accounts of their reporting as amusing, even admirable, lapses in ethical reportorial practices. But the nervousness of the *Post* editors about the methods Woodward and Bernstein used during their investigation (as well as the widespread uneasiness among journalists about the *Post*'s loose use of unidentified sources in their Watergate stories) illustrated how much a shaky trust between editor and reporter rather than a clearly articulated code of ethical conduct had come to guide the news-gathering process of the 1970s.[20]

This tenuous bond was ruptured a few years later in an equally celebrated incident involving Woodward, as the *Post*'s city editor, and a young reporter he supervised who won a Pulitzer Prize for her series about a child heroin addict. When it was discovered that Janet Cooke had fabricated much of the story, chagrined *Post* editors returned the Pulitzer and set off a nationwide debate in journalism circles about whether the freedoms granted to reporters had grown too great. The Janet Cooke incident played into a backlash already underway among news executives, who, in reasserting their management authority, had sent the message that the "heyday of autonomy has ended" for reporters, as James Boylan declared in 1982.[21] Proposals for a host of tactics to restore news organization credibility—including ombudspeople, correction columns, the adoption of ethics codes, and the impaneling of citizen forums—became the preoccupation of news executives, who, ever more aware of their newspapers' problems with stagnant circulation and reader alienation, were turning increasingly to market-oriented, customer-pleasing solutions. It is important to note how often the debate over ethical issues, while posed in moral terms, was really a reflection of the business interests of the news organization and the desire of news executives not to risk their credibility with their audience.

After the press's Watergate triumph, it seemed that one incident of ethical lapse after another cascaded down on the profession. In 1977, Laura Foreman, a reporter for the *Philadelphia Inquirer*, was investigated by her own paper and drummed out of the business for taking gifts from a politician-lover and a source, Philadelphia state senator Henry J. "Buddy" Cianfrani, who was later convicted of mail fraud and racketeering. The columnist and ABC News commentator George Will coached Ronald Reagan in a 1980 debate with Jimmy Carter and then did TV commentary afterward without disclosing the connection. R. Foster Winans, a *Wall Street Journal* reporter, was convicted of insider trading in 1985 for passing along information from his stock column for stock trades. The *Newsweek* columnist Joe Klein wrote an anonymous novel about the presidency and then lied about it to protect his publishing interests. The *New*

Yorker journalist Janet Malcolm was sued for doctoring quotes and then defended herself by saying everyone in the press does it. And a number of journalists
at such publications as the *New Republic,* the *Boston Globe,* and the *Cincinnati
Enquirer* were caught fabricating stories or quotes or breaking the law to ob-
tain information. Each time, news organizations wrung their hands, held professional forums on the matter, and adopted tighter ethics codes and conflict-
of-interest rules. But even as journalistic organizations focused ever greater
attention on journalistic integrity, the media business found its standing with
the public ebbing. Polls consistently have shown that the American public has
serious questions about the news industry's contribution to the erosion of public
morals and its willingness to follow the same moral code that it uses to judge
and criticize others.

To try to assess the role of religion in the running of the modern news operation—or even to identify the residue of Judeo-Christian ethics in the activities of today's journalists—can be a tricky task. Many journalists clearly do not
have much use for what is perceived as Christian righteousness and intolerance,
and they do not always follow the dictates of Judeo-Christian morality, even if
they endorse it in the broadest sense. The news organization as a secular island
in a sea of religious sanctimony has a long-established tradition, one that stretches from the days of the "Moral War" against James Gordon Bennett to the attitudes that most journalists hold about today's evangelist-politicians, such as
Jerry Falwell and Pat Robertson. The admiration journalists hold for, and the
amusement they get out of, Ben Hecht's tale of Hildy Johnson's breaking all the
rules in search of her exclusive in the play *Front Page* is matched only by the
satisfaction they feel when the *Charlotte Observer* wins the Pulitzer Prize for
exposing the PTL scandal that led to the imprisonment of the evangelist Jim
Bakker. Most journalists today tell with pride the occasional tale of how they
bent the rules to bring back the story, and most tend to believe that, if on occasion they forget to apply ethical principles to their practices, so-called profess-
ing Christians are even worse.

Journalism, after all, is a practical business, and many journalists have been
willing to pursue the greater good in any way they can—whether it means pro-
tecting the public good or just getting the story. The ends-versus-means debate
is a lively one in most newsrooms, one that takes place on a regular basis. The
standard operating principle at most mainstream news organizations is that
journalists are not supposed to lie or break the law, even if tempted by the opportunity to use less than honest means to pin down information. However,
journalism ethics books are filled with examples of the "gray areas" where the
ethical issues are not settled in the profession—when is it proper to pose as
someone other than a reporter, to use deception and mislead sources, to pay for
information, to exchange information with sources, to use material from anonymous sources, et cetera? In general, most journalists would subscribe to some
variation of Immanuel Kant's categorical imperative (itself a variation of the

Golden Rule) that says we should never engage in moral actions that we do not believe should be binding on everyone. "How can newspapers be for honesty and integrity when they themselves are less than honest in getting the story?" is the way the former *Washington Post* editor Ben Bradlee put it.[22] But Bradlee's own newspaper has been both praised and criticized for its ethically debatable decisions, such as its reporting tactics during Watergate and the printing of the Pentagon papers, which were stolen and then passed along to the *Post*. Like most editors, Bradley reserved the right to make these judgments on a case-by-case basis, and few editors hold up their ethical code as binding precedent that cannot be altered under changing circumstances.

While the public may damn journalists for their hypocrisy and their fixation on the outward forms of morality, one must acknowledge this: the "guts" on which journalists today rely to make moral and ethical decisions, as Scripps liked to put it, can be a powerful internal barometer of right and wrong. With all its shortcomings, journalism is still one of the strongest bastions in a society where moral and ethical frameworks direct and motivate professional activity—even though, unlike law and medicine, it does not have formal oversight organizations with the power to punish transgressors or kick someone out of the profession. In this circumstance, typical journalist professionals, no matter what their religious beliefs, recognize their internal moral regulator as a vital tool in guiding them through the difficult, day-to-day decisions of their business. Within the daily framework of their occupational activities, journalists have been taught to trust their ethical instincts and to recognize the importance of their moral integrity as a centered place that must direct them in their professional decision making. This trust in their professional integrity as a grounded source directing them in their daily activities can be seen as a faith of sorts, particularly for people who tend to rely on their individual natures rather than institutional regulations as the source of moral authority. "My father once told me that in attempting to decide if a given action is right or wrong, you may think you do not know . . . but you know," the former *Time* magazine editor Ray Cave once said. "Follow that kind of guidance . . . and you will never lose faith in yourself as a journalist."[23]

Even with the spread of ethics codes in newsrooms, industry panels examining ethical questions, more ethics courses in university journalism training, and higher standards of professional conduct among journalists, journalism remains an unpredictable business, at least when it comes to the moral and ethical questions that descend on the newsroom on a willy-nilly basis. Journalism is not a licensed profession; it operates with no widely accepted code of professional conduct beyond what news organizations voluntarily adopt or individuals voluntarily subscribe to as members of professional journalist organizations; and precedent—that is, the decision the news organization made yesterday—does not bind journalists when it comes to what they decide today. This aspect of the news business often drives lawyers and others crazy, but, in the broadest sense, it is what gives journalism an enormous range of latitude when it comes to dealing with moral and ethical questions. The First Amendment freedoms granted to the press are the reason why the American media operate with so few restraints, and those freedoms granted the press are still widely cherished (at least, in the press itself). However, one only has to look at the morally sober and civic-minded stands on the typical editorial page to be reminded of how journalists still line up with the framers of the Constitution, some of whom may have had their own doubts about conventional Christian theology but who believed that there could not be a successful democracy if people lost touch with religious values and who looked to the ethics inherent in religious teachings to provide the restraints and the moral purpose to keep the nation's public spirit strong. As Benjamin Franklin once put it, the great mass of people "have need of the motives of religion to restrain them from vice, to support their virtue, and retain them in the practice of it till it becomes habitual."[24] (Or, as he added more pithily, "If Men are so wicked as we now see them with Religion, what would they be without it?")[25]

Many journalists—both optimistic and pessimistic about human nature—could be expected to relate to this utilitarian view of religion, even with their doubts about Christian orthodoxy. The declining nature of public morality has been very much on the mind of both the public and the press in recent years. While some of the blame for the decline has been laid at the door of the media, the journalism community should, in fairness, be credited for continuing to articulate fundamental moral and ethical values on its editorial pages, launching investigations when corruption and inequities are discovered in the public body, and taking important steps in cleaning up the ethical standards of the profession. Although far more secular in orientation than it was in the nineteenth century, the journalism profession has done much to put its own ethical house in order—to such a degree that the ethical values of the typical journalist today would almost certainly impress a nineteenth-century pastor more than a grab-for-the-main-chance journalist of that period. Yet, as will be seen, the confusion surrounding the basis of those ethical values has made it more difficult for the press to assert its role as a moral force and to convince the public that it is a worthy guardian of public morality.

"I Will Show You My Faith by What I Do": A Survey of the Religious Beliefs of Journalists and Journalists' Faith Put into Action

Ralph Cipriano is the prototype for the modern religion reporter, at least in the minds of those who believe the media have become secular in orientation, implicitly anti–church establishment in outlook, and interested in covering religion only when it involves the bizarre, the entertaining, or the shocking. "I hung out with a voodoo group and watched them do a goat sacrifice," Cipriano told the *American Journalism Review* in explaining his editors' desire that he "liven up" the religion beat he covered for the *Philadelphia Inquirer.* "I wrote about a 300-pound former night watchman who was a Baptist preacher and would proselytize with prostitutes, a story about a rabbi who rap sings and a Mormon who spoke Vietnamese to get converts. I didn't want to do stories about anybody sitting around a table talking about theological stuff."[1]

It is difficult to tell which troubles the critics of the media's coverage of religion more: journalism's Enlightenment values of skepticism, rationalism, and empiricism, which has led conservative critics to label journalists the "secular humanists" par excellence, or the commercial press's fixation on controversy, which tends to put religion in the news mostly when it pits science against religion or involves contentiousness, scandal, or the offbeat. In this context, journalists routinely have been portrayed as unchurched social liberals who are indifferent, if not antagonistic, to religion, particularly Christianity.

The conservative press critic Marvin Olasky, for example, has called press coverage of American evangelicals "the result of a materialist world view hostile to Christianity. . . . Most journalists see leftist guerillas, homosexual parades, and anti-Christian textbooks as the good news of our era."[2] Olasky, like many conservative Christians, believes that the press has substituted a humanistic perspective for a God-centered one and that there is little hope for the mainstream media's redemption. "If a person who had not had that experience [of the Christian person] is unwilling to accept the testimony of others, and thus assumes internally-generated psychological change rather than God's grace, he will see Christian fact as imagination, and Christian objectivity as subjectivity," Olasky stated. "In the long run, journalistic differences between Christians and non-Christians are inevitable."[3]

For years, these critics have relied on a 1980 study by S. S. Robert Lichter, Stanley Rothman, and Linda S. Lichter, who surveyed 238 journalists in top media positions and found that 86 percent of them seldom or never attended religious services and that half said they had no religious affiliation.[4] Critics have also accused the media of lacking a basic understanding of religious matters or covering religion only when the subject involves conflict or can be sensationalized. A common critique is that three impulses tend to motivate journalists when covering religious issues: ignorance, indifference, or downright hostility.[5]

However, this picture of journalism as identified with secularism, agnosticism, and cultural division has been questioned by other researchers in more recent years. A 1993 Freedom Forum study, for example, found that 72 percent of the 266 editors surveyed said religion was very important or somewhat important in their lives.[6] A 1992 study by David H. Weaver and G. Cleveland Wilhoit, who found similar results in a nationwide survey of 1,400 journalists, led some observers to wonder whether modern journalists, contrary to their public image, may be more religiously oriented than previously believed.[7] Even Rothman updated his assessment of journalists' irreligiosity in a later study, which indicated that the proportion of major journalists who attended religious services had jumped from 14 percent in 1980 to 30 percent in 1990 and that journalists who reported no religious affiliation had dropped from 50 to 22 percent in that same period.[8]

No matter what their conclusions, none of these studies examined the nature of journalists' religious values in great depth or probed the relationship between journalists' expressed views of their religious beliefs and the ways those beliefs may be translated into their professional activities. In particular, the studies have tended to draw conclusions about journalists' religious orientation based on narrow measures, such as church attendance or church membership, and all have relied on what journalists say about their religious values without probing further into how those values may show up, consciously or unconsciously, in their work.[9] The lack of research in this area has made it easier for journalism's critics to pigeonhole journalists in terms of their religious values and to make generalizations that imply journalists' religious orientation is fairly one-dimensional and can easily be put into such categories as believer or nonbeliever, Christian or agnostic, spiritualist or secularist.

Scholars have concluded that—contrary to the image of religion reporting as something relegated to the "ghetto" of the Saturday religion page—religion coverage has improved in recent years. In 1986, all of the religion editors surveyed indicated that there was more space devoted to religion coverage than there had been ten years earlier, reported Ernest Hynds in a survey of religion editors at large newspapers—if for no other reason than that editors have become convinced that religion is a saleable beat. Stewart M. Hoover, in his book *Religion in the News,* documented what he believed was a resurgence in religion reporting and improved media coverage of religious matters in the waning years of the twentieth century.[10]

This picture is complicated even further if one thinks of journalists—as Mark Silk did and as I have hypothesized throughout this book—as "covertly" religious people.[11] Their seemingly secular professional standards are, this hypothesis goes, rooted strongly, if unconsciously, in the Judeo-Christian heritage of the country. On the surface, journalists may look like Enlightenment-bred rationalists, pragmatic skeptics, and empiricism-loving modernists, but they really are idealists, moral crusaders, and social reformers who at core are motivated by a powerful religious value system.

The dearth of authoritative data about journalists' religious orientation raises a large question, though: how exactly should one describe the religious views of journalists? Should their beliefs be seen only in the context of how much they subscribe to the views of religion identified with the orthodox interpretations that have grown out of the Judeo-Christian tradition? Is it important to examine the personal values of journalists only as a reflection of the religious teachings of the church establishment, or is something more at work? If so, is it possible that journalists' religious values may need to be measured in ways that go beyond the narrow frames of analysis applied to them in the past?

If one looks at the professional exhortations of well-known journalists—some of which have become famous maxims in journalism—one might conclude that the professional values of journalists cannot be fully understood without considering the religious undertones. Take the comments of the nineteenth-century editor James Gordon Bennett, whose sensationalistic tactics as an early proponent of the penny press once provoked members of the New York City religious and civic elite to wage a "Moral War" against his newspaper. Bennett, who once trained in a Catholic seminary, responded to his critics that it was in his newspaper, not in the teachings of the churches, where the "facts" of religion and morals could be found. Neither "true religion nor real Christianity [consists] in believing the dogmas of any church," Bennett wrote. "The Bible is before me. Have I not a right to read that book—to draw out from it religious opinions—and to create a belief and a church of my own?" Or consider the seemingly paradoxical statement of E. W. Scripps: "Old atheist and infidel as I am, my convictions are such, that no teachings of the Christ are repugnant to me, and when he bids us, as he is constantly doing, to be meek, to be merciful and to abstain from judging our fellows, I feel that I cannot help but obey."[12]

So what were Bennett and Scripps saying? Were they contending, as many critics of modern journalism do, that journalists are "atheists and infidels," as Scripps described himself, and a force for irreligion in society? Or were they indicating that journalists, proud and independent-minded people that they are, may actually believe that they, rather than the voices of the religious community, hold to a higher and more sophisticated view of religious principle?

With these questions in mind, my University of Washington colleague Keith Stamm and I undertook a survey of journalists in the United States and Canada to see if we could identify what, if any, links existed between journalists' professional values and their religious heritage. We hypothesized that, given the findings of the Freedom Forum and Weaver and Wilhoit studies, today's journalists would be more religiously oriented than their critics claim and that they would respond positively to the underlying religious values inherent in many journalistic maxims and professional ideals. Considering the harsh comments Bennett, Steffens, and others have made, we also speculated that journalists might reject those same sentiments if they were posed in overtly religious language or doctrinal form. In our study, we paid special attention to the role of the "reform" type of journalist. We thought that since journalism drew much of its professional inspiration from the muckrakers and the Progressive and Populist advocates of reform in the late nineteenth century and early twentieth (who, in turn, were often advocates of the Social Gospel movement and looked to the "prophetic" message of social justice in the Bible for their guidance), we might find similar attitudes still alive in journalism today.

At the same time, we recognized that the complex nature of journalists' professional orientation would make it difficult to describe the religious aspect of journalists' value system. We suspected journalists' religious values could not be easily pinned down or reduced to a single descriptive factor, and we wanted to find a way to present an accurate portrayal of journalists' relationship to the country's religious tradition. This was a key point in our conceptual analysis. It is remarkable how much has been concluded about journalists' religiosity from such scant evidence. Earlier studies have tended to be decidedly one-dimensional, and we recognized how much this has contributed to misleading conclusions about journalists' religious beliefs.

To carry out our project, we mailed a questionnaire probing the connection between journalism and religion to 1,413 daily newspaper journalists in the United States and Canada in the summer of 1998.[13] The mailing included the full roster of the Investigative Reporters and Editors organization (267 journalists) and the total membership (184 journalists) of the Religion Newswriters Association. The remaining journalists were selected from a random sampling of daily newspapers taken from *Editor and Publisher Year Book*. Questionnaires were sent to three journalists (a police reporter, a city editor, and an editorial writer) at the newspapers selected. Since many news organizations base their staff size on journalist-to-circulation ratios, an additional three journalists were sampled for each additional 100,000 in circulation for newspapers above 100,000 circulation as a way to ensure that the staffs of the bigger metro dailies received proportionate representation in the study. For journalists who did not initially respond, a second mailing of the questionnaire and then a reminder card were sent out. In the end, 432 journalists responded to the mailing (a 31 percent response rate).[14]

The journalists we surveyed tended to support our hypothesis that journalists are more motivated by religious values than they may realize, and they demonstrate this in clear although complex ways. We discovered, for example, what other researchers have noted—that journalists more openly embrace religion than their critics would expect. In our questionnaire, journalists were asked a number of basic questions about their religious practices: which faith they were raised in, whether they were currently members of a church or religious organization, how often they attended. A key measure of religious orientation (because it has been used in other studies) was one asking our respondents how important religion/spirituality was in their lives. Consistent with the Freedom Forum and the Weaver and Wilhoit studies, 72 percent of our respondents indicated themselves to be religiously or spiritually oriented, and they reported relatively high levels of church attendance and church membership (see tables 1–3).

The subcategories of the surveyed group deviated very little from this picture of respondents as a religiously oriented group. As has been the case in other studies of journalists covering religion, we found that the great preponderance of religion reporters said that religion was important or very important to them (85 percent), followed by investigative reporters (73 percent) and the other journalists surveyed (67 percent).[15] Journalists at large newspapers were only slightly less willing to say religion or spirituality was important to them than were journalists at smaller newspapers (69 percent compared with 74 percent, respectively), thus challenging the notion that journalists at the large urban newspapers are more secular in orientation than their counterparts in

Table 1. Journalists' Religious Views: Frequency and Percent of Responses to the Statement "Religion or Spirituality Is Important in My Life"

	Not Important	Indifferent	Important/ Very Important	Total Sample
Religion reporters	6 (7%)	7 (8%)	76 (85%)	89 (100%)
Investigative reporters	14 (19%)	6 (8%)	55 (73%)	75 (100%)
Other journalists	37 (15%)	47 (18%)	174 (67%)	258 (100%)
Canadian journalists	5 (18.5%)	5 (18.5%)	17 (63%)	27 (100%)
American journalists	52 (13%)	56 (14%)	289 (73%)	397 (100%)
Large-paper journalists	26 (16%)	23 (15%)	107 (69%)	156 (100%)
Small-paper journalists	31 (12%)	38 (14%)	199 (74%)	268 (100%)
Total sample	57 (14%)	60 (14%)	305 (72%)	422 (100%)

Note: Of 432 questionnaire responses, 422 were usable for the factor analyses. Other responses fit into some subcategories but did not contain enough information to be included in the factor analysis and the total sample. That means there may be more responses in some subcategories than in the total sample. Those who responded "no answer/don't understand" were not included in the table. Newspapers over 100,000 in daily (Monday–Saturday) circulation were considered large papers.

Table 2. Attendance at Church or Religious Organization

	Frequency	Percent
Never	62	15.0
Rarely (a few times a year)	109	26.5
Occasionally (1–2 times a year)	57	13.8
Frequently (once a week)	137	33.3
More than once a week	47	11.4
Totals	412	100.0

Table 3. Membership in Church or Religious Organization

	Frequency	Percent
Yes	250	59.7
No	169	40.3
Totals	419	100.0

smaller communities. Although the number of Canadian respondents was very small, they, too, did not differ much from their American counterparts in endorsing religion or spirituality as important to them (63 percent versus 73 percent, respectively). The strong, across-the-board religious orientation of the journalists surveyed held among the subgroups. It also is interesting to note that investigative reporters were only slightly more religiously oriented than the general group of journalists, thus adding additional credence to Steffens's belief that the reform values of journalism are rooted in religious tradition not just for investigative reporters but for journalists of all stripes.

But we also discovered that to understand the complex manner in which religion is interwoven into journalists' professional value system, we needed to go beyond these findings and look at more than just what journalists report as their religious beliefs and practices. It became apparent from our study that religious values permeated the journalistic value system in powerful ways. Journalists who said religion was important in their lives tended to see it as the underlying basis for their professional values. At the same time, we found that journalists in all categories of religious belief tended to embrace the reform tradition of the profession and to endorse the prophetic warnings against injustice and corruption that can be found in the Bible. Perhaps our most interesting finding was that, while journalists can be differentiated in terms of a wide range of religious beliefs, they responded in highly similar fashion to calls to put traditional Judeo-Christian values into practice in their profession. In responding positively to the religious elements in many of the questions we asked, our respondents largely substantiated our hypothesis that unspoken and unconscious religious impulses tend to motivate members of the journalism profession, including those who think of themselves as nonreligious.

The results of our survey contradict many of the assertions made by those who see journalists as an irreligious lot. But the way journalists reflect their religious values is not always easy to interpret—just as we had hypothesized. To understand the role that religion plays in their value system requires more than a simple examination of what journalists say about their religious beliefs and their church involvement. At the level of their expressed religious values, our respondents displayed an array of mixed and varied beliefs, and few of the journalists could be placed in a "pure" category. Even though we confirmed recent findings that a large percentage of journalists see religion as important to them, our data indicated that this conclusion needed to be probed in more depth, too.

To help us with our in-depth examination of journalists' religious orientation, we included in our questionnaire a series of questions that allowed us to examine not only our respondents' general religious beliefs but which elements of religious teaching they tended to identify with, if any. The survey consisted of two parts: one asked respondents direct questions about their religious views; the second measured their attitudes about religion in a less direct manner by seeking journalists' responses to a series of "moral exhortations" by famous journalists. Among the questions in the first part, one set asked the extent to which the religious beliefs of our respondents were derived from a range of sources: formal teachings of their church, personal experience, and a range of theologies and philosophies (six items). A second set asked about belief in God, ranging from not believing to definite belief (five items). A third set inquired about various sources of ethics and morals: the Bible, other faiths, universal ethics, gut feelings, and the like (ten items). A fourth set asked specifically about their views of Jesus, whether he was divine, human, a wise teacher, and so forth (five items). In a fifth set of questions, respondents were asked for their reactions to a series of well-known biblical statements selected to represent a range of moral and theological values (10 items). Finally, a key measure of religious orientation used in other studies was a question asking our respondents how important religion or spirituality was in their lives. The items in all six sets were based on a five-point scale from "strongly disagree" to "strongly agree" and an option for no answer/don't understand.

Since a large proportion of the population is still Christian in orientation, we directed many of our questions at two main elements of Christian teaching found in many areas of American life. The first—or "Christian"—element drew on that aspect of Christian teaching that focuses on the hope for personal salvation, the faith in Jesus as one's personal savior, and the belief in the tenets of Christian faith presented by the church establishment as a prerequisite to gaining salvation.

The second element of teaching we focused on drew from both the Christian and Jewish tradition and was what we called "compassionate." This strain of thinking—which is strongly represented in both the Hebrew scriptures and the New Testament—puts less emphasis on saving one's own or others' souls

than on ameliorating the social conditions of the world. "Compassionate" journalists could be expected to embrace the elements of the Bible's teachings that
emphasize the importance of putting faith into deeds, the elimination of injustice, and the notion that God's love lives and works within humans in their relationships with one another.

We also recognized that some journalists do not identify with the Jewish or
Christian tradition and may be followers of other religions, and we wanted to
probe their belief systems, too. We speculated that there would be secular journalists who would not identify themselves as religious people and who would
likely indicate that their ethical principles were based in nonreligious values
(such as the laws of the state, personal conscience, and the like).

To help us identify dimensions of journalists' religious belief that we may not
have anticipated and to aid in interpreting the findings from these 37 items, we
decided to employ a factor analysis using principal components extraction followed by varimax rotation for better interpretation of factors. This method was
used by Don Ranly in his 1979 study of fifty-seven religion editors at large daily
newspapers, and it led to his successfully identifying a multidimensional religious value system at work among journalists. Since we speculated that journalists are likely to hold complex views about religious matters, the factor analysis provided a tool to aid in identifying as fully as possible the individual
dimensions making up the belief system of journalists.[16]

Our factor analysis yielded the three anticipated dimensions of journalists'
religious values—the "Christian," the "compassionate," and the "secular"—plus
two others: an "eclectic" dimension, reflecting values stemming from faiths and
philosophies other than Christian theology, and a "diffident" dimension, reflecting a lukewarm and uncertain relationship to religious teaching altogether (see
table 4). (Even though the "eclectic" and the "diffident" dimensions had low
measures of reliability and a small number of factors, we kept the "eclectic"
dimension in our analysis because we wanted to include the journalists who
drew their religious views from faiths other than Judaism and Christianity.)

On the basis of this analysis, it is tempting to focus our discussion, in terms
of religious values, on these four kinds of journalists—"Christian," "compassionate," "secular," and "eclectic." But that would be misleading because these dimensions are not mutually exclusive; they mingle and intertwine. To test for this,
we ran a cross-tabulation to see how they overlapped (see table 5). We discovered that it was not unusual to find journalists who subscribed to both "Christian" and "compassionate" beliefs (14 percent) or to "Christian," "compassionate," and "secular" beliefs (11 percent). In fact, the cross-tabulation revealed that
a majority of journalists scored above the median on two or more dimensions
(69 percent). Where religious values were concerned, there were few "unidimen-
sional" journalists (24 percent). A large number of journalists endorsed three or
more of the dimensions of religious values identified in this analysis (32 percent),
thus demonstrating the complex nature of their religious outlook.

Table 4. Factor Loadings for Dimensions of Journalists' Religious Values

Questionnaire Items	Christian	Compassionate	Secular	Eclectic	Diffident
Definitely believe that God or some ultimate reality exists.	.85				
Believe Jesus was both divine and human.	.83				
"Do not doubt but believe. . . . Blessed are those who have not seen and yet have come to believe."—John 20:27,29	.75				
Don't believe it is possible to know whether God exists.	−.75				
Believe Jesus was human but not divine.	−.70				
Ethics and morals are based upon teachings of Jesus.	.69				
Uncertain, but lean toward not believing in God.	−.67				
Can't know anything about Jesus because his life is shrouded in mythology.	−.67				
Don't believe in God or some ultimate religious reality.	−.65				
"If anyone is in Christ, there is a new creation: everything old has passed away; see, everything has become new!" —2 Corinthians 5:17	.65				
"If any want to become my followers, let them deny themselves and take up their cross daily and follow me." —Luke 9:23	.64				
Religious beliefs derived from the formal beliefs as set forth and interpreted by my church and/or faith tradition.	.64				
Ethics and morals are based upon Ten Commandments.	.61				
Religion or spirituality is important in my life.	.60				
I have no particular religious beliefs.	−.58				
Ethics and morals are based on fear of God's punishment.	.55				
"For the whole of the law is summed up in a single commandment: You shall love your neighbor as yourself." —Galatians 5:14		.77			
"Do not despise the words of the prophets, but test everything." —1 Thessalonians 5:20–21		.74			
"Faith, by itself, if not accompanied by action, is dead. . . . Show me your faith without deeds, and I will show you my faith by what I do."—James 2:17–18		.71			
"What does the Lord require of you but to do justice, and to love kindness, and to walk humbly with your God." —Micah 6:8		.70			

Table 4. Con't.

Questionnaire Items	Christian	Compassionate	Secular	Eclectic	Diffident
"If we love one another, God lives in us [and] love is perfected."—1 John 4:12		.67			
Ethics and morals are based upon universal ethics.			.74		
Ethics and morals are based upon laws of state/nation.			.73		
Ethics and morals are based upon gut feelings.			.65		
Ethics and morals are based upon personal conscience.			.50		
Ethics and morals are based upon a code from other faiths.				.80	
Religious beliefs are derived from a combination of my experiences, interpretations, and concepts taken from a wide range of theologies and philosophies.				.66	
Religious beliefs are derived from the formal beliefs of my church/faith tradition's teachings but with my own interpretation where there is room for it.					.69
Religious beliefs are mainly my own but influenced by my church/faith tradition's teachings.					.68
I am uncertain but lean toward believing in God.					.41
Alpha	.94	.86	.65	.63	.42
Eigenvalue	12.9	4.26	2.84	2.04	1.92
Percent of variance	19.3	6.4	4.2	3.0	2.9

Table 5. Overlap between Four Dimensions of Journalists' Religious Values

Secular/Eclectic	Christian/Compassionate				Totals
	Neither	Christian	Compassionate	Both	
Neither	7.3	4.1	0.8	14.1	26.3
Secular	5.2	3.5	1.4	10.6	20.7
Eclectic	14.1	2.4	6.0	6.5	29.0
Both	9.2	3.3	3.8	7.6	23.9
Totals	35.8	13.3	12.0	38.8	99.9

Note: Percentages do not total 100.0 due to rounding.

As complex as our respondents' stated religious views were, we thought it would be helpful to examine their religious value system in more depth by seeing how they applied their faith in their journalistic activities. To do this, we analyzed the second part of our survey, where we asked our respondents for their reactions to a series of professional exhortations that we thought captured important elements of the journalistic "credo" or professional value system. In selecting the twenty quotations, we examined the biographies and autobiographies of many of the important and recognizable journalists in American history and selected the "calls to moral action," so to speak, or what might be called "applied morality." To better understand the relationship between journalistic and religious values, we chose quotations that contained strong religious themes, albeit expressed in informal language with which journalists are comfortable. In a number of cases, this allowed us to compare the journalists' reactions to the professional maxims with their responses to biblical passages containing similar, if more theologically worded, sentiments.

When we examined the way these journalists applied their religious values in their job—or put their beliefs into action—we came up with equally interesting but complex findings.[17] Our analysis identified four "types" of journalists-in-action: a "faithful" type based on the responses to a number of quotations that emphasized putting Christian faith into action; an "ambivalent" type based on responses to quotes, most notably from the muckrakers, who embraced many of the moral teachings of Jesus while scorning religious orthodoxy and accusing the religious establishment of not living up to the Bible's own teachings; a "reform" type that responded positively to maxims calling for social justice and the rooting out of corruption; and an "independent" journalistic personality that endorsed quotations indicating journalists should operate out of conscience and a value system not necessarily connected to religion or institutional dictates (see table 6).

Again, journalists did not fall easily into just one category when it came to the application of their religious views in their jobs. The largest single group (16 percent) of journalists were those who did not strongly endorse any of the four dimensions (see table 7). "Faithful" values applied to journalism tended not to overlap with "reform" (1.3 percent) or "independent" (2.4 percent) but overlapped somewhat more with "ambivalent" (7.4 percent) and with "ambivalent" plus one or more of the other two factors (27.9 percent). It appears that the transference of religious values to journalism is anything but straightforward for journalists.

To try to gain some additional insight into the relationship between journalists' religious beliefs and their application in journalism, we asked which of the four dimensions of religious beliefs were most closely associated with the four dimensions of journalistic belief put into action. The findings proved to be somewhat predictable in places. "Faithful" journalists in their professional practices tended to endorse "Christian" and "compassionate" (but also "secular")

Table 6. Factor Loadings for Dimensions of Journalists' Religious Values Applied to the Practice of Journalism

Questionnaire Items	Faithful	Ambivalent	Reform	Independent
"The world needs a Jesus more than it needs anything."—Upton Sinclair	.75			
The great mass of people "have the need of the motive of religion to restrain them from vice, to support their virtue, and retain them in the practice of it till it becomes habitual." —Benjamin Franklin	.66			
Human beings are "by primal necessity" transformers and reformers. "Yes, I will say it—Christian social order is not impossible."—Horace Greeley	.61			
"The Book of Nature tells us distinctly that God cares not a rap for us—nor for any living creatures."—Mark Twain	−.58			
"I have never heard Christianity, as Jesus taught it in the New Testament, preached to Christians."—Lincoln Steffens	−.54			
Humans are "the religious animal." A man "is the only animal that loves his neighbor as himself, and cuts his throat if his theology isn't straight."—Mark Twain		.64		
"My quarrel with the churches is a lover's quarrel; I do not want to destroy them, but to put them on a rational basis and especially to drive out the money changers from the front pew."—Upton Sinclair		.58		
"Mystical experiences are as direct perceptions of fact for those who have them as any sensations" are for the rest of us. —William James		.53		
The proper definition of a journalist is someone who "comforts the afflicted [and] afflicts the comfortable." —Finley Peter Dunne			.76	
It is the job of the journalist "to spur the lazy, watch the weak, [and] expose the corrupt." —Drew Pearson			.69	
"My father once told me that in attempting to decide if a given action is right or wrong, you may think you do not know . . . but you know. Follow that kind of guidance . . . and you will never lose faith in yourself as a journalist."—Ray Cave				.64
"The recognition of truth and the clear statement of it are the first duties of an able and honest reporter."—Hal Boyle				.63
The ideal journalist "resists all controls," "observes the law," renders "unto Caesar what is Caesar's" but morally is their own person. Even the boss "can't touch" them. —John Merrill				.55
Alpha	.68	.47	.52	.35
Eigenvalues	2.87	2.49	1.40	1.24
Percent of variance	14.4	12.4	7.2	6.2

Table 7. Overlap between Four Dimensions of Religious Values as Applied
to Journalism

	Faithful/Ambivalent				
Reformist/Independent	Neither	Ambivalent	Faithful	Both	Totals
Neither	16.1	8.2	2.9	7.4	34.6
Reformist	6.1	7.6	1.3	5.3	20.3
Independent	8.2	5.3	2.4	7.1	23.0
Both	3.9	7.6	2.6	8.2	22.3
Totals ($n = 380$)	34.3	28.7	9.2	28.0	100.2

Note: Percentages do not total 100.0 due to rounding.

beliefs; "ambivalent" practitioners tended to endorse "compassionate" and
"eclectic" beliefs; "independent" journalists tended to embrace "compassionate" and "secular" beliefs (see table 8). Note, however, that all four groupings
by application of faith endorsed the "compassionate" beliefs, thus indicating that
journalists of all religious views tend to embrace the social justice elements of
religious teachings.

At this point, we thought it would be productive to simplify our analysis to
see if we could come up with a clearer picture of the way that our respondents'
religious views and journalistic values worked together in forging their professional outlook. Although ten different groups of journalists could be distinguished based on different measurements of religious faith (such as church attendance, importance placed on religion, and religious philosophy), a detailed
breakdown of the ten categories led to a simpler and more efficient three-cate-
gory classification.[18] Those few journalists (about 5 percent of the sample) with
a purely "secular" orientation reported the lowest church attendance, attached
the least importance to religion, and expressed more liberal religious and political philosophies (see table 9). A second group (42 percent of the sample) was
made up of various combinations of "secular," "compassionate," and "eclectic" orientation distinguished by the absence of a "Christian" orientation. These
journalists attached greater importance to religion but were otherwise similar
to those with a purely "secular" orientation. The third group (52 percent of the
sample) was distinguished by a "Christian" orientation accompanied by one or

Table 8. Correlations between Religious Values and Religion Applied
to Journalism

	Religious Values			
Application	Christian	Compassionate	Secular	Eclectic
Faithful	.45**	.37**	.11*	−.08
Reformist	.05	.16**	.02	.12*
Ambivalent	−.08	.17**	.09	.31**
Independent	−.04	.11*	.12*	.06

Note: * = $p > .01$; ** = $p > .001$

9.* Some Defining Characteristics of Three Broad Classes of Religious Orientation

Characteristic	Religious Orientation			F Test (df = 2)
	Secular (*n* = 19)	Secular/Compassionate/ Eclectic (*n* = 155)	Christian (*n* = 192)	
Church attendance	2.26[a]	2.34[a]	3.80[b]	F = 92.9, $p < .001$
Importance of religion	2.79[a]	3.53[b]	4.63[c]	F = 59.7, $p < .001$
Religious philosophy	4.00[b]	3.85[b]	2.74[a]	F = 49.9, $p < .001$
Political philosophy	3.47[ab]	3.66[a]	3.03[b]	F = 18.3, $p < .001$

Note: For religious and political philosophy, higher values are more liberal, lower values more conservative. Means with single superscripts are significantly different from means with different single superscripts by Scheffes's test at $p < .05$ (i.e., differences would occur by chance fewer than 5 times in 100). Means with double superscripts are not significantly different from means with either single superscript.

more of the other orientations. This majority group reported the highest church attendance, attached the most importance to religion, and had more conservative religious and political philosophies than did the other two groups.

A further refinement of our analysis yielded an important finding: while these groups were quite distinctive in their religious views, they were not much different in their feelings about the way religious values should be applied to the practice of journalism (see table 10). All three groups—despite their different religious orientations—responded in similar fashion to three of the four categories ("faithful," "reform," and "independent") in which we grouped our journalistic maxims (or journalistic versions of spiritual calls to action). The only difference was the tendency of the middle group (those with a mixture of "secular," "compassionate," and "eclectic" orientations) to respond more positively to the quotations that reflected an "ambivalent" attitude toward Christian teaching. It did not make much difference whether journalists were "secular," "Christian," or some middle combination when it came to putting religious values into action in their practice of journalism. In other words, our

Table 10. Applications of Religion to Journalism by Three Broad Classes of Religious Orientation

Application	Religious Orientation			F Test (df = 2)
	Secular (*n* = 19)	Secular/Compassionate/ Eclectic (*n* = 155)	Christian (*n* = 192)	
Faithful	3.00	2.97	3.02	F = 0.43, n.s.
Ambivalent	3.54[a]	3.74[b]	3.49[a]	F = 4.32, $p < .01$
Reformist	3.47	3.54	3.54	F = 0.05, n.s.
Independent	4.02	4.00	4.03	F = 0.12, n.s.

Note: For the "ambivalent" application, means with single superscripts are significantly different from means with different single superscripts by Scheffes's test at $p < .05$ (i.e., differences would occur by chance fewer than 5 times in 100).

respondents—no matter what they said they believed when it came to religion—tended to respond in the same fashion to the calls to put faith into action uttered by famous journalists.

We thought it would be instructive to further compare these findings with what journalists openly acknowledged as their views about the issue of mixing religion with their journalistic practice. To do this, we turned to another section of our survey where we had selected a series of items from current journalistic discussion representing a wide range of views about whether religious values should be mixed with journalism in the news-reporting process.[19] In our analysis of these questions, the journalistic responses fell into three groups: those who were comfortable intermingling journalistic and religious values, those who wanted to keep them separate, and those who felt that journalists should simply be knowledgeable about religion to promote public discourse (see table 11). Here, our results were somewhat more predictable and easier to interpret: journalists with stronger religious views were more comfortable with the notion of intertwining journalistic values with religious values, while more secular journalists more strongly endorsed keeping the two separate (see table 12).

At the same time, our findings pointed to a major difference between our respondents' uniformly positive responses to the religious elements implicit in the journalistic maxims and the mixed nature of their explicit views about the role of religion in the practice of journalism. As noted earlier, journalists of all religious views responded positively to calls for putting belief into action when these calls were couched in exhortatory language familiar to journalists. But they fell into more predictable camps of religious orientation in endorsing or reject-

Table 11. Factor Loadings for Treatment of Religion in News Coverage

Questionnaire Items	Together	Keep Separate	Knowledgeable
Morals should be based on religious values.	.82		
Christian values should underpin journalism.	.80		
Nonbelievers can do a good job of covering religion.	−.61		
Journalistic values should draw on all great religions.	.49		
Journalists should be suspicious of those who impose values on others.		.68	
Separation of journalism and religion should be as important as separation of church and state.		.66	
Reporters with strong religious beliefs should not be assigned the religion beat.		.65	
Journalists should have good knowledge of religion.			.75
Journalists bear responsibility for public discourse on the role of religion in society.			.72
Alpha	.66	.49	.44
Eigenvalues	2.36	1.37	1.22
Percent of variance	23.6	13.7	12.2

Table 12. Correlations between Religious Values and Treatment
of Religion in News Coverage

| | Religious Values | | | |
Treatment	Christian	Compassionate	Secular	Eclectic
Together	.06	.24**	.08	.10
Keep separate	−.36**	−.18	.14**	.18**
Knowledgeable	.18**	.14**	−.11*	−.04

Note: $* = p > .01$; $** = p > .001$

ing the idea of mixing religion with the practice of journalism when asked about it directly (see table 13).

It also should be noted that investigative reporters—whom we speculated would be most likely to carry on the "prophetic" reform values of the muck-rakers—proved to be more "reform" oriented than their general journalistic colleagues were. At the same time, religion reporters almost equaled the investigative reporters in the "reform" orientation, and the religion reporters proved to be more "Christian" and "compassionate," as other research indicated they might be expected to be (see table 14). However, the variations among the subgroups were not enough to conclude that there are major differences in religious outlook among different types of journalists.

It is perhaps no longer surprising to find—as we did—that journalists are not anything close to the image of "heretics" and religious "debunkers" that critics have described. In confirming the findings of earlier research, we can add our results to those that have found journalists to be largely religiously oriented people. In other respects, our study also drew conclusions that can be seen as somewhat predictable. Journalists who were more secular in orientation said they wanted to keep religion separate from news coverage and professional ethics; those who were more religiously inclined were more comfortable intertwining them. Those journalists who were more "Christian" in their beliefs tended

Table 13. Preferred Journalistic Treatment of Religion by Three Broad Classes of Religious Orientation

| | Religious Orientation | | | |
Treatment	Secular ($n = 19$)	Secular/Compassionate/Eclectic ($n = 155$)	Christian ($n = 192$)	F Test (df = 2)
Together	2.75[a]	2.73[a]	3.31[b]	$F = 29.9, p < .001$
Keep separate	3.30[b]	2.97[b]	2.45[a]	$F = 15.8, p < .001$
Knowledgeable	3.74[ab]	3.60[a]	3.95[b]	$F = 3.16, p < .04$

Note: For each treatment, means with single superscripts are significantly different from means with different single superscripts by Scheffes's test at $p < .05$ (i.e., differences would occur by chance fewer than 5 times in 100). Means with double superscripts are not significantly different from means with either single superscript.

Table 14. Religious Values by Type of Journalists

	Type of Journalists			
	Religion ($n = 89$)	Investigative ($n = 74$)	All Others ($n = 245$)	F Test
Religious values				
Christian	4.04[b]	3.45[a]	3.63[a]	$F (2, 419) = 8.4, p < .001$
Compassionate	4.57[b]	4.26[a]	4.28[a]	$F (2, 403) = 5.7, p < .004$
Secular	3.45	3.62	3.58	$F (2, 421) = 2.0$, n.s.
Eclectic	2.78	2.86	2.77	$F (2, 386) = 0.2$, n.s.
Religious values applied to the practice of journalism				
Faithful	2.89	2.93	3.00	$F (2, 404) = 1.3$, n.s.
Reformist	3.56[a]	3.76[a]	3.38[b]	$F (2, 417) = 5.2, p < .006$
Ambivalent	3.59	3.63	3.54	$F (2, 396) = 0.4$, n.s.
Independent	3.89	4.07	4.01	$F (2, 411) = 1.6$, n.s.

Note: For selected religious values, means with single superscripts are significantly different from means with different single superscripts by Scheffes's test at $p < .05$ (i.e., differences would occur by chance fewer than 5 times in 100).

to define themselves as more politically and philosophically conservative and to see religion as more important in their lives.

But perhaps the most important finding in our study is the way the journalists we surveyed reflected their religious values and the intricate way those values were interwoven with their professional outlook. It is significant that while journalists could be distinguished in terms of their religious beliefs and practice, they were not that much different when it came to supporting the notion of putting belief into action in their journalistic activities. It is interesting, for example, that journalists we defined as "secular," "Christian," and a combination ("secular," "compassionate," "eclectic") responded in like fashion to the "reform" category of quotes (the role of the journalist is to "comfort the afflicted [and] afflict the comfortable"), the "independent" category (the ideal journalist "resists all controls" and "morally is their own person"), and the "faithful" category ("Christian social order is not impossible"). Journalists of all religious orientations, it seems, respond similarly to calls to put belief into action, as long as these calls are framed in a way that makes them seem to be a part of the journalistic, rather than the religious, tradition.

It also is noteworthy that journalists—again regardless of religious orientation—responded most positively to the maxims we labeled "reform" and "independent" (as well as "ambivalent") and less positively to the "faithful" maxims. It appears that righting injustice and taking social action that are so strongly articulated in the prophetic passages of the Bible, as well as in the utterances of the muckrakers and the journalist-reformers we quoted, still resonate with today's journalists, as do the passages urging journalists to follow their conscience and to remain true to an independent vision of their professional duty. At the same time, journalists of all religious orientations—even

"Christian" ones—were somewhat more wary of calls to action that sounded too explicitly religious (or Christian) in tone. One can expect journalists—even religiously oriented ones—to act on their religious views in ways that do not compromise their professional integrity.

One might go so far as to say that journalists share the same belief in the social justice values of the Bible and the importance of putting belief into practice, regardless of their own personal religiosity. Our respondents, it is true, were somewhat more "reform" oriented than "faithful" in practice, which makes perfect sense. It is not their business to tell others how to transform the world, they seemed to be saying; but the application of moral values to community life (i.e., applying fundamental moral teachings found in the Judeo-Christian tradition by correcting injustice and social inequity) is their business. The notion of journalism as defined as moral activism appears to be embraced by journalists of all stripes, regardless of whether they identify themselves as people of faith.

It also makes sense that most journalists, regardless of religious orientation, would see the value of exercising independent judgment. In our survey, journalists across the religious spectrum responded most enthusiastically to the maxims we labeled as "independent." Our respondents also generally indicated high levels of openness and tolerance toward religious matters (although less so among those of "Christian" views). One cannot discount the impact that the practice of journalism—with its emphasis on conscience and independent thinking in one's professional activity and balance and fairness in news coverage—has on the religious expression of members of the profession.

Finally, our analysis suggests a reexamination of the claim that journalists are "hostile" toward religion because there is much evidence that they have great sympathy for religious values.[20] But we must be careful not to mistake this sympathy for an overt embrace of religion in their work or explicit support for the expression of religious viewpoints in their professional activities. The high levels of support for the "ambivalent" maxims (the ones where journalistic figures showed sympathy for core Judeo-Christian calls for justice and self-sacrifice but not necessarily orthodox theology) indicate that many journalists are uncomfortable with evangelizing or credal confessions.

The results of our survey reflect the dynamic and complex history of the relationship between media and religion. This shows up in the multifaceted nature of modern journalists' religious views and the forceful ways that journalists advocate putting them into practice. Yet it is important to recognize that today's journalists may reflect a strong religious orientation in their professional value system while not universally acknowledging their religiosity or even liking the idea that religious ideas might be operating in their work life. Clearly, religious currents—both visible and less visible—run through the moral value system of journalists. But one should never make the mistake of not recognizing the complicated manner in which religion comingles with professional principles in the day-to-day operations of modern journalism.

Religion, Morality, and Professional Values: A Study of the Ethical Sources of Today's Journalists

In recent years, journalists have appeared somewhat at a loss when faced with ethical conundrums and perplexing moral problems, particularly when they recognize that the public does not necessarily view journalists, as they often view themselves, as guardians of public morality. This can be seen in the frustration many members of the media—especially those in the Beltway culture of Washington, D.C.—experienced with the political scandals that obsessed the nation's capital after the election of President Bill Clinton in 1992. Washington journalists played a key role, either as the original investigators or as a pipeline for partisan accusations, in such controversies surrounding Clinton and his wife, Hillary, as the "Whitewater" scandal involving the Clintons' land transactions in Arkansas; the "Travelgate" scandal that erupted after Clinton dismissed a number of longtime staffers in the office handling White House travel; the Paula Jones and Monica Lewinsky affairs, where Clinton was accused of lying under oath and sexual misconduct; and the investigations of allegations that Clinton misused his office for fund-raising purposes.

Throughout much of Clinton's term, journalists scratched their heads over polls that showed the public did not necessarily share journalists' outrage over the conduct of a president who was widely viewed as morally suspect and an ethical hairsplitter. But what journalists did not appear to recognize, I believe, is that they have become widely perceived to be on the side of a ritualistic, rule-bound morality that has more to do with the Washington, D.C., outlook on the world than with morals or ethics. In the public's mind, journalists' intense response to every peccadillo and misstep in public conduct appeared to be a demonstration of something very much different from high-minded civic virtue. The public seemed to feel, at some visceral level, that when everything is a scandal, then, in the broadest moral sense, nothing is a scandal. The propensity of the press—as well as the increasingly partisan groups that orchestrate the latest scandal through congressional hearings, special prosecutor investigations, and headline-making leaks to the press—to tack the term *gate* onto almost any controversy may demonstrate a dubious moral outlook on public life rather than a lofty one.

Some observers of public life in the United States see this situation as part of the culture of "civil religion" that has come to dominate the discourse of the country's political elites—as well as the press corps that covers them. According to this theory, journalists easily deal with religious morality and religious moral judgments as long as these judgments reflect some amorphously perceived public viewpoint about proper moral behavior, not journalists' own religious or moral values.[1] In this scenario, journalists—convinced that there is a deep religious righteousness among the citizenry—were waiting for the public to rise up to punish Clinton for behavior that journalistic insiders know is commonplace among the political high and mighty. This led to the anomalous situation where a jaded and irreverent press corps came to believe that Judeo-Christian moral standards should be applied to a president who wore his religious beliefs on his political sleeve, while the public, its theology imprecise and its interests more down-to-earth, never really took Clinton's religious pose seriously and judged Clinton on more practical grounds (such as his presiding over a good economy).

As interesting as this analysis is, I believe something more is at work. Journalists are influenced, as our research has shown, by the remnants of Judeo-Christian ethical values in a now highly secularized professional culture, but the confusion over their application of moral standards shows how little they often understand the source of their ethical instincts. It is easy for journalists—as well as the news organizations for which they work—to treat ethics as detached from religiosity, and many a-religious journalists would argue that one can follow a personal ethical code without holding any particular religious beliefs. Anthropologists, philosophers, and historians have debated which came first—religion or morality—and many see ethics as an inherent human impulse drawn from tribal codes in existence long before the evolution of advanced theological systems that assimilated ageless moral precepts into their belief structures. In this view, people act ethically toward one another because it is the only way to ensure the perpetuation of a civilized social order, and it is in each person's self-interest to do so. Walter Lippmann argued much the same thing when he wrote that "for the modern population the old rules are becoming progressively unsuitable" and that people today must piece together a moral code from "what the sages have prophesied as high religion, what psychologists delineate as matured personality, and the disinterestedness which [modern society] requires for practical fulfilment." The modern person, Lippmann said, cannot "permit the old symbols of faith and the old formulation of right and wrong to prejudice his insight. Insofar as they contain wisdom . . . he will return to them. But he cannot return to them with honesty and sincerity until he has himself gone and drunk deeply at the sources of experience from which they originated."[2]

Whether or not they subscribe to Lippmann's view, many journalistic organizations today operate quite comfortably with the idea that professional codes of conduct and secularized institutional standards can do a more than adequate job of enforcing ethical standards and that religion—while it may have once served a purpose in ensuring a civilized society—can now be treated as little more than a nominal factor in maintaining decency and proper moral conduct.[3] Yet, precisely because it has become commonplace to see ethics as disconnected from religion, I thought it was important, as part of my examination of the data from our nationwide survey of journalists' religious beliefs, to focus specifically on the source of journalists' ethics and its connection to their religious outlook.

As is the case in other places in the book, my hypothesis is influenced by my view that the loss of the sense of a conscious connection with the religious tradition in the media profession only confuses matters when ethical decisions come to the forefront. As with complex political campaign disclosure laws, modern journalistic organizations have promulgated ethics codes and improved the "appearance of morality" in conducting their professional duties. But if a larger moral spirit proves to be missing in the profession, as the public appears to believe is the case, then no amount of regulation and rule making will, in the end, serve as a substitute.

In looking at the dilemma facing journalists worried about their standing with the public, it is tempting once again to draw a religious parallel. Jesus reserved some of his harshest rebukes for the Pharisees, the Jewish holy men who held themselves up as morally righteous by following the letter, as opposed, in Jesus' view, to the spirit of the Jewish law. Journalistic righteousness can often look dangerously like the rule-bound sanctimony of the Pharisees, particularly when it draws on ambiguous and legalistic standards for regulating ethical standards. Journalists can be a proud lot, puffed up with fame, high salaries, and even higher opinions of themselves (more journalists have been ruined by self-righteousness than by drink, a wag once said), and their willingness to condemn the misdeeds of others can appear downright gleeful at times. Particularly when journalists judge human conduct in ways that make them look holier-than-thou and do it without acknowledging their own "sin," if one can borrow from the concepts of Christian theology, they can appear to be complicit in the morally dubious behavior they so willingly criticize in others.

Despite this, there is good reason to be suspicious of the arguments of those who would portray journalists as moral relativists who have abandoned traditional religious values for a humanistic, secular outlook that applies shifting modern standards of moral behavior on a case-by-case basis. Even though elements of the media are rightly castigated for their sensationalism, commercialism, and insensitivity to the feelings of the targets of their coverage, most mainstream media organizations adhere to a highly principled value system in their editorial policies, their professional codes of conduct, and their expectations for the conduct of those in the community whose activities they monitor.[4] Journalists and journalistic organizations unquestionably can be exploitative, hypocritical, and crassly acquisitive in the pursuit of profits and stories. But a close examination, I contend, will show that the bedrock values of the business are drawn from a moral and ethical code that is anything but hostile to Judeo-Christian morality.

What I am hypothesizing here—and what we set out to test as part of our nationwide survey of journalists—is that the basic moral and ethical admonitions found in the Judeo-Christian tradition still hold their authority, even among the most irreverent and contrarian of American journalists. I speculated at the outset of our research that, stripped to their core, the governing moral principles of the journalism profession in United States can be found in elemental form in the Bible: the Ten Commandments; the Sermon on the Mount (which contains Jesus' reinterpretation and deepened points of emphasis regarding the Ten Commandments); and important biblical passages that reflect generalized ethical and moral sentiments subscribed to beyond Jewish and Christian circles ("For the whole law is summed up in a single commandment: You shall love your neighbor as yourself"; "Faith, by itself, if not accompanied by action, is dead"; "What does the Lord require of you but to do justice, and to love kindness, and to walk humbly with your God"). However, I also postulated that this commitment may be less than self-evident to those outside of journalism (and even, I should add, to many inside the profession).

I recognize that this may not seem like startling stuff. Professional and ethical standards in a wide range of professions, as well as the underpinnings of our modern legal system, are rooted in values that grew out of fundamental religious notions. The core ethical principles of the Judeo-Christian tradition are shared with others of the world's major religions (Islam, Buddhism, Hinduism, Confucianism) and appear to reflect an innate human sense of morality and community that crosses religious and cultural lines.[5] But it also is true that the Bible's strong emphasis on social equity, humane treatment of the downtrodden, and the threat of bringing down God's wrath on those in power who do not treat the powerless with justice and mercy is distinctive in its teachings. American journalists, as our research has already shown, show great sympathy for these moral teachings. I thought it would be interesting—if not ironic—to find that journalists, with their reputation in certain quarters of being cynical, callous, and indifferent to moral convention, draw their ethical inspiration from a religious tradition that, it is believed by some, they reject.

I also realize that my hypothesis is largely a refinement of the one I used in the previous chapter—although focused specifically on the question of journalistic morals and ethics. In dividing questions of journalists' religious beliefs and their moral and ethical outlook, I hoped to be able to sharpen my examination

152   FROM YAHWEH TO YAHOO!

of the contention—made both inside and outside journalism—that modern, secular society has more than adequately absorbed the ethical role of religion and that one can be a moral person without maintaining any connection to religious systems or beliefs. In probing my hypothesis, I especially wanted to look closely at the ethical values of those journalists who did not identify religion as important to them or who took a largely nonbelieving stance toward many items in the questionnaire. In similar fashion to my hypothesis in the previous chapter, I speculated that this group of journalists would generally endorse fundamental Judeo-Christian ethical values, even if they did not acknowledge themselves to be religious people, as long as those sentiments were not posed in overtly religious form or language. But I also expected to find that—given their ambivalence about religious matters—the relationship between journalists' ethical values and their religious beliefs would be less than completely transparent, just as the earlier examination of journalists' religious beliefs showed them to be anything but simplistic or one-dimensional, and would contain unconscious connections that might not always be readily apparent to today's journalists, their critics, or the public.

The focus of the analysis of journalists' ethical views was centered on the questions in the survey that asked journalists to indicate their level of agreement with the ideals expressed in the twenty quotations from important journalistic figures, as well as the ten biblical passages.[6] A number of the journalistic quotations were chosen because they explicitly or implicitly reflected moral and ethical values associated with Judeo-Christian teachings, but they were couched in a professional idiom familiar to journalists. The biblical passages, in turn, were selected to reflect commonly held sentiments to which journalists might be expected to subscribe ("Do not despise the words of the prophets, but test everything") as well as more orthodox beliefs that could be expected to garner less universal agreement ("If anyone is in Christ, there is a new creation . . . see, everything has become new!"). Some of the journalistic and biblical passages were picked because they contained similar moral and ethical sentiments, even though the journalistic maxims (The proper definition of a journalist is someone who "comforts the afflicted" and "afflicts the comfortable") were expressed in language quite different from the biblical version (The Lord said, "I will bind up the injured and I will strengthen the weak, but the fat and the strong I will destroy. I will feed them with justice."). This provided an opportunity to test whether journalistic responses to fundamental moral statements and ethical principles varied depending on whether those statements were couched in traditional religious language or in expressions that have grown out of journalistic tradition.

The survey found—similar to the results in the last chapter—that journalists, no matter what their religious orientation, responded positively to the religious principles embedded in key precepts of their profession as expressed by important historical journalistic personalities. On a number of measures, journalists of varying religious orientations demonstrated themselves to be uniformly supportive of these core ethical values as long as they were articulated in ways that sounded journalistic rather than religious in nature; at the same time, journalists who identified themselves as less religiously oriented responded much less positively than their more religiously oriented colleagues when these same values were expressed in an orthodox or clearly theological manner. Once again, a gap could be seen between what journalists said was the basis of their moral and ethical outlook and what could be discerned from an analysis of their responses to the journalistic and biblical quotations. However, focusing more closely on the moral and ethical side of the religious tradition revealed some interesting insights about the transformation of ethical values from a religious to a secular context in the journalistic setting, as well as the tendency of journalists to identify themselves as more secular in ethical orientation than other indicators may signal.

When asked directly about the basis of their ethical values, the journalists surveyed sounded largely like the secular, individualistic lot that they are often portrayed to be. Journalists by the highest proportions said their ethics were based on such factors as "personal conscience," the "Golden Rule," "universal ethics," the "laws of state/nation," and "gut feelings" (see table 15). None of these categories is explicitly linked with any religious tradition (including the Golden Rule that, notwithstanding the common understanding, is not biblically based). Such religious sources as the "ethical teachings of Jesus," the "Ten Commandments," "codes from other faiths," "fear of God's punishment," and "eye-for-an-eye, tooth-for-a-tooth" were cited by fewer respondents as the source of their ethi-

Table 15. Source of Journalists' Ethical/Moral Values

Source	Not at All/Slight	Some	A Good/Great Deal
Personal conscience	6 (2%)	40 (9%)	379 (89%)
The Golden Rule (Do unto others as you would have them do unto you)	16 (4%)	40 (9%)	366 (86%)
Universal ethics	39 (10%)	74 (19%)	281 (71%)
Laws of state/nation	42 (10%)	90 (22%)	279 (68%)
Gut feelings	51 (12%)	100 (24%)	265 (64%)
Ethical teachings of Jesus (e.g., Sermon on the Mount, Parables)	75 (18%)	82 (20%)	263 (63%)
Ten Commandments	79 (18%)	104 (25%)	240 (56%)
Code from other faiths (Buddhism, Islam, Hinduism, Confucianism, etc).	222 (54%)	122 (30%)	65 (16%)
Fear of God's punishment	281 (72%)	73 (19%)	37 (10%)
Code of eye-for-an-eye, tooth-for-a-tooth	310 (74%)	82 (20%)	24 (6%)

Note: Percentages may not total 100.0 due to rounding.

cal values, although the ethical teachings of Jesus and the Ten Commandments ranked high on the list, particularly among those who gave them "a great deal" of emphasis. Of the ten categories, the only ones that did not receive strong support from a majority of our respondents were "codes from other faiths," "fear of God's punishment," and "eye-for-an-eye, tooth-for-a-tooth." Since our respondents ranked so many of the categories as important to their ethical philosophy, it is clear that many see the basis of their ethics as coming from multiple origins, including ones rooted in both secular and religious sources.

As interesting as these findings were, it was important to examine the sources of journalists' ethics beyond just what they identified them to be. If one hypothesizes that journalists draw on an ethical value system that is rooted in religious tradition but has been transformed into something less explicitly religious in form, it is useful to see whether those connections to religious values can be identified and whether they play a role in journalists' ethical decision making, even if journalists may not always be aware of it.

To test for this, we undertook a detailed examination of the way our respondents indicated their level of agreement with the ethical ideals expressed in the biblical passages and the quotations from important journalistic figures. The key question chosen to measure respondents' religious orientation was one asking them how important religion was in their life. Mean values were calculated, and the response to this question was then measured against the responses to the twenty journalistic quotations and the ten biblical passages.[7] The goal was to determine if journalists' religious beliefs made any difference in the way they responded to the ethical and moral values expressed in the journalistic maxims and the biblical quotations. Particular attention was paid to journalistic quotations that contained strong religious sentiments or moral implications but were phrased in ways that would not be off-putting to journalists who did not identify themselves as religiously oriented.

On six of the twenty journalistic quotations, the journalists surveyed responded in remarkably similar fashion, whether they identified themselves as religious people or not. With these six quotations, there were no significant statistical differences in responses between journalists who identified religion or spirituality as important in their lives and those who did not. These six quotations included what Lincoln Steffens might have called prophetic admonitions, which he saw as central to the reform tradition in journalism (see table 16). The most prominent is the Finley Peter Dunne quote (The proper definition of a journalist is someone who "comforts the afflicted" and "afflicts the comfortable")— probably the clearest translation of the prophetic mission into journalistic terms familiar to reporters and editors—as well as a Drew Pearson quote (The job of the journalist is to "spur the lazy, watch the weak, [and] expose the corrupt"). In addition, note the uniformly high level of support for Sinclair's notion that the church establishment needs to be "reformed" of its money orientation, including among religiously oriented journalists.[8]

Table 16. Quotes to Which Journalists Responded Similarly Regardless of Religious Orientation

	Religious Orientation			F Tests
	Low	Moderate	High	
The proper journalist is someone who "comforts the afflicted [and] afflicts the comfortable." —Finley Peter Dunne	3.32 ($n = 114$)	3.35 ($n = 105$)	3.43 ($n = 198$)	$F (2, 414) = 0.35$, n.s.
The job of the journalist is to "spur the lazy, watch the weak, [and] expose the corrupt." —Drew Pearson	3.63 ($n = 113$)	3.50 ($n = 103$)	3.70 ($n = 196$)	$F (2, 409) = 1.10$, n.s.
My father once told me in deciding whether you are right, "you may think you do not know . . . but you know. Follow that kind of guidance and you will never lose faith in yourself as a journalist." —Ray Cave	3.64 ($n = 109$)	3.54 ($n = 94$)	3.64 ($n = 187$)	$F (2, 387) = 0.29$, n.s.
The ideal journalist "resists all controls," "observes the law," renders "unto Caesar what is Caesar's" but morally is their own person. Even their boss "can't touch" them.—John Merrill	3.83 ($n = 113$)	3.61 ($n = 93$)	3.74 ($n = 182$)	$F (2, 385) = 0.91$, n.s.
"I still recommend people to re-read the New Testament as I read it, without reverence, with feet up on a desk and a pipe in the mouth, as news. It is news." —Lincoln Steffens	3.42 ($n = 104$)	3.40 ($n = 97$)	3.55 ($n = 189$)	$F (2, 387) = 0.73$, n.s.
"My quarrel with the churches is a lover's quarrel; I do not want to destroy them, but to put them on a rational basis and especially to drive out the money changers from the front pew." —Upton Sinclair	3.63 ($n = 102$)	3.73 ($n = 95$)	3.68 ($n = 187$)	$F (2, 381) = 0.21$, n.s.

Note also how strongly our respondents—regardless of religious orienta-tion—responded to the quotations calling for an independent, even a "gut lev-el" approach to ethical decision making (the Cave and the Merrill quotes). It is important to recognize that this ethical independent-mindedness was shared by the religiously oriented respondents, which indicates that even religious jour-nalists prize the freedom to make moral decisions above any obligation simply to follow religious dictates. One may believe in the fundamental moral precepts of the Judeo-Christian tradition, as many of our respondents indicated they did, but the process for arriving at an ethical decision is still apparently seen by jour-nalists as something that should be settled in one's own conscience.

There was a second group of journalistic quotations—fourteen in all—in which the respondents' religious orientation appeared to play a role in their responses to ethical values. For the most part, these quotations triggered signifi-cantly different responses from journalists, depending on their religious orien-tation. Six of the quotes largely drew higher agreement from journalists who identified religion as important to them (see table 17). Note that a number of these quotations, even though uttered by journalists, included some explicit endorsement of religious theology, belief, or values. It is also worth pointing out the uniformly strong support for the quotes endorsing truth-seeking as part of the journalistic mission (the Boyle quote and the second Franklin quote) and how religiously oriented journalists were more inclined to view religion as an ethical restraint on misbehavior, while less religious journalists were less likely to do so (the first Franklin quote), thus indicating the degree to which many journalists have grown comfortable with the idea of secular values serving as an adequate check on misconduct.

Eight other quotes mostly received responses in the opposite fashion—that is, the less journalists identified themselves as religious in nature, the more they agreed with the sentiments expressed in table 18. Again, note that most of these passages contain expressions that could be considered irreverent, even irreli-gious, and certainly challenge traditional religious views, although there are interesting variations in support among them (including relatively high levels of support for Twain's jaundiced view of human beings as prone to religious righteousness and hypocrisy and very low levels of support for the outright endorsement of pragmatics over ethics by the Florida journalism student).

There were no mixed results when it came to the biblical passages. By the strongest of measurements, journalists with a positive orientation toward reli-gion were in significantly greater agreement with all ten biblical passages (see table 19). This finding is hardly surprising, since journalists with a favorable attitude toward religion (particularly Christianity) could be expected to respond most enthusiastically to key biblical statements.

However, an interesting pattern emerged in the responses to the biblical pas-sages. Unlike religiously oriented journalists, journalists who were not religiously inclined tended to let their reaction to biblical language color their responses

Table 17. Quotes to Which Journalists Responded Differently Depending on Religious Orientation

	Religious Orientation			F Tests
	Low	Moderate	High	
Human beings are "by primal necessity" transformers and reformers. "Yes, I will say it—Christian social order is not impossible."—Horace Greeley	2.80^a ($n = 99$)	3.00^a ($n = 92$)	3.41^b ($n = 186$)	$F (2, 374) = 12.2, p < .05$
"The world needs a Jesus more than anything,"—Upton Sinclair	2.92^a ($n = 103$)	3.42^b ($n = 98$)	4.09^c ($n = 191$)	$F (2, 389) = 32.3, p < .05$
"The recognition of truth and the clear statement of it are the first duties of an able and honest reporter."—Hal Boyle	4.44^a ($n = 112$)	4.50^{ab} ($n = 105$)	4.70^b ($n = 196$)	$F (2, 410) = 5.1, p < .05$
"Mystical experiences are as direct perceptions of fact for those who have them as any sensations" are for the rest of us.—William James	3.08^a ($n = 62$)	3.42^{ab} ($n = 78$)	3.52^b ($n = 205$)	$F (2, 350) = 4.8, p < .05$
The great mass of people "have the need of the motive of religion to restrain them from vice, to support their virtue, and retain them in the practice of it till it becomes habitual."—Benjamin Franklin	3.02^a ($n = 108$)	3.48^b ($n = 97$)	3.69^b ($n = 188$)	$F (2, 390) = 14.2, p < .05$
"When truth and error have fair play, the former is always an overmatch for the latter."—Benjamin Franklin	3.84^{ab} ($n = 111$)	3.59^a ($n = 96$)	3.96^b ($n = 184$)	$F (2, 388) = 3.9, p < .05$

Note: Means with single superscripts are significantly different from means with different single superscripts by Scheffes's test at $p < .05$ (i.e., differences would occur by chance fewer than 5 times in 100). Means with double superscripts are not significantly different from means with either single superscript.

Table 18. Journalists' Responses to Irreverent Professional Maxims

	Religious Orientation			F Tests
	Low	Moderate	High	
"The Book of Nature tells us distinctly God cares not a rap for us—nor for any living creatures." —Mark Twain	2.93[a] (n = 107)	2.31[b] (n = 96)	1.57[c] (n = 191)	$F(2, 391) = 52.1, p < .05$
Humans are "the religious animal." A man "is the only animal that loves his neighbor as himself, and cuts his throat if his theology isn't straight." —Mark Twain	3.69[a] (n = 108)	3.71[a] (n = 100)	3.46[b] (n = 191)	$F(2, 396) = 2.0, p < .05$
"A newspaper can send more souls to Heaven, and save more from Hell, than all the churches or chapels in New York—besides making money at the same time." —James Gordon Bennett	2.67[a] (n = 106)	2.40[ab] (n = 99)	2.20[b] (n = 194)	$F(2, 396) = 6.2, p < .05$
"Reporting the great dramas of a murder story 'may come to speak more eloquently to the minds of thousands than the sermon preached to a hundred in the church on Sunday.'" —Jacob Riis	3.82[a] (n = 109)	3.53[ab] (n = 98)	3.45[b] (n = 197)	$F(2, 401) = 3.7, p < .05$
"If you're too ethical and nice, you're never going to get anywhere in journalism. . . . As a journalist, you do whatever you have to for a story. That's your job." —Florida journalism student	1.62[ab] (n = 113)	1.68[a] (n = 103)	1.42[b] (n = 196)	$F(2, 409) = 4.2, p < .05$
"I have never heard Christianity, as Jesus taught in the New Testament, preached to Christians." —Lincoln Steffens	2.94[a] (n = 94)	2.67[a] (n = 90)	2.11[b] (n = 188)	$F(2, 369) = 16.1, p < .05$
"One can always talk to a journalist 'with full confidence' that one is talking to someone 'who is at least free of moralistic mush.'" —Theodore Dreiser	2.54[a] (n = 112)	2.31[ab] (n = 100)	2.11[b] (n = 191)	$F(2, 400) = 5.3, p < .05$
"The Bible is before me. Have I not the right to read that book—to draw out from it religious opinions—and to create a belief and a church of my own?" —James Gordon Bennett	3.65[a] (n = 109)	3.70[a] (n = 100)	3.37[b] (n = 193)	$F(2, 399) = 3.0, p < .05$

Note: Means with single superscripts are significantly different from means with different single superscripts by Scheffe's test at $p < .05$ (i.e., differences would occur by chance fewer than 5 times in 100). Means with double superscripts are not significantly different from means with either single superscript.

Table 19. Journalists' Responses to Biblical Passages

	Religious Orientation			F Tests
	Low	Moderate	High	
"Faith, by itself, if it is not accompanied by action, is dead. . . . Show me your faith without deeds, and I will show you my faith by what I do." —James 2:17–18	4.09[a] (n = 106)	4.14[a] (n = 99)	4.67[b] (n = 192)	F (2, 394) = 22, p < .05
"Do not despise the words of the prophets, but test everything." —1 Thessalonians 5:20–21	4.36[a] (n = 107)	4.01[b] (n = 99)	4.41[a] (n = 193)	F (2, 396) = 7, p < .05
"What does the Lord require of you but to do justice, and to love kindness, and to walk humbly with your God." —Micah 6:8	3.85[a] (n = 100)	4.21[b] (n = 96)	4.62[c] (n = 192)	F (2, 385) = 23, p < .05
"Do not doubt but believe. . . . Blessed are those who have not seen and yet have come to believe." —John 20:27, 29	2.65[a] (n = 104)	3.18[b] (n = 100)	4.31[c] (n = 191)	F (2, 392) = 75, p < .05
"For the love of money is a root of all kinds of evil, and in their eagerness to be rich some have wandered away from their faith and pierced themselves with pains." —1 Timothy 6:10	3.83[a] (n = 108)	3.82[a] (n = 100)	4.79[b] (n = 190)	F (2, 395) = 6, p < .05
The Lord said: "I will seek the lost, and I will bring back the strayed, and I will bind up the injured and I will strengthen the weak, but the fat and the strong I will destroy. I will feed them with justice." —Ezekiel 34:16	3.04[a] (n = 92)	3.11[a] (n = 92)	4.15[b] (n = 185)	F (2, 366) = 47, p < .05
"If we love one another, God lives in us [and] love is perfected." —1 John 4:12	3.67[a] (n = 97)	4.06[b] (n = 99)	4.64[c] (n = 189)	F (2, 382) = 40, p < .05
"For the whole of the law is summed up in a single commandment: You shall love your neighbor as yourself." —Galatians 5:14	4.17[a] (n = 109)	4.26[a] (n = 101)	4.70[b] (n = 189)	F (2, 396) = 17, p < .05
"If any want to become my followers, let them deny themselves and take up their cross daily and follow me." —Luke 9:23	2.98[a] (n = 92)	3.35[b] (n = 94)	4.30[c] (n = 187)	F (2, 370) = 52, p < .05
"If anyone is in Christ, there is a new creation; everything old has passed away; see, everything has become new!" —2 Corinthians 5:17	2.96[a] (n = 85)	3.11[a] (n = 87)	4.21[b] (n = 184)	F (2, 353) = 43, p < .05

Note: Means with single superscripts are significantly different from means with different single superscripts by Scheffe's test at p < .05 (i.e., differences would occur by chance fewer than 5 times in 100).

to the moral and ethical admonitions contained in the biblical passages. Biblical passages containing sentiments similar to key journalistic maxims received lower support from less religiously oriented journalists than when the same sentiments were expressed in journalistic language. For example, journalists of all religious orientations responded similarly to the Dunne quotation on comforting the afflicted and afflicting the comfortable. But when these same moral sentiments were expressed in biblical passages (such as the quote from Ezekiel 34:16), journalists responded in ways that reflected their religious orientation: positively if they identified religion or spirituality as important in their lives, negatively if they did not.[9]

Although journalists of strong religious orientation tended to endorse all ten biblical passages strongly and significantly, journalists who were less religiously inclined did endorse some of the biblical passages more strongly than others. These passages tended to reflect more generalized ethical and moral sentiments that could be expected to receive support beyond the domains of Judaism and Christianity. An example is Paul's comment from Galatians 5:14 ("For the whole law is summed up in a single commandment: You shall love your neighbor as yourself"), which is similar in principle to Kant's categorical imperative or the nonbiblically based Golden Rule ("Do unto others as you would have them do unto you"). At the same time, the endorsement gap between journalists who identified themselves as religiously oriented and those who did not was greatest for the biblical passages that reflected strong Christian orthodoxy, such as 2 Corinthians 5:17 ("If anyone is in Christ, there is a new creation; everything old has passed away; see, everything has become new!"). In this sense, one can conclude that journalists of all backgrounds, whether religious or not, respond positively to core moral and ethical values contained in the Bible but tend to let their religious views influence the way they respond to more theologically loaded statements.

One can conclude from these results that Judeo-Christian ethical values are embedded deeply, if not always consciously, in the professional values of many of today's journalists. But one must be careful not to take this conclusion too far. For example, over 67 percent of the respondents disagreed with the statement "Christian values should underpin journalistic values," while over 53 percent agreed with the statement "Journalistic values should draw upon the ethical and moral traditions of all great religions" (see table 20). In the survey, a high proportion of respondents reported growing up in homes that were Christian (about 85 percent) or Jewish (about 5 percent)—thus linking them, at least by background, to the Judeo-Christian tradition in the United States and Canada.[10] Yet one must be wary of assuming that biblical values provide the sole foundation of journalists' morals and ethics, at least in the explicit sense. Journalists, it appears, have expanded their definitions of what religion coverage means in an increasingly diverse and pluralistic society, and few seem to want to connect their professional principles with only Christian moral teachings.

Table 20. Religious Values in News Coverage

	Christian Values Should Underpin Journalistic Values		Journalistic Values Should Draw upon Ethical/Moral Traditions of All Great Religions	
	Frequency	Percent	Frequency	Percent
Strongly disagree	227	54.0	73	17.7
Disagree	55	13.1	54	13.1
No opinion	55	13.1	66	16.0
Agree	46	11.0	121	29.4
Strongly agree	37	8.8	98	23.8
	420	100.0	412	100.0

E. W. Scripps's comments—in which he embraced Christian ethics while shying away from identifying himself as a Christian believer—still appear to go some ways in explaining the ethical and moral value system of today's journalists. Despite the secular directions of society and the skeptical and irreverent traditions of their profession, the journalists we surveyed seem solidly connected to the system of moral values growing out of the nation's religious heritage. This is demonstrated not only by the relatively high levels of religious orientation the journalists themselves reported but also by the positive ways in which even nonreligiously oriented journalists responded to core ethical principles found in both the Bible and their professional maxims. It is no surprise to find that modern journalists—so influenced by the scientific revolution and the rational skepticism of the Enlightenment—might spurn the notion that their ethical obligations grow out of religious duty. But regardless of whether they explicitly affirm it, journalists can still be seen as personifying the old religious virtues in their ethical and moral stances.

In both the American culture at large and the profession of journalism, we are reaching the end of a two-century drift away from the Puritan rigidities that bound us together in rules for conduct. What we have substituted in their place, however, has become a subject of great soul-searching in the culture and in journalism. The old America that reflexively celebrated Christian virtues and the Puritan conscience is no longer sustainable in a nation that has grown demographically diverse, religiously pluralistic, and culturally divided. Very few among us (at least, in journalistic quarters) would argue that the solution to the nation's moral questions is to simply reimpose the old values of traditional American religion. Journalists and editors—seeking market success, if nothing else—have made the adjustment to the new circumstances of a more diverse America. Journalists can no longer afford to identify with one particular religious belief or portray America as monolithically Christian in outlook.

Still, journalists would profit from pondering more deeply what constitutes the core of their moral vision. A hundred and fifty years ago, Judeo-Christian values were at the center of the way journalists judged the world, and few involved in the journalism business would have denied it. Today, the widely accepted ethical and moral precepts of the profession are remarkably similar to what they were then, even if the consensus on the theological underpinning of those values has disappeared. Is this something we should be concerned about or even interested in? What difference does it make if journalists no longer recognize that their ethical principles are rooted in the nation's religious heritage? If the Judeo-Christian tradition as the avowed source of journalistic ethics has disappeared from the consciousness of many journalists, only to be replaced by a complex web of professional, institutional, and collegial guidelines, so what? Since this same phenomenon has taken place in so many other professions in our increasingly secular culture—in law, in medicine, in academics—it only makes sense to ask, so what is lost? If some people have abandoned religious belief, what relevance is it as long as a key element of religion—its ethical commands—has been subsumed into the professional guidelines of the secular social order?

Jesus faced somewhat similar questions when the Pharisees questioned him about why he was not following the strict, ritual practices of the Jewish law. Time and again, Jesus refused to be pinned down, often answering his followers' or his critics' questions in parables or riddles. Jesus' point was that genuine ethical practice requires a commitment to something that is greater than simply following rules and regulations laid down by external authority. Journalists, one might like to believe, would recognize the dilemma. The unpredictability of the news, the demand to deal with unusual circumstances and predicaments that have not been encountered earlier, and the flow of unexpected events out of which journalists must make ethical decisions are never-ending facets of a journalist's career. No matter how many guidelines for ethical conduct or professional responsibility codes are developed, journalists know how much they must rely on their own wisdom to guide them in their ethical and moral decision making. But what is it that guarantees the journalist's "gut" will continue to make the right call? Most journalists would resist using explicit religious terms to describe this phenomenon—as we probably should expect. But external rules, regulations, and guidelines can take a person only so far when it comes to moral and ethical choices. After that, the conscience rules, and one can only trust it is grounded in a place where something more than guesswork can be drawn on for guidance.

PART 3

Secularism and the Newsroom
Search for Substitute Faiths

CHAPTER 11

The Cult of Science and the Scientifically Challenged Press

The way the *New York Times* reported it, Dr. Stephen Hawking—despite being confined to a wheelchair, completely paralyzed from Lou Gehrig's disease, and able to communicate only through a computer synthesizer—managed a broad grin during a Chicago convention of physicists. Hawking, like his fellow "cosmologists" in the audience, was showing his amusement at a comment from a colleague that, at least in broad outline, their scenario of the history of the cosmos was a lot like St. Augustine's sixteen hundred years ago. The moment of "laughter" and "humility," as the reporter described it, was something that might have been predicted from a group that sees parallels between science and religion drawn on a routine basis in the press.[1] No one more than Hawking inspires reporters to grand metaphorical reaches of language, where modern science is framed in terms of the theological notions it has ostensibly come to supplant.

Few reporters openly say they believe science has replaced religion as the domain where the search for answers to the mysteries of the universe is carried out in modern life, but they seldom hold back, as was the case in the above story, in using such terms as *astonishing, bold,* and *breathtaking* in explaining the theories advanced by modern scientists or in treating someone like Hawking with near reverential awe.[2] An examination of more than two dozen stories in major newspapers focused on Hawking over the last ten years revealed that more than half (16 out of 26, or 62 percent) used religious terminology to describe Hawking (he is most commonly referred to as "oracle"-like) or used the term *God* or one of Hawking's well-known references to God in the story (Hawking has sought in his theorizing, he once said, to know "the mind of God" and has made a play on the famous Albert Einstein quote that God does not play dice by saying, "God not only plays dice but also sometimes throws them where they cannot be seen.").[3] Hawking's theories about black holes in space and his efforts to develop a unified theory of physics that eluded Einstein—combined with his sly use of religious language to draw attention to his theories—have led reporters to wax eloquent about his cosmic speculations, as was the case with the *Washington Post* reporter who wrote that Hawking believed he had expanded Einsteinian physics to the point that "he may have made contact with God or at the very least his mathematical equivalent."[4]

Hawking is only the latest in a line of "superstar" scientists who have been unabashedly promoted by a media that, despite struggling to comprehend the technical details of scientific breakthroughs, have been eager to popularize the achievements of great scientific celebrities. Sir Isaac Newton, Charles Darwin, and Einstein all became greatly revered figures in the press of their time. Yet, as Abraham Pais pointed out, Einstein's "magical stature" with the press and the public was built on the basis that few comprehended what he was really saying. This, Pais said, was illustrated in an eyewitness account of one 1921 concert hall appearance by Einstein: "'People were in a curious state of excitement in which it no longer matters what one understands but only that one is in the immediate neighborhood of a place where miracles happen.'"[5]

Journalism has made many contributions to the ironies of history but none more so than in the realm of modern science. Journalists have contributed greatly to the mystification surrounding scientific developments in the public mind, largely because they do not understand the mathematical truths underlying these grand theories or have not figured out how to convey them. It is fair to say that journalists, who have served over the centuries as debunkers of religious orthodoxy and critics of theological claptrap, have done much to create in the "mysteries" of science a new altar for people to worship at, a veritable cult of belief that has many of the earmarks of religious devotion.

If asked, most journalists would probably deny this, as they might the contention (which I would make) that science receives more worshipful coverage in this day and age than does religion. If that is the case, as perhaps a few members of the press would concede, they would say it is for good reason. Theories of God cannot be proven in scientific ways, leading to opposing views of the divine that stir up deep, seemingly irreconcilable issues among believers and encourage journalists to hesitate to cover religion for fear of offending various groups in their audience. Some of the most skeptical journalists might go even further than this. Scientific reason refutes or at least calls into question the picture of God portrayed in the historical teachings of the world's major religions. This justifies downplaying religion coverage to matters of controversy, where one side says one thing and the other says another, while treating science with the deference due a subject that is objective and empirical in nature and whose discoveries are tested in ways that can be verified. Besides, science is about what is new and experimental and future-oriented, and it has led to technological advances that "work." In contrast, religion is old and out-of-date and, even when it emerges in fresh new movements, deals with hoary philosophical questions— do people have "souls," can we be "saved," what happens to us after we die— that no one ever expects to be answered anyway.

Yet many of the media's problems with coverage of religion do—or, at least, should—apply to science, too. Much of science cannot be "proven" in the commonsense way that journalists usually define as proof, particularly the complex theories involving modern physics and quantum mechanics. In addition, many of the views of modern science involve matters of opinion, even among scientists themselves, who often carry on lively debates about the validity of theories and the credibility of experimental proofs. Finally, many scientists, despite their empirical training and their reason-based approach, actually believe in God or some form of higher power, and they often see the complex harmony of the universe as pointing to a transcendental force that cannot be fully understood in scientific terms. It is often laypersons, as much as scientists, who have come to worship science as a replacement for religion and as a wondrous source for keeping mystery alive in the world.

Ideally, the advances of modern physics should have led journalists into a profound and soul-searching reexamination of the fundamental elements of their professional methodology, but, for the most part, they have not. Journalism, as a profession, sees itself rooted in the open-minded and experimental traditions of the great empiricists and rationalists, such people as Galileo, who was persecuted mightily for his persistent belief in proofs and demonstrations rather than theological speculations;[6] John Locke, who saw the human mind as a "tabula rasa" that was filled in through experience and experimentation and the God-given capacity for reason; Voltaire, who championed the causes of freedom of individual conscience, tolerance, and the scientific method; John Stuart Mill, who believed passionately in the many-sided nature of truth and the virtue of nonconformity; and William James, who rejected dogmatic or final answers to the great cosmic questions and embraced a process where pragmatic guidelines would determine the right course of action. These practical philosophers all helped lay the groundwork for the journalist's viewpoint that reality is discernible and sensible through the use of reason, good sense, intellectual persistence, and devotion to the common good.

But the stance of today's journalist vis-à-vis modern physics forces us to consider how much modern journalism may need to look to its intellectual roots in a less optimistic, less straightforward philosophical manner. From the time of Plato, who maintained that the human mind had the capacity to glimpse only a dim and imperfect impression of the true nature of things (with his famous image of the shadows of light cast on the cave wall), to Thomas Hobbes (who rejected belief in an objective world and felt that without names and words there was no truth), to David Hume (whose philosophy of skepticism applied to the mind's imperfect ability to go beyond limited "impressions" of what the world might really be), to Immanuel Kant (who believed that our comprehension of reality is limited and that time and space are forms our mind imposes on what we experience through the senses), another strain of philosophers has argued that it is the human imagination more than the true nature of the world that shapes our experience of existence and that we can rely only on our limited reasoning capacity and our uncertain will (as well as, in Plato's case, our spiritual powers of understanding) to extend the mind's idea of order to a world that we cannot fully know.[7]

Walter Lippmann, the great twentieth-century newspaper columnist, picked up this line of thinking in his highly influential criticism of the modern, commercial press. Lippmann, in the tradition of Hume, was a pessimist about the press's capability to comprehend what was happening in the world in all its manifest complexity. In applying the term *stereotyping* to the press, Lippmann argued that, while journalists may think of themselves as reason-based empiricists who only want to discover the facts, they tend to portray the world through the prism of preconceived notions, prejudices, and standardized judgments rather than in the clear light of truth. Sadly perhaps for journalism, Lippmann's critique has found a greater following in academic circles than in the press itself, where journalists resist criticisms that they tend to resort to distortions, simplifications, and shallowness in conveying a complex reality.[8]

Nowhere can Lippmann's critique be better seen than in journalism's coverage of modern science, where looking for the "gee-whiz" science discovery, creating scientific celebrities, and covering the controversies generated by scientific theory have preoccupied journalists to a much greater degree than trying to convey the true complexity of modern scientific discovery. Journalism today still bears much of the responsibility for creating the image of the world's prominent scientists, foremost among them Einstein, whose visage on billboards and magazine covers is associated with everything from nuclear weapons to space travel to the most recent discoveries about subatomic particles. Largely because of the media, however, the public's idea of the theories of the great scientists may bear only a tangential connection to what those scientists actually say about the workings of the universe. The popular images that have been perpetuated in journalism articles, movies, television, and advertisements—Galileo dropping weights off the leaning tower of Pisa; Newton watching the apple fall; Benjamin Franklin flying his kite; the brainy Einstein with the bushy hair mumbling $E = mc^2$—often serve as the cartoon symbols and the media age folklore that express our sense of the superiority of science and scientists as the icons of our time.

There has been no better example of a scientist with a "superstar" problem than Einstein had with the press of his day. Unknown outside of physics until 1919, Einstein, a Swiss government clerk, was suddenly catapulted into the world limelight by the headlines in British and American newspapers about his "fantastic" and "marvelous" theories about the nature of matter and the universe. After two groups of scientists in Brazil and Africa had witnessed the bending of starlight predicted by Einstein's general theory of relativity, headlines blazed across England and America: "Revolution in Science, New Theory of the Universe, Newtonian Ideas Overthrown," proclaimed the *Times* of London on November 7, 1919; "Lights All Askew in the Heavens, Men of Science More or Less Agog. . . . Einstein Theory Triumphs," exclaimed the *New York Times* two days later.[9] By 1929, Einstein—already a cult figure of monumental celebrity—was inspiring such headlines as "400 Bewildered as Einstein Speaks" and "Einstein Is Amazed at Stir over Theory. Holds 100 Journalists at Bay for a Week."[10]

In no time, Einstein became a "media sage" and a living legend, courted the world over, particularly by reporters, who found him not an abstruse academic but a "wild-haired eccentric" with "rumpled charm and a mocking sense of humor." With his opinions sought on every conceivable subject, Einstein soon found that everything he said became a fuss in the newspapers. The excitement Einstein could cause in a society titillated by scientific celebrity is captured in the account of his visit to the Geneva Peace Conference in 1932. As Einstein walked into the palace, hundreds of people followed at a respectful distance; when one Bulgarian delegate questioned his right to be there, he was hit in the mouth by the paper pad of one American correspondent; another young reporter "almost fainted with excitement" when Einstein asked him to rekindle the cigar he was smoking.[11]

Part of Einstein's appeal came because he—like Newton and Darwin before him—seemed to capture the mood of an age. But where Newton's science had gained such universal acceptance because it appeared to confirm popular wisdom, Einstein's appeal came largely because he confounded it. Newton became the scientific figurehead for the Age of Reason, a period when enlightened and progressive minds used a popular version of Newton's picture of the universe as a predictable, clockwork apparatus ultimately penetrable by human reason to undercut the oppressive authority of church dogma as the basis for explaining the workings of the universe. Einstein appeared in a world in which certainties had been shattered by the disillusionment of World War I and where his theories about warped space and the bending of light—his "strange new order, in which little was what it seemed"—captured, as the biographers Roger Highfield and Paul Carter put it, "the disturbed mood of the times."[12]

While only a few journalists have really grappled with them, Einstein's theories presented the world of journalism with a profound dilemma. Einstein's postulates portrayed the nature of the universe in ways that appeared to be so bizarre and so defied common sense that it required journalists (like most everyone else) to fall back on imperfect spatial metaphors and mind-stretching imaginative techniques to convey the mathematical principles by which Einstein expressed his theories of the physical world. At the most superficial level of understanding, Einstein's ideas seemed to challenge daily experience at every turn: that the flow of time is not an absolute or universal property but varies depending on the location and the velocity of the observer; that space is not a

fixed and neutral medium through which objects move but is a hybrid property that must be combined with time into an object called space-time; that gravity
is not a force like other forces but the product of the fact that space-time is not
flat but warped by the distribution of mass and energy within it; that matter at
the subatomic level contains the seemingly contradictory quality of both particles and waves at the same time. Time and time again, it seemed that Einstein
solved the most vexing problems in physics by discarding the time-honored and
commonsensical notions that seem self-evident to earthbound humankind and
by soaring into mathematical dimensions where seemingly hypothetical notions
(such as the nature of things as we approach the speed of light) become critically important in ascertaining how the universe actually works.[13]

The key point in comprehending Einstein's impact on popular wisdom is that
relativity became a code word for the twentieth-century view that appearance
and reality were not quite what they seemed to be and that all sorts of human
principles (morality, ethics, cultural values) were to be treated as subjective and
variable depending on where one was positioned. As unrelated as it may be to
Einstein's own moral beliefs (which were not necessarily at all relative in nature), Einstein has been appropriated by modernist intellectual forces in the
same way that Newton was embraced by the Deists and the Enlightenment
philosophers and Darwin by the social Darwinists and the proponents of laissez-faire economics. However, as Bertrand Russell pointed out, Einstein was
preoccupied with finding the unity and the harmony in the workings of the
universe. While it is possible to maintain that everything in the physical world
is relative to an observer, this is not what the theory of relativity is about, Russell observed. On the contrary, Einstein was interested in developing a theory
that excluded what is relative, Russell argued, and arriving at a statement of
physical laws that was not dependent on the circumstances of the observer. "A
certain type of superior person is fond of asserting that 'everything is relative,'"
wrote Russell. "This is, of course, nonsense. . . . Perhaps the name is unfortunate; certainly it has led philosophers and uneducated people into confusions."[14]

As accurate as this may be at the theoretical level, Einsteinian physics has still
left journalists with the tricky task of explaining this complex material to the
public and trying to decide what, if any, implications it may have for journalistic methodology. To comprehend the fundamental order and symmetry underlying Einstein's theories, one simply must be trained in mathematics—which
few journalists are. Without that training, journalists, like most of the rest of
the public, are left to take his findings on faith and the testimony of experts in
the field. Even more difficult is the challenge journalists face in trying to convey the theories of Einstein, which have undercut the Newtonian notion of the
way the universe works, with a journalistic methodology that is still Newtonian
in its epistemological foundation. Journalism, more than any other field, is committed to the notion that the average mind (with the journalist showing the way,
of course) can comprehend the physical world as it truly is. Even today, no oth-

er field is more locked into a persistently outdated quasi-Newtonian (or, more accurately, Newton as interpreted by the Enlightenment philosophers) worldview, all the while left with the increasingly baffling duty of trying to interpret twentieth-century scientific developments with their abrupt departures from the comforting certainties of Newton's picture of the universe.

With this heritage, it is no surprise that the discoveries of twentieth-century physics—so alien to the commonsensical perception of the world around us—should come as such a challenge to the mind-set of the typical journalist. Milic Capek argued that the mind's instinctive tendency to cling to the concrete patterns of Euclidean geometry and Newtonian mechanics—the "Newtonian-Euclidean subconscious," in his words—is psychologically understandable because the roots lie deep within the human heritage and are too obstinate to be modified by mere mathematical formulations about the nature of the universe so different from our experience of it. Journalists—as well as most of the rest of us—live in a "zone of the middle dimensions," as H. Reichenbach described it, somewhere between "the world of galaxies and the microcosm," where Newtonian physics does apply and where mastery of three-dimensional space and submission to the inexorably forward-moving clock dial are necessary to complete the fundamental business of life. Most journalists would be inclined to call this place "the real world" or "real life" and simply dismiss the explanations of relativity physics and quantum mechanics as irrelevant to the demands of daily life (including the task, ironically, of having to explain these theories to the public in terms it can understand). As a result, journalists find it easy to retreat to their tried-and-true formulas for attracting an audience by describing scientific matters in terms that can be understood—even if that understanding is based on conventional wisdom, popular falsehoods, and oversimplistic truisms.[15]

With so little true understanding of Einstein's science, it is no surprise to find him treated in a dual fashion—held up to us, on the one hand, as the symbol of the triumph of human reason and the scientific imagination and, on the other hand, as a brilliant but bewildering figure whose bizarre and fantastic conclusions about the true nature of things mostly baffle us. It is here that the parallels between science and religion—and the media's contrasting coverage of science and religion—come forcefully into play. Although the original overly exuberant coverage of scientific developments like those Einstein first elucidated was toned down somewhat during the twentieth century, newspapers still tend to present matters of modern scientific discovery as if they are discussing fantastical events that defy normal human comprehension. While it is not quite the same thing as reporting on bodies rising from the grave and the birth of monsters, as the seventeenth-century press was prone to do, the reporting of modern scientific developments in the popular press seems to have brought us full circle, where people are told to set aside their regular experience of day-to-day life and accept once again that reality is an awe-filled and fantastical place where, from the grandest reaches of the cosmos to the smallest microscopic levels of

matter, our senses deceive us and our minds are not perceptive enough to comprehend the true design of creation.[16] "Everybody thinks he or she knows what
'space' means, everybody knows what a warp is," wrote Pais. "Yet hardly anyone understands the meaning of warped space. . . . I believe that it is precisely
this nearness to mystery unaccompanied by understanding which accounts for
the universal appeal of the man who created all this novelty."[17]

Of all journalists, science writers invariably are the most knowledgeable about
the field, and, as Ted Anton and Rick McCourt pointed out, there are some highly trained and respected science writers working at newspapers around the country. This has come about partly because of a boom in science-writing programs
in recent years.[18] But most of the recent social science literature examining scientific issues and media performance concludes that the press accounts of scientific advances still tend to be simplified, incomplete, or misleading. Researchers blame this on a variety of factors, including the minimal number of full-time
science writers, the lack of science understanding by reporters and editors, the
limited space for science news, journalists' tendency to rely too much on sources
with credentials, and scientists' poor communication skills and lack of understanding of how the media work.[19] More than anything, however, science writing tends to show that journalists fall back on the formulaic conventions of the
business to convey scientific information if it is necessary to please an editor or
to appeal to a popular audience. This has resulted in science writing as a flawed
product, researchers say, with the journalistic fare in even the most august publications often "uneven, overhyped, and occasionally downright wrong," in the
words of Anton and Court.[20]

This gap between scientific theory itself, journalism's portrayal of the great
scientists and their theories, and the public's perception of scientific advancements can be seen as far back as 1727, when Voltaire, who as a journalist had
written much about Newton's revolutionary theories, visited the estate where
Newton lay on his deathbed.[21] In making Newton's theories accessible to the
popular mind, Voltaire displayed an intellectual depth rarely found in journalists today (Voltaire, for example, spent more than a decade studying Newton's
science and had fully digested his most challenging work, *Principia Mathemat-
ica*); Voltaire could not, however, resist a bit of entertaining journalistic storytelling that was partly responsible for one of the most enduring legends that still
defines Newton in our age: that Newton's inspiration for his theory of gravity
came when, while sitting in a contemplative mood in his garden, he watched
an apple fall from a tree. Newton's biographers have pondered for centuries
whether this story is true (Voltaire's apparent source was Newton's niece, who
helped care for the celebrated scientist during his last days).[22] As a good journalist, Voltaire indulged in reporting other anecdotes that "humanized" (and
some would say "scandalized") the memory of Newton.[23] Still, when it came to
Newton, Voltaire recognized the challenge that journalism faces when conveying scientific developments to the general public. Few people, Voltaire knew, had

the technical competence to understand Newton's most complex works, yet that did not stop people everywhere from believing they understood the importance of Newton's breakthroughs.[24] As Voltaire put it, "Newton . . . has very few readers, because it requires great knowledge and sense to understand him. Everybody however talks about him."[25]

No one understood better than Newton how much his contemporaries were trying to impute to his scientific discoveries. Even an intellectually sophisticated journalist such as Voltaire could not resist putting Newton's theories to work in reinforcing Voltaire's philosophical worldview and in attempting to undermine the prevailing explanations of the universe offered by Christian orthodoxy.[26] However, as Newton often pointed out, he never believed his theory explained why the galaxies operated as they did. Gravity, Newton believed, was a principle of attraction based on his observations, not an explanation for the cause of the solar system's workings. His theories were a set of geometrical theorems deduced from experimental phenomenon, not a mechanical model of a predictable universe operating free of God's direct intervention and only distantly connected to a prime mover, as the Deists conceived of it.[27] Newton was interested in what happens, and he did not see anything he discovered as contradicting the principles of Christian faith. "You sometimes speak of gravity as essential and inherent to Matter," he once wrote to a colleague. "Pray do not ascribe that Notion to me; for the Cause of Gravity is what I do not pretend to know."[28]

Newton, in fact, was a mystic, a loyal Anglican, and a believer in an all-powerful, unpredictable God who could intervene to correct the occasional flaw in Newton's otherwise mathematically predictable model of the solar system.[29] Newton, it turns out, produced volumes of odd and eccentric religious writings in which he struggled to explain his ideas about God and the universe in nonmathematical prose, and he welcomed those who defended his scientific theories as supportive of Christianity and a weapon to use against atheism. Voltaire might have wished that Newton, like Voltaire himself, had rejected the orthodox Christian doctrine of religion and had put his faith in "the natural law" that "nature teaches all men,"[30] but he was too honest a journalist not to recognize the distinction. "Sir Isaac Newton was firmly persuaded of the Existence of a God; by which he understood not only an infinite, omnipotent, and creating being, but moreover a Master who has made a Relation between himself and his Creatures," Voltaire wrote.[31]

In retrospect, we can see that the division between science and religion was only in its infancy in the eighteenth century, at least compared with the thundering nineteenth-century disputes that took place over the discoveries of Charles Darwin and the threat that Darwin's theory of evolution posed to the traditional Christian explanations for the origin of the human race. To see Darwin's science linked to religious controversy tells us much about how powerfully religious viewpoints persist in the culture, no matter what happens in the way of scientific discoveries. But it is also interesting to see how Darwin's ideas about natural selection not only challenged Christian views of sin, salvation, and the afterlife but also precipitated a transformation of press attitudes in favor of science coverage over religion. While it would not be fair to describe the nineteenth-century British press as unanimous in its initial hostility to Darwin's theory—a number of important publications reviewed Darwin's first major publication, *The Origin of Species,* favorably—many editors and editorial commentators, although largely scientifically illiterate, were gravely suspicious of a theory that appeared to cast doubt on the Christian dignity of humankind.[32] The *London Times,* for example, was vigorous in denouncing Darwin's 1871 publication of *The Descent of Man,* where he most explicitly espoused his view that humans, despite their "god-like intellect" and evolutionary advancements, are linked in fundamental ways to lower forms of life and still bear the "indelible stamp" of their "lowly origin."[33] Over two days, the *Times* condemned the book as "reckless" for its incomplete evidence, its reliance on hypothesis rather than facts and its unscientific conclusions.[34]

As the years went by, however, the progressive quarters of English society—including the higher reaches of the press establishment—began to tilt toward Darwin and his theories. Just as they had with Newton, the progressive elements of the Christian community came to realize that Darwin's evolutionary theories could be used to buttress, rather than undermine, prevailing Christian attitudes about human progress and religious hope. Like Newton's theories, Darwin's science became intertwined with the spirit of his age, and natural selection soon was touted as a positive thing, a sign that humankind had evolved from the primordial ooze and was headed to greater things. Nowhere was this transformation of attitude more explicit than in the British press, which by the time Darwin died in 1882 was hailing him as someone who had made it possible to synthesize the findings of science and religion and to reformulate Christian faith based on progressive scientific thought. At Darwin's funeral—like Newton's, held with great pomp and circumstance in Westminster Abbey—the newspapers virtually canonized him as one who had brought honor to the English name, proclaiming, as one did, that Darwin's doctrine was quite consistent "with strong religious faith and hope."[35] Even the *Times* declared the clash between Darwinians and Christians to be "ancient history" and held up Darwin as one of Britain's immortal figures on a par with Newton.[36]

Yet it would be a mistake to think that religion emerged from this controversy on equal terms with science—at least in terms of the attention paid to the two fields by the press. While editorialists might have seen the possibilities for fusing Christian faith with Darwinian explanations, the news pages increasingly held up science, as well as scientific discoveries, as the source of high reverence, and discussions about religion increasingly were banished to the back sections of the newspaper. Darwin's triumph in the columns of the newspaper industry (in the United States, too, he was grandly praised at the time of his death, with the *New York Herald* comparing his life to Socrates and calling him a "giant among his fellows") can be seen as setting the tone of journalism's attitude, even today, in support of science's ascendancy over (or perhaps one should say, assimilation of) religion.[37] The fusion of evolutionism with Christian thought that took place in the minds of many nineteenth-century Christians may have righted the old church order for a time, but clearly it was science, not religion, that had gained the upper hand. While a new strain of Christian liberalism developed that was open to the tenets of modern science, it was really the scientific outlook—with its optimism, its sense of discovery, its fundamental faith in human progress—that replaced the old religious worldview in many intellectual quarters, including much of the press.

If Darwinism was a challenge to the nineteenth-century imagination, it was the darker strains of continental European thought—combined with the terrible shocks of two world wars, state-sponsored genocide, and nuclear weapons development—that provided the bleak intellectual landscape upon which twentieth-century scientific discoveries made their appearance. In many respects, it proved to be easier to remake Darwin's theories into a Christian positivist framework than to reconcile Christianity with the pessimistic elements of philosophical thought that permeated Europe in the late nineteenth century and throughout the twentieth. The biggest blow to the optimists' worldview came not from Darwin but from such thinkers as Søren Kierkegaard, the nineteenth-century Danish philosopher who questioned whether either religion or science led to an objective knowledge of nature and whose existentialist advocacy of a "leap of faith" into belief reflected his view of a universe that was, at heart, irrational. Kierkegaard's forswearing of a religion of reason as well as the reason of science—views that were echoed in even more atheistic fashion by such nineteenth-century German philosophers as Arthur Schopenhauer and Friedrich Nietzsche—dovetailed in remarkable ways with the demoralizing historical developments of the twentieth century. The confusion in the common mind caused by the developments of modern physics (which, after all, had led to the development of "the bomb") contributed greatly to a mood of angst, uncertainty, and doubt that led to such pessimistic modern philosophical and literary movements as nihilism, existentialism, and postmodernism.

Journalists may be pleased to know that even Einstein, as bold and pioneering as his thinking was, was not free from the human tendency to hold on to old metaphysical notions and the need to believe in a harmonious pattern of things. One of the most fascinating episodes in modern science was the dispute between Einstein and Niels Bohr, the Danish physicist who took some of Einstein's early postulates about quantum mechanics and developed them in ways that Einstein could not accept for much of his life. Bohr and others discovered in their experiments that subatomic particles were subject to an "uncertainty principle" that made their motion predictable only by the application of probability laws—an essentially "irrational" underpinning to material reality that appeared to defy common sense, including Einstein's.[38] Einstein publicly resisted

Bohr's discoveries about quantum mechanics for many years. In his now famous statement, Einstein declared that Bohr believed in a dice-playing God and that he (Einstein) preferred to believe in a universe that operates under the force of "perfect" laws. He worked to the end of his professional life vainly attempting to find a unifying theory of the universe that could incorporate his relativity theory into the laws of subatomic matter.[39]

The dispute between the two twentieth-century science giants is a reminder —to journalists as well as others—that matters of science are often as much about faith as about objective reality. The surprising frequency of religious allusions in the Bohr-Einstein exchanges made the debate fundamentally theological in certain important respects. Bohr, for example, accused Einstein of insisting that God must have a design that coincided with Einstein's theories of the universe and said that Einstein should not tell God how to behave. Einstein, for his part, said that Bohr thought very clearly, wrote obscurely, and thought of himself as a prophet.[40] But what both men seemed to understand was that scientific discovery had not ended the discussion of the great questions that religion always has addressed.

While ministers' statements about God may be found less frequently in the news columns, Einstein's comments about spiritual matters have become famous. Among his many oft-quoted comments about the spiritual source of the scientific quest, Einstein was fond of saying that he did not believe in a god concerned with the fates and actions of individual human beings, or in an afterlife, or in religious texts, dogmas, or creeds.[41] "I cannot conceive of a God who rewards and punishes his creatures, or has a will of the kind that we experience in ourselves," Einstein declared. Instead, Einstein articulated his religious views in the form of a vague scientific pantheism, an experience of a mystical force from which the "finer speculations" and the "noblest motive for scientific research" spring. "The scientist is possessed by the sense of universal causation," Einstein said. "His religious feeling takes the form of a rapturous amazement at the harmony of natural law, which reveals an intelligence of such superiority that, compared with it, all the systematic thinking and acting of human beings is an utterly insignificant reflection."[42]

Einstein's view has become quite popular with scientists and has contributed (in its fusion of modern scientific ideas and more traditional notions of the divine at work in the universe) to such movements as the Point Omega philosophy of the Catholic theologian Pierre Teilhard de Chardin, where evolution is explicitly incorporated into a scheme of Christian end-time, and the process theology of A. N. Whitehead, in which God is identified as party to every event and every possibility that unfolds in experience.[43] This kind of generalized religious metaphysic—attached to the remnants of spiritual feeling in many modern people—has been reflected in a whole host of late-twentieth-century religious movements, from New Age thought to the popularity of Native American religions to a revival of occult and pagan worship ("I am a deeply religious nonbeliever," Einstein once said. "This is a somewhat new kind of religion").[44]

Journalism, then, finds itself at an interesting juncture in this post-Newtonian, post-Darwinian, post-Einsteinian world of the post–twentieth century. In one respect, journalists believe they have adjusted their moral and philosophical outlook to fit with the advancements of science, absorbing the theories of Newton and Darwin and (although to a much less comprehending degree) Einstein and Bohr into their methodological systems for interpreting the world. But any scientist who reads daily journalism (or knows many journalists, for that matter) would laugh at the notion that modern journalism connects with the methods of modern science in any way other than the most superficial. In its belief in pragmatism and the practical, in its commitment to no-nonsense observation of everyday life, in its trust of the senses to render the world an intelligent place, journalism rests squarely in an eighteenth-century worldview. Everything about the printing of newspapers, magazines, and periodicals, as well as the regularized news schedules of broadcast companies, follows the rhythms of absolute Newtonian time. The organization of the traditional news business, with its top-down organizational structure, its assembly-line production schedules, and its highly rational news product, reflects a belief in the solidity of matter in real space; the professional values of journalists, with their belief in empiricism and the objective search for truth, demonstrate a confidence (dubious as it may be) in a tangible world that can be comprehended by our five senses and can be interpreted accurately for others. It is true that journalists may appear willfully "agnostic" about the world—doubting what is presented to them, searching out controversy and disagreement, always reserving their right to change their minds. But this is only a surface impression. Beneath their external stance as skeptics and doubting Thomases, journalists operate with a virtually total and complete faith in themselves as empiricists and in the capacity of their professional methodology to present an accurate recounting of reality that, if it is good enough for the daily newspaper, must be pretty close to what reality is.

This belief system can be seen as not only religious in the sense that it stipulates metaphysical propositions that can only be asserted but even obsolete, since modern science has largely discarded it as the framework for interpreting the way the universe works. Yet, if it is the popular picture of developments in science and technology that tends to change journalists' worldview more than their theoretical understanding of scientific ideas does, then we may be at the dawn of a new day in journalists' professional attitude. The fast-moving and unsettling advances that computer technology has brought to the news business are forcing journalists to alter their fundamental view of their profession. In symbolic ways, if nothing else, the way the "new media" work mimics the chaos theory that (along with quantum mechanics) is at the forefront of modern theories of physical predictability, and the indeterminacy principle could be just another name for what media executives face when they try to gauge the future prospects of their industry.[45] The classical, three-dimensional models of the news business—the inverted pyramid, the scannable news page, the old-fashioned news lead of the five *w*'s and an *h*—are under assault from hyper-text, network

browsers, and search engines, all operating on a grid system that, metaphorically at least, seems to extend into multiple dimensions diverging endlessly off
into cyberspace. Everything about the Internet seems, at least to minds still
wedded to classical modes of thought, to invite anarchy and chaos, a webbed
world where information spins in endless giga-bytes pulsing through millions
of miles of electronic current. Most of this, of course, has very little to do with
cutting-edge theories of physics. But the mental image called forth by the Internet seems to agitate the orderly mind and lead to visions of a whirling vortex of mounting information engulfing our collective consciousness in the same
way that big bangs, black holes, and antimatter stretch the imagination.

It is hard to believe that the march of science and technology—always so
influential in the religious picture of the universe—will ever fully absorb the
religious impulse into the culture's rapidly changing communications systems
in the way that Marshall McLuhan once imagined. But the fast-proliferating
digitized consciousness of our interactive and interconnected collective life is
certainly going to exercise its influence on the shape of the religious imagination of the twenty-first century—as well as on the journalistic profession and
the way journalists imagine the methodologies of their profession to work. The
news profession—as connected as it is to a peculiar blending of science and
religion in modern thought—is facing the prospect of a major transformation
under the pressures of the perpetually self-reinventing world of science and high
technology. One wonders if journalists—often seemingly oblivious to the philosophical and religious underpinnings of their professional methodologies—will
survive the changes in the form and content of news that are, as the media critic Ben Bagdikian put it, "similar to the old theological upheavals."[46]

CHAPTER 12

The Mind of the Inquiring Reporter: Psychology and the Science of the Soul

Like many famous people, Sigmund Freud had little use for the popular press. "Why [do] you still believe anything you read in an American newspaper?" he grumbled to a disciple in 1928. The article that had provoked Freud's scorn was a *New York Times* account of the controversy created by Freud's latest book, *The Future of an Illusion,* where the Viennese founder of psychoanalysis contended that religion amounted to little more than a childish illusion and the projections of wish fulfillments of ancient peoples. The headlines of the article read "Religion Doomed/Freud Asserts/Says It Is at Point Where It Must Give Way before Science/His Followers Chagrined/Master Psychoanalyst's New Book Deplored for Dissension It Is Expected to Cause."[1]

In a figurative sense, Freud was having done to him what his critics say he did to religion. The press's tendency to stereotype and simplify yet to believe itself the organ of objective science mirrors Freud's own tendency to reduce complex human behavior into tidy psychological formulas that he offered up as scientific explanations. Freud's hostility to religion consistently was dressed up in his work as scientific inquiry. Yet today, in many academic and intellectual circles, Freud's claims about religion are perhaps the only aspect of his psychoanalytical theories that are not seen as anachronisms—brilliant but outdated ideas about the functioning of the human personality that succeed as philosophical speculation and literary symbolism more than as scientific explanations for the operation of the psyche.

Ironically, Freud's theories and the religion he so detested share the same lack of scientific basis, no matter how much "projection" and "wish fulfillment" (favorite Freudian terms) went into Freud's own hopes to see his ideas treated as empirical fact. Freud based his theories about the workings of the human

psyche on interviews with neurotic Viennese women and presented these theories in a fashion that cannot be decisively proven or disproven in the empirical sense of the term, just as there is no way to prove or disprove elements of
faith based on reports of religious experience.

Largely because of Freud's scientific pretensions and the press's desire to see
its own methodology treated as a form of empirical science, psychological speculation constitutes a major part of the media's coverage of everything from
crime to politics to lifestyle. In much of its coverage, the press treats psychological theorizing about why people behave as they do—asking experts why
people go on a killing spree, why people are unhappy in the workplace, why
married couples fight and what can be done about it—as if it is a reflection of
precise scientific analysis. In embracing Freud or at least the psychological field
that Freud did much to advance, many journalists have found a comfortable
place from which to probe life's imponderables and to discover patterns in
human behavior. In doing this, the press has elevated psychology to such an
honored position in the social order that some would see it as new theology to
explain human mystery and enshroud the meaning of life.

Although Freud may have had reason to object to the inflammatory headlines and the dramatizations in the *New York Times*'s reaction to his book, he,
in fact, was an atheist and an implacable foe of organized religion who believed
that the premises of science are incompatible with religion and that religion was
a failure in the face of modern scientific advancements. Religion, in Freud's
schema, was a powerful symbol for the drama taking place in the human subconscious, but his reflections on the subject barely disguise the contempt for
religious belief that he shared with many nineteenth- and early-twentieth-century members of the intelligentsia who were in rebellion against Victorian moral
and religious attitudes.

Freud also had good reason, as have many intellectual pioneers, for disliking
and distrusting newspapers of his day. Freud's theories were initially belittled in
the Victorian atmosphere of the late nineteenth century and early twentieth, when
the press spread "confusion and facile judgments," particularly about Freud's
contention that the sexual drive, transformed into a whole range of subconscious
and irrational compulsions, explains the behavior of human beings. Like Einstein and Darwin, Freud was subject to caricature in the popular press; he was
"the grave, bearded Herr Professor, complete with droll, heavy Central European
accent, who had put sex on the map," as the biographer Peter Gay put it. Puritanical elements of the press in both Europe and the United States castigated
Freud, like Darwin, for undermining Christian notions of humans as rational
beings capable of making free and conscious choices and occupying a special
status among God's creatures. As late as 1926, the *London Times* was demanding
a medical investigation of psychoanalysis and refusing to print letters from psy-
choanalysts defending themselves from attacks against them.[2]

But as with Darwin, Freud experienced during his lifetime an enormous transformation in the public response to his theories, especially in the popular press. Although Freud's ideas about the power of the sexual and subconscious impulses in humans at first shocked Victorian sensibilities, including those of editors and publishers, the press soon came to see Freud as a fellow rationalist in the great Enlightenment tradition—debunking religion, pushing reason into the realm of the irrational, and asserting the primacy of science as a way to understand human behavior. Freud's hostility to the traditional religious explanations for human activity and his determination to see psychoanalysis as a science and a legitimate medical method to treat emotional illness fit in nicely with the empirical, pragmatic mood of the age, particularly the press's desire to find plausible (and marketable) explanations for the antisocial and deviant acts that provided the grist for its pages.

The popular press had much to do with the fact that psychoanalysis soon became all the rage among a population that generally understood very little about it and, particularly in the United States, quickly became the material of faddists and profiteers. "Most unfortunately for Freud's repute, his theories lend themselves with terrible ease to the uses of ignorance and of quackery," the *New York Times* noted in 1926.[3] The highbrow *Times* might have been referring to its lowbrow competitors, who were eager to exploit the popularity of psychoanalysis in legitimatizing the coverage of titillating information, particularly in the lucrative market of stories that traded on sex, crime, and violence. In 1924, for example, Freud was offered $25,000 by the *Chicago Tribune* publisher Colonel Robert McCormick if Freud would go to Chicago and psychoanalyze the murderers Nathan Leopold and Richard Loeb. This "grotesque" recognition of the stature of Freud's new science of the mind, as another Freud biographer, Giovanni Costigan, put it, was upped, in true tabloid fashion, when William Randolph Hearst promised Freud any fee he might care to name and the use of a special liner to cross the Atlantic to go to Chicago for the trial. The next year the movie mogul Sam Goldwyn offered Freud $100,000 to act as technical adviser for a film about Anthony and Cleopatra, and a few years later several American publishers urged Freud to undertake a psychoanalysis of the Bible.[4] (All of these overtures were spurned by a slightly amused Freud.)

Freud also had a large following among individual journalists, who were seeking new ways to explain human behavior without relying on the old religious formulas. In 1912, Walter Lippmann, the prominent newspaper columnist, described his enthusiasm at first reading Freud "as men might have felt about *The Origin of Species*" and recounted how in rereading William James (the philosopher and early psychologist with whom Lippmann studied as a young man) he was struck with "a curious sense that the world must have been very young in the 1880's."[5] "Serious young men took Freud quite seriously, as indeed he deserved to be taken," Lippmann wrote. "Exploitation of Freud into a tiresome fad came later and generally from people who had not studied him and had only heard about him."[6]

Interestingly, James—the father of the pragmatic philosophical movement so embraced by journalists and yet also a professional student of religion with a deep interest in mystical experience—was filled with qualms at the "programmatic, obsessive hostility to religion" that he found among Freudians, even though he generally applauded Freud for his contributions to understanding dream life and the psyche. It is probably no surprise then, in the years since his theories first burst onto the scene, that many of Freud's critics have found in his fervent promotion of the premises of psychoanalysis—that reason can conquer superstition, that religious conceptions resemble the mental states of primitive people, and that the premises of science are incompatible with religion—an almost messianic belief in the power of his psychoanalytical movement to replace religion as the wellspring of human understanding. Peter Gay pointed out that the philosophers of the Enlightenment, with their deep skepticism toward traditional religion, reverberate throughout the pages of Freud's writing. "Your substitute religion is in essence the Enlightenment thought of the eighteenth century in proud, fresh, modern guise," his friend Oskar Pfister once told Freud.[7]

Freud did not believe he was advocating a substitute religion, but he did often speak with almost religious certitude of his psychoanalytical theories.[8] He urged the Swiss psychologist and one-time colleague Carl Jung, for example, to help him "make a dogma . . . an unshakeable bulwark" of his sexual theory,[9] and he once wrote to a colleague, "We possess the truth; I am as sure of it as fifteen years ago."[10] Asked about the eventual break with his two former disciples, Jung and Alfred Adler, Freud explained it this way: "Precisely because they too wanted to be Popes."[11] The most notable dispute of his professional life was with Jung, who contended that human actions were based on something more than just the sexual impulse, as Freud believed, and that religious belief was a fundamental human need, not just a distorted response to childhood fears and unresolved psychological fixations, as Freudian theory insisted.

Almost from the start of their relationship, Jung was troubled by Freud's insistence that human instincts were virtually all rooted in the sex drive and that religion was an unhealthy perversion of that drive. Throughout his life, Jung exhibited a strong interest in mysticism, parapsychology, alchemy, and the occult, as well as Christian and pagan mythology, and he came to believe that some form of religious belief or at least the embrace of a force or power that transcended one's own ego was vital to the process of becoming one's true self and developing an integrated inner life. In contrast, Freud believed the appeal of religion could be traced back to the unhealthy influence of unmet childhood needs, and he scorned people who needed the "illusion" of religion to deal with life's vicissitudes. Freud viewed with increasing alarm what he felt was the spiritual turn in Jung's thinking, and he worried that Jung would have to incur the "disgrace" of having turned into a mystic. Freud grew especially contemptuous of Jung for deemphasizing the centrality of the sexual instinct in subconscious life and emphasizing that God is a primal experience of the human being—

something that Freud believed Jung did to make psychoanalysis more palatable to a prudish public that felt psychoanalysis was atheistic and perverted.[12]

When Freud and Jung split over the importance of religion, the press, in figurative terms again, chose Freud. The dispute between Freud and Jung broadened into the two principle currents of the psychoanalytical movement in the twentieth century: the psychological rationalism of researchers and practitioners who, although seldom Freudians anymore, still thought of psychology as a scientific pathway to unlocking the cures for emotional and mental distress, and the other more mystical psychology of Jung that emphasized the spiritual dimensions in the activities of the subconscious. The rationalist wing—where most elements of the press still reside today—treats psychological matters as an exercise in intellectually based, Enlightenment-rooted analysis that focuses the light of reason on the otherwise hidden, distorted, and irrational impulses of human beings. Freud's view of the sexual impulse as the source of subconscious human drives has a particular appeal to the world of journalism, where news (focusing on conflict, crime, controversy, personality, oddity, and, increasingly, sex) requires a steady flow of "analysis" that tries to make sense of the strange and bizarre things going on in the world. Applying a "logical" theoretical pattern to seemingly inexplicable human behavior has an irresistible attraction to journalists, and doing psychological journalism or quoting psychological experts has become a staple of journalists who write about crime, politics, or personalities.

Freud's tendency to see symbolic patterns that can be almost mechanically applied to human activity or interpreted as the subconscious motive for human behavior lent itself to the press's tendency, as Lippmann complained, to simplify life's events into compelling yet easily comprehensible formulas. As the popular understanding of Freud's ideas has spread, the reductionism inherent in Freud's theories has dovetailed nicely with the press's zeal for stereotyping. Much of what Freud did—looking out at the world and discovering patterns of subconscious meaning in individual and collective activity—is exactly what journalists hope to do when they assess the human landscape about which they report. Freud found repetitive models for working out unconscious psychic tensions everywhere he looked, all fitting into formulas—involving such concepts as the Oedipal complex, castration anxiety, the Electra complex, the death wish, the clash between the ego, superego, and id—that he treated as empirical discoveries. Freud's desire to see psychoanalysis treated as a science is rivaled by the press's determination to see itself as an "objective" force in uncovering truth. Paradoxically, modern psychology has moved far beyond Freudianism into a wide array of schools of thought and psychotherapeutic movements, as well as drug and behavioral treatment, and it has long since rejected the notion that Freud's theories and insights (brilliant and foundational as they were) can be called science by the prevailing standards of empirical verification. Yet today's journalists (while abandoning many of Freud's psychological concepts) still are tempted to rush in with formulaic psychological explanations whenever faced with curious or deviant human behavior.

It is not surprising, given the press's propensity to see psychology within the empirical tradition, that Jung's more spiritually oriented theories have never captured the imagination of the journalistic community, even though they became popular with the public during the latter half of the twentieth century. Jung's ideas about human archetypes and the mythological unconscious have won him many followers, particularly among liberal Christians, universalists, holistic health counselors, self-help organizations, and the New Age movement, and his concepts have been blended with religious doctrine to produce what has become known as the Jungian spin on modern religious belief. Many members of the press, in accepting Freud's notion of psychology as based in science, share Freud's discomfort with the idea of religion as a necessary factor in the integration of the healthy personality and his rejection of Jung's notion of the religious impulse as a wellspring of healing and recovery in the human psyche. Freud—with his emphasis on sexuality and human deviancy, his psychological formulas that have seeped into the popular consciousness, and his distaste for religion—provides a more compatible psychological system for a profession like journalism that prides itself on its skepticism and its irreverence, focuses much of its attention on aberrational personalities and events, and can find in Freud as much to mock and ridicule as to pattern its coverage after. Journalists have never evinced much overt interest in the rivalry that developed between the Jungian and Freudian wings of psychology, but, in the development of their reporting methodologies, they have, perhaps without always realizing it, revealed a clear preference for the Freudian notion that almost every human impulse, including the religious impulse, stems from a distorted transformation of a more fundamental drive. Freud's formulas for how the sex drive can become manifested (penis envy or anal retentiveness, for example) might be expected to bring chuckles from journalists, but not because they do not subscribe to the fundamental concept.

Yet the practice of psychological journalism—while, in some respects, growing more sophisticated since Freud's time—still falls prey to what the Freudian scholar Philip Rieff saw as a key failing of Freud's system: mistaking interpretations of human motivation for fact. Freudian analysis, like journalistic objectivity, is far from the expression of value-free notions that Freud considered his science. With Freud, "one can always get from description to judgment in a single short step," Rieff wrote.[13] Freudian interpretation is, in essence, a poetic act or, to stretch the analogy even further, an act of faith—although admittedly, a new kind of faith in the power of human understanding to unlock the repressed emotions of the unconscious. Journalism, relying on the judgments of experts, has never held quite such lofty goals for itself, but its determination to simplify, popularize, and make accessible complex intellectual concepts to its market of readers and viewers has done much to give the veneer of fact to the art of psychoanalysis. While it would be exaggerating somewhat to posit a direct parallel between Freud's case histories and the typical use of psychological theories in newspaper profiles or crime stories, one would be myopic not to see how Freud's fundamental tenets—particularly his belief that conscious knowledge and unconscious motive may run on two different tracks—have influenced the journalistic presentation of the world.

Like many others in the sciences, philosophy, and literature during the nineteenth century and early twentieth, Freud was engaged in establishing an "all-embracing" replacement for the traditional truths of Christian culture, one of the "great formulation[s] of nineteenth century secularism, complete with substitute doctrine and cult," as Rieff put it. For Freud, great synthesizer that he was, psychoanalysis offered a new interpretation of virtually the entire spectrum of human intellectual activity—religion, history, literature, philosophy, anthropology, sociology, civics, and, of course, psychology. But as an aggressive atheist, Freud was preoccupied with the hold that religion maintained over human imagination, and he devoted much of his literary output to portraying religious belief as merely a disguise or rationalization for deeper emotions and patterns of psychic activity. Like so many of the Enlightenment rationalists, as well as such romantic philosophers as Nietzsche and Schopenhauer, Freud believed it was not enough that religion gave people confidence, comfort, and a sense of security. In Freud's view, "religion bestows the very fears and anxieties that it then appeases," as Rieff put it. "Religion may have been the original cure; Freud reminds us that it was also the original disease."[14]

It would be unfair to hold Freud responsible for having fostered psychology's usurpation of religion in many of the accounts of human activity on the typical newspaper page. The increasing secularization of society in the eighteenth, nineteenth, and twentieth centuries and the newspaper industry's involvement in that trend have multiple explanations, and the spread of psychological theories is but one of them. But journalism, as a powerful organ that both reflects and defines popular thinking, illustrates in one of the most visible ways not only how the tenets of psychology have come to replace religious terminology as the common parlance of our individual and collective lives but also the largely superficial nature of this transformation. Nowhere more than in the media do we see the popular drift of psychological science, where, in Rieff's words, "psychological doctrine, filtered down into textbooks, daily newspaper columns, salesmanship manuals, and the mental hygiene movement, overtly anti-religious and carrying all the pomposity of an immature science in its train," teaches us that individual psychic adjustment and freedom from internal emotional stress are the keys to self-realization or the explanations for deviancy.[15] Against this backdrop, "pop" psychological journalism—practiced from newspaper crime reporting to tabloid television to the personality profiles and self-improvement advice in such magazines as *Self* and *People*—can be seen as additional evidence that the old-fashioned search for God's will (or, contrarily, the recognition of the places where the devil is at work in the world) has been replaced in modern life with the belief that it is only our interior "hang-ups" and our psychological stuck places that keep us from realizing our fullest potential or hold us down in our repressed condition.

It is far too glib to say that Freud's theory of the implacability of the unconscious has replaced in the minds of modern people the Christian church's notion of an omnipotent and an omniscient God working providentially in the lives of humans and human society. Religion, to say the least, has survived the onslaught of the psychological sciences (as the press's recent "discovery" of its audience's interest in religion demonstrates), and, in many ways, psychology has been adapted to the uses of religion as much as the opposite. A large literature has grown up among enlightened clergy and progressive religious thinkers seeking to balance the insights of psychology with the revealed truths of the major religious traditions. Jung himself is strongly identified with that wing of liberal Christianity, and Jungian interpretations of the Christian message can be found quite readily among the writers and ministers of the major Christian denominations. The hero's quest—whether it involves Jesus, Buddha, or Odysseus— where great religious or mythological figures come face to face with their demons, both external and internal, blends, in Jung's thinking, with the heroic demands of our own life journeys and has made Jung a highly popular figure among those who are attracted to the idea of harmonizing theology, mythology, and psychology. However, the fact that Jung, too, has been subject to so much popularization makes him suspect in many quarters, certainly among those tougher-minded critics (as Freud was) who find in Jung a fuzzy mythologizing that allows the libido to be portrayed not as a fierce and awesome force that may work against us but as a sort of élan vital out of which life's fulfillment can be gained.

Freud's tough-mindedness is a closer reflection of the stoical and hardened view of life found in the newsroom than is Jung's happy embrace of the religious impulse as essential to the achievement of an integrated personality. Freudianism's rejection of religion's comforts—combined with its insistence on empirical proof of anything so "irrational" as mystical assertion—makes it a better model for a profession that, in many quarters, operates by the principle that religion should be treated, at best, as just another enthusiasm in a modern world filled with a myriad of lifestyle options or, at worst, as a vestige of a more primitive time that can be happily discarded. In contrast, psychology—which provides an "empirical" analysis of the world that dovetails so nicely with journalism's marketing formulas—is embraced unquestioningly as a foundation for the intrepid journalist seeking to shine the light of "reason" on the crazy events of the world.

The respectability of psychological analysis has become so unchallenged in news organizations that it is safe for a reporter to treat a psychological theory about human action as if it is a "fact" that fits into the canon of journalistic objectivity, particularly if it has been advanced by an expert in the field. Just as journalists rely on experts and official sources in politics, police work, government, and business, they are quick to seek out the theories of academics, clinicians, and researchers in psychology—most of whose observations are used alongside the most elemental facts about the who, what, when, and where of a news story. That people are convicted (in the press and in the courtroom) on the basis of their psychological profile has become so commonplace in modern life that few question its applicability.

The case of Richard Jewell, the hero-turned-suspect-turned-press-victim in the 1996 Atlanta Olympics bombing, brought this tendency to public attention in a dramatic fashion. Jewell's journey into fame and then into infamy, when he was first hailed as hero for reporting the pipe bomb and then fingered as a suspect for planting it, led to much handwringing and mea culpas in journalistic circles. After the FBI backed off from its suspicions of Jewell, the spotlight turned to the press, which had headlined leaks from the bureau that pinpointed Jewell as the chief suspect. While much of the debate centered on the propriety of using leaked information on uncharged suspects, the controversy surrounding Jewell also highlighted journalists' habit of accepting unthinkingly a proposition that has become widespread in modern society: experts, guided by the science of psychology, can produce a psychological profile of a person who might be prone to commit a crime. In Jewell's case, the profile—of a loner and a frustrated gun enthusiast, a law enforcement "wanna-be" whose need for attention propelled him to commit a crime so that he could emerge the hero—seemed to fit so exactly with society's preconception of a psychologically driven personality that both the FBI agents and the reporters who ran with the leaked information could not resist pointing the finger at Jewell.[16]

That this speculation about Jewell's propensity for deviant behavior upon further investigation turned out to be nothing more than pop psychology gone awry was largely ignored in the critics' condemnation of the press coverage in the Jewell case. The working principles of journalists, as well as those of police investigators, social workers, personnel managers, and educators, have come to reflect a world in which psychological insight and analysis are treated as objective science—whether it is in the administration of personality tests by institutions and businesses, the production of self-help books, or the use of expert witnesses in court cases. Yet what are we to make of "psychological" journalism if we accept that Freud can be viewed, as he now is in many scholarly quarters, as a philosopher of the psyche who refashioned the tenets of eighteenth-century Enlightenment rationalism and nineteenth-century romanticism into a twentieth-century "science" of the soul? Might we not discover—as we did with Enlightenment thought and nineteenth-century romanticism—that psychoanalysis can be viewed largely as another reaction against, but ultimately as a another substitute for, the prevailing Judeo-Christian explanations of human behavior? Might we not conclude that the "psychological" press—like Freud, desirous of viewing itself as empirical, objective, and scientifically respectable—

is actually operating in an environment in which a transformed religious impulse is working (in true Freudian fashion) at the deepest, subconscious levels?

Reporters and editors who have distilled a variation of Freud's insights into a journalistic version of newsroom pop psychology would do well to pay attention to those who note how potent it is, and how dangerous it may become, to believe in an "objective" science of psychological patterns to deduce the subconscious motives of human behavior. Freud thought of the unconscious as something like a "hidden god," Rieff pointed out, indifferent, impersonal, unconcerned about its impact on the life of the individual. Freud inherited this view of the unconscious as the blind will of the instinctual life from his romantic predecessors. In particular, his view of the unconscious mirrors Schopenhauer's notions of women and Nietzsche's fascination with the "Dionysian" side of the human personality—the Greek god of passion, ecstasy, and emotional frenzy.[17] But, unlike Nietzsche, who urged that we embrace and live out our darkest drives and instincts, Freud—like the many journalists he has come to influence—proved himself to be an Enlightenment rationalist more than a romantic advocate of a cult of the irrational. Just as journalists are influenced by the vestige of romantic ideals, Freud shared with the romantics his belief that subconscious mental activity is rooted in some earlier memory—particularly those having to do with childhood needs and traumas—and that neurotic symptoms are a mask for this memory. Unlike the romantics, however, Freud never denigrated reason as a powerful blight on spontaneity. In the Freudian schema (as it is in the Freudian-influenced formulas of much crime reporting), it is reason that must master the unconscious.

Looking at Freud and his influence on journalism from this perspective enables us to see why Jung's followers might find it curious that Jung, instead of Freud, is portrayed as the advocate of treating psychology in terms usually reserved for religious belief. Jung defended himself as a scientist in the empirical tradition in the sense that he acknowledged the observed power of religious experience in human life. "I practice science . . . and I have neither the competence nor the desire to found a religion," he said. "My interest is a scientific one. . . . My concern is to point out in a scientifically responsible way those empirically tangible facts which would at least make plausible the legitimacy of Christian and especially Catholic dogma."[18] As an empiricist, Jung looked to personal experience and direct observation first, and those told him that the religious impulse and the images of God played a profound part in the individual's journey to emotional wholeness. Jung believed that psychoanalysis for Freud had come to be little more than a substitute religion that replaced theological explanations of human behavior with psychological theories about inner compulsive drives. In his autobiography, Jung chose explicitly religious language to describe his differences with Freud: "Freud, who had always made much of his irreligiosity, had now constructed a dogma; or rather, in the place of a jealous God whom he had lost, he had substituted another compelling image, that of sexuality."[19]

Jung's approach, I would argue, can serve as a model for journalists on how to write honestly and respectfully about religion no matter what their religious orientation. Not many journalists have been interested in Jung, but one of the most notable was the muckraker (and mystic) Upton Sinclair.[20] Jung underwent his own mid-life crisis, precipitated in part by his break with Freud (some would call it a breakdown), a painful descent into the depths of his dreams and his inner emotional torments, from which he emerged with the firm belief that mysterious forces had prepared the ground for a new stage in his psychic odyssey. In confronting a multitude of self-revealing fantasies in his subconscious and "discovering my own myth," as he put it, Jung felt compelled to base his developing psychological theories on his own encounters with the realm of the spiritual.[21] This is something Jung believed, as he indicated in correspondence to Sinclair, that a journalist, who often bases a theory on firsthand observation, might understand.

It is fascinating to see how far Jung, despite his strong distaste for Christian dogma, went in defending the meaningful role of Christian symbolism against the efforts—so common during his lifetime—to redefine Christianity along the lines of the rationalist, humanist values so fashionable with the modern intelligentsia. For example, Jung was gentle but incisive in critiquing Sinclair's efforts to reinterpret the meaning of Jesus in the rational and enlightened terms of a progressive American journalist. Jung chided Sinclair for attempting to tell a "better" story about Jesus, "something nice and reasonable" that did not repeat those "ancient absurdities," such as the "Virgin Birth, blood and flesh mysteries, and other wholly superfluous miracle gossip." Jung chastised Sinclair for creating a portrait that discarded too many statements of Jesus that "do not fit in with your premises," particularly the eschatological and messianic elements of Jesus' message. "Surely, we can draw a portrait of Jesus that does not offend our rationalism" but at the same time retains "loyalty to the textual authority" of the New Testament, Jung wrote.[22]

As with Freud (although in quite different ways), Jung was accused by his critics of trying to psychologize religion along the lines of his own theories and of promoting a new form of psychologized religious humanism ("To become human seems to me to be the intention of God in us," Jung wrote). But Jung actually occupied an important position between the defenders of traditional Christian belief and the rationalist debunkers of Christian dogma, such as Freud and Sinclair. Jung did comment, sometimes sarcastically, on the contradictions in the Hebrew scriptures and the similarities between the Christ stories and pre-Christian myths. Unlike Freud and those who used the anomalies in the Bible to write off religious experience as subjective illusion or projections of neurotic needs, however, Jung recognized the power of biblical stories to influence individual lives and the culture at large, and he was adamant in his view that the human soul is a "vessel for an ultimately inexhaustible content that is beyond the reach of the ego."[23]

Perhaps fittingly, while the spiritual aspect of Jung's thinking may not have had much impact on journalists' thinking, the press did its best to do to Jung what it did to Freud, which was to celebrate him as a great seer or a soothsayer, at least in a superficial sense. With little comprehension of or real interest in his theories, journalists made pilgrimages to the residence of the amiable, pipe-smoking, white-haired Swiss doctor (Jung's stereotype was slightly different from the Herr Doctor Freud's) to ask him for a psychological interpretation of world events. The impression Jung made on H. R. Knickerbocker, a reporter for Hearst International's *Cosmopolitan* magazine, after their 1939 Zurich interview, for example, was symptomatic of the general influence psychoanalytic theory exercised on the press by World War II. "Over and over he said that Jung was the only person who really knew what was going on in Europe, that none of the statesmen or politicians had any idea at all of what the growing volcanic rumbling on the European scene heralded," wrote a colleague about Knickerbock-er's reaction. "Only Jung knew it."[24]

Yet as much as journalists like to apply psychological interpretations to others, they have resisted it when psychological theories are used to analyze them. At least one behavioral psychologist applied psychoanalytical analysis to the operation of the modern newsroom and found it lacked collective psychological health. The Harvard organizational psychologist Chris Argyris came to conclusions about human nature almost as pessimistic as Freud's when Argyris was brought in to improve the management operations of the *New York Times* in the 1970s. In his book *Behind the Front Page*, Argyris wrote that he gave up on the possibilities for healthier and more forthright ways for journalists to interact in the workplace, and he concluded that journalistic management systems were so neurotic and impermeable to change that there was little hope for the future of the newspaper industry. Argyris found the executives he worked with to be compulsive, insecure, dominating, defensive, emotionally closed, averse to risk-taking, and inflexible. In Freudian fashion, Argyris ultimately despaired of introducing honest and unrepressed methods of communication into the system, and he left resigned that the newspaper business would labor under management systems that would reflect the press's "organizational paranoia" and the unhealthy psyches of newsroom leaders.[25]

It is only natural that journalists wince when they see themselves psychoanalyzed in the same way they psychoanalyze others, but the lesson is an obvious one. Psychology, like religious systems it was to supplant, applies a series of interpretative categories to the often unfathomable activities of the human psyche. Journalists too often pretend to rely on psychology as fact when it is, in reality, only one more symbolic method of describing and interpreting human behavior. Many journalists—believers in their own empirical methodologies—have become more comfortable with the categories of psychology than with the categories of religion. But journalists need to tread softly in this territory of the human unconscious. Much about modern life has convinced people to abandon the belief, which Freud held at the outset of his career, that reason is the ineluctable guide to conquering the inner impulses that drive us. Freud himself modified this notion in his later, more pessimistic writings.[26] Lots of journalists, in their own personal philosophy, have done the same thing, even as they continue to use convenient, psychoanalytical categories as part of their writers' arsenal. But, in this way, psychology survives as just one more journalistic shorthand way to try to make sense of the mysteries of the soul. To claim more for it would be to pretend, as St. Thomas Aquinas did, that one had succeeded in the task of reconciling reason with the ways of God.

CHAPTER 13

The Press, Politics, and Religion
in the Public Square

It was such a good piece of political gossip, even back in 1950, that reporters probably could be excused for not focusing on the religious angle: Drew Pearson, liberal Quaker and the preeminent investigative journalist in the nation's capital, was kneed twice in the groin in the cloakroom of a private Washington, D.C., club by the angry and drunken Senator Joseph McCarthy, the anticommunist inquisitor of the early cold war years. The fight—with McCarthy slapping Pearson around "movie-villain fashion" after exchanging insults at a dinner party—was broken up by Senator Richard Nixon, evangelical Quaker, McCarthy's ally in the hunt for communists in government, and a fellow despiser of Pearson and his muckraking journalism. "Let a Quaker stop this fight," Nixon is said to have announced as he pulled McCarthy away from the fallen Pearson.[1]

A few days after the national publicity about the incident, Nixon received a note from Herman Perry, the son of a Quaker minister and Nixon's most powerful backer among his Republican supporters in his hometown of Whittier, California. In it, Perry joshed Nixon about a "letter of censure" the Whittier Lions Club had "almost" sent him for intervening to save Pearson, who had regularly gone after McCarthy and had criticized Nixon and his anticommunist campaign for the Senate in 1950. "They definitely feel that you should not have shown your Quaker training in stopping the fight," Perry wrote.[2]

For anyone who views politics through the lens of religion, this incident was rich in symbolism, replete with clues about the tensions between Nixon's political and religious values, and instructive in the way that the complexities of American religious belief influence our political leaders, even in a supposedly secular age when most politicians deal with matters of religion in a highly calculated manner and with great caution. It can be argued that, in never fully understanding the nature of Nixon's Quakerism and the role it played in his life, the press missed out, as it has with many presidents and other top American political leaders, in explaining how religious background and belief help illuminate the motivation and character of one of our important political personalities.

Journalists, of course, were amply aware of Nixon's Quaker background, and they emphasized it repeatedly in portraying Nixon as a flawed and compulsively ambitious personality whose moralistic public image contrasted with a vindictive private nature that led him, in the nature of a Greek tragedy, to be brought down by his criminal involvement in the Watergate scandal.[3] Castigated in bestselling books by the Watergate investigative journalists Bob Woodward and Carl Bernstein and blockbuster movies by Robert Redford and Oliver Stone, Nixon was defined in the popular imagination by his statement, "I am not a crook," his resignation from the presidency in 1974, and his efforts in retirement to rescue his place in history from disgrace. Journalists have pictured Nixon as the son of a "saintly" Quaker mother whose pious advice he spurned and his Quakerism as a contradictory backdrop for his sanctimonious public pronouncements, his mean-spirited political machinations, and his paranoia about his political enemies. "Nixon seemed to have a soul," the journalist-historian Garry Wills once wrote, in summing up the press corps' general attitude toward Nixon, "even if a damned one."[4]

But this is a simplistic caricature, particularly in the presentation of Quakerism as a pious religion that could have produced a Nixon only if he proved to be a wayward product of the faith in which he was raised. In fact, while the press seems sometimes inordinately focused on the religious beliefs of presidential candidates (particularly if they can then be deemed by their actions to be untrue to their faith), journalists often have a limited and superficial understanding of presidents' religious beliefs and the role that denominational differences play in their theological and political outlook. This often means that the press's portrayal of the role that religion plays in politics is flawed, stereotyped, and subject to misleading interpretation, particularly when the press, always on the lookout for falseness and phoniness in politicians, portrays religion as something that candidates simply use to impress voters.

Where Nixon may have been blinded by overweening ambition, the press's blindness to the nuances of religious life in the United States deprived its audience of the fullest possible understanding of the religious wellsprings of Nixon's inner nature and the way these translated into his political actions. The press is even more cynical in its judgments about religion, particularly the religious beliefs of politicians, than about the motivations of politicians. It is almost axiomatic among reporters that most politicians' positions on religious questions are not reflections of true belief as much as they are efforts to manipulate public opinion and curry favor with voters and religious groups; if, however, their political views are seen as a reflection of deeply held faith, then they are probably a product of religious extremism and should not be trusted. This cynicism reflects three impulses in the press: to present religious belief as if it should be a private matter and to respond suspiciously when politicians use it on the public stage; to ignore denominational or theological differences while providing pro forma accounts of politicians' "religiosity," presumed to be packaged largely for public consumption; and to treat religious faith that appears to drive a politician's political objectives as something potentially dangerous to the Republic. As a result, the press is usually interested in the religious beliefs of political figures only to the extent that they reflect on questions of hypocrisy, generate political controversy, or can be framed in terms of political zealotry. At the same time, the press seldom acts on the basis of these cynical assumptions and rarely probes the ways politicians dress up their religious faith to serve their political ambitions. Politicians' religious faith is seldom presented as sincere or insincere because members of the press often cannot or do not want to try to draw distinctions between religious belief that is genuine and that which is convenient. In the end, the press's blind spots about religion often mean that it abdicates its responsibility to help the public better understand and perhaps distinguish between the public pronouncements of faith made by politicians and to better comprehend the complex role that faith plays in politics beyond the superficial religious categories into which journalists prefer to fit politicians.

The saga of Richard Nixon—as told in the typical journalistic accounts of his political career—exemplifies these tendencies in the press. Behind the media portrayals of Nixon as venal political opportunist, tortured psychological personality, and callous betrayer of the public trust lies the religious personality of Richard Nixon, one that owes much to the complicated and often contradictory transformations in the theology and value system of American Quakerism as it adapted to the peculiar historical circumstances of American life. Unquestionably, Nixon's unscrupulous ways and his ethical transgressions had more to do with his personal character or his lack thereof than with his Quaker background. But the religious elements of his complex personality also reflect the splits, the schisms, and the struggle for a modern identity that has plagued American Quakers (also known as Friends), as it has many Christian denominations during their history on American soil.

Understanding Nixon's evangelical, southern California Quakerism makes it easier to understand how someone with such conflicting ethical principles, such moral cross-currents working within him, and such a bitter sense of persecution could fail after rising to the highest office in the land. Nixon's conversion at a fundamentalist revival and his pietistic interpretation of political and constitutional issues fit with the classic experiences of those raised in the evangelical wing of Quakerism that was transformed by the nineteenth-century revival movement, the Methodist holiness campaign, and the various great awakenings in American history. The high ideals and the strict rules of upright behavior Nixon inherited from his Quaker heritage—and Nixon's inability to live up to them—are commonly viewed as the backdrop to his contradictory behavior. But the

transformation of those ideals within evangelical Quakerism points to the turmoil that has occurred within Quakerism as it has adapted its teachings under
pressure to conform to mainstream elements of American social and political
life. In Nixon's case, this tension within his own religious tradition may have
contributed to a sense that his goals were too high to be reached by normal means,
that his mission was too important to let himself be bound by traditional ethical restraints, and that his tortured self was never good enough.

At the same time, in looking at his bitter rivalry with Pearson and the "liberals" Nixon believed were always out to get him, it is important to examine the
other, better-known wing of American Quakerism—the liberal, nonevangeli-
cal, peace activist–oriented branch centered largely on the East and West coasts
and in cities with college campuses—to which Pearson belonged. Many people
unfamiliar with the splits that have divided American Quakers have not recognized that Nixon's brand of Quakerism is very different from the one associated with social activism, antiwar and antideath penalty stands, and tolerant attitudes toward gays. It helps to look closely at the history of American Quakerism
to better comprehend what led two men of the same faith to operate with a
barely suppressed contempt for each other's politics.

Southern California Quakers, with whom Nixon associated, are conservative,
anticommunist, Republican-oriented people who approved of Nixon's politics
if not—in the end—his political ethics. Honesty and integrity are values embraced by evangelical Quakers, just as they are for the liberal branch of Quakerism, with which Pearson affiliated. However, in other ways, the two groups
reflect the deep split in Quakerism that grew out of the early-nineteenth-cen-
tury dispute between American Quakers over which should be treated as the
most trustworthy guide for the faithful—the scriptural authority of the Bible
or the personal "inner light" of direct revelation from God. The controversy,
which led to the first great separation in American Quakerism in 1827–28, focused on the ministry of Elias Hicks, a New York Quaker, and Joseph John
Gurney, a charismatic English biblical scholar and evangelist who traveled widely
in the United States. Ultimately, the Hicksite branch of Quakerism came to be
known as the liberal wing of Quakerism—theologically tolerant, less traditionally Christian, and committed to such historical Quaker traditions as silent
worship, pacifism, and the lack of a professional ministry. The Gurneyite branch
(or orthodox branch, as it is also known)—deeply influenced by the Great
Awakening and the evangelical mood that swept up many American churches
in the nineteenth century—has come to resemble other Protestant denominations with its emphasis on biblical teachings, personal salvation, and the centrality of Jesus in worship. Soon after the Hicksite-Orthodox separation, many
orthodox congregations were also influenced by Methodist revivalist circuit
riders teaching holiness doctrines who converted Quaker meetings to their
forms of worship, which included more traditional Christian services with a
sermon, hymns, and a formal worship program. That history, combined with a

growing inability of Quaker farmers and merchants to perform the voluntary ministerial work required in traditional Quaker meetings, led many orthodox churches to employ full-time pastors and to abandon the Quaker tradition of gathering silently at worship.

Nixon's Quakerism—like that of Herbert Hoover, Nixon's political patron in his early career and the other Quaker president—was linked to the most conservative of these movements. The East Whittier Friends Church, which Nixon and his family attended, is allied with the evangelical association that grew out of the Gurneyite tradition, and many southern California Quakers, like Nixon, grew up in an atmosphere of revival gatherings, prayer meetings, and close alliances with other evangelical churches. The Quakers in the modern evangelical movement lay claim to the enthusiasm for preaching and witnessing of the early Quakers, such as George Fox, who were exuberant evangelists and strong believers in Christ's saving capacity. But in other ways, the traditional elements of Quaker belief survive only in highly diluted fashion in the conservative evangelical tradition. The historic Quaker peace testimony, which led Quakers to forswear taking up arms in military service to the country, is still subscribed to by some orthodox Friends but not all. For example, when Nixon attended Whittier College, an orthodox Quaker institution, the college maintained a memorial honoring both the alumni who had been pacifists and those who had died fighting in World War I, but the flag honoring the pacifists would later be defaced and eventually removed. Nixon himself gave only brief and passing consideration to becoming a conscientious objector in World War II (which, despite his mother's wishes that he not compromise his Quaker peace principles, he apparently decided would be fatal to a political career).[5]

On a personal level, Nixon was influenced as much by the evangelical and revivalist impulses that came to dominate southern California Quakerism as he was by traditional Quaker doctrine. His father, a grocer/gas station owner and a convert to Quakerism, became a fervent and emotional believer who took his children to the Aimee Semple McPherson revivals, and Nixon himself went through a public conversion at a large Los Angeles gospel rally. Nixon's public image depended little on his religious identification, though. It was widely known that Nixon was raised a Quaker, but, by the time he was elected president in 1968, Nixon seldom attended Friends or any other church, and he was seen, even among many of his followers, as a nominal believer. When he did mix religion into his political appeal, many observers (certainly those in the press) viewed it as little more than a crass grab for votes among the religiously inclined.

As a Hicksite Quaker, Pearson, who emerged as one of Nixon's chief press critics in the 1950s, was a member of a group that tended to attract well-educated, individualistic, and theologically heterodox members—philosophical and political liberals, for the most part, like Pearson. In ways that were to be mirrored in their politics as much as in their religious beliefs, the Hicksites and the Gurneyites each saw the other as the symbol of a rising tide of infidelity engulfing Quakerism. The split is so complete that today members of one branch may have only the slightest awareness of what the other is about (the orthodox usually accuse the liberals of not being Christians, and the liberals counter that the orthodox are closer to Methodists than to Quakers in their religious practices). Predictably, it was largely over the issue of authority that the Hicksites and the Gurneyites split—with the Hicksites insisting that each member be free to follow his or her own "inner light" in matters of conscience and belief and the Gurneyites demanding that biblical authority, as interpreted by church leaders, govern the discipline of membership.[6]

Although Nixon and Pearson shared the same religious heritage, Pearson's brand of Quakerism—theologically liberal, only vaguely Christian, centered on the East Coast, sympathetic to civil liberties and the causes of the underprivileged—had come to symbolize everything that Nixon despised about the eastern intelligentsia and led him once to describe Pearson's wing of Quakerism as "tinctured basically with communism and socialism or whatever you may call it."[7] (The liberal Quakers returned Nixon's enmity, with the Philadelphia Yearly Meeting once unsuccessfully trying to make a "pastoral visit" to the president-elect in the midst of the Vietnam War in 1968. Nixon declined the visit, leaving his relationship with the pacifist wing of Quakerism, which regularly denounced his conduct of the Vietnam War, "awkward and often strained," as his biographer Charles P. Henderson Jr. put it.)[8]

Pearson became the first and in his day the most prominent press critic of Nixon and a focus of Nixon's deep hatred for large portions of the media that covered him. Pearson, "the muckraker with the Quaker conscience," as he was described by the *Washington Post*, occasionally used "thee" and "thou" at home with relatives, was a pacifist, and served on an American Friends Service Committee reconstruction unit in Serbia after World War II.[9] But, like Nixon, Pearson was filled with contradictions (his admirers once described him as someone who was "personally peaceful" but "professionally warlike"), and he nettled Nixon unmercifully in his column, "Washington Merry-Go-Round," which led to what another biographer called "an acrid, quarter-century running battle" between the two men.[10]

As is the case with Nixon, the religious undercurrents that run through the lives and the careers of America's major political figures have seldom received proper attention from the political chroniclers of the times. In his book *Under God*, Garry Wills—one of the few journalists to pay close attention to the ubiquity of religion's place in the American political system—cites example after example of the role religion played in the lives and careers of Ronald Reagan, Gary Hart, Michael Dukakis, the senior George Bush (as well as the more obvious cases of Jimmy Carter, Jesse Jackson, and Pat Robertson). Wills faults the press for its obliviousness to the underlying religious significance of the way politicians have conveyed their messages and carried out their programs. "Religion embarrasses the commentators," Wills declared. "It is offbounds."[11]

The press's lack of understanding of the religious dimension of political life, along with its overriding cynicism about public piety and politicians' open expressions of faith, leads to two forms of coverage, both of which do a disservice to the public. The first was illustrated during the presidency of Bill Clinton, when the press tended to treat Clinton's Baptist views as something apart from his politics, thus making it easier to see the Monica Lewinsky scandal as reflective of behavior that was anomalous with his religious beliefs (the press loved, for example, to talk about Clinton's ability to compartmentalize his life).[12] The second was illustrated during Ronald Reagan's presidency, when a jaded press corps took Reagan's concept of politics dressed up as religion so much for granted that few journalists seriously undertook to explain Reagan's public expressions of faith and his political overtures to the religious Right in the context of Reagan's lack of church attendance and his largely lip-service commitment to the legislative agenda of the Christian conservatives (a maneuver on Reagan's part that, to a great degree, was of little interest to more liberally oriented journalists).

Chief among political journalists' discomfort with religion in politics is their fear that it will breach the wall of separation between church and state—a journalistic twist to the complaint Stephen Carter made in his best-seller, *The Culture of Disbelief*. In his book (incidentally, a favorite of Bill Clinton), Carter argued that the culture's zeal to keep religion from dominating political conversation has led to discounting the legitimate role religion can play in American life and that many Americans mistakenly think the separation clause in the First Amendment means religious motivation has no place in American public debate. In fact, Carter asserted, America's founding figures expected individuals' religious values to play a vigorous role in political life. What they did not want was government to be officially linked with a state church or dominated by formal religion of any kind—which is an entirely different matter.[13]

Since Jimmy Carter's presidency—when his born-again status "disconcerted" liberals, as Garry Wills put it—much of the press has treated political candidates' expressions of religious belief with thinly veiled contempt, particularly if they sound inspired or emotional, stray too far from consensus moral expressions, or go beyond the vague religious sentiments that have come to be expected from politicians.[14] After Carter retired from office, his reputation underwent something of a rehabilitation, and it is now vaguely okay for journalists to salute the religious motivation in his work for Habitat for Humanity and his freelance, international mediation missions. Sadly, what was lacking in Carter's coverage by the press, which treated him with withering scorn for his holier-than-thou attitude while in office, was an appreciation for the way Carter took on difficult, no-win political challenges (such as his support of the unpopular treaty to give the Panama Canal back to the Panamanians, his attacks on pork-barreling by powerful members of Congress, and his criticism of the American public for its waste of energy resources) and how this reflected the cross-bearing side of his religious nature. Certainly, Carter was justly criticized for his vacillations on public policy, his tendency to be politically expedient when it served him, and his sometimes inept approach to political problems. But no matter how one views Carter in retrospect, his case illustrates how difficult it is for a cynical press corps to credit a president with genuine religious faith—or to see a connection between faith and political character—while in office.[15]

But can this critique be right, you may be asking yourself? Haven't political reporters become ever more riveted to the "hot-button" themes and controversies that have mixed religion and politics during the past two decades—the rise of the religious Right, the anti-abortion movement, the "family values" campaigns of the Christian Coalition? Journalists, it is true, do comment extensively on the more blatant aspects of religion's involvement in the political realm—on the evangelicals' resentment at the moral "relativism" of modern culture, their fear of the secular menace represented by a rights-oriented liberal establishment, and their campaigns against homosexual marriage, radical feminism, and multiculturalism. But, when they do this, as Stephen Carter observed, the media "typically make a mess of matters," by "exultantly" choosing up sides, pitting liberals against conservatives, and "implying that only external political forces can explain the way the battle lines have been formed."[16] What characterizes the coverage in all these areas is political journalists' stance that they are above the fray and detached from the religious nature of the controversy—as if the greatest service they can perform is to extract the religious elements from the debate and reframe them in political terms. By focusing on religious matters that can be recast in political controversy, journalists lose sight of many of the elements of religion that are most deeply important to the American public. Moreover, as much as political journalists see their handling of religion in this manner as part of their "objective" professional duties, they fail to recognize how their efforts to be neutral and a-religious are laden with assumptions that, on closer analysis, can only be called quasi-religious in nature.

As we have seen time and again in this work, the operating principles of the journalism community are strongly connected to religious values, even if most journalists are not particularly cognizant of this. Unfortunately, problems can arise when journalists—beholden to a set of unspoken religious principles—believe they are operating out of a tradition of neutrality and detachment. Mark Silk noted how morality in the United States is inextricably bound up with religion, but in the American tradition, with its fervent religious movements and fractious history of religious dissent, maintaining the moral order means not only endorsing religion (at least, in its broader, civic form) but also keeping religious enthusiasm at arm's length. "Journalists know that religion is dynamite," Silk observed. "They use . . . moral packaging designed to keep the explosions to a minimum." The news media coverage of much religious news that falls into the category of the controversial or the sensational—unconventional religious groups, expressions of religious radicalism, the overt campaigns by religious groups to influence government policy, the fundamentalist reaction against modernism and urban cultural influence—reflects, Silk contended, an instinctive and a largely unreflective desire to defend the moderate religious values of mainstream society. This, by unconscious design perhaps, is what makes the news palatable to the mass of moderately political, moderately religious viewers and readers. "People fail to register what gives no offense," Silk noted. "A lot of religion news does not strike most consumers of news as reflecting any point of view, precisely because it is a point of view they share."[17]

Silk's explanation both describes the impulses of the media when they encounter religious expression outside the mainstream and implicitly defends them. This, in turn, helps explain why religious language—at least in the forms that have been absorbed into the civic language—is embraced by the press, as long as it has been sanitized, so to speak, of any excessive, sectarian, or divisive elements. In its most benign form, religious language has been accepted as a routine—some might even say obligatory—element of political dialogue, including among the media. From the beginning of the nation, when General George Washington invoked religion to the revolutionary cause (calling on "every officer and man . . . to live and act as becomes a Christian soldier"),[18] Americans have grown accustomed to hearing religious appeals from mainstream politicians covered matter-of-factly by the press. Even beyond the acceptable public platitudes that pass for political religion in campaigns, Americans have been accustomed—well before Carter and Reagan—to having religious controversy appear in presidential races. Thomas Jefferson and John Adams received scathing criticism from conservative Christians, as well as in the partisan press of their day, for the "heathenism" of their Deist and rationalist humanist beliefs and the irreligiosity of their followers; Republican President Ulysses S. Grant's opposition to state support of church-operated schools spawned the phrase that the Democrats were the party of "rum, Romanism, and Rebellion"; appeals to the evangelical vote were critical in the presidential races of Andrew Jackson in 1828 and William Jennings Bryan in 1896 and in the selection of Aaron Burr as Jefferson's vice presidential pick in 1800; Catholic-Protestant rivalries played a major role in the campaigns of Bryan and William McKinley in 1896, Herbert Hoover and Al Smith in 1928, and Richard Nixon and John F. Kennedy in 1960; promotion of the social gospel was prominent in the campaigns of Bryan and Theodore Roosevelt; and a call for Christian moral values applied to international affairs became the trademark of the Woodrow Wilson administration. The churches, both liberal and conservative, have played major and often catalytic roles in such historical national controversies as the development of the Bill of Rights, abolition, prohibition, the civil rights movement, the debate over prayer in public school, and abortion and homosexual rights—and few politicians (along with the press that covers them) have escaped the politico-religious disputes of their day.

Despite the seemingly more secular nature of society, there are a number of ways in which America's top politicians—and much of the editorial voice of the press—have not changed much in their embrace of certain broad, widely accepted religious concepts. Perhaps the most universally acclaimed principle—avowed openly by the founding figures and still acknowledged (although in a more disguised tone) by today's editors—is that valid social law depends ultimately on religious sanction and that, in the word of John Adams, "a patriot must be a religious man." Adams, like Jefferson, doubted some of the tenets of orthodox Christianity, but he believed that theistic religion is indispensable for republican virtue and that freedom is founded on morality and religion. "We have no government armed with power capable of contending with human passions unbridled by morality and religion," he wrote in 1789. "Our constitution was made only for a moral and religious people. It is wholly inadequate to the government of any other."[19]

The rhetoric of the nation's founders also drew on another religious viewpoint—traceable to Jonathan Edwards and the Puritans—of an America chosen by God to launch the world's salvation. This attitude—again still strongly expressed in modern political speeches and on editorial pages—so infuses American assumptions about the country's place in the global order that it is seldom questioned (including by editors) when it comes to examining the underpinnings of American foreign policy. It is no coincidence that some of the most aggressive advocates of an America-first overseas policy—John Adams, James Monroe, Andrew Jackson, Theodore Roosevelt, Richard Nixon, Ronald Reagan—were prone to mixing Christian and biblical symbolism into their political oratory ("We stand at Armageddon and we battle for the Lord," Theodore Roosevelt once said of his candidacy; in his first inaugural, Abraham Lincoln invoked "intelligence, patriotism, Christianity, and a firm reliance on Him, who has never yet forsaken this favored land" as a means for dealing with the crisis of secession).[20]

In the same vein, a progressive newspaper editor, such as Walt Whitman in his journalism days, could write, "Let our arms now be carried with a spirit which shall teach the world that, while we are not forward for a quarrel, America knows how to crush, as well as how to expand," in justifying his vision of America's manifest destiny at the outbreak of the Mexican War in 1846. ("The people of the United States are a newspaper-ruled people," Whitman also wrote in the *Brooklyn Eagle,* who have cut their ties with "kingcraft," "priestcraft," and "the old and moth-eaten systems of Europe" but depend on editors to lead them, sometimes against their will, to "light and knowledge" and "noble reforms.")[21] This unquestioning tie between religion and politics gets the United States in trouble—despised by many around the world as arrogant and self-serving, called upon by others to get involved in hot spots around the globe—not the least because the American press corps tends to end its pledges of neutrality at the American shore and to reflect the prevailing foreign policy establishment view when covering overseas conflicts that involve the United States.

The explicitly inspired language of the eighteenth and nineteenth centuries

has been reduced in our age, for the most part, to a safe and carefully crafted rec-
itation of public pieties by political leaders who calculate religious viewpoint into
their formula for high office—and the patriotic bromides of editorial pages that,
although rooted in religion, no longer fully acknowledge their debt to the exalted vision of America as the world's redeemer. This is why Reagan and Bush Senior could indulge in "an old American habit," as Stephen Carter put it, of linking America's cause to God's will—as Reagan did in routinely associating God
with conservative political causes or Bush did when he claimed God's approval
for the Gulf War. Stephen Carter called this phenomenon "political preaching"—
something that Frederick Mark Gedicks defined as the utterance of "faintly Protestant platitudes which reaffirm the base of American culture despite being largely void of theological significance." However, Carter maintained the problem
comes when "one's theology always ends up squaring precisely with one's politics. At that point, there is reason to suspect that far from trying to discern God's
will and follow it in the world, the political preacher is first deciding what path
to take in the world and then looking for evidence that God agrees."[22]

Journalists, of course, should be exposing this kind of duplicity, but too often,
with their tin ears to the role of religion in American life and their blanket cynicism about religion in politics, they simply do not. Within their own peer group,
journalists are always safest adopting a skeptical stance—and that applies especially to religion. To discuss religious hypocrisy (or religious sincerity) intelligently requires a careful understanding of the issues of faith and religion, and
most journalists, particularly political journalists, would prefer not to venture
into such complex terrain. It is easier for political writers to avoid religious
matters, unless they take shape in the familiar forms of controversy and claims
and counterclaims, or to adopt the view that all religious utterances by politicians are bogus and thus should be dismissed as predictable and unimportant.

Nixon came out of this tradition of the political preacher advocating a divinely
sanctioned agenda for the nation and routinely chose "the moral and religious
argument over the political" in his rhetoric, as Charles P. Henderson Jr. put it.[23]
It is clear that Nixon's conservatism was based, at least in part, on what one biographer called his "pietistic interpretation" of the Constitution. This view, which
Nixon first espoused as a Whittier high school student competing in an oratory
contest, meant that the American Constitution "came down from Mt. Sinai along
with the Decalogue," as one contestant described the substance of Nixon's address.[24] This philosophy, which Nixon later in his political career refined as the
"strict constructionist" reading of the Constitution, originates in the same impulse that has led certain Protestant groups to be accused of worshipping the Bible
and to interpret its texts in strict accord with their conservative tenets. A favorite conservative variation of this—Constitution worship—is not just habitual
with the political Right (civil libertarians and politicians on the left also are prone
to embrace the Constitution as a pristine reflection of their own beliefs), but it
seems to create the most fervency in those conservative circles where politics is

mixed with the moralism and the zealotry of the crusading evangelist. Nixon "perfectly illustrates the curious inbreeding of patriotism and piety, the Protestant ethic and liberal pragmatism that has been so pervasive in this nation's history," wrote Henderson. "Lacking a transcendent God, he seems to make patriotism his religion, the American dream his deity."[25]

Much has been written about the rift between the press and Nixon, particularly the divide that occurred after his vice president, Spiro Agnew, attacked the media as dominated by privileged, liberal commentators who were ignoring the political views and news preferences of Middle America. Agnew's populist conservative rhetoric was symptomatic of a hostility that, in the broadest cultural and religious sense, goes to the heart of the public's "mistrust" of the modern media and the suspicion with which journalists and the members of Nixon's "silent majority" (who are still very much with us) view each other. In Nixon's and Agnew's view, the news of their time—about the civil rights movement and ghetto disturbances, the Vietnam War and antiwar protests, drugs and hippies and social ferment—was a constant assault on the ancestors of Jonathan Edwards and their evangelistic inheritors whose vision of America (the "city upon a hill [where] the eyes of all people are upon us") was a nation that stands as a beacon of industry, purity, and moral rectitude for the world.[26] The Nixon and Agnew contention that many Americans resented the press as the harbinger and promoter of all that was unhealthy, immoral, and unpatriotic in American culture had a chilling effect on the press and bred both fear (that maybe Nixon was right) and resentment (that, even if he was right, he was exploiting the public's mistrust for his political gain). The media sociologist Herbert Gans argued that journalists' response to Agnew's charges was to pay closer attention to balancing the news and making Middle America, white ethnics, and Agnew himself more newsworthy for a time. But Gans also noted the journalists' defensiveness about the attacks, and he predicted that the conservatives' unhappiness with American press coverage would likely have little impact because journalists already "discount that audience."[27]

Gans's comment hints at the cultural divide that separates many journalists from a major segment of their audience and helps explain the resentful and worried attitude in many press circles about the role of religion in politics. Today many journalists (although demonstrating a wide range of unconscious Christian-based assumptions in their own professional mind-set) tend to identify Christian involvement in the political arena with the efforts by right-wing groups to influence the political agenda. Conservative organizations' dedicated effort to identify Christianity with conservative causes has succeeded among many secular-oriented media people, whose recognition of the role that religion plays across the political spectrum is often minimal. This split—between journalists who see themselves as cosmopolitan commentators on the contemporary scene and their audience, which they believe is made up in important ways of people who are frightened of modernity—makes it easier for journalists to ignore those who complain when the press fails to recognize the good religion story in politics.

If Nixon's religion was not fully understood by the press corps at large, it was by one man—fellow Quaker Pearson. The mutual antagonism felt between Nixon and the press can be seen early in his tempestuous relationship with Pearson—a relationship that, in the zealousness of its feeling, reflects an equally intense rivalry between their two respective branches of the Quaker faith. Although by the end of his own career, Pearson could be called only a nominal Quaker, too (he seldom attended his own Quaker meeting in Swarthmore, Pennsylvania), he had grown increasingly upset at what he felt was Nixon's lack of commitment to Quakerism, particularly what he viewed as Nixon's un-Quakerly hawkishness on issues of war and peace. This feeling became the foundation for many columns attacking Nixon for his efforts while in office to reward his campaign supporters, criticizing his red-baiting and his role while on the House Committee on Un-American Activities, and helping expose the Nixon special campaign fund that led to the Checkers speech, where Pearson (called by some the "Scorpion-on-the-Potomac") put his stinger into Nixon.[28]

Pearson—in a very real way—was a reflection of a rival culture to Nixon's, one that has become entrenched in the Washington, D.C., press corps of today. While Pearson did base his journalistic mission on his liberal Quaker beliefs, his loyalties were much more to the professional ethic of journalism, particularly the ethic of muckraking, with its certainty that corruption in high places is everywhere and must be exposed. Pearson was, for the most part, a political liberal but in the journalistic, not in the partisan, sense. He campaigned against the Klan, warred with the House Committee on Un-American Activities, and even went after such patriot icons as General Douglas MacArthur and Dwight Eisenhower (according to Jack Anderson, these reports were censored by a great majority of the pro-Eisenhower press). Pearson's distaste for Nixon grew out of the same distaste that great numbers of press people, particularly those who covered Nixon in the latter stages of his political career, came to feel for what they believed was Nixon's false piety, his political opportunism masking as moralism, and his petty vindictiveness. Pearson hated hypocrisy, and hypocrisy is at the top of the chart when it comes to journalistic condemnation.[29]

After Pearson's death (he died just months after Nixon took occupancy of the White House in 1969), a whole succession of events—Nixon's continuation of the Vietnam War despite campaigning on a peace plank, the antiwar protests aimed at him, the divisive 1972 reelection campaign against Democrat George McGovern, and the Watergate revelations—solidified the divisions between Nixon and what he viewed as the liberal press that wanted to bring him down. As always, few in the press saw the confrontation as the reflection of a religious rivalry, but religious scholars have. "Significantly, it was not the churches but the press that in full cry led the forces of moral indignation over Watergate," wrote Richard John Niehaus. "Jonathan Edwards had nothing on 'investigative reporters' such as Woodward and Bernstein or the editorialists of the prestige papers. . . . When the incorrigible moralism of the American people is no longer articulated by the establishment churches, that expressive task 'circulates' to the establishment media."[30]

One can see Nixon and Pearson as products of their religious tradition, but it would be misleading to measure their careers and their actions solely in the context of their religion. Both men, in their own ways, shared the view that the end justifies the means, which contradicts the most fundamental of Quaker values. Both showed that even religious people resort to tactics that are sometimes dubious, in the case of Pearson, and immoral and illegal, in Nixon's case. The nation's judgment of Nixon's conduct is a matter of record. But Pearson's journalistic techniques have been questioned, too, even by his admirer and protégé Jack Anderson. Said Anderson (himself a devout Mormon), "I objected frequently, and am not yet reconciled to, his subordination of the rules of journalism to 'larger' considerations—his mixing of reporting with political activism, his getting into bed with what he judged the lesser offender in order to get help in bagging the greater, his occasional use of deduction to carry on from where investigative fact left off."[31]

Sometimes, in reading about the hard-nosed journalistic pursuits of Pearson and the ruthless political strategizing of Nixon, it is hard to believe that religion really had anything much to do with the exploits of these two rivals. Again, one is reminded of the founding figures' concern about what American life would become if morality were divided from religion (or if morality were forgotten by the religious). In this respect, Pearson was probably unlike many of his colleagues; he did give a bow to religion and acknowledged it as an element in his journalistic motivation. Still, few of Pearson's fellow journalists would have recognized his zeal for scandal and his zest for muckraking as originating in religious sources. Yet, if it is the press that hopes to take on the role of moral guardian for the nation, Pearson certainly stepped up to the task with enthusiasm. One can see Pearson in the tradition of George Fox, looking to rid the world of its moral impurities and not caring whose feathers he ruffled in the process.

Nixon, of course, did not think much of Pearson's brand of Quakerism—just as Pearson did not think much of Nixon's. Politicians would certainly look askance at the notion that the press corps that sometimes bedevils them has become a principal advocate for the reform tradition that grows out of America's religious heritage. But, if that is the case, and I believe it is, then things have turned out much different from what was envisioned by John Adams, Benjamin Franklin, and the others who were convinced that only explicit religious faith would keep America moral.

CHAPTER 14

Foundations of Sand: Technology Worship and the Internet

It was meant as a parody, but the *Boston Globe* still called the wire story about Microsoft's acquisition of the Catholic church a "serious" statement about the higher power of the Internet and Microsoft's reverential status within it. In 1994, soon after the Internet had burst into the consciousness of journalists and the public, a spoof Associated Press story datelined the Vatican was put out on the Web, saying that Microsoft planned to buy the Catholic church and had made Pope John Paul II a senior vice president of religious software. Microsoft was so concerned that it issued a press release disavowing any responsibility for the cyberprank.[1]

Religious metaphor—whether meant tongue-in-cheek or seriously—seems to surround Microsoft and its leader, Bill Gates, as it has many of the aspects of the emerging "new media" industry. For example, the now famous Bill Gates "retreat" in 1994—when he went away to ponder the potential meaning of the Internet and returned with the revelation that Microsoft must jump into the world of interactive communications in a big way—was rich with the religious symbolism of a modern sage going up the mountain for a religious vision.[2]

As the multibillionaire guru of personal computing software, Gates has proved himself to be the master proselytizer (particularly among the journalists who hang on his every word) of the gospel of the personal computer as the shaper of future human destiny. In his book *The Road Ahead,* Gates predicts the Internet will lead to even more revolutionary changes than did the spread of the personal computer business from which Microsoft so greatly profited. "We are all beginning another great journey," Gates declared. "We can't be sure exactly where this one will lead either, but I'm certain it will touch many lives and take us all even further. . . . There is never a reliable map for unexplored territory, but we can learn important lessons from the creation and evolution of the $120 billion personal computer industry."[3]

While users of the Internet still appear to prefer to find their religious inspiration in more traditional ways (*Time* reported, for example, that Gates turned up only 25,000 Web references on one major search engine compared with Christ with 146,000 hits and God with 410,000), Gates has, in very interesting ways, invited observers to see religious parallels in his mission to sell personal computing to the world.[4] Gates, like would-be gurus of the past, has found it easy to tap into people's zeal for new forms of human-to-human contact but also their anxieties, fears, and hopes about the future, particularly their desire to get on the right side of coming technological developments.

To see Gates as personally responsible for his elevation to the status of religious seer leading us into the future would be an exaggeration. But Gates has an intuitive feel for how deeply our sense of the importance of communications technologies has become intertwined with our spiritual values and our hopes for the future. In a world where media systems are being transformed at such a rapid pace, it is easy to understand why people hold up technological change as something to exalt. Our anticipation of future electronic communications developments has much to beguile us if we are willing to yield ourselves to their grand inevitability. This devotion is even easier to come by when we realize that the mythologizing now surrounding communications advances contains so many elements that tie into people's need to venerate things that they cannot fully control and that seem to have such overwhelming power over them.

In one respect, on-line communications seem supremely human and all about fulfilling a basic human need—to reach out and touch other human beings in ways that assuage loneliness and satisfy curiosity and the need for self-expression. But these very human interactions also can elicit the feeling (in both the individual and the collective experience) that there is something transcendent going on, that some higher level of spirituality is being attained in these communications. If this is so, should we take seriously the claims of those who experience on the Internet some sort of mystical high?

Humankind has long been prone to believe that the latest tools of communication will lead to a wonderful, new spiritual revolution. The media historian John Durham Peters has traced the history of what he calls the "dream of communication" that has captured the imagination of people throughout the ages who have longed for a medium that will provide a perfect mechanism for allowing the communion of human souls and minds. This impulse to find a way to escape "the gross and oppressive bonds of space and time," as the sociologist Charles Horton Cooley put it, has been manifested as a deep mythic hope for the possibilities of each advancing form of communication—from writing to the telegraph to the telephone to modern electronic media—and has even become entangled through history with people's belief in angels, spiritualism, mental telepathy, psychic research, communication with the dead, and ghosts. "The sus-

picion that each of us dwells in a heart-shaped box is a product not only of fren-
zied philosophical imagination but of lived conditions—in architecture, religion,
the organization of work and leisure, public and private, and . . . the structure
of communications," Peters contended. "In a world in which we routinely 'communicate' with others whose bodily presence is out of reach and out of sight,
where delivery is never assured, the anguish of dubious contact can take hold."[5]
    The Internet fits right into this historical pattern. There has been a surge of
enthusiasm that the exponential growth of the Internet is multiplying the possibilities for binding together human community in ways that offer great opportunities for new forms of religious dialogue. Some observers—as *Time* magazine
did in December 1996—even proclaim the experience of signing onto the Internet a "transformative act" in itself, "a marriage of God and the global computer
networks." In the news magazine's frothy and hyperventilating prose, *Time* discussed the exploding use of the Internet by religious adherents, ranging from the
pope to religious proselytizers to the many people surfing religious Web sites. "We
stand at the start of a new movement in this delicate dance of technology and
faith," the magazine said. "There's no sure way to measure how much the Internet will change our lives, but the most basic truth about technological revolutions is that they change everything they touch. . . . Will the Net change religion?
Is it possible that God in a networked age will look, somehow, different?"[6]
    The quickness of *Time* to capitalize on the growing frenzy surrounding the
Internet, combined with the perceived upsurge of faith and interest in religion
among the public, may be explained as its seizing an opportunity to put another portrait of Jesus on its cover, always a sure seller. But the eagerness to see a
spiritual dimension in the expansion of the World Wide Web is an extension of
Marshall McLuhan's notion that the religious attitudes of a culture are inextricably bound up with the development of media technology.[7] Something about
the Internet—with the lure of its chat rooms, its interest group bulletin boards,
and its interactive "communities"—has spawned a particularly extravagant bout
of religious metaphor spinning in the press. For some of the religiously inclined,
the new medium promises to transform the very essence of religion. For example, for proponents of "process theology," who believe that the earth and its
inhabitants are participants in the divine process and that God evolves with
humankind, the Internet vastly expands the opportunities to reshape the face
of God. "If God doesn't change, we are in danger of losing God," William Gras-
sie, a religion professor at Temple University, told *Time*. "There is a shift to [the
idea of] God as a process evolving with us. If you believe in an eternal, unchanging God, you'll be in trouble."[8]
    I have talked throughout this book about the role that religion has played in
the development of the mass media and the value system of journalism professionals. But with the advent of what is called new media, the traditional media
industry's hold over a one-way flow of information controlled by journalists and
dispensed to the public from the perspective of journalism professionals is un-

dergoing a dramatic change. Not only do the new, networked, interactive, computer-based information systems draw in average people as participants in the creation and the direction of news and information, but traditional mass media organizations are migrating on-line as if their future existence depends on it. With everyone using e-mail, building Web sites, and searching on-line for everything from archival information to e-commerce products, it only makes sense to ask—with perhaps a bit less exuberance than in the popular press—whether the latest transformation in communications technology will have the same impact on the development of religion (and vice versa) that it has had in the past.

McLuhan set the stage for this discussion with his image of modern society as a networked system of electronic pulsations that, in near mystic fashion, resonate through the communications grid in a way that mimics the human nervous system. McLuhan anticipated the giddy enthusiasts of the Internet in the way he equated human involvement in modern media communications with something akin to religious experience itself. "If the work of the city is the remaking or translating of man into a more suitable form than his nomadic ancestors achieved, then might not our current translation of our entire lives into the spiritual form of information seem to make of the entire globe, and of the human family, a single consciousness?" McLuhan asked.[9] McLuhan's musings about electronic communications invite one to see in them a techno-mystical vision for the modern media age. "McLuhan had a new version of the myth of Christianity," wrote Herbert Altschull. "Paradise was lost in Eden; the Fall was completed in Babel when a multiplicity of tongues destroyed human communication. But with the arrival of new media, Paradise is regained. . . . In McLuhan's vision, Babel is conquered by cybernetics; the communal world of the ancient villages is reconstructed through the global village that has been established by the new media."[10]

Already, the grandiose claims of those who are promoting the Internet as a new religious influence on the culture are in full force. Jennifer Cobb, the author of *Cybergrace: The Search for God in the Digital World,* wove strains of Eastern and Western religious thought into a "theology of cyberspace," where human consciousness is portrayed as moving toward God in an evolutionary process that is advancing through the universe of digital communication. Throughout the book, Cobb used religious metaphors to describe the Web, referring to the "soul of cyberspace," with "deeper, sacred mechanisms" that are a "medium of grace" and a place that has "a fundamental role to play in the ongoing movement of soul and spirit through the universe." This leaves cyberspace, Cobb contended, as a place where humans can reconcile the major division of our time—the division between science and spirit—and move us to a place of higher spiritual consciousness.[11]

If, as I have argued earlier, religious values permeate the traditional process of producing news and information, why shouldn't we be comfortable simply calling on-line, interactive communications a transcendental experience that has the potential of transforming everybody who participates in it? This would mean that everyone—journalist or not—could be seen as influenced by the way the Internet is opening up new possibilities for spiritual experience. By redefining religion to suit the evolving nature of human communications, we would have to worry less about how traditional journalism ties into the old religious values and simply set about looking to some future, emerging moral vision for our new religious and communications patterns.

Advocates of process theology would be very comfortable with this idea. By the very definition of God's process at work in the world, process theologians would see the Internet as an immense new stage in the divine process that is shaping the future by expanding opportunities for human interaction today. Process theologians—most of whom are disciples of the philosopher Alfred Whitehead—say that many modern people can no longer believe in an all powerful, unchanging God and that humans must not abdicate their power and responsibility in favor of the passive notion that everything unfolds according to God's plan. Instead, they believe that everything and everybody together make up God and that the past, the present, and the future—and the decisions each human being makes that shape the flow of human affairs and the earth's condition—are the interrelated aspects of what constitute God's activity in the world. In their view, it is humans choosing from among life's possibilities, not a fixed, distant power, that ultimately determine the future. In this conception, it is logical to see the Internet as a vital new force in the scheme of human interaction—perhaps, as predicted by McLuhan, "by technology a Pentecostal condition of universal understanding and unity."[12]

However, before we cede this territory to the techno-mystics, we should examine some of the places where the theology of cyberspace does not offer answers. Techno-mysticism—like process theology—is only one of a number of modern religious systems that have changed the definition of God to meet the needs of modern people who cannot believe in the view of God presented by traditional religious systems but do not want to abandon the concept. While a fascinating notion, techno-mysticism (like process theology) does not offer much insight into such questions as the role of spiritual transformation in the human community, how divine revelation occurs, the nature of sin, how religious values contribute to the building of moral character, or the source of ethics. If God is the sum of human activity, what is going to determine truth—the majority will? Process theologians prefer not to discuss these questions in ways that the average person can follow, instead opting to advocate a more sweeping theology that views all people—and all historical developments—as part of divine activity. In the end, process theology is a system that appeals to the human intellect: neat, tidy, comprehensive in philosophical scope, attractive in commanding a sense of human dignity and responsibility. But it is not something that warms the heart, compels one to take a stand, or demands one's deepest commitment and loyalty. Nor is it something that could give much guidance to a journalist trying to decide whether to right a wrong or to do the ethical thing—other than to justify that journalist in looking to some vague internal pull (what some process theologians have called the "lure" of God) in nudging them into action.[13]

As a skeptic of process theology, I would suggest that one might also want to view with some reservations the hyperbole of those who believe that human participation in the media process can serve as a substitute for the transcendent elements of faith. The idea of the Internet as a replacement for religious practice is fraught with fallacies and pitfalls. As people begin to worship the Internet as some sort of transformative spiritual experience, one can only be reminded of that Hebrew scriptural warning of mistaking the medium for the source— of focusing so much on the channel through which spiritual impulses are directed that one forgets the higher source from which spiritual meaning is derived. When people proclaim the new media to be something that is potentially changing the nature of religion itself, what does that mean? Does it mean the Internet will change people's attitude toward religion or toward media or both? If it changes the nature of religion, what exactly will people be worshipping? The Internet itself? The experience of participating on the Internet? Or one of the many religious Web sites that are made accessible on the Internet?

With these questions in mind, it is instructive to look behind the evangelistic zeal in which the Internet has been embraced in many quarters and to examine what it is about the nature of communications technology that makes it a subject of near reverential awe—particular within the press itself. That a mythic, McLuhanesque vision of new media has become so attractive to modern members of the press is probably no surprise, given the way it flatters them and their role in the world. After all, journalists' fascination with the workings of their own business—along with their fixation on the flux and uncertainty that come with working in the modern communications field—makes the communications process a natural focus for media workers. As the media historian Mitchell Stephens observed, "Indeed, the currently common view of the present as uniquely exciting and frightening may owe as much to the spell woven by journalists as it does to the reality of technology development. And journalists see change nowhere as evident as in journalism itself."[14]

The concept of God as the Net—so avidly embraced by technology worshipping futurists—is reminiscent of other moments of major communications advances, when enraptured journalists (as well as other citizens) held up the new communications technology as connected to the divine. In one of the most famous examples, the invention of the telegraph was hailed by Samuel Morse with a credit to the divine ("What hath God wrought," Morse reportedly uttered at the first successful transmission) and was rhapsodized about by techno-mystics of the time ("Piercing so the secret of Nature, man makes himself symmetrical with nature. Penetrating to the working of creative energies, he becomes himself a creator."). This was followed by other paeans to the power of electronic communications, which was treated, as Carolyn Marvin put it, "as an extension of religious revelation." In 1880, *Scientific American* magazine, for example, described the newly invented telephone as a device that would lead to "nothing less than a new organization of society," and, as one telephone counsel put it, a new "epoch of neighborship without propinquity," where utopian yearnings for community with socially distant persons would be fulfilled. Similar outbursts of rapture were uttered about radio ("Unwittingly then, had I discovered an invisible Empire of the Air," proclaimed Lee De Forest, an early radio developer who promoted his inventions with a biblical and missionary zeal) and television (which the TV critic Jerry Mander described as appealing to believers in the "techno-mystical-unification" mode, "a nationwide, one-mind experience, previously thought to reside only in the realm of the mystic").[15]

Somewhat soberer voices have chanted a counterveiling mantra that these new communications technologies are simply devices and that we should not elevate them to spiritual dimensions until we see to what uses they are put. Henry Thoreau is the most notable, with his famous comment about the telegraph ("But Maine and Texas, it may be, have nothing important to communicate")—a sentiment echoed by C. K. Chesterton at the internationalization of radio, which, he said, came just as the nations had nothing to say to one another.[16] But McLuhan had an answer for this criticism—one that is embraced by today's techno-mystics. The focus on the content of a media source (or lack of content) is secondary to the power that media have over our nervous systems and our imaginations, McLuhan liked to say, whether we think we are attentive to the influences or not. Content analysis, McLuhan maintained, offers "no clues to the magic of these media or to their subliminal charge," nor can it reduce the "spell" of the media, which can occur "immediately upon contact, as in the first bars of a melody."[17]

So what is it about the capabilities of newly emerging forms of media that make humans ready to herald that they have seen the divine at work in the latest communications gadget? Walter Ong, a Jesuit priest and a former teaching colleague of McLuhan at St. Louis University, fashioned McLuhan's celebration of technology and his own Christian mysticism into a highly optimistic thesis about communications technology as the key to bringing about a world of dialogue, peace, and global fellowship. Ong's work is reminiscent of the work of an earlier Catholic theologian, Pierre Teilhard de Chardin, who took the seemingly anti-Christian elements of Darwinism and the theory of evolution and refashioned them into a framework of life moving toward an "omega point" of Christian perfection.[18] The key for Ong, in his techno-Christian vision, is the advancing capability of electronic communications to bring about human-to-human contact—"where my voice . . . calls not to something outside, but to the inwardness of another" as a "primary point of entry for the divine." The sense of presence and participation these new media promote, Ong said, enlarges the ground in which God's presence is felt and allows us to share more and more in one another's "inwardness" (a concept for Ong that, like Teilhard's concept of "interiority" in the evolutionary process, is a divine element in living creatures that becomes ever more revealed as God moves the world toward perfection). While traditional one-way television has the capacity to expand these contacts by increasing our cross-cultural sense of one another and exposing us to new levels of global understanding, the new forms of two-way electronic communications systems promise the person-to-person dialogue where the "Word" (in Ong's broadly mystical Christian sense) can break through. With computerization, "thus far the last stage in the quantification of man's life-world, is it possible that we are moving toward some new realization of the personal and thus new opportunities for Christian living and giving in our time?" he asked.[19]

If McLuhan had been as open about his Christianity as Ong was, he might have injected a similarly explicit blend of Christian doctrine into his writings about technology. Little known to those who came to know McLuhan as a pop figure and a high-profile guru of the glories of global communication, McLuhan was a quite devout person—a Baptist-reared convert to Catholicism who held fairly conventional beliefs about the importance of Pentecost, the Incarnation, and the Resurrection. McLuhan's synthesizing impulses and his enraptured prose were rooted in a fascination with such Christian figures as St. Thomas Aquinas and C. K. Chesterton, whose comprehensive philosophy and rhetorical flourishes were of great inspiration to him. "It was a long time before I finally perceived that the character of every society, its food, clothing, arts, and amusements are ultimately determined by its religion," McLuhan once wrote, later confiding to a colleague, "I deliberately keep Christianity out of all these discussions lest perceptions be diverted from structural processes by doctrinal sectarian passions."[20]

There is no doubt that McLuhan and Ong have to be aligned with a long list of thinkers and philosophers who have attempted to interpret communications technology developments in ways that make them consistent with Christian positivism. Still, it is a mistake to treat modern electronic communications systems as omnipotent, to bow to their inexorable hold over history, or to view their influence over us as somehow foreordained by a divine plan, as McLuhan and Ong did, without recognizing the ways in which this interpretation can undermine important aspects of the religious message. The Hebrews banned the worship of Baal not just because it was idolatrous but also because it had such a powerful attraction for a people who were struggling against the temptation to assimilate with the tribes around them. Perhaps even more meaningful is Jesus' admonition about the spiritual perils facing those who build a foundation on sand—something that, it should be noted, can be applied to the ingredients of the silicon chip.[21]

The Hebrews felt strongly that corruption can come to a culture when the experience of the transcendent is replaced with the worship of human-created devices. The pull of the material world and the way it has been translated into the worship of the good life are no better reflected than in modern humankind's instinctive genuflection before the spectacle of advancing technology. For many modern, secular people, bereft of faith in any other sense of the divine, it has become too easy to believe that the swirling, confusing, exciting, and overwhelming flux of technological change is worthy of worship in itself—just as people of the past have been prone to worship powerful forces that appeared to be dictating the direction of their lives in ways that could seem overwhelming. McLuhan—in what seems to contradict his otherwise mystical enthusiasm for electronic communications technology—understood the problem when he wrote, "It is this continuous embrace of our own technology in daily use that puts us in the Narcissus role of subliminal awareness and numbness in relation to these images of ourselves. By continuously embracing technologies, we relate ourselves to them as servomechanisms. That is why we must, to use them at all, serve these objects, these extensions of ourselves, as gods or minor religions."[22]

In the end, Ong's argument, as with McLuhan's broader embrace of electronic media, neglects the reality that modern electronic communications are too much about profit, economics, and corporate-marketing objectives to have religious value so casually imputed to them. We should not presume that just because we have invented so many wondrous new instruments of communications—and just because they have engendered such flights of mystic verbal fancy—that we can necessarily find God's purposes looming behind them. Television allows us to increase our global understandings of one another, the personal computer makes it possible to intensify one-to-one dialogue, and multimedia and virtual reality immerse us in powerful moving images that can fully absorb us, but we should not forget what is human in these transactions and should not presume that what is going on is principally about the divine.[23]

Throughout history, people have confused their own motives with those of God—and nowhere more so than in humankind's often ecstatic embrace of new communications technologies. McLuhan and Ong, in their celebration of electronic media as the pathway for God's plan, risk falling into the trap of others who waxed exuberant about the mystical possibilities of new communications technologies only to neglect to notice the way idolatry can creep into their expression of it. Ong is certainly no idol worshiper; he does not advocate that we revere electronic communications as transcendent in itself. But in his nearly exclusive focus on electronic media as a means to human kinship and Christian communion—and his inattention to the economic motives that are mixed in—he invites us to ignore the darker implications of a communications system that is operated in the service of the very human motives lurking behind the inspired talk of the Information Age.

So is the zealous embrace of new media just another form of dancing around the golden calf? While I would agree that much of the history of religion is about mistaking the medium of religious worship for the source of it, I would hardly put myself in the camp of those who view the Internet as positively malignant (one must also beware of seeing the devil behind all new developments in communications, too). But to enthusiasts who would impute to the new technology a mythic lure and power of divine proportions, I would suggest that it is worth remembering the lessons of Faust and to ponder that it is human pride in unlocking the secrets of the universe that most tempts us to celebrate our inventions as transcendent and to invest them with grand-scale spiritual meaning. As Theodore Roszak, the author of *The Cult of Information,* put it, we may think the computer is all about creating a perfect, mechanical system that will unlock the universe's mysteries, but it is really about something quite different. "It is important to realize . . . that these foolish simplifications, just as they stand, even without the hope of eventual elaboration, are useful to certain forces in our society [which] . . . make good use of computerized data to obfuscate, mystify, intimidate, and control," Roszak observed. "Because they overwhelmingly own the sources and machinery of data, the cult of information lends a mystique to their dominance."[24]

The Gospel of Public Journalism: The Newsroom Communitarians and the Search for Civic Virtue

I learned recently what James Carey meant when he referred to the use of the word *public* as the "god term" of journalism.[1] While on a panel at a conference of journalism teachers and academics a few years ago, I warned that the "public journalism" movement was in danger of degenerating into just another newsroom marketing tactic at some newspapers. A woman in the audience, her voice breaking with emotion, asked me if I had any understanding of how many people had given their hearts and their souls to the concept of public journalism and how much hope it gave them for the future of the field. I responded by noting I had not realized until that moment how much public journalism had taken on the elements of a religious cause.

I should have known that I was not the first person to whom this idea had occurred. Writing in the *American Journalism Review,* Alicia Shepherd entitled her article "The Gospel of Public Journalism" and described the movement as "the hottest secular religion in the news business."[2] Rosemary Armao, the former director of Investigative Reporters and Editors, once called the people involved in public journalism "a cult." ("It was like being born again in Jesus," she said. "If you hadn't experienced the conversion, you just couldn't understand.")[3] Then there are the prophets of the movement—ranging from Carey, the influential media scholar, to the educator-sociologist John Dewey to the European media critic Jürgen Habermas—who are revered for their efforts to restore a meaningful "public sphere," in Habermas's well-known phrase, where news organizations would be expected to stimulate intelligent civic dialogue and to take seriously their role in democratic institution building. Even Jay Rosen, the New York University academic described as the intellectual force behind public journalism, has expressed his annoyance at those who see the movement as "a new religion, complete with true believers and traveling evangelists."[4]

In promoting a deeper, more "responsible" form of news reporting, public journalism advocates have used polls, focus groups, citizen panels, and "solution-oriented" journalism to generate greater public participation and active civic involvement from readers, viewers, and listeners. The movement's goal is to enlist citizens in establishing community agendas that address difficult social and political problems and to position the news organization at the center of a campaign to restore vitality to American civic life. While it has caught the imagination of academics, politicians, foundation officials, and certain journalists, public journalism is controversial with other journalists who see it as an abandonment of news organizations' traditionally detached and "objective" stance. It might be even more controversial if its supporters admitted, as Dewey openly did, that the building of community and the improved communication among citizens fulfill an avowedly religious purpose.

Despite Rosen's disavowals of public journalism as a religious movement, he has used the term *spiritual alarm* in describing the reaction of people to the "hardened realism" and the "ethos of disgruntlement" that he believes is turning public life into a poisonous climate where reporters' "snarling and relentless cynicism" begets politicians' manipulations, which begets public apathy and so on. Rosen's use of the concept may have a more secular meaning than it did for Dewey, but Rosen approved of public journalism to help address the "lack of any affirmative vision, something inspiring" that journalists can work toward and believe in. "What reporters are likely to fear is not the corrosion of their souls, but the judgement of their colleagues that they have been 'naive,'" he wrote of the movement's critics.[5]

The religious dimensions inherent in Rosen's thinking have been made explicit by other advocates of a more "communitarian" form of journalism. In criticizing the excessively individualistic, Enlightenment-based approach of modern journalism and calling for a new moral imperative based on the media's recognition of community values, Clifford Christians, John Ferré, and P. Mark Fackler described a journalism they would like to see practiced in a "humanized workplace," where the value of "servant leadership, spheres of stewardship, and a welcoming disposition toward the public voice" would be recognized. Citing the theologian H. Richard Niebuhr, they insisted it is important to recognize the role of religious discourse in communicating world views, and they argued for a journalism that would capture the religious dimension often manifested in ordinary experience. "Typically, the root metaphors that shape our world views must be manifested in sacred symbols in order for values, feeling, and history to be recast toward integrity," they wrote. "As religious words—ordinarily in the first person—open up the divine-human relationship, our visions of life are nurtured toward moral rectitude."[6]

Most practitioners of public journalism would shy away from using explicitly religious language to describe the movement, even though—in its activism
and in its willingness to get involved trying to solve community problems—
public journalism taps into very genuine religious traditions in the country.
However, in not fully acknowledging the religious basis of their outlook, advocates of public journalism have sidestepped the moral demands required of
those who take on the work of solving the most difficult task facing the American community—namely, addressing the structural inequities in American life.
The religious zeal that motivated the muckrakers, for example, to challenge the
social and economic status quo and to call for a fundamental redistribution of
wealth of the country is missing, for the most part, in the campaigns of public
journalism, as is the prophetic outlook that would require journalists—and even
journalistic organizations—to consider the potentially radical consequences of
a genuine and thorough examination of the causes of society's ills.

With so much of the debate about public journalism in the profession focusing on its lack of "objectivity," defenders of the public journalism movement often point to the reform tradition in American journalism to rebut those who
claim that news organizations should never stray from their historical stance of
detachment in news coverage. But when one looks closely at the causes taken up
by the public journalism movement and the journalistic product produced in
its name, the movement's solutions often become little more than bromides for
do-good campaigns that few would challenge and relatively harmless agendas for
good citizenship that most corners of society would embrace. The "causes" usually taken on by mainstream media companies practicing public journalism are
what must be called safe ones, where one could expect to find a high degree of
public consensus about the problems and often the solutions.[7]

If prophetic journalism is defined as that which challenges, shakes up, or even
outrages the community with its call for reform and higher standards of justice
and equity, then public journalism does not meet this mark. The Pew Center for
Civic Journalism, which supports many of the public journalism projects at news
organizations around the country, provides a good catalogue of the kind of issues taken up by advocates of public journalism. According to Pew's *Civic Catalyst* and other publications from 1998 and 1999, major public journalism projects
were being tackled at news organizations on such topics as the decline of local
leadership (three); juvenile crime and problems of young people (three); better
interaction with members of the community (eleven); voter access and voting
(three); the local economy (two); troubles in the schools (one); the problems of
poverty (two); problems with the police (one); drinking (two); aging (one); taxes
(one); literacy (one); and race relations (one). Most of these topics fall well inside the range of what would be considered safe, good citizenship topics. Although there may not be a consensus on the answers, few readers (and few advertisers) would be offended if a news organization examined these issues.[8]

I also question some of the underlying motivations of a campaign that is, for the most part, being carried out in the newsrooms of the large media corporations that now dominate the news industry. News organizations, particularly those controlled by large, corporate conglomerates, are unlikely to tackle tough issues that might offend important elements of their audience or engender controversy that could lead to anger or strong emotions directed against the news organization. Commercial media companies, deeply vested in the economic system, are seldom willing to pose questions about inequities in the economy or social justice issues and are virtually certain to bend the laudable values of public journalism to tame ends. One has only to take a look at the kinds of public journalism projects undertaken around the country to see how seldom news organizations fulfill the prophetic role of "speaking truth to power."

Critics of public journalism also have noted that the movement uses many of the tools of, and blends easily into the goals of, the movement toward market-oriented journalism, which, along with public journalism, has been one of the news media's favorite, faddish approaches to dealing with problems caused by demographic change and audience stagnation.[9] Advocates of public journalism have coined a slogan—treat the audience as citizens rather than as consumers—as a way to distinguish their campaign from the trendy marketing movement with its audience research, its packaging schemes to lure readers and viewers, and its emphasis on news as a product in the marketplace. Still, this mantra can disguise how easy it is for market-minded editors to mouth the slogans of public journalism while fulfilling their marketer's goals. With its citizen panels, community forums, and citizen polls, public journalism can look disturbingly like boosteristic, "chamber-of-commerce" journalism or the "good news," "reader-friendly" news coverage that distinguishes market-driven journalism. "Two decades ago, outspoken editors in the South who denounced Jim Crow and endorsed civil rights were hated in their communities," wrote John Bare in the *Media Studies Journal* in discussing the shortcomings of the public journalism movement. "If those editors had established their news agenda by survey research, however, they certainly would have found that citizens wanted something else."[10]

To their credit, public journalists usually recognize that—in concept anyway—they are operating in a philosophical tradition that cuts against the grain of safe, traditional media practice. Perhaps not so widely recognized is that the first attempt at what today we would identify as public journalism was not only highly unconventional but also highly unsuccessful. The driving force behind it was Dewey, whom public journalism advocates today still look to as the inspiration for their campaign to restore a sense of community as the driving element in revitalizing society ("The world's shortest definition of public journalism is actually three words: 'what Dewey meant,'" noted Rosen).[11] However, an equally important figure in the annals of public journalism is Robert Park, one of Dewey's close colleagues and a former journalist who had much to say about the promise and limitations of the "communitarian" journalism of his time—and whose insights can still be applied to today's public journalism movement.

Park and Dewey were partners in the creation of "Thought News," an idealistic scheme for launching a newspaper that, if it had fulfilled its founders' vision, would have put the news organization at the center of a philosophy of social action and a journalism of sociological depth. An urban reporter before becoming a renowned sociologist, Park joined Dewey in planning what can only be termed a late-nineteenth-century effort at realizing what public journalists today hope to accomplish in bringing to the world a journalism that would give profound insight into social events, inspire civic virtue and civic action, and realize the dream of the news organization as the catalyst for community solidarity. "If we propose to maintain a democracy as Jefferson conceived it, the newspaper must continue to tell us about ourselves," Park wrote. "We must somehow learn to know our community and its affairs in the same intimate way in which we knew them in country villages. The newspaper must continue to be the printed diary of the home community."[12] But in 1892, when the "Thought News" project fell apart before it got off the ground, it was Park—despite never fully letting go of the dream of a higher journalism—who as a journalist most fundamentally recognized the limitations of daily newspapering in serving the lofty goals he and Dewey had envisioned. (Although it was Dewey who commented drolly, "The idea was advanced for those days, but it was too advanced for the maturity of those who had the idea in mind.")[13]

The public journalism movement has tapped into an old impulse both in the progressive tradition and in the American spiritual ideal. Davis "Buzz" Merritt, the former editor of the *Wichita Eagle* and Rosen's partner in developing the modern incarnation of public journalism, described it as at the center of the "emerging communitarian movement," where "the frustration" and "malaise" felt by Americans at the loss of civic life is "boiling over" on many fronts. "It is no coincidence that the decline in journalism and the decline in public life have happened at the same time," he wrote. "In modern society, they are codependent: Public life needs the information and perspective that journalism can provide, and journalism needs a viable public life because without one there is no need for journalism."[14]

Merritt, in reality, would have been more accurate if, in discussing public journalism, he had talked about the "reemergence" of the communitarian impulse that breaks out periodically in visible form in American life. Merritt's comments mimic, for example, the themes of William Allen White, his fellow Kansan, in lamenting the loss of community in the America of nearly a hundred years ago. White's position as editor of the *Emporia Gazette,* which he owned from 1895 to 1944, became the vehicle for touting the values of small-town, rural life and made him the spokesperson for a vision—which White did not hesitate to articulate in explicitly spiritual terms—of a journalism that served the interests of Americans, not simply as individuals but as members of community. "Our children grow up with the feeling of community strongly upon them," White wrote in 1910. "The 'we' feeling is pressed upon them in common schools, in the common playgrounds and in homes, linked to humanity as no other homes have ever been joined. The electric wire, the iron pipe, the street railroad, the daily newspaper, the telephone . . . have made us all of one body. . . . There are no outlanders. It is possible for all men to understand one another. . . . Indeed it is but the dawn of a spiritual awakening."[15]

Although communitarian thinking has been transformed from one rooted in the Judeo-Christian tradition, it is still no less a spiritual expression of Americans' perennial faith in community rootedness, the importance of "the land," and the character that is built in rural, small-town, and neighborhood living. The desire to articulate the American dream in terms of grass-roots citizenship crops up again and again throughout American history, particularly as a response to rapid urbanization, industrialization, and technological change. It is this belief in native American democracy, the nobility of the common person, and the importance of the human collective that can be found in the writings of such figures as Thomas Paine, Ralph Waldo Emerson, Henry David Thoreau, Walt Whitman, Horace Greeley, George Ripley, Theodore Parker, Margaret Fuller, Frederick Jackson Turner, and Booth Tarkington. Brook Farm, Walden Pond, the ideal of equality, the gospel of America, the frontier thesis, and the escape valve theory were all recognitions, of one kind or another, of Americans' desire to escape the encrustments of civilization and to be reborn in the experience of simple living and the harmony of community life. While many of these figures were not orthodox believers, they did not hesitate to use biblical or Christian terminology as metaphors for their faith in human freedom and reform ("My country is the world; to do good, my religion," Paine said; "The World is young. We too must write Bibles, to unite again the heavens and the earthly worlds," wrote Whitman.).[16]

At least three epochs in the early evolution of American communitarianism can be identified: the colonial and Revolutionary War days of the late 1700s, when such folks as Thomas Jefferson and Benjamin Franklin openly expressed their belief that life in small communities and pastoral settings, in combination with education and Christian training (as well as the absorption of a few simple homilies and proverbs, such as those in *Poor Richard's Almanack*) would create the American individualism needed to make democracy successful; the period of American Transcendentalism in the early to mid-1800s, when universalist attitudes and the rebellion against Puritan moral rigidity, combined with the embrace of pantheistic views of nature, led certain people (mostly high-bred intellectuals and artists) to seek solace in a romanticized rural community life; and the period of progressivism and populism in the 1890s and early 1900s that led discontented reformers to advocate turning away from the corruption of urban politics and the economic inequalities of the Industrial Age to find solutions in the organic life of the community, whether it was the small town, the neighborhood, or the worker-owned business enterprise.

Probably the most celebrated public manifestation of the communitarian movement was this last one, when Dewey, Park, White, the sociologist Charles Horton Cooley, and the urban reformers Frederic Howe and Jane Addams sought to find in community settings the "spiritual meaning" that would satisfy the utopian yearnings and the idealistic desire for reform that has animated progressives throughout American history. During this period, a number of these reformers believed that two disciplines for which they held out near mystic hope—journalism and sociology—could be brought together to serve "as a model for realizing a liberal utopia through communication," as Fred Matthews put it. Or, as one of Dewey's biographers described the form of journalism that would constitute the "Thought News" project, "[It] involved a moral commitment with a religious meaning, for the project was conceived as a strategy for idealizing the world in and through social science and journalism."[17]

Never had such high hopes been held out for a newspaper that would never issue a single edition. The project had been instigated by Franklin Ford, a visionary former newspaperman who recruited Dewey and Park, Dewey's former student at the University of Michigan who took a break from his journalism career to participate. Park saw "Thought News" as a way to do what he had come to believe was impossible in daily commercial journalism: analyze the day's news in terms of long-term historical trends that went beyond the immediate and the superficial; interpret current affairs for the average person according to the insights of sociology and philosophy; and elevate the communications process to its full potential in creating a liberal and enlightened democracy. The illumination of deeper sociological forces, the improvement of society through the production of high-level journalism, the reduction of the chasm between academic ideas and real life—for Park (using language that foreshadowed Marshall McLuhan, a global communitarian in his own right), "the solution of all the problems of our social life is the extension of the nervous system of the social body."[18] In reality, Park and Dewey saw their newspaper venture as nothing less than the production of a spiritualized form of journalism that could touch people at their deepest levels and inspire them to build a better society.

The project was abandoned in 1892 soon after it had stirred up a blast of publicity with a press release announcing the first edition (the first issue—costing the then exorbitant price of $1.50—was written but never published). Both Dewey and Park were distracted by other activities—Dewey with his social science research, Park with his return to daily journalism. One of Park's biographers called the plan an example of "touching naivete" but acknowledged the profound impact that the planning of the newspaper had on the development of both Park's and Dewey's communal beliefs and their near worship of social science as a "secularized deity" at the center of a philosophy of social activism and community building.[19]

The religious orientation of the participants in "Thought News" was largely a transparent one, particularly in the context of the late-nineteenth-century and early-twentieth-century communitarians' expressions of spiritual enthusiasm for the social sciences and the developments in communications technology. The mercuric Ford, for example, made no secret that the idea for the new newspaper began with the premise that "the means of communication are in place but . . . could not be brought to the highest use until the realities flowing out from the locomotive and the telegraph, their spiritual meaning, should be wrought out" by a new form of newspaper publishing.[20] The University of Michigan English professor Fred Newman Scott, an ex-student of Dewey who also collaborated on the "Thought News" project, gave the most explicitly Christian rationale for the founding of the new newspaper in an address to a Christian student association. "The newspaper is the most powerful ally that Christianity has ever had," Scott told the group. All newspapers "should band together into one great organism bent upon conveying the truth of life to the minds of men," he said, concluding on this exalted note: this transformed newspaper could be "for us today, the voice of the real, the living Christ."[21]

In Dewey's work, one can see the preliminary shape of a philosophy wedding technology and communitarian ideas that would emerge in McLuhan's "global village" concept. But whereas McLuhan was less public in acknowledging Christian influences, Dewey interjected his Christian impulses and his Christian values into his vision of the sociological mission, and he saw the union of the scientific spirit and its application to solving moral and social problems as the goal of Christianity. Dewey saw Christ's work on earth as the attempt to reveal truth and make it manifest to humanity—which Dewey increasingly came to identify with the social scientific method. In identifying Christianity with the disclosure of practical truth, Dewey said, the new symbols of social science inquiry had begun to replace the old, supernatural Christian symbols that no longer give meaning to life. "Jesus had no special doctrine to impose—no special set of truths labeled religious," Dewey wrote. "The only truth Jesus knew of as religious was Truth. . . . His doctrine was that Truth, however named and however divided by man, is one as God is one; that getting hold of truth and living by it is religion."[22]

Dewey's faith in social science, his belief in the organic connection between the individual and society, and his sunny democratic view that each person becomes most fully realized through social interaction are best recognized for their impact on education; many American public schools still operate according to Dewey's philosophy of learning-by-doing and educating the student as a social being. But it also is no surprise to see Dewey exercising such an influence on today's advocates of public journalism. Dewey's faith in pragmatic learning and his commitment to scientific methods of discovering and transmitting truth are reflected in the importance he placed on the function of the newspaper and the communications process as a whole in society. Dewey's call for the union of the daily press and up-to-date social science methods was a key underpinning in his belief that everyday people must have a way to encounter the truth experimentally, apply it to their lives, and then seek to institutionalize it in the democratic organizations of society. Ultimately, the communication of truth is absorbed into the functions of democracy, and a "community of truth" develops that leads to "the spiritual unification of humanity, the realization of the brotherhood of man, all that Christ called the Kingdom of God," he wrote.[23]

Park breathed in this same intoxicating atmosphere of transposed Christian mysticism and faith in the social sciences that his friend Dewey did, but he was far more restrained in his views of it. Park and Dewey shared a similar small-town, pious, church-going upbringing, but Park was always less explicit (and less mystical) than Dewey in incorporating his religious beliefs into his philosophical framework for pursuing the investigation of truth in the world. Park was an "agnostic moralist," as one biographer described him, with only a "nominal" interest in religion for much of his life, as another biographer put it.[24] However, Park's biographers probably underestimated the role of religion in his outlook on life. Park, in a letter he wrote to a colleague who had inquired about Park's religious beliefs late in Park's career, explained that—despite trying out different creeds earlier in his life—he had come to see himself as "essentially and fundamentally orthodox," as someone who had "come finally to believe in religion itself; believe in it, that is to say, as an essential element in a wholesome individual and social life." What that meant, Park went on to explain, was that he was "no longer greatly concerned either about my own or other souls. I was in fact more concerned about the world because I had come to realize that it was in this world that souls are lost and saved."[25]

Like his fellow communitarians, Park believed information organized around the scientific method could be transmitted in a way that would elevate journalism to a position superior to the superficial journalistic practices of the period. But Park, perhaps because he had actually spent so much time in the newspaper business, grew to become less certain about exactly how the newspaper would achieve this lofty objective. Park's ultimate disillusionment with the practice of sociological journalism foreshadowed the criticisms of modern public journalism, which, while it may be motivated by the right ideals, is not often hailed for the brilliance of the journalism itself. While Dewey believed that the ideal newspaper would read much like a daily installment of an encyclopedia of the social sciences, Park came to wonder whether the prose that moved sociologists would find a following among a large reading public. In the end, while other communitarians retained their idealist's faith in the potentially redemptive role of the press, Park worried that news organizations would never rise above the sensationalized story, the stereotypical angle, and the attention-grabbing headline that, as Walter Lippmann complained, kept the deeper truth of the social order from coming to light.[26]

It may seem strange to see theology undergirding a debate about the methodology of the feature story in journalism, but, in the communitarians' incorporation of journalistic methodology into their philosophy, this is an example of how far their thinking had gone. As a reporter, Park had developed a sense of urgency for the survival of the local community within the urban environment, and some of his fellow communitarians urged him to look at the dynamic of the feature story itself as a device to convey emotional empathy and moral enlightenment from the subject of the story, via the journalist, to the reader. Cooley, for example, saw in the human interest story the machinery of communication conveying the dramatic reality of another person as an almost mystical bonding experience for the reading citizen, and he welcomed the use of the color story in journalism. "One who entertains the thought and feeling of others can hardly refuse them justice," Cooley said. "He has made them a part of himself."[27]

On this issue, however, Park was not quite so enthusiastic. Park, who grew up in Red Wing, Minnesota, had learned the excitement of the city in his early reporting years; the classical small-town-boy-turned-itinerant-journalist, he had worked as a court reporter, police reporter, and feature writer for newspapers in Minneapolis, Detroit, Denver, and New York.[28] Working in the heyday of the city reporter, when the city beat was full of glamour, Park thrilled at the drama of the city's street life. "Walking on upper Broadway or down to the Battery on a bright afternoon, or watching the oncoming and outgoing human tide as it poured morning and evening over Brooklyn Bridge, was always for me an enthralling spectacle," Park once wrote. Despite the limitations of daily reporting, Park had found the city beat to be a place that "fulfilled the role of the informal and intuitive sociologist," where reporters wrote about murders, elections, and other news of urban life.[29] Park could see journalism as a profoundly fulfilling and socially important profession if only journalists had more opportunity to chronicle the slower changes that underlay colorful events—the growth of new urban neighborhoods and institutions, the influence of interesting personality types, the ways that social and political forces shaped city life.

But it was for this reason that the human interest story, Park felt, had its limitations. It was a throwback, he believed, to the evangelical tradition that put sentiment before utility and aroused feelings in ways that were not always socially useful.[30] Park recognized the pragmatic reasons for journalists to find ways to connect personally with readers and to hook them into a story, but he wondered if that demand would make the kind of journalism he envisioned—richer in sociological details, deeper in historical context, more rigorously connected to the discoveries of social science research—incompatible with the commercial mission of the typical news organization. Unlike many of the public journalists of today, Park recognized the difficulties of serving two masters—economic reality and the cause of "higher" journalism—and he acknowledged that it would be no easy task to produce a newspaper that would be successful in both realms.[31]

However, Park never abandoned his hope in the newspaper as an agency for controlling public opinion and strengthening public agencies that attempted to integrate the life of the individual in a society where family and neighborhood controls had grown weak.[32] After he returned to journalism with the demise of the "Thought News" project, he talked about setting up a foundation to bring university people and journalists together to discuss how academic theories and ideas could be put into practice, and he proposed organizing a bureau to disseminate dispassionate information about crime and social pathology to counter the way it was dealt with in the popular press. Ultimately, Park's calm and ironic detachment toward the urban scene was what would lead him to abandon a ten-year journalism career and in 1913 come to the safe academic haven of the University of Chicago, where he began his second career as a pioneering sociologist. When he left journalism in 1898 to pursue his graduate education, Park had still not lost his interest in the notion of the press as a source of scientific knowledge about social problems, even though he had been unable to advance the concept as a member of the journalism profession. "One might say that a sociologist is merely a more accurate, responsible, and scientific reporter," Park later said as an established sociologist.[33]

If there is any group of journalists who could be expected to feel a resonance with the spiritual aspirations that were reflected in the communitarian journalists of the Dewey and Park era, it should be the modern practitioners of public journalism. To produce intelligent, captivating, and illuminating journalism free of formula writing and sensationalism and to make those stories the catalyst behind meaningful social change are still animating forces in journalism and motivate many serious journalists (including those who support public journalism and those who do not). Still, it is the public journalism movement of today that draws so directly on the spirit of community renewal that inspired the communitarians a century ago. Carey, the media scholar, articulated this connection when he described the "ritual" view of communication (which he contrasted with the commercialized, "transmission" view) as a "redemptive" act for Americans, where the exchange of information carries with it emotional, spiritual, and cultural value. Reading a newspaper, he said, should be seen as similar to "attending a mass." "We recognize, as with religious rituals, that news changes little and yet is intrinsically satisfying; it performs few functions yet is habitually consumed," Carey wrote. "Like any invented cultural form, news both forms and reflects a particular 'hunger for experience,' a desire to do away with the epic, heroic, and traditional in favor of the unique, original, novel, new. . . . Under a ritual view, then, news is not information but drama."[34]

Sadly, public journalism faces another obstacle: it has turned out to be very boring and predictable. Much of what has accompanied the public journalism movement—public forums, reader involvement groups, polls and surveys about reader attitudes about community and community priorities—does not translate into very challenging journalism or even very interesting storytelling. It is unfortunate to see public journalism—held out by many as the hope for a new kind of journalism—included in accusations that news organizations produce too many accounts of the safe or the obvious and do it in ways that are formulaic and predictable. At a time when news organizations are criticized for not emphasizing what is fresh and original as a way to revitalize their link with the public,

public journalism too often has produced tedious, bland, and tendentious accounts of the newspaper's efforts to help define community concerns and little else. To try to turn this kind of material into exciting, reader-grabbing journalism has been an uphill challenge in the same way that Park wondered how well the public would be captivated by sociology translated into journalistic prose. As with so many other fashionable new directions in the journalism business, the promotional rhetoric surrounding the public journalism movement begs the question that the production of high quality, citizen-engaging journalism can be very difficult to achieve—even when journalists are motivated to do it.

In Seattle, for example, I have watched with interest as the *Seattle Times*—along with the public television and one of the public radio stations—has taken a stab at public journalism with what the *Times* calls its "Front Page Forum." While the program has led to laudable community forums discussing important local issues, the journalism has generally been about the process itself, including long pieces examining the role of leadership in the community and the substance of polls that show Seattle-area citizens are greatly concerned about sprawl and growth, family values, the loss of social morality, the well-being of children, and crime.[35] What has been missing are imaginative, in-depth stories illuminating community concerns in "prophetic" ways that might challenge the power structure. For example, instead of predictable accounts of the well-documented community concerns about growth, what about stories that question the policies of local political bodies (largely supported by newspaper editorials) that promote growth: convention center expansions, taxpayer subsidized port and foreign trade projects, legal changes that allow cruise ship dockings, and special tax and regulatory exemptions for high technology companies and real estate developments throughout the city? Or instead of running superficial wire stories about the debate in Congress over welfare reform, what about stories showing the impact on the "family values" in poor communities where single parents will be forced to go to work at minimum wage jobs that do not support day care or family health insurance? Or, at the time of the reparation payments to Japanese Americans locked up during World War II, where were the stories about the powerful local interests that profited (and still do) from the land confiscated from Japanese American families? Or how about more articles that probe who profits locally from illegal immigration (powerful agricultural interests, the high technology industry) or the war on drugs (the police and the military), or that look at the social and economic consequences of chain and conglomerate ownership of so many local businesses (including chain newspapers themselves), or that ask the consumer questions that might threaten advertisers (for example, are the sales at the large department stores that advertise in the newspaper really sales and how do the discounts compare with those in other stores)? It does not take a commitment to public journalism to do this kind of reporting; it takes a commitment to aggressive, no-fear-or-favor journalism. It also takes a prophetic journalist's willingness to challenge power, to scrutinize the sacred cows, and to risk some economic losses for the sake of principle.

In fairness, though, it should be pointed out that the communications academic community, in its idealism and its relentless criticism of the overly commercial orientation of the mass media, has tended to embrace public journalism in ways that are no less worshipful than are certain sectors of the media. Not only have such prominent academicians as Carey, Rosen, and Theodore Glasser become boosters of the movement, but it has become identified with the thinking of Habermas, who has been elevated to a prophet status in certain academic quarters. Habermas has tapped into a strong vein of romanticism and nostalgia among communications academics, who long for the ideal of a civic dialogue modeled on the eighteenth-century café society so exalted by Habermas, the New England town meeting, or the civic forum of the ancient Athenians. Habermas's view of the high point of the operation of a successful "public sphere"—eighteenth- and nineteenth-century salons in England and France where educated elites gathered to discuss public affairs and where the early periodical press exercised wide influence—offers an intellectual model for modern-day academic followers of public journalism who, like Habermas, believe that the public sphere has been badly eroded by the image creation and opinion management of the modern, commercial press. Habermas's vision of a long-lost café society (one, that if one looks more closely, was never as richly communitarian or as politically influential as Habermas's followers like to imagine) has only tenuous historical connections to the problems facing modern "mediated" society. But here, too—whether it comes through the theories of Habermas, the advocacy of Carey and Rosen, or the enthusiastic articles about public journalism that have proliferated in academic publications—the academic community's zealous endorsement of public journalism looks a good deal like the conversion process that has won over so many true-believing journalists.[36]

There is a field of academic research that, in a much more practical sense, may provide clues that could help make public journalism work. The communitarian movement of the last century also left its impact on media scholarship, some of which provides the most effective analysis of what it takes for news organizations to reconnect with their readership and to help people integrate with their community. The scholarship—known as "community ties" research—offers an alternative analysis to the way market-oriented news executives use audience research and provides a more dynamic method to analyze what gets citizens involved in the community and how it relates to the media they consume. The media research specialist Phil Meyer, for example, has noted that, despite years of doing market research, media companies often have difficulty translating data about audience taste into clear and effective strategies for doing something to fix their readership problem.[37] Community ties researchers, such as my University of Washington colleague Keith Stamm, avoid this trap by looking at the problem from a different angle. Taking their cue from Park (and later the sociologist Robert Merton), they first study the patterns involved in the way individuals and families become connected to their community—such as in their relationships with the public schools, local political organizations, churches, and other community institutions—and then provide news organizations with information about how to better serve as a primary mechanism in fostering integration into the community.[38] Unfortunately, only a few media organizations (and not necessarily the ones involved in the public journalism movement) have shown much interest in this line of research, despite the failure of traditional market research approaches to stem the mainstream media's audience decline.

As public journalism advocates in both academia and the media know, it is difficult to change the orientation of a professional culture or the business approach of an industry. Park and Dewey came to recognize the folly in trying to bring their idealized version of a community-cultivating, social science-inspired journalism to reality in a culture that was not ready for it. Today's public journalism movement—circumscribed by the dictates of the commercial press—has made some strides in demonstrating that journalism can be done with a greater attention to community building. However, the controversy it has stirred up—as well as the dearth of quality journalism that has been produced in its name—may prove to be the movement's downfall. Executing high quality journalism that truly makes a difference to the community is a daunting, even a courageous, task. Releasing the spirit of community, as we have seen, has long been one of religion's greatest challenges, and journalism faces enormous hurdles in openly embarking on this mission. News organizations cannot and should not be expected to see their role in explicitly religious terms. But whenever they hold up the communications process as a catalyst for building the bonds of community, they at least should be aware that they are operating in sacred space.

PART 4

Journalism after Jesus

CHAPTER 16

Jesus without Journalists: Miracles and Mysteries, Minus Media Reports

In 1945, an Egyptian peasant unearthed an urn that contained what turned out to be one of the greatest finds in the history of Christian scholarship. But before the Nag Hammadi gospels came into the hands of authorities, a key, middle section of one of the discovered texts—the "Gospel of Mary," ostensibly based on a vision of Jesus that came to Mary Magdalene after Jesus' crucifixion—was found to be missing, apparently burned by the peasant's family to kindle the breakfast oven.[1]

The missing parts of the "Gospel of Mary" will be forever tantalizing to scholars fascinated with the Gnostic texts that had been buried after they were declared heretical by the early church. In this text, Mary Magdalene, one of Jesus' closest companions, was just beginning to recount to the disciples a special revelation she said she had received from Jesus when he came to her in a vision after his crucifixion. Without the missing sections, we get only a small sample of Jesus' sayings, which were dismissed as "strange" and unauthentic by the disciple Andrew. Peter also was skeptical of Mary's account and questioned whether Jesus would speak to her secretly. This position, as we now know, was to become a key element in the assertion of church authority by Peter and his successors in the apostolic tradition.[2]

When I first read the "Gospel of Mary," I found myself wondering how a modern journalist trained in today's reportorial methodologies would deal with the claims of the early Christians that seem such an affront to modern notions of science and logic? The question, I had come to realize while researching the relationship between religious and journalistic history, was not entirely an academic one. Journalists, as we have seen, are believers in "facts," and it is often religion's lack of the factual proof of its claims that makes journalists skeptical.

A close examination of the methods of the mainstream press, however, shows rather conclusively that journalism reports not facts but only what people report as the facts. Nor does journalism apply any independent methodological examination to claims made by those who contend there are more things happening in the universe than can be verified by the empirical method. When it comes to coverage of the supernatural, mystical, or faith-based elements of religious experience, journalists grow particularly wary and cautious and avoid the issue of factual proof whenever possible.

This question has become increasingly relevant for journalists who in recent years have been caught up in the controversy surrounding the "search for the historical Jesus," as it has become known. The "Gospel of Mary"—as well as the discovery of the Gnostic gospels themselves—is only one in a cascade of new articles, books, research projects, archaeological finds, reinterpretations of old and newly discovered texts, and scholarly debates that have engulfed the Christian community in an unprecedented reexamination of the nature of Christian orthodoxy and the claims of historical truth attributed to the Christian gospels. Although the "historical Jesus" issue has been around practically as long as the Christian church, most explicitly since the publication of David Friedrich Strauss's *Life of Jesus Critically Examined* in 1835, journalists have only recently begun to evince any particular interest in the historical questions surrounding the ministry of Jesus.[3] Journalists have been especially fascinated by the work of the Jesus Seminar, an organization of liberal scholars and academics who practice what is known as the "historical-critical method" in analyzing biblical texts. As part of a high-profile challenge to the evangelical position on the inerrancy of the Christian gospels, this group has gained headlines with its dismissal of the historical validity of such claims as the virgin birth, Jesus' proclamations of his divinity, his working of miracles, and his resurrection.[4]

Ironically, as journalists have covered the debate, they have found themselves—and their own practices and professional methodologies—dragged into the controversy. On a superficial level, the criticisms lodged against the press by the critics of the Jesus Seminar sound much like what is often said whenever the press finds itself caught between two highly polarized groups hotly contesting issues of deep emotional feeling. But the juxtaposition of the ways orthodox Christians and academic scholars debate questions of faith and historical truth with the methods used by journalists raises important questions about the methodology of journalism, too. In fact, the methods of modern journalism present journalists, just like the scholars of the Jesus Seminar, with the dilemma of any group that believes it is employing the tools of modern scientific analysis in examining factual claims.

In pondering the controversy surrounding the press coverage of the Jesus Seminar and its search for the historical Jesus, I found myself wondering if journalists would have any better luck in applying their methodology to the thorny questions surrounding the lives of Jesus and his followers. In doing this, I came to realize that I had to spend as much time examining the nature of modern journalism and the attitudes and assumptions that have gone into the construction of the methodology of modern journalists as I did trying to understand the cultural framework of those early Christian writers. I discovered that journalists, like other modern rationalists, are every bit as susceptible as those early Christians to allowing unconscious attitudes about the nature of truth and the operation of the universe to seep into their thinking. If we apply a little historical perspective and imagination to the question, we will find that these journalistic assumptions are every bit as extravagant and problematic as the interpretations Jesus' followers imputed to his life and his teachings two thousand years ago.

Journalism—if we define it, as we do today, as instantaneous or even contemporaneous chronicling of the events of a time—did not exist in Jesus' day. By today's standards, the systems of communication in the ancient Middle East were slow and crudely developed. Few people beyond the priesthood, a handful of government administrators, and a small number of professional scribes could write, and only a slightly greater number could read; letters and other forms of written communications circulated slowly over the ancient roads; and most information traveled by word of mouth and was spread from village to village by travelers and storytellers. Jesus' ministry was very much a part of this world—an oral ministry in a largely oral culture, in which he taught mainly through parables that in their use of paradox and the unexpected were easy for an illiterate audience to remember and pass along. We have no direct eyewitness accounts of Jesus' life or his teachings by his contemporaries; Jesus himself left no written accounts; and there is no indication that any of the original twelve disciples (with the possible exception of Levi, the tax collector) were literate. The closest thing we have are a few references by Roman and Jewish historians who made brief mention of Jesus soon after his death. The gospel accounts of Jesus and the heretical Gnostic texts were written anywhere from 70 to 150 years after his death, most scholars believe. From the standpoint of journalism then, it looks like a pretty fruitless effort—at least, if we want to establish who Jesus was, based on any surviving record of him written by him or his contemporaries.

If, as Harold Innis and Marshall McLuhan believe, the spirit tends to flourish most intensively in oral cultures, the ministry of Jesus offers a fascinating glimpse into what can emerge when a culture is undergoing a profound shift in communications media. Jesus' world not only was a cauldron of social, political, and economic change but also was witnessing a dramatic transition from a primarily oral culture to a written culture. Jesus' life was circumscribed with the trappings of print learning—a temple life built around the oral and written interpretation of Jewish religious texts by Hebrew rabbis, a Graeco-Roman system of administration and education for the ruling and social elite, and a developing system of letter writing and written communication over long distances that after Jesus' death would be instrumental in memorializing him for the ages.

At one level, Jesus' ministry was aimed primarily at the largely uneducated population of Palestinian Jews. But Jesus also was an avid participant in the learned disputes among the rabbinic community of the temple. No one knows for sure the level of Jesus' literacy, but most scholars believe that he could read scripture (even though it was possible to learn the sacred texts from hearing them read aloud in synagogue), that he spoke Aramaic, some Greek, and probably Hebrew, and that he might have had at least a rudimentary ability to write (there is no record that he wrote anything, beyond a brief mention of his writing with his finger on the ground, as described in John 8:6–8).[5] But Jesus' legacy was forged by his literate followers, such as the writers of the gospels and the Apostle Paul, whose writings were not penned until one-half to three-quarters of a century after Jesus' death.[6]

Despite Rome's great military, engineering, and administrative prowess, it was never able to fully control the heart of its subjects, and it was here that Christianity burst onto the scene. The Roman religious system offered conquered peoples little that spoke to their deeper human needs. Although intermingled with Hellenistic mystery cults and various forms of indigenous religions, the Roman gods, for the most part, simply existed above the heads of subjugated populations as the imposed religion of the ruling elite. By the time of Jesus' crucifixion during the reign of the emperor Tiberius, the Roman religion served largely as a symbolic backdrop for the military control of Rome and held little personal meaning for the ruled people in the lands of Jesus' ministry. At the same time, the bitter political, economic, and social conditions suffered by the subjects of Roman territories left them ripe for a message that would emphasize personal salvation, spiritual equality, and, most important, the notion that they were loved by a divine power no matter what their social status.

Some scholars believe that Jesus was able to capture the imagination of both his contemporaries and posterity in such dramatic fashion precisely because he was positioned at this fulcrum point in communications history. For Walter Ong, the "word"—in the Jewish and Christian meaning of the word—is what it is today because of the unique mix of oral ministry that Jesus employed and the evolving written tradition that memorialized Jesus' message for posterity.[7] Other scholars, such as Thomas Boomershine, have suggested that it is the mystification of Jesus that occurred during the period when his followers circulated their oral stories about him, combined with the written accounts that emerged years later, that has given Jesus his status as a lasting spiritual figure. Yet this analysis also implies that if people had been able to experience Jesus firsthand, as might have been the case if anything like the modern mass media had existed in his day, or if there were eyewitness accounts of his ministry, as might be the case if modern journalists or historians had been around, we might have a very different impression of his life and the legacy of his message.

Intrigued by these uncertainties and these unanswered questions, I found myself speculating what it would mean to imagine the search for the "real" Jesus in modern journalistic terms or at least in ways that would be familiar to, say, an investigative reporter or perhaps a religion writer (or a combination of the two, if there were such a thing). If we accept the writings about Jesus as the nearest thing to journalism that we have, then we can ask ourselves how these accounts differed from modern journalism and in what ways. How was the picture of Jesus "framed," to use a favorite word of modern communications scholars, and how might it be "framed" in the methodologies of today's reporting? How would our picture of Jesus have been different had we had complete access to the accounts that may have been buried or burned because they did not fall within the accepted interpretations of the early church?

Many of us have pondered from time to time what Jesus might experience if he were to encounter our modern commercial and materialist culture—if he walked into the ornate church buildings of the Vatican in Rome, say, or visited a Christian theme park, or attended a drive-through suburban Christian church. It is commonplace to hear people speculating about what would have happened if Jesus had launched his ministry in a modern media age. Would he not have been dealt with like just another cult leader, self-proclaiming evangelist, or street-corner prophet? Even if he were to rise to the media stature of a Mother Teresa or a Martin Luther King Jr., would he have been able to carry out his mission in today's complex, pluralistic world or been taken seriously for what he said? Could he have gained a following of hundreds of millions across the world who would come to believe in him as their savior? Or in our modern "mediated" era, would he have been forced to make the talk show circuit to get his message out, set up his own religious broadcasting network, or just hire some good public relations operatives? Books have been written and movies and television shows made spinning out this scenario. In most, the conclusion is that the circumstances of the modern world and the sophistication of the modern media environment would offer little that would be receptive to the figure of a Jesus or little opportunity for him to gain the spiritual stature that he did in history.

If it is true that we might have a very different picture of Jesus if we had been able to experience him during a film clip on the six o'clock news or in a *People* magazine profile, what does that say about the possibilities for religion and the prospects for a truly transcendent religious figure in our culture today? Is it possible that the essence of religious belief is inextricably bound up with the nature of the media that convey to us our impressions of things? Even if Jesus were exactly the person portrayed in the gospels, would we experience him in the same way if we knew him as a personality in our television age? If Jesus' world were not exactly as it was and if it had not been in the exact stage of media development that it was, might not Jesus seem to us to be a very different person? If McLuhan is right that the medium is the message, there had to be something unique about the way people communicated—and Jesus' appearance at just such a point in the evolution of media systems—that made it possible for him to emerge as a profoundly memorable religious figure. Is it necessary that we see Jesus as a product of a particular media environment, as Innis's theories imply, or to believe that he might have had a much different profile, as Joshua Meyrowitz's ideas suggest, if he had lived after the mass media, particularly the electronic media, reduced the awe and the respect that once shrouded the great and the mighty?[8] And what of Ong's notion that the development of media systems, as well as Jesus' special place within it, is itself part of God's plan?[9]

With these ideas in mind, the account of Mary Magdalene's testimony to Peter and the disciples would present any chronicler—whether a modern journalist or a chronicler of that time—with not only major challenges but also interesting possibilities. For the sake of our discussion, let us suppose we had no first-hand knowledge of or acquaintance with Jesus. It is, of course, interesting to speculate on the implications for Christianity if Jesus had been the subject of direct, eyewitness media coverage, and I will do that later in this chapter. But for the moment, I want us to imagine that, as journalists operating under modern professional reporting methodology, we are encountering the controversy after the key supernatural events of Christian tradition (such as Jesus' divine birth, his performance of miracles, and his crucifixion and resurrection) reputedly have taken place. As we shall see, in imagining ourselves writing about Jesus but never knowing him personally, we are in a position not that different from what journalists face when they write about events they have not witnessed. By imagining ourselves operating in the time soon after Jesus' crucifixion, we also can imagine ourselves in the middle of a controversy—where journalists usually are—that would turn out to have profound repercussions for posterity.

It is important to remember that truth, in the methodology of the modern journalist, can be ascertained in three ways: first, by directly observing events; second, by recounting the claims of what others say they have observed or believe to be true; third, by examining documents, texts, or other accounts in which people record what they claim to be the truth. After the information is collected, the standard reportorial methodology (at least in the American context) would be to lay out the claims of one side of a controversy in the news pages and to balance them off against the claims of the other. The reader is then free to decide what is the truth.[10] The journalist's position is detached, skeptical, uninvolved in the event at hand. Television journalists are allowed some commentary, but the "visuals" of the event would be relied on to convey the story. Print journalists doing a typical story for the news section of the daily newspaper would give the subjects of the controversy little personalized treatment so that they would not influence the reader. The quotes and the factual details would carry the piece.

A reporter operating by today's professional norms probably would have approached a story about the dispute between Peter and Mary warily and with a good deal of discomfort. We can presume that the subject matter would meet at least some of the tests of modern newsworthiness. There was certainly controversy attached to Jesus' crucifixion by the Roman authorities; there was some degree of uniqueness to his followers' claim of Jesus' messiahship and resurrection from the dead; and it appeared to matter to people. But the other tests would be much more problematic. Could the claims be demonstrated to be "factually" true? Was there demonstrable evidence of their truth? Could the issue be settled by scientific analysis? Would "experts" on the topic be in agreement? Since this would almost certainly not be the case, a reporter would likely fall back on the bare essentials of reportorial methodology: lay out the claims and the counterclaims and let readers make up their own minds. Skepticism, belittlement, or downright disbelief might be left for the columnists or the editorial page writers, but we are talking about the news pages now.

As thorough and enterprising journalists working in the early Christian era, we would have prepared for our story by checking the archives for any previously written material on the subject. Unfortunately, in our imagined scenario, we would not find much to help us there. While Jesus did operate on the edge of an emerging print culture, he received only scant attention in the recorded texts of his time—or at least, those that have survived. A search of the ancient histories of the early Christian period might prove interesting, but it would not help us much, either. None of the ancient historians who mentioned Jesus— the Jewish historian Josephus, and the Graeco-Roman historians Suetonius, Pliny the Younger, and Tacitus—were contemporaries of Jesus or wrote about him from direct observation. Their commentaries came from observing or hearing about the movement that grew up in his name (which, incidentally, did not impress them as particularly important or interesting).[11]

An imaginary reporter in this period soon after Christ's death might ask, what about consulting the Christian gospels themselves to gain an authoritative account of Jesus' life and teachings? Unfortunately, this is the point in which our hypothetical exercise grows complicated—but also intriguing. Scholars have largely concluded that none of the four gospel accounts of Jesus' life (Matthew, Mark, Luke, and John) and none of the books sometimes attributed to the disciples who traveled with Jesus (James, the two letters of Peter, and the four other accounts of John) as well as Acts, usually attributed to Luke, were written by people who knew Jesus during his ministry, even though some were written in their names.[12] Scholars speculate that this was because so many of his original followers had seen and heard Jesus firsthand; because they felt little need to put oral tradition into writing even if they could; and because there was such strong expectation of Jesus' imminent return.

To confuse matters even more, the books of the New Testament were selected from dozens of sacred accounts produced by vying communities of Christians, many of which contained very different interpretations of the religious significance of Jesus' life and teachings. Slowly over a period from the end of the first century A.D., when Paul's letters were collected and circulated, to the end of the fourth century, when Jerome translated the scriptures into Latin, the New Testament that we recognize today took shape as the orthodox text of the Christian church. Among the books that did not make it into the canon were the many texts of the Gnostics, a mystical faction that offended the eventual orthodox victors by downplaying the significance of the resurrection (in the Gnostics' view, Jesus was a spirit anyway and only seemed to die) and emphasizing elements of magic, visions, and strange supernatural cosmologies that were highly syncretistic with other occult beliefs of the time. Included in those heretical texts was the "Gospel of Mary."

Let us continue with our scenario by imagining that this book is an important account of a confrontation among the early Christians. Let us suppose that there was an encounter between Mary Magdalene and Peter and the other disciples and that, in our hypothetical modern journalist's role, we were present at it. Let us assume that we recognize Mary as a potentially powerful, rival personality within the early Christian movement—a person who the biblical scholar Elaine Pagels argued was very likely a central figure in the life of Jesus but whose influence may have been squelched by the male apostles[13]—and that we sense the potentially dangerous "Gnostic" elements in her vision. In our imagined scenario, we sense that we are witnessing an important moment in the history of the Christian movement. Jesus, as risen savior, has made an appearance to answer some of the disciples' questions but has departed, according to the account in the "Gospel of Mary," leaving the disciples confused and uncertain what to do next. Mary Magdalene rises to speak and is recognized by Peter as a favorite of Jesus and someone who has gained special wisdom from him. Mary, in an effort to raise their spirits and strengthen their resolve, promises to reveal what has been "hidden" from the disciples. She then recounts her vision of her dialogue with Jesus where he describes the soul rising until, free of its physical bonds, it has attained eternal rest. The dialogue is typical of Gnostic "wisdom" material attributed to Jesus, and it clearly offends Andrew and Peter, whose reaction induces Mary to respond, weeping, "Do you think that I thought this up myself in my heart, or that I am lying about the Savior?" The passage ends with the disciple Levi chastising Peter for treating Mary like "the adversaries" and entreating the disciples to be ashamed and to go out and teach as Jesus taught them.

A modern journalist covering this story would be facing something of a challenge. From a newsworthiness standpoint, there probably would be two main elements of the story to choose from—the vision Mary claims to have experienced and the beginnings of the controversy that would ultimately pit Mary and her Gnostic followers against the prevailing orthodox forces, as represented by Peter and Andrew. It is amusing to speculate about which aspect of the story different publications might emphasize (the *National Inquirer* would quite probably choose to focus on Mary and her vision or the nature of her relationship with Jesus, and the sober and politically minded *New York Times* would emphasize the complex, political aspect of the story). But the point is that a modern journalist (even at the *Inquirer*) would be severely constrained in dealing with the supernatural elements of the story. As any journalist knows, the events that underlie most controversies are not something that the journalist has witnessed (particularly if the "event" involves something supernatural). Secondhand accounts—what people say is true or tell a journalist that they have seen or know—are staples of the news business.

In a sense, as journalists covering this "controversy," we would find ourselves in a position not much different from that of reporters covering modern claims of the supernatural—the cloak at Turin, the visions of the Virgin Mary that crop up frequently (which are discussed in more depth in the next chapter), the claims of divinity of cult leaders. It is an interesting aspect of modern journalism that, with its reputed claims to scientific objectivity, the more controversial the subject matter, the more detached and careful the accounts of the event become, and the more journalists shy away from making bold claims about what may have happened. Journalists are taught to be suspicious of sources with a vested interest in their interpretation of events, particularly sources who make claims about the divine or the supernatural. In reality, however, the "objective" journalism found in most daily mainstream newspapers in the United States is far from the meaning of objective in scientific terms. The standard news-reporting methodology is not to demonstrate whether a claim is true or false but simply to present the claim and then let the other side present the rebuttal. Readers are left to sort out for themselves what they believe is the truth. This type of reporting, which developed in the nineteenth century in the United States for practical and largely economic reasons (newspapers, seeking larger audiences, did not want to offend any segment of their reading public; wire services, serving many clients, wanted to be as neutral as possible), is now the staple of a mainstream press that relies on a cautious and largely uncritical process for conveying news and information. Today no segment of the news is treated more gingerly by the press than religion—with its emotionally charged, hot-button issues and passionate people on both sides of many debates.

If we take this one step further, we can see why issues of faith end up being treated so warily in the news pages. I have assumed in our hypothetical scenario that no reporter would be privy to a visit from the risen Christ, who could have confirmed the "truth" of the matter by his firsthand witness. Of course, one is free to hypothesize that, as reporters, we were witness to Jesus' postcrucifixion appearance to the disciples. But imagine what trouble that could cause a journalist if that had happened. Editors like to say that they trust nothing more than a firsthand account by a reporter, but imagine trying to get that into the news pages. Whether or not one takes seriously the possibility that a person (journalist or otherwise) could experience supernatural phenomena, it is clear there is little place in modern "objective" newspaper methodology for such a report. (I would suggest that such an account would even have trouble getting printed in the typical letters-to-the-editor section.)

So let us imagine that we have now returned to the newsroom and that we are about to tackle this story—cognizant that even though we personally did not witness the visit from the resurrected Jesus, we have just been present at a powerful moment in the history of a controversial new religion. As we sit at our computer keyboard, we know that we want to be respectful in what we write, but we also recognize how powerfully the modern mind-set exercises its hold over the newsroom. Few of our newsroom colleagues, we know, take seriously a claim involving supernatural occurrences or divine revelation. But we also know our article will be scrutinized carefully, particularly by believers who are on the lookout for antireligious bias in the newspaper. Since professional caution is the byword among most journalists, we ponder the best way to convey what we have been covering without sounding overly impressionable, on the one hand, but not overly dubious, on the other. Fortunately for us, the methodology of modern journalism provides us with safe and easy devices for formulating our story.

A radical Jewish prophet who was executed by Roman authorities has returned to earth in a vision to comfort and to advise his followers, according to a key member of the Jesus sect.

An apparition of the prophet, Jesus of Nazareth, came to Mary Magdalene recently and revealed to her how the soul gains enlightenment, Magdalene told a gathering of Jesus' inner circle on Sunday.

Magdalene's comments were met with skepticism by Peter and Andrew, two leaders of the Jesus sect, who questioned whether their master would appear to her in a private revelation. Jesus' followers preach that his crucifixion by Pontius Pilate was followed by a miraculous resurrection—and his return from the dead is a sign that he is the Jewish messiah and God's favored one.

"Did he prefer her to us?" asked Peter. Peter acknowledged that Magdalene was especially close to Jesus, but he questioned her claim of a special visit from the resurrected Jesus. Peter and other members of Jesus' inner circle believe they have witnessed the appearance of Jesus since his crucifixion—but always when Jesus' intention was to prepare them to be gathered together so he could openly instruct the group.

"Do you think I thought this up myself in my heart, or that I am lying about the Savior?" Magdalene responded.

Roman authorities question the legitimacy of the Jesus movement and have cautioned citizens to avoid contact with Jesus' followers. The group also has fallen out of favor with Jewish authorities, who contest the sect's claim that Jesus is the Jewish messiah and who urged Pilate to execute him.

The Romans note there are many groups in Palestine that lay spurious claim to divine status, and they urge citizens instead to honor the emperor and to worship the Roman gods.

Sources within the Jesus movement say there are indications of a rift within their midst. Some of Jesus' followers, like Magdalene, believe they are privy to special revelations from Jesus, and these guide them in their spiritual search. Members of the old-line leadership, led by Peter, assert the right to determine proper doctrine within the group, and they argue that Magdalene's individualistic views threaten group cohesion and their collective experience of the resurrected Jesus. Women, they say, are inclined to this line of thinking and therefore are lacking in leadership skills.

I could go on, but this is probably as much as this story would have warranted. As anachronistic as this may seem—trying somehow to blend ancient belief with modern journalistic style—the exercise still illustrates how difficult it is to arrive at a "journalistic" assessment about matters of faith. Notice how in our modern mainstream newspaper account, the readers are still left to decipher what to make out of this story. We might think that the modern press would deal forthrightly with what many newsroom employees would view as the clearly fantastic claims made by Jesus' followers. But this would not likely happen, even in our enlightened times. No matter what journalists themselves believe, the methodology of modern news coverage requires that these kinds of supernatural claims be treated seriously and reported in a way that ultimately presents journalists as throwing up their hands and saying to readers, "You decide." This is held up as a good thing—as an example of the fairness, balance, and open-mindedness of modern journalistic inquiry.

This is the point at which we have to look at television and its role in reshaping attitudes about religion, as well as many other matters. Regardless of methodology, one of the underlying assumptions about modern media in many quarters is that technology is certain to expose fantastic and supernatural claims for the foolish fancies they are. Implicit in this thinking is the speculation that, if television had been around, we would have known the true story about a lot of things that supposedly happened long ago—including whether Jesus did the miraculous things the Bible claims he did—because we would have had it on tape. Forget scientific evidence, forget archaeology and anthropology, forget biblical scholarship, forget our more sophisticated attitudes about the role of mythology and folklore among ancient peoples—all it would have taken, this line of reasoning goes, was a television crew to have shown up when Jesus was performing one of his miracles, and, many modern-minded people would be confident, the fiction would have been exploded, and we would have learned that some perfectly plausible, rational explanation accounted for what happened. The explanations themselves might be scientific, but it would be television that would expose the ruse.

One of the most widely held beliefs in our culture is that the camera never lies. This assumption underlies much of the cultural superiority that we as moderns bring to questions of historical veracity. Even those who are skeptical of Christian claims will acknowledge that there is really very little that modern historians can prove about Jesus or the events of his life. But, at heart, the typically secularist, cosmopolitan, show-me-the-proof personality—as so many journalists see themselves—knows these things could never have happened, not just because they do not fit into normal life experience, not just because modern science declares them to be impossible, but because we have never seen anything like them on television. Even though television spends most of its programming time entertaining its audience with fictional material and technological tricks, the "box" has traditionally been trusted by large segments of the public as the most honest conveyer of news and information. Studies show that people believe what they see on television news more than they do any other news medium, mostly because of the widely shared illusion that through the camera lens they can see things for themselves.[14]

I am not going to go into the countless studies that have shown that this notion of television as an accurate reflector of reality is a skewed one. Suffice it to say that, from its earliest uses as a conveyor of live events and a recorder of the news of the day, television's "bias" as a medium shows up in all sorts of ways—from the way television reporters tend to cover events so that the story fulfills audience expectations, to the distortions in coverage caused by the logistical difficulties of dispatching camera crews, to the need for dramatic visuals and emotional stories that will drive up ratings and simple, understandable themes that present all news items as pat little dramas.[15]

In this context, we have to consider the possibility that, with its formula for attracting viewers, television simply might not have been terribly interested in covering the events surrounding Jesus. As big as the Jesus story became in history, it was not really much of a story in its time—at least not the kind of story television would have wanted to cover. From the perspective of the gospel writers, of course, the crowds Jesus attracted, the parables he repeated, and the miracles he performed make him seem very much the superstar of his day—but that, too, is something of a distortion. Jesus was just one of many messianic figures whose movements multiplied during a period when the Roman authorities and their client kings suppressed a series of uprisings in support of a coming Jewish kingdom, and we know from the number of bones at Golgotha that the crucifixion of one more Jewish transgressor was hardly an event of great moment.[16]

It is hard for us to imagine—given the grip the Christian story has on our culture—that the drama of Jesus' life and the power of his teachings would not have attracted the attention of television editors and reporters. But if such people had been around two thousand years ago and had been operating by today's television news standards, it is very possible they simply would not have been interested. Religious teachings would be viewed as so boring that they could not possibly make the airwaves (how would you titillate viewers with a news story built around a public gathering where such sentiments as "Blessed are the poor in spirit, for theirs is the kingdom of heaven" or "Blessed are the pure in heart, for they will see God" were expressed?). Instead, it would be in the category of crime news or perhaps political news where Jesus might have the possibility of breaking into coverage. Perhaps the controversies surrounding his association with the beheaded John the Baptist would have attracted media notice, or his celebrated entrance into Jerusalem, or his dispute with the money changers in the temple, or possibly his sentence and his crucifixion—although these kinds of things were much more commonplace than we might imagine. In today's big urban areas, certain crimes—bank robberies, car jackings, suicides—do not make it to the level of news coverage simply because they are seen as such routine events. At the time of political and religious turmoil in ancient Palestine, with repeated uprisings against the authorities, religious zealots everywhere, and crucifixions on a daily basis, it is quite possible that Jesus would not appear on the media's radar screen (although one can imagine violent crime–obsessed local television news operations quite delighted with daily crucifixions, which they might never tire of reporting).

But what of Jesus' reputation for performing miracles, casting out demons, or curing the ill—would that not have aroused some intrigue in television newsrooms? What of raising Lazarus from the dead? Or Jesus' walk on water? Or the creation of wine and bread to feed the multitudes? Television's propensity for preplanned and predictable events and the logistical difficulties of coverage would have made it very unlikely that television cameras would have shown up for one of Jesus' "performances." Everything we know from the gospel accounts indicates that Jesus performed his miracles spontaneously—and, even then, sometimes reluctantly. One can hardly imagine him sending out press notices, calling a press conference, or otherwise bringing attention to himself so that he could demonstrate his skills to the viewing public. One might imagine a lonely television journalist (perhaps some determined documentary maker working for a public television station) traveling with Jesus and hoping to present "proof" that he could perform the miraculous when the cameras were around. The greater likelihood is that the whole business would have been dismissed as preposterous in the first place by news workers—or, if not preposterous, so ordinary that it would not warrant coverage at all. The Hellenistic world was much like ours—rife with mystery cults, wandering prophetic figures, and rival sects tussling in a culture that had no overarching sense of religious or spiritual consensus. Just as in our day, a religious figure—despite a large following or purporting to possess supernatural powers—could have just as easily been ignored as noticed. After all, the countryside today is filled with religious figures (both within and outside Christianity) who claim to be operating by divine inspiration, to have healing gifts, or to have the power of tongues, and modern journalism hardly takes notice. Outside of occasional mentions in movies, entertainment television programs, and the tabloid press, the topic of the supernatural in any form—from the occult to the exotic beliefs of other world religions to the metaphysical aspects of Christian story—seldom receives attention in mainstream journalism.

It is easy to see that the assumption I made at the start of this chapter—that some element of the media would have been interested in Jesus—involves more than just a hypothetical leap of imagination. By supposing that we might bring modern journalistic methods to bear on Jesus' life, we have been forced to make the biggest presumption of all—namely, that Jesus' name or his story would have shown up in the journalistic accounts of the time, had there been any. Journalists, I imagine, would like to surmise that, if there had been modern journalism in Jesus' day, many issues would have been settled for us, but that is not necessarily so. Hard as it may be to accept (certainly for journalists), journalism may not be the surest path to truth—at least, when it comes to matters of faith—and it may not even be the best source for determining what history finally decides was really important about an era. That does not mean that journalists cannot apply their news judgment and their traditional truth tests, but, as we have seen, that can leave gaping holes in what gets covered, what gets presented as news, and what ends up constituting the historical record. We can always take refuge in our modern notions that in ancient times, people did not understand enough about science or medicine to recognize, for example, that an epileptic attack was not demons at work—but that begs the point. Making modern, post-Enlightenment assumptions about the world and then applying them in our news judgments is not the same as going out to find the "whole" story in the broadest sense of the word. It certainly is not the same as keeping our minds open to the possibility that the whole story might mean something more than just going out and confirming our original assumptions in the first place.

One can always trust that "good" journalism might have enlightened us to the deeper truths of Jesus and his message, but there is precious little of that kind of journalism around today (and certainly little of it in television). Even today's best journalists are bound by the methodologies, the traditions, and the editorial demands of their profession, and it would probably be an uphill fight to find much news hole for an itinerant carpenter who preached that the kingdom of God was all around us and that we should love our enemies. Any journalist who might have been at the confrontation between Mary Magdalene and the disciples and was sophisticated enough to note it would be reporting at a depth much beyond what we usually find in the press.

But look at the product of our journalistic venture—the studied neutrality, the careful phrasing, the conscious effort to balance one viewpoint off with another. How sterile that seems when compared with the moving, panoramic, powerful accounts in the biblical (or even the Gnostic) literature. Is it possible that spiritual meaning—with its verification in experience and emotion, its emanations from a dimension beyond logic and reason, its persistent but intangible hold on the human imagination—is simply too difficult to be transmitted in standard journalistic reporting? Is it possible that there is something inherent in the way modern journalism is practiced—something in its methodology, in its style, even in the very social and economic purposes it is trying to serve—that is inimical to the authentic conveyance of matters of faith? I do not believe that is necessarily so, but I do find that today's journalism that touches on religious matters lends credence to this view.

It is revealing that Luke Johnson, in his critique of journalism's superficial coverage of the controversy surrounding the "historic" Jesus, simply wrote off the modern media—with its sound bites, its fascination with the spectacular, and its tendency to treat religion as "an afterthought," as he put it.[17] An orthodox Christian, Johnson held out little hope for press coverage that is more knowledgeable or sensitive in its approach to issues of faith. Johnson's resentment of the self-promotions of the Jesus Seminar leaders is matched only by his annoyance at the media for exacerbating the culture wars. The two hundred academics who participate in the Jesus Seminar and vote on whether they believe a gospel saying of Jesus is authentic by dropping red, pink, gray, and black beads into a box have reduced the debate about Jesus to little more than a publicity stunt, Johnson complained. But, as far as the press is concerned, he seemed to be saying, "Well, what more can you expect?" With little interest in or knowledge about religion, with little more required than to recognize a controversy when they see one, journalists, he declared, cannot help framing the issue as they do.

As with journalists, scholars need to be wary that they do not become so fixated on trying to establish the historical "facts" that they, too, forget that their methodologies have severe limitations. It would be something if we could rely on two hundred scholars voting with colored beads to determine the scope and the origins of Christian faith. But we cannot—and I do not think we would really want to. Most people who have explored the issues surrounding the historical Jesus soon come to the realization that no one (including academics) can know for sure who the historical Jesus really was and that there is an enormous amount of speculation involved when scholars "reconstruct" the historical Jesus from their research. I must confess I find that many of the Jesus Seminar's conclusions fit my own instincts about Jesus and his teachings. But I share Johnson's concerns that scholars sometimes overreach the evidence in trying to present provocative and publicity-gaining portraits of Jesus. I also respect Johnson's contention that, no matter what the historical facts, the Bible presents a marvelous and coherent portrait of Jesus that allows his spirit to penetrate the lives of those who are open to it far beyond questions of academic or journalistic methodology.

Within my own Quaker tradition, there is a concept known as "continuing revelation"—a belief that God's work was not just done in the past but continues into the present. Quakers believe in the reality of direct revelation, but they also acknowledge the Bible, along with the spirit that permeates the text, as a vital way to help experience this divine presence. Modern biblical scholars, like journalists in a different fashion, tend to put such an emphasis on their research methodologies and their academic conclusions that they often miss the point of faith. The "truth" of the text of the New Testament may have nothing to do with establishing the historical facts of Jesus' life—or with believing that we could have known for sure if only the modern press had been there. As Johnson put it, Christian faith is established not by "facts about the past, but by the reality of Christ's power in the present."[18] That is an assertion that one cannot prove or disprove beyond the testimony of human experience.

CHAPTER 17

Visions of Mary and the Less
Than Visionary Press: Religious
Apparitions in the Framing
of the Modern Media

The way the *Columbus (Ohio) Dispatch* described it, there can be little doubt that the sightings of the Virgin Mary are a big and modern business.[1] A Web site devoted to apparitions of Mary and Jesus lists dozens of religious sightings all over the world dating back to 1347, with a star indicating full Catholic church approval, a Bible denoting bishop's approval, and a thumbs down indicating "discouraged by bishop." In a droll interpretive dig, the columnist Mike Harden added how disappointed he was that his favorite sightings—Jesus on an oil storage tanker in Fostoria, Ohio, and Christ on a burrito in Lake Arthur, New Mexico—did not make the list.[2]

In recent years, a virtual industry has grown up around spiritual sightings—particularly those of Mary—from around the world. Sites in Portugal, Bosnia, Egypt, Ireland, and the United States, among many others, have garnered press attention and attracted large crowds of people. In Puerto Rico, a site draws 100,000 pilgrims a year, and church leaders are planning a tourism complex, called Mystical City, with a 93-meter statue of the Virgin Mary. At a site in Bosnia, where thousands of visitors a year come, there are new hotels, restaurants, and souvenir shops. On Britain's Achill Island, the church was the target of angry local residents who have seen business and tourism dry up after the church declared a local woman who saw a vision of Mary was a fraud, leading her to shut down her prayer house and shrine. In May 2000, the Vatican made headlines when it disclosed the third secret of Fatima, a prophesy based on an apparition of Mary that appeared to three Portuguese shepherd children and has been tied to doomsday cults, terrorism attacks, and the assassination attempt on Pope John Paul II.[3]

But anyone who expects the American press to cover this phenomenon with even the faintest hint of Harden's gentle, almost tongue-in-cheek skepticism would be mistaken. Those critics of the press who presume that the secular doubters making up the press corps would cover the visions of Mary phenomenon with dubiousness or impiety do not understand the dictates of the traditional American journalistic reporting methodology or the media's deep desire not to offend any portion of their audience. It is true that journalists are empirical in orientation and define themselves as debunkers of myth and demanders of hard facts. But when it comes to people claiming to have had religious visions, journalists often present little skeptical, and often no balancing, material in their reporting.

An analysis of three years worth of representative stories about the sightings of Mary bears this out.[4] The stories were often one-sided, presenting only the religious claimants' point of view; respectful to the point of pandering; and bereft of context, analysis, or perspective about what might have led to such a widespread phenomenon. Most of the stories simply reported what enthusiasts said and left it at that. Left unsaid were not only the views of skeptics outside the community of believers but also the insights of people of faith who might have had interesting and important things to say about why these sightings seem to have increased in recent years, why so many people make pilgrimages to the sites, and who these people may be.

Typical were such stories as a *Louisville Courier-Journal* column about the many believers who said the Blessed Mother has appeared to them on a local hillside where Rosary beads are draped on the hands of a grotto statue built by volunteers. "The second and the twenty third each month are when the apparitions are, and there's usually a pretty good crowd," said one visitor. Skeptics may scoff, wrote the reporter (in the only reference to skeptics), but believers say this only means people today do not have enough faith to follow a star.[5]

A Knight-Ridder report appeared in the *New Orleans Times-Picayune* about how an image resembling the Virgin Mary that shimmers on an office building has become a shrine for pilgrims, with crowds reaching 80,000 a day. The reporter noted that the flawless image, which is thirty-five feet tall and fifty feet wide, cannot be explained by scientists. "How can nine panes of glass come together so perfectly?" one visitor was quoted as asking.[6]

A brief *USA Today* story told of a crowd of 100,000 or more who sat on lawn chairs and stood shoulder-to-shoulder to listen to a woman on a farm outside Atlanta, Georgia, tell of her annual sighting of an apparition of Mary and her claim that Mary wants a Catholic cathedral built on the site. "This is the greatest experience I've ever had and nothing is going to keep me away from here," declared the only other person quoted for comment in the story.[7]

A *Miami Herald* story about an image of the Virgin Mary that the Miami relatives of Elian Gonzales said appeared on a mirror in their house was reported without comment from anyone but the boy's relatives and supporters. However, the reporter added it was only the "latest mystical twist" in the story that included another sighting of the Virgin Mary on a bank building nearby and the boy's belief that he had survived his ordeal at sea because he had been protected by dolphins.[8]

Untypical was a story in the *Financial Times* of London that provided in-depth perspective on the Vatican's difficulties with its visionaries, pilgrimage sites, and growing reports of apparitions and miracles; the church's fear of frauds and charlatans; and the pilgrims, often converted by powerful emotional experiences, who have come looking for more intimate spiritual connections than those provided by the institutional church.[9]

Of the 75 Marian vision stories analyzed from major English-speaking newspapers in the general news index of Nexis between spring of 1997 and spring of 2000, 72 (96 percent) included material that emphasized what enthusiasts or believers felt about the visions, while only 18 stories (24 percent) presented any balancing material from skeptics (including skeptics in the Catholic church). Interestingly, 11 of those balanced stories, or more than half, were in non-U.S. newspapers in England, Canada, and New Zealand. Remarkably this meant that only 17 percent—or 7 out of 41 stories—in U.S. newspapers reporting on Mary visions in this time period even bothered to include any balancing material from those who raised questions about the phenomenon.[10]

What explains this lack of balance and perspective even in a media whose methodology requires balance and perspective for most other stories? In the United States, there are probably a number of factors at work. First, American news organizations may maintain that the "objective" truth of a matter involves presenting both sides of an issue, but that often is not achieved because common journalistic "framing" of stories simply does not require it. Many of the stories about the Marian apparitions were reporting on an event—large numbers of people gathering or going on a pilgrimage to a site—and journalists might have felt that covering the event was enough in itself. Second, American journalists place an enormous amount of weight on what people say they believe, or experience, or feel strongly about, and this often gets top priority in stories, without finding anyone to challenge it. Third, it takes extra effort to call up experts or official sources, and journalists often do not bother, or editors cut out that material for lack of space.[11] Fourth, journalists may simply feel that skeptics can read between the lines and can import their own doubts into the story without the journalist explicitly pointing it out. This is particularly the case as U.S. newspapers have become exceedingly sensitive to insulting any portion of their audience, and editors recognize that anything less than credulous coverage of certain aspects of religion will be heatedly criticized by religious followers.[12]

Finally, the Marian visions story appears to have burned out as a phenomenon that interests American journalists. After a burst of news stories and television reports in the 1980s and early 1990s, the story of new sightings became commonplace, and journalists—always interested in what is new—moved on, except for their increasingly pro forma coverage of the crowds and apparitions.[13]

Normally, this would mean ho-hum stories that cover both sides of the controversy, but in this case, many news reports did not bother to cite the critics (even though there are many, including both Protestants and Catholics who have questioned the legitimacy of the movement).[14]

What is lost by this approach to the coverage of religious visions? Public understanding of religion suffers by the superficiality and lack of perspective in this kind of reporting. In only a few stories was there any discussion of why this phenomenon was taking place and who were the people so moved by it. In a handful of stories, the reader learned of the Catholic church's concerns about the spread of the phenomenon, how the church has struggled to distinguish between what it considers legitimate and bogus visions, and how the pressure from enthusiasts was influencing the church's decision making. At the same time, readers were rarely privy to any discussion of the kinds of people who went on these pilgrimages and what it was about their religious beliefs, their conversion experiences, or the things they might find missing in more traditional religion that was influencing them. Most frustrating, nothing in any of the stories discussed why Mary is such a figure of reverence—which, for the noninitiated, is an intriguing question, one that should be of fundamental interest to anyone who wants to grasp the meaning of the phenomenon.[15]

The spirit of evangelism and mysticism that continues to sweep through Catholic believers is one of the truly interesting, ongoing religion stories of our time and a telling commentary about the hunger for powerful, personal religious experience among religious followers. The story of Marian visions has fascinating roots that are intertwined with Latin American history and modern-day politics, Vatican intrigue and infighting, growing movements of Catholic fundamentalism across Europe and the rest of the world, and a heightened interest among Catholics in miracles, spiritual signs, and the mystical significance of historical events. That so many media reports would cover this in such cursory and formulaic ways is a reflection of how jaded and routinized much media coverage of religion is. One cannot even presume that religious believers would find much that was satisfying in the pro forma accounts that convey little of the richness of the experience for followers of Mary or the nature of the phenomenon for those outside the circles of the convinced.

As Mark Garvey pointed out, a phenomenon is not the same thing as a miracle.[16] Unfortunately, the press—always baffled by how to deal with a miracle—has even lost interest in the phenomenon, at least in terms of the events surrounding the sightings of Mary. The public's understanding of religion in our times has been the loser for it.

Proselytizing and Profits: The Growth of Televangelism and the Collaboration of the Mainstream Press

In the early 1980s, when I was a legislative correspondent for the *Seattle Times*, I witnessed what to me was a startling event on the steps of the Washington state capitol in Olympia. Jerry Falwell, the well-known televangelist and the founder of the Moral Majority, brought to the Washington legislature his crusade to inject conservative Christian moral and family values into politics. Replete with a choir singing patriotic and religious hymns, banners draping buses and other vehicles, and well-scrubbed followers passing out literature to the crowd, Falwell spoke to the audience in God- and Christ-laden terms while laying out a political agenda that he described as the good Christian's program for national renewal.

There was much murmuring and head-shaking among my fellow reporters as we listened while Falwell mocked the liberals and the liberal press that he so loathes and issued forth with a fiery, southern preacher's rhetoric that gave his caravan visit the feel of a cross between a revivalist tent meeting and an old fashioned, Huey Long–style political rally. Although few of my colleagues were church-going people or particularly knowledgeable about Christianity, they knew enough about basic Christian tenets to be highly skeptical of Falwell's implication that the Prince of Peace might embrace weapons of war in the name of a strong national defense (Falwell was strongly advocating the building of the B-1 bomber at the time). They were also suspicious of the theocratic implications in Falwell's forceful efforts to inject the issue of God's will into matters of politics. Adding to their unease, Falwell brought to the podium the impact of his media celebrity, a power that expanded his influence through his religious broadcasting network to the phalanx of Christian viewers who shared his fears about the direction of modern, secular life and the modern commercial press.

The anxiety I sensed in the Olympia press corps at Falwell's appearance was my first, up-close encounter with the emotions that helped launch what we now call the "culture wars" in the United States. Falwell's willingness to clothe religion in politics and politics in religion has been commented on exhaustively and used as a cudgel by liberal political groups that have exploited the specter of the Christian Right to spur their own supporters into action. Yet, in the years since that event, we have come to learn that television exposure in itself cannot win the nation over to a political message. Christian conservatives have seen only modest political successes since the Reagan years; the Moral Majority itself has been disbanded; and Falwell's television network has suffered bankruptcy and serious funding problems.

Still, Falwell's and other televangelists' use of television as a medium to prod the political establishment to pay attention to the voices of alienated, conservative Christians was one of the most important political developments of the late twentieth century. Christian television has given Americans of all political stripes a glimpse of a once withdrawn and pietistic religious population that has been drawn into political action by the perceived horrors of the secular world it has witnessed in commercial television programming, movies, and other parts of the media. Yet conservative Christians—despite their loathing of the mainstream commercial media and the media's "secular humanist" bias—have shown themselves more than willing to exploit a medium they otherwise abhor. That religious broadcasting has led to the coining of a neologism—televangelism—is a tribute to the wide-scale acceptance of the role television now plays in promoting religion and religious causes. Today, this irony—where a religious communications network thrives in the midst of the broader commercial media environment that much of the religious community condemns—is exemplified in the role that religious television broadcasting has come to play in linking together members of the Christian community (mostly the conservative Christian community) through religiously oriented talk and variety shows, broadcast revivals and church services, and fund-raising appeals.

In concert with this, the commercial press, in seeking out controversy and discord, has done much to both magnify and distort the influence and the image of Christian conservatives. The press has tended to overestimate the numbers and the political potency of the movement; it has focused attention on such divisive and easy-to-televise events as abortion demonstrations, antigay rallies, and other hot-button controversies; and it has set up such one-time luminaries in the conservative Christian movement as Jim Bakker and Jimmy Swaggart for ridicule and contempt when they were brought low by scandal. Just as important, the rise of televangelism in the 1970s (along with some key decisions by federal regulators) gave the commercial television networks and most local network affiliates the excuse to drop virtually all free, public service religious programming and to rely instead on the programming provided by the growing numbers of conservative, evangelical preachers who were more than happy to pay for their time on the airwaves.

This, combined with the steady growth of televangelist programming that migrated to the cable and satellite television networks during the 1980s and 1990s, has led many Americans—including some members of the mainstream press—to identify Christianity with the conservative, evangelical Christian viewpoints that they have been exposed to on television and increasingly to see Christianity itself through the lens of Christian televangelism and the political causes of the Christian Right. That identification often has not been a flattering one. The much discussed characterization by the *Washington Post* writer Michael Weisskopf of the followers of Jerry Falwell and Pat Robertson as "largely poor, uneducated and easy to command" often is held up as an example of the stereotypes that mainstream journalists carry around (analysts point out that, with the growth of Christian higher education institutions and the post–World War II economic expansion, modern evangelical Christians do not fit any of these characterizations).[1] While the press has grown more aware of and interested in the evangelical phenomenon in the United States, conservative Christians continue to see the media as one of the secular forces they most loathe and resent.

Although the critics are not sure who is to blame—the press or the Christian conservatives—they insist that the impact of the Christian conservative movement has contributed to mainstream journalists' shallow and distorted coverage of Christianity, Christians, and their relation to politics. Journalists, wrote the British religion commentator Ann Wroe, are already skeptical enough of religion as it is, and the extremism of Christian conservatives has only exacerbated the situation. "Journalistic diffidence towards religion is not always possible; and, where it is not, a thinly veiled hostility often replaces it," she observed. "Ralph Reed, Pat Robertson and their cohorts have much to answer for. By politicizing God, by claiming to know how he would vote if asked, by appealing to the authority of the Bible above that of the Constitution, by making Christians appear to be bigots, zealots, and primitives, they awaken the anti-religious tendencies that might otherwise lie dormant in the pages of the American press."[2]

More sympathetic observers (at least of the press) acknowledge that the conservative, evangelical Christian forces have effectively captured much of the press's attention, often to the exclusion of other Christian viewpoints, but they blame it on factors that have more to do with journalistic methodology than with journalists' religious or political attitudes. The authors of the Freedom Forum's *First Amendment Guide to Religion and the News Media* acknowledged that there is a "chasm of misunderstanding and ignorance" separating news media professionals and the church community and that the existence of the "two alien cultures," "separated by wind-blown waters as difficult to cross as the Red Sea," leaves reporters ill-prepared to deal with matters of religion. However, the report implied that the primary reasons moderate Christian denominations are so seldom visible in the news pages or broadcast reports—and the Christian Right is so often the focus of press coverage—are the news media's appetite for controversy and their penchant for publicizing the activities of organized groups that do not shy away from conflict in promoting their agenda.[3] The real workhorse in giving structure to a daily news story is the "us versus them, veterans versus upstarts, good guys versus bad guys" shape of the news, wrote Cullen Murphy, managing editor of the *Atlantic Monthly*. "One result is that any contemplative tendencies that manage to survive in the media environment are largely engulfed by the pursuit of conflict."[4] Murphy's view was echoed by Mark Coppenger, the public relations director for the Southern Baptist Convention, who said he wished the news media would not always choose such "radioactive" personalities to represent the evangelical position. "There are measured voices on both sides," he said.[5]

The Freedom Forum report was one of the more ambitious undertakings in a burgeoning cottage industry of criticism and analysis about the failings of the mainstream press to cover religion in the United States with thoroughness, fairness, and comprehension. The report went to great lengths to document its contention that, while many religious practitioners believe the press holds negative feelings toward them, the press actually tends to fail its religious readers by operating with minimal understanding in covering matters that it finds foreign to the empirical tradition and alien to the worldview of most journalists. The report (issued from an establishment, corporately founded press foundation) tended to find good faith everywhere—journalists admitting to their failings and their unfamiliarity with religion, acknowledging the limitations of their professional outlook, and urging the industry to do a better job of covering religion in-depth; religious figures conceding that they need to give some latitude to the press's professional norms and recognizing that some of what appears anti-Christian in the news pages is simply the press's reflecting a growing pluralism and changing mores and lifestyles in contemporary America. "Mainstream journalists mostly ignore religion because they do not understand it and because they are worried about misinterpreting it," the report quoted the well-known TV commentator Bill Moyers, one of the few journalists in the broadcast industry who has done thoughtful and sympathetic stories on religious themes. "They do know it's a subjective series of subcultures for which there is no common language. It's the Tower of Babel to a mainstream journalist—everybody's speaking in tongues."[6]

The press's fixation on conflict appears to go some way in explaining why the press coverage of the "religious Right" or "Christian conservatives" vastly outweighs the coverage of "liberal Christians" or the "religious Left" (despite conservatives' suspicion that the "liberal" media tend to be more sympathetic to liberal groups of all kinds). A Nexis search of a typical period of daily news stories from January to June 2000 showed a nearly four-to-one imbalance of stories involving Christian conservatives versus Christian liberals and nearly two stories about the Christian Coalition, the most prominent lobbying organization for conservative Christians, for every story about the National Council of Churches, the religious organization most widely identified with liberal causes.[7]

Drawing comparisons from this analysis is a somewhat tricky matter, how-

ever, and to explain the differences in coverage requires more than just count-
ing stories. To begin with, virtually all the stories examined involved controversy
—as so many stories do in the press. It is therefore not always beneficial to be
covered by the press, particularly in the case of the Christian Coalition. More
than a third of the stories about the conservative lobbying group contained some
kind of pejorative language or description of the group by critics, analysts, or
journalists (using such words as "bigoted," "extreme," "divisive," "mean-spirited," "moralistic").[8] Only about 13 percent of the stories about the National
Council of Churches contained negative references (the description "too liberal" was most often used).[9]

Perhaps it is not entirely surprising that this was the case. The Christian
Coalition was established as an activist lobbying group to challenge the political establishment by proposing to ban abortion, promote prayer in public
schools, repeal gay discrimination ordinances, and require Internet pornogra-
phy filters in libraries. Needless to say, these proposals generate—and are designed to generate—news coverage in the context of the divisions and the hostilities of the "culture wars."[10] The National Council of Churches—while not
shying away from controversy—does not have the same kind of activist agenda
that thrusts the organization into the media spotlight. The council, like many
other more traditional church organizations, performs a lot of the "do good"
activities that do not generate the kind of controversy that is going to pique the
interest of the press. Only when the council jumped into the Elian Gonzales
controversy (on the side of the boy's family in Cuba) did its profile in the press
increase during the period surveyed.[11]

The press may be fascinated with the religious Right because of the controversy surrounding the Christian Coalition, but there is also a major difference
in the tone of its coverage of the two organizations. An investigation of the more
analytical press coverage and comments of columnists revealed the Christian Coalition was analyzed respectfully but negatively in 55 percent of stories, nonrespectfully and negatively in 24 percent of the stories, and respectfully and positively in 21 percent of the stories.[12] Even when the organization received some
positive coverage, the stories tended to appear in more conservative publications,
such as the *San Diego Union-Tribune* or the *Arizona Republic,* which had family
or business connections to conservative causes. The same investigation showed
the National Council of Churches was analyzed respectfully and positively in 62
percent of the stories and respectfully and negatively in 38 percent of the stories; there were no nonrespectfully and negatively analyzed pieces.[13]

Does this prove that the press is liberal in its leanings when it comes to covering religious conservatives? Perhaps, but only up to a point. In virtually all the
cases, the press coverage was keyed to the organizations' involvement in political controversy, and there was little coverage of either organization on its own
terms (such as covering organization meetings and speeches by officials) and
little discussion of the organizations' viewpoints on faith matters.[14] Liberal re-

ligious groups do not appear to get much more coverage for their noncontro-
versial activities on the news pages than do conservative religious groups. Whatever the press's political orientation, the first rule seems to be to cover religion
largely through the prism of public disputes.

Given these circumstances, it makes sense that religious conservatives would
come to feel it was necessary to control their own broadcast channels. But it was
not so much concern about their image in the mainstream press as it was their
recognition of the potential of the airwaves for proselytizing that propelled
Christian conservatives into the broadcasting business. Religious proselytizers
have long recognized the evangelical possibilities inherent in media technologies. Bishop Fulton J. Sheen, an early television preacher, for example, once said,
"Radio is like the Old Testament, hearing wisdom, without seeing; television is
like the New Testament because in it the wisdom becomes flesh and dwells
among us."[15] Sheen's views were only the latest stage in the commonly held
evangelical outlook that technological developments, particularly those in the
communications area, are gifts from God to be used to God's advantage. "I have
added the ocean steamer, and the rail-way, and the steam printing-press, and
telegraph," wrote one nineteenth-century Christian writer who imagined God
urging Christians to take up new technology as their own. "Employ all these for
my glory and for the establishment of my kingdom! Use them, till it shall be
announced along the lightning wires that encircle the globe, 'Their line is gone
out through all the earth, and their words to the end of the world.'"[16]

Since those early days, evangelicals have adopted the electronic media with an
unapologetic enthusiasm. The former head of the National Religious Broadcasters proclaimed in 1979 that religious broadcasting had "broken through the walls
of tradition" and "restored conditions remarkably similar to the early church."[17]
The broader culture of media marketing—where the $300 million gospel music
industry, the prodigious evangelical book publishing industry, and the building
of religious theme parks, colleges, and drive-through churches now dominate
evangelical outreach efforts—has been embraced for its capacity to popularize
the Christian message. One evangelical writer compared this "market orientation" with Christ's own approach to people and suggested that contemporary
popular culture is simply a distorted version of something that God meant to
be good.[18] Quentin Schultze noted that this uncritical faith in media and marketing technology among evangelicals is widely held, despite the general evangelical critique of popular culture as something destructive to Christian moral
values. "As a result of this popularization, evangelical culture generally mirrors
the secular culture that Evangelicals often criticize," Schultze wrote.[19]

In historical terms, though, it took the entrance of some of these broadcast
preachers into the political arena to arouse the interest of the mainstream press
in the field of religious media. Father Charles Coughlin, a bellicose Catholic
priest who provoked cries of demagoguery with his pro-Nazi attacks on Jewish
influence, international bankers, and Roosevelt administration policies, is the

most notorious figure from the days of early radio ministries. Coughlin's ministry led the network broadcasters to drive him from the air in 1940 by refusing to lease him airtime and the National Association of Broadcasters to adopt a code of ethics that barred "controversial" speakers.[20] In many ways, Coughlin (who continued his broadcasts from a network of independent stations linked by telephone lines) was only operating in the tradition of other early radio evangelists, such as Aimee Semple McPherson, Billy Sunday, and "Fighting Bob" Shuler, who played major roles in convincing the federal government and the radio industry in the 1920s that government regulation of the airwaves was needed. For example, when Secretary of Commerce Herbert Hoover moved to withdraw McPherson's license after her radio station started broadcasting all over the bandwidth, McPherson resorted to "otherworldly defenses," as the media historians Stewart M. Hoover and Douglas K. Wagner pointed out, by wiring Hoover: "Please order your minions of Satan to leave my station alone Stop You cannot expect the Almighty to abide by your wave length nonsense Stop When I offer my prayers to Him I must fit into his wave reception Stop Open this station at once."[21]

In the end, the mainstream church establishment was able to negotiate provisions in the Radio Act of 1927 and the Communications Act of 1934 that provided public service access on commercial stations for such "respectable" voices discussing the broad truths of religion as Harry Emerson Fosdick, S. Parkes Cadman, Ralph Sockman, Joseph F. Newton, and David H. C. Read and established some controls over the evangelical preachers who had begun to flood the airwaves. One of the reasons the mainline churches negotiated this arrangement was that it succeeded in getting the strident voices of conservative evangelicals off the air—at least for a time. Partly in response to the controversy over Father Coughlin and other "Bible-thumping" preachers, the early radio networks—led by NBC and CBS—moved to replace paid religious broadcasts (including Coughlin's) with free programming offered to the major ecumenical and faith groups for programming that focused on broadly Christian moral, ethical, and spiritual issues. The National Association of Broadcasters' code said that radio should not be used to "convey attacks upon another's race or religion" and instead should seek "to promote the spiritual harmony and understanding of mankind and to administer broadly to the varied religious needs of the community."[22] However, in many parts of the country (particularly in the South), the tradition of the fiery radio evangelists flourished, and such radio ministries as those of Carl McIntire, Billy James Hargis, Dean Clarence Manion, Dan Smoot, Edgar Bundy, Gerald B. Winrod, and Frederick C. Schwartz were replete with attacks on politicians who were "soft on communism" and were modeled on the notion that evangelical progress could not be separated from a conservative political agenda.[23]

The parallels linking commercial journalism and the present state of Christian broadcasting are historical as well and are tied together more closely than the casual observer of the two seemingly distant traditions might imagine. The critics of commercial television's indifference to organized religion like to blame it on the fact that mainline denominations are just so boring—or so "quiet," as one commentator put it the Freedom Forum report[24]—that there is little sizzle-and-pop-oriented broadcast news reporters can grab hold of. But the reality is that religious broadcasting from the mainstream churches was once prevalent on the airwaves and disappeared from television only in the late 1970s, as a result of a ruling by the Federal Communications Commission (FCC) in 1960 that paid religious programming could count as public service broadcasting and that station owners could get credit for selling airtime to evangelicals.[25] In the early days of television in the 1950s and 1960s, Sunday mornings were often set aside on local commercial stations and the networks for programming—such as *Look Up and Live, Lamp unto My Feet, Frontiers of Faith,* and *The Catholic Hour*—that was produced in cooperation with the mainline religious organizations and was broadcast free as part of commercial television's public service obligation.[26] But after the FCC's 1960 ruling and faced with evangelists eager to buy airtime, local commercial television stations began to phase out the free public service religious programming, and paid televangelism programming came to dominate the airwaves, particularly as cable television came onto the scene.[27]

It is important to understand how troubled mainline churches have been by the spectacle of evangelical proselytization on first radio and then television. The mainstream churches clearly find the idea of doing fund-raising on the air distasteful, and some even have had qualms about using the airwaves at all, given the widespread view (in both mainline and conservative Christian churches) that the commercial mass media have done much to undermine the moral fiber of the social order. Many mainstream churches are not comfortable with going much beyond the occasional televising of traditional church services. The economic and class divisions between mainline and conservative, evangelical Christians cannot be ignored, either. Most mainline Protestant and Catholic traditions "find the thought of begging for money on the air to be quite repugnant," observed Jeffrey K. Hadden. "Thus they repudiated both the motives and the methods of evangelical preachers."[28]

Televangelism must be seen in the context of the divisions within Christian circles over religious proselytizers using the latest communications technology to promote religion's interests. Virtually from the time the printing press was invented, the religious community has been of two minds about using for its own purposes the latest tools of communications, which it sees as responsible for so much of what is wrong in the world. For many defenders of the traditional religious order, the rise of mass printing in the United States was one of the most pernicious manifestations of the market revolution, and the spectacle of religious leaders using mass publication for the purpose of evangelism and community building meant little more than "fighting fire with fire," as the media

historian David Paul Nord put it. Mainstream Christians were particularly troubled as they saw Christian enthusiasts—particularly conservative evangelicals—
eagerly embrace whatever communications tools became available for their
proselytizing and political rabble-rousing. "For religious leaders the times could
be both frightening and exhilarating," Nord wrote. "The marketplace could
appear as problem or solution. . . . To the conservators of traditional values and
authority, enthusiastic commercialism and enthusiastic religious populism
seemed equally horrifying."[29]

It was this dual-mindedness that in the 1800s led the American Tract Society—an organization containing both mainstream and Christian evangelical
influences—to print millions of Bibles and other religious material for free distribution while at the same time campaigning against "foul and exciting" romance novels, the "satanic press," and the "intoxicating" effects of modern
novel-reading. Even though many of the religious publishers were "obsessed
with the morally corrosive power" of the commercial press, as Nord put it, they
developed many of the key technological and business techniques that contributed to its growth. "Again and again, from the 1820s on, the answer [of the religious publishers] was repeated: If the devil works fast, let us work faster," Nord
remarked.[30]

Even while the culture of the mass media and the culture of evangelical Christianity may seem at odds, it is fascinating to see the ways in which the two worlds
work by certain similar principles. Whether the gulf between the two worldviews
is caused by ignorance, hostility, or people who have experienced life in radi-
cally different ways, one thing binds them together: journalists and evangelical
Christians (or at least the evangelical Christians who come into Americans' living rooms via the religious television networks) have made their peace with the
prevailing communications technology and are willing to use it single-mind-
edly in service to their respective missions. Journalists—many of whom are
attracted to the "higher calling" of the profession—perform their duties with
the trappings of commercialism surrounding them everywhere: the extravagant
profit expectations of media owners, stories treated as filler between the advertisements, ratings and marketing surveys that circumscribe their professional
lives, and the earnings pressures from Wall Street and the stockholders of publicly held media companies. Christian broadcasters exist in a somewhat different environment, but money, in the form of fund-raising appeals and marketing ventures, is increasingly what drives the religious networks and is used (as
it was by Falwell or Bakker, for example) to build grand-scale religious empires
that may also include universities, residential communities, and theme parks.
The perils of pursuing the almighty dollar are criticized by the moralists in both
enterprises, but both enterprises profit immensely from the very evils they condemn. "Although Christian broadcasters and church leaders are . . . quick to
point out the banality and offensiveness of modern television, they are no less
eager than their secular counterparts to exploit television's idioms—talk shows,

game shows, cartoons, formulaic dramas—for the purposes of ministry and
mission," observed John W. Kennedy.[31]

Steve Bruce, author of *Pray TV: Televangelism in America,* noted that the cost
of broadcasting time (money, of course, that goes into the pocket of the commercial broadcasters) is what requires some televangelists to spend as much as
25 to 35 percent of the money they take in simply to keep the programming on
the air. The "opportunity structure" of the evangelical's worldview, Bruce added, means that there is a long tradition in revivalist and fundamentalist circles
of "supposing that the Christian message is flattered rather than insulted by being
linked in metaphor with commerce and selling." The "health and wealth gospel" of televangelists and the focus on material success by many of their followers grow out of a stress on certain biblical texts, Bruce explained, but it lessens
the edge of the critique when conservative evangelists complain that it is others
who have been corrupted by the commercialism of modern American life.[32]

This theme was picked up by both William Fore and Quentin Schultze, who
lamented the way that the culture of today's modern mass media has captured
religious organizations themselves, despite church leaders' complaints about the
pernicious influence of the mass media. Although Christians have traditionally found themselves in conflict with the secular culture, too many church organizations have been willing, Fore argued, to subordinate the religious message
to image-making designed to advance all-too-human goals, such as soliciting
funds and promoting the expansion of religious ministries. The feeling in many
religious quarters, he observed, is that the religious center is not holding anymore amid a media vortex that is pulling everything—the religious community as well as the culture at large—into its powerful influence. "Unfortunately,
the church has tended to fall into the trap of technology mythmakers and ask
what works and how to get results, rather than what is true and how to increase
insights and perceptions that lead to the truth," Fore concluded.[33] Schultze added, "Much Christian TV has lost track of the gospel and is really oriented toward building constituencies and entertaining audiences and raising money. The
gospel is not always fashionable, even in Christian circles, particularly the sin
side of the gospel. The positive thinking and name-it-and-claim-it messages are
still widely preached instead of the gospel."[34]

It is too easy, however, to point the finger only at the evangelical broadcast
preachers and to forget it is the commercial media, particularly the commercial television industry, that play a powerful, symbiotic role in the exigencies of
religious broadcasting. Although originally troubled by the tone of early evangelical broadcasting and even willing to forego payment for airtime to get away
from it, the broadcasting industry has become very comfortable accepting the
money that now flows in from religious broadcasters and doing away with virtually all its unpaid mainline religious programming. In listening to the handwringing commentaries by journalistic pundits about the threats to a pluralistic society from the growing influence of the Christian Right, one could almost

forget that the bottom-line driven policies of the commercial television industry (with some quiet help from the federal government) have provided the exposure that has allowed high-profile televangelists to push themselves into the public limelight. The scenario is a reminder, as Jeffrey Hadden pointed out, that at certain basic levels a capitalistic media industry and an aggressively proselytizing religious community have much in common. "At the heart of the evangelicals' success in monopolizing air time is a confluence of theology and the free-market principles of broadcasting in the United States," Hadden wrote. "On the one hand, evangelicals believe passionately in the commandment to take the message of Jesus Christ to all. On the other hand, broadcasting in America, almost from the onset, has been an instrument of a free-market economy. . . . Evangelicals, like automobile and personal-hygiene manufacturers, have a product to sell and the airwaves are a marketing instrument."[35]

The ties that bind may be as profound as those that seem to break asunder. Evangelistic broadcasters' growing orientation toward marketing, popular entertainment, feel-good themes, and money-raising, despite their claim that the gospel message is what the whole enterprise is about, sounds a familiar refrain for those who watch what is taking place in a commercial press that lays claim to a higher mission but puts its emphasis on the bottom line. Journalists and Christian conservatives each hold the other responsible for bringing more contention, hypocrisy, and hucksterism into the world. I would suggest the two antagonists could profit from examining what they do not like about their adversary and then applying the analysis to themselves.

Pluralism and the Press's Blind Spots: The Coverage of Religious Diversity at Home and Abroad

It did not take the *Boston Herald* long to speculate that the October 1999 crash of the EgyptAir flight might involve terrorism. There was no shortage of suspects, the newspaper wrote on the day after the disaster: the terrorist leader Osama bin Laden, the al-Jihad organization that assassinated Egyptian president Anwar Sadat in 1981, the groups responsible for the 1997 tourist massacre in Luxor or the 1993 bombing of the World Trade Center in New York.[1]

The *Herald*'s coverage was only the beginning of a steady flow of stories in the U.S. media suggesting that terrorism was involved in the crash of the Egyptian jet in the ocean off New York. Of 772 stories found in a Nexis search for the week after the crash, 45 mentioned "terrorism" or "terrorist" (almost exactly equal to the 46 that speculated about "mechanical" failure).[2]

However, it was not this speculation that generated the most controversy in the wake of the EgyptAir crash. Within a week of the disaster, stories began to appear that, quoting unnamed American government sources, blamed the plane's downing on a copilot suspected of committing suicide. In the week following the crash, 72 stories (roughly 10 percent of the total) mentioned "suicide" in connection with the tragedy.[3]

The tone of most of these stories was ominous and the implications clear: there was something sinister about an Islamic prayer uttered by the copilot of the doomed airliner. No matter that the investigation into the cause of the crash had only just begun, that previous stories in the American press speculating about the involvement of Arab terrorists (such as those surrounding the bombing of the Oklahoma City federal building) proved to be unfounded, that this kind of reporting and similar coverage around the country would foster a diplomatic rift in the relations between Egypt and the United States. The frame in which the U.S. media cover Islam and perceived Islamic terrorist activity is clear: jump to conclusions first, put out reports based on them, and then worry about correcting the record later, if at all.

One thing must be said for the U.S. media's approach to religion reporting. Christianity is not singled out for problematic coverage. Other religions often are treated with the same confusion, negative stereotyping, and lack of sympathetic understanding that can make their way into press reporting of Christianity. In particular, Islam and its adherents are presented almost exclusively in the context of the hostilities and violence that have come to be associated with Middle East politics. It is something of an irony that the U.S. news media—which can demonstrate such discomfort in dealing with issues growing out of Christian belief—still so readily relate to Islam through the prism of the rivalry between Islam and Christianity that dates back centuries. (The Canadian press also has this problem, at least according to a 1999 study by the Canadian Islamic Congress that found Muslims were persistently portrayed as violent in the Canadian media.)[4]

Even when Arab extremists are behind terrorists acts, the American media often do not do enough to distinguish between the actions of terrorists and the views of the rest of the Islamic world. The media enthusiasm for comparing the attacks on the World Trade Center and the Pentagon to Pearl Harbor and emphasizing such cries as "The U.S. is at war" tended to agitate rather than illuminate and made it easier for the public to get the idea that a people or a culture—or more to the point, the adherents of a particular religion—might justifiably become a target for retaliation. Despite voices of sympathy for the United States from moderate Arab and Palestinian groups, the tone of much of the press coverage certainly helped fan the anger that led to assaults on Islamic mosques and hostile acts directed at people of Arab descent in the United States. The attacks directed at Islamic places of worship are evidence that some Americans—taking their cue from the American media that tend to use *Islamic* as an adjective for a host of pejorative terms (*terrorist, extremist, fundamentalist*)—see Islam in political rather than religious terms. They mistake Arab antipathy for U.S. policy as antipathy toward Americans and view that antipathy as something inherent in Islamic beliefs.

The media's coverage of the world's religions is complex, though, and not subject to uniform analysis. For example, while Islam is treated with great suspicion, Buddhism—along with the Tibetan Dalai Lama, a prominent Buddhist religious leader—receives largely favorable treatment in the media. Compare, for example, the *Los Angeles Times* article headlined "Dalai Lama: Humble Man Inspires Awe. . . . The Exiled Tibetan Buddhist Leader, Who Describes Himself as a Simple Monk, Is Globally Respected" with the many articles linking the EgyptAir crash to the so-called death-prayer of the plane's copilot.[5]

At first glance, this may look like just another example of an old pattern of

American news reporting: the press's preference for presenting religious discussion in political terms and its tendency to present anything in negative terms that collides with U.S. foreign policy interests. The Islamic fundamentalist revolutions are depicted in the contexts of their threat to U.S. economic and diplomatic interests—oil, Israel, the safety of U.S. citizens, American overseas investments, the push for modernism and economic growth in the Third World, and the like. In contrast, the Dalai Lama is portrayed as a hero because he is the symbolic figure of resistance to China's occupation of Tibet and a promoter of peace and spiritual values in the face of a communist government that has a troubled relationship with the United States.

As with Christianity, however, it seems that other, unconscious factors also dictate the way the religions of the world are presented in the American press. It has to be noted that coverage of religion in U.S. newspapers has become more open and diverse, if for no other reason than that news organizations recognize the "market" for their reporting is no longer an exclusively Christian one. The changing demographic face of American society and changing religious attitudes—with in-migration from non-Western cultures, the establishment of non-Christian houses of worship, the spread in popularity among Americans of nontraditional religions, the rise of the "New Age" movement, the popularity of self-help and personal spirituality programs—have forced religion reporters and editors to expand their definition of religion beyond traditional ones. In addition, the global reach of television has made Americans more aware of the multitude of religions in the world and has exposed them to religious views that might once have been treated only as exotic or strange.

That said, the media's growing sensitivity to religious pluralism has not been extended to religious movements that are seen as a threat to the secular order or the economic and political status quo. Although American journalists probably would not describe their mission as "Christian" in nature, critics in the Muslim world often accuse the U.S. press of portraying Islam through the perspective of its historical competition with Christianity. There seems "to have been a strange revival of canonical, though previously discredited, Orientalist ideas about Muslim . . . which have achieved a startling prominence at a time when racial or religious misrepresentations of every other cultural group are no longer circulated with such impunity," the Columbia University media critic Edward W. Said observed. "Malicious generalizations about Islam have become the last acceptable form of denigration of foreign culture in the West."[6]

In the case of the EgyptAir crash, American reporters relied on unnamed government sources (who never did publicly confirm their claim) in the early days after the crash to pin the blame on the plane's copilot. Egyptian authorities complained vehemently when American news accounts labeled the copilot's prayer found in the cockpit voice recorder a suicide prayer. Translators have never been able to arrive at a conclusive interpretation of the copilot's words, but that did not stop the flow of American media reports that hypothesized the prayer amounted to a suicide statement.

This gave reporters another "frame" to carry forward the story. One of the few times that religion makes it into front page news accounts is when it has something to do with something else (such as politics, terrorism, or disaster). In this case, American press accounts diligently followed up Egyptian authorities' complaints that the American media treated an Islamic prayer not as a plea for help but as evidence of evil plans.[7]

This led the *Los Angeles Times* to dispatch its religion reporter to cover the story. She covered a press conference of Southern California Muslim leaders who complained that their religion was being unfairly tarred with the brush of violence. They pointed out that the copilot's words—"I put my trust in God"— are routinely uttered by Muslims as a public prayer and that it was unlikely a devout Muslim would ask for God's support before killing himself.[8]

Muslim media critics point to a tendency in the U.S. press that may explain why fundamentalist movements in both Islam and Christianity are viewed so critically. The commitment to secularism and modernism runs so strongly in the Western media that anything smacking of theocracy or an intrusion on press freedoms arouses instant hostility. As a result, many Islamic traditions and values—ranging from Arab governments that see themselves as arms of Islamic nationalism to an Arab press that, in its media codes and press charters, proclaims that the first duty of journalists is to be defenders of Islam— are treated as inherently inimical to Western political values and Western press notions of objectivity and detachment.[9] The Western media, added Said, assume that the West "is greater than and has surpassed the stage of Christianity, its principle religion" and that "the world of Islam—its varied societies, histories, and languages notwithstanding—is still mired in religion, primitivity, and backwardness."[10]

This tendency often plays itself out in the ways the American press takes the U.S. government's accounts involving Islam or the Islamic world at face value if they fall within the stereotypical Western attitudes toward the Middle East. The press's probing of unfounded government statements about a wide range of incidents, such as the initial explanations for the U.S. Navy's downing of an Iranian airliner or the U.S. military attack on a Sudanese chemical plant falsely accused of producing material for chemical weapons, has often been slow, lax, or nonexistent, and erroneous government leaks are often passed off as facts. In the frenzy of press coverage that followed the attacks on the World Trade Center and the Pentagon, reporters fell over themselves running with government leaks that focused on Osama bin Laden as the straight-from-central-casting villain behind the assaults and avoided the thornier and more complicated discussions of how American foreign policy failures, political and religious divisions within Arab countries, and poverty and cultural alienation throughout the Middle East have led to such an entrenched and extensive terrorist network throughout the world.

"For years, Muslims have complained that Americans are ignorant of Islam and quick to assume the worst about Muslims and their religion," noted the *Los An-*

geles Times writer John Daniszewski in analyzing the "cultural chasm" that has led westerners to see Islam as a violent religion and Muslims to see the West as a place that trusts only science and technology rather than God. "Muslims òften appear distrustful of the West," Daniszewski added, "assuming at some basic level that Westerners are out to get them, and have been since the Crusades."[11]

There are other religions, though, that are portrayed much more favorably by the American media, particularly if they seem open, tolerant, and passive and do not threaten the political or economic order. Buddhism, for example, gets generally good press in the United States, partly because Buddhist leaders (with the exception of the Dalai Lama) are not usually involved in national politics in Asia or other parts of the world. Buddhism is a religion that stresses individual detachment, the search for inner peace, and values of cooperation and tranquility, and, on only rare occasions, has it been the religious inspiration for those trying to change the political order or in any way threaten American global interests.

Even in the Dalai Lama's case, his "mastery of the media," as one analyst put it, is largely because his role as a symbol of Tibetan resistance to the Chinese government is viewed favorably by both American conservatives (who excoriate China for its suppression of religious movements and its human rights record) and liberals (who have made "Free Tibet" one of their cause célèbres). That the U.S. government does not endorse a free Tibet as a policy matter is seen by many as mere capitulation to the powerful economic interests that have a stake in appeasing the Chinese government and only serves to enhance the Dalai Lama's stature as a figure of principle and as someone the press feels no hesitancy in enshrining.[12]

In addition, Buddhism and Hinduism were favorite religions in the counterculture movement of the 1960s, and many older journalists, who came of age in that period, still view them positively. Even today, certain critics of the U.S. economic system look fondly on Buddhism and Hinduism as religious systems that offer alternative visions to the work and success orientation of Protestant Christianity. Within Islam, the Sufi movement—with its stress on mysticism, the attainment of personal wisdom, and peace and nonviolence—is treated with a respect the Western media do not accord other Muslim sects. Only in recent years—as Hindu radicalism and fundamentalism have begun to stir up political discord in India—has the Western press begun to present Hinduism as something other than an exotic but appealing form of meditative religion that has attracted such celebrities as the former Beatle George Harrison.

The Western press's proclivity for stereotyping also plays a powerful role in the presentation and coverage of religions that advocate values running counter to what are seen as the progressive views of the Western world. The harsh treatment of women by the Taliban Muslim fundamentalists in Afghanistan, the death sentence put out on writer Salman Rushdie by fundamentalist Islamic leaders in Iran, the heightened attention to the caste system in India, the killing of women unwilling to submit to traditional attitudes of marriage in Muslim and Hindu countries, and female genital mutilation in Africa have all been portrayed as repugnant aspects of the religious systems of those regions. In reality, many of these practices are not integral to any religious system but are a blend of tribal or local customs, political exploitation of the religious culture, and controversial interpretations of religious texts that are by no means settled issues among adherents. Yet the Western press's eagerness to highlight controversy, extremism, and the bizarre has led to associating global religions in the news with some of the most problematic practices of the cultures in which their followers reside. At the same time, the values of commercialism, moral license, and unfettered expression are so imbedded in the worldview of the Western media that few Americans fully grasp how the constant global exposure to news and entertainment programming emanating from the West collides with other cultural and religious assumptions, particularly among Islamic people.

While the Western press sees itself as valuing religious diversity, it also tends to be dismayed at the influx of a host of new and nontraditional religions. The proliferation of so-called cults in the United States has been consistently portrayed in the American media as part of the breakdown of values that threatens everything from social unity to cherished individual freedoms. Concepts such as "mind control" and "brainwashing" of members—as well as the relentless attention paid to the horrific incidents associated with such groups as Jim Jones and his followers, the Heaven's Gate community, and the Branch Davidians— have set the tone for the way the U.S. press presents seemingly strange, new sects. In this respect, the press seems reflexively to prefer mainstream worship as the benchmark of religious practice in American life, even as it evinces only a passing interest in what actually is going on in traditional religious institutions.

Perhaps the most uniformly enthusiastic portrayal of religion in the U.S. press these days is the presentation of Native American spirituality. The connections between the environmental movement and Native American religious beliefs revolving around valuing the land and emphasizing human harmony with nature have played a large role in this, as has the perception that it was exploitative European cultural and economic practices growing out of Christian belief that led to the mistreatment of Indians and the ravishing of the landscape. Journalism's traditional support for romantic rural values, as well as for the politically oppressed and downtrodden, has reinforced media sympathy for Native Americans and their religious values, as has the perception that Native American outlooks about the symbiotic relationship among humans, animals, and natural forces are more "politically correct" than the dualities, growing out of Greek and Judeo-Christian thought, that objectify the natural world and other life forms and treat them as things over which humans should maintain dominion.[13]

Scholars of international communication have written much about the way the Western mind-set has come to dominate the global news framework. This, too, can explain something about the way global religions are portrayed in the Western press. Critics in developing countries complain about how news flows throughout the globe and how the developed world controls the manner in which news is framed while developing countries are mentioned only if there are conflicts, catastrophes, or civil unrest. This state of affairs—which can be seen as mimicking old colonization patterns—has led, unconsciously or consciously, to treating Christian viewpoints as the norm and other religious outlooks as something on the margin.[14]

Despite these differences, journalists in the West tend to endorse certain ethical and moral principles that they see as universal to most of the world's religions—and, in fact, are willing to acknowledge journalism's debt to these "universal" religious principles rather than to Christian values alone.[15] Clifford Christians attempted to distill what he believes are the basic moral principles of all the major religions of the world, including respect for human dignity, truth telling, and a commitment to nonviolence, and to apply them to what he sees as a universal ethic in the global communications systems. Christians, a critic of what he sees as excessive Enlightenment individualism in Western journalistic attitudes, would like to see the press adopt more communitarian values in its professional ethics. But he also maintained that "a commitment to universals" can advance common citizenship in global communications systems and will not do away with important elements of cultural pluralism.[16]

How the world's religions will be covered in a pluralistic environment may depend on the media's marketing orientation in the future. Historically, religion has often served the economic interests of the ruling elite, and even in today's more secular climate, this is likely to continue to be true. On the one hand, this may lead to a continued growth in the sensitivity of media organizations and their religion correspondents to diverse religious viewpoints, if for no other reason than to accommodate the multicultural marketplace of a changing audience. On the other hand, the powerful figures who control the media may find it serves their purposes to encourage the shaping of global religion coverage in ways that will benefit the corporate agenda.

One only has to be reminded of the comments about the Dalai Lama by Rupert Murdoch, no friend of communism, at least until his purchase of Star TV, which controls much of the satellite communications market in Asia, including China. In a magazine interview after the purchase, Murdoch excused China's human rights record on the grounds that the average Chinese person cares more about "his next bowl of rice" than democracy. Then, in an effort to ingratiate himself with his new Chinese business partners, the normally politically conservative Murdoch went on to note how cynics sometimes called the Dalai Lama "a very political old monk shuffling around in Gucci shoes."[17]

Afterword

The television journalist David Frost always seems to elicit the most candid self-revelations from the Americans he interviews, perhaps because he is British or because his questions are so probing and unexpected. Clearly, he surprised Bill Gates, the multibillionaire software superstar and our era's most celebrated capitalist, when he asked Gates during a television interview if he believed in God. Gates, who was promoting his new book, *The Road Ahead,* stammered out a vague and what was intended to be deflecting answer (which, in effect, indicated he was skeptical of the concept), but the expression on his face registered his clear discomfort with the question. "I've been too busy building a software empire," a viewer could almost sense him thinking, "to have time for a question like this."

Only in a country that has come to worship science and technology as the path to economic success could Gates be startled by a question that might connect his speculations about the future to his religious beliefs. After all, Gates had recently married and had lost a mother to cancer; he was talking at the time about having children and what to do with his fortune in the future; and, in his early forties, he was at a natural point to start thinking seriously about the larger questions that grow out of a sense of life's finiteness. The computer industry, in which Gates's company is a leading force, was making possible a rapid advance into realms that were once the domain of philosophers and theologians: virtual reality, artificial intelligence, robotics, biotechnology, genetic manipulation, deep space travel, even cryonics. And Gates, a relentless self-promoter, had found his personal life a subject of intense fascination in a nation that had come to welcome fabulously wealthy computer geeks into the shrine of media celebrity.

Frost, in the end, did not have much success in luring Gates into a discussion of his personal theology. But, in his efforts, Frost presented a tantalizing picture of what it might mean if journalists regularly engaged their subjects in a deeper, more profound probing of the realms of personal belief and inner experience. It is perhaps fitting that Gates—who succeeded so brilliantly in anticipating and then dominating the software market that made the personal computer revolution possible—has emerged as the symbol of the threat facing the journalism industry. Gates's determination to continue to be the master of the world of new media can be seen not only in economic and technological terms but in theological terms as well. It is interesting to muse on the fact that the computer's operating system has been, in effect, the soul of the personal computer network, while the multiplying interconnections of the Internet—which Gates's company has been seeking to master as aggressively as it came to dominate the computer software industry—can be seen as that soul writ large. If, as Marshall McLuhan speculated, we are simply extensions of our culture's dominant communications technology, Gates can be viewed as the technological version of that person who is reaching out his finger to touch the divine (to borrow from the image in Michelangelo's famous painting in the Sistine Chapel). If that is the case, Gates's ambition to push on into the frontiers of cyberspace (he hardly needs to add to a multibillion-dollar personal fortune that has made him one of the world's richest people) amounts to much more than just a business person's ambition to corner the market.

Like Faust, Oedipus, or Milton's Satan (as some of his competitors think that he is), Gates can be viewed as the high technology person of unbounded ambition determined to expand human capacity as far as the powers of the universe will permit. Of course, it may be an exaggeration to find classically tragic or theological meaning in Bill Gates's aspirations, but it is no exaggeration to see Gates as a symbol of a hubris—of a near worshipping of technology and a faith in the power of the human computing devices—that is leading in a direction where, if the divine forces operate as they do in classical literature, some humbling might be in the works.[1] In this context, it may be no surprise that Gates does not want to be troubled with thinking about the religious implications of his grand ambitions.

Frost's questioning of Gates had another highly significant implication, too. Gates is now a journalist; almost overnight, he has become the head of one of the key players in the news business. With the entry of Microsoft into the world of news (with MSNBC and its on-line alliance with NBC-TV News), the world's dominant computer software company is now on the cutting edge of where the news business is headed. Journalists everywhere are wondering who will decide the design of tomorrow's information: journalists, or the technology wizards of the computer industry, or perhaps some blend of the two. Suffice it to say that Bill Gates, with his bloodless technocratic outlook and his unrelenting business acumen, now represents a major new challenge to the once complacent and comfortable circles of journalists and media owners.

All this could have repercussions for the world of faith, not only in the way the news media have traditionally covered religion but also in the role religious values play in the journalistic mission. In previous chapters, I have lamented that modern journalists— products of the Enlightenment tradition of doubt, empiricism, and rationalism—have come to see the role of religion in society in narrow, formulaic, and unmindful ways. However, even with the shortcomings of mainstream journalism's coverage of the role of religion in society, journalists, I have contended throughout the book, are still animated by a religious spirit that draws on the traditions of biblical prophesy and the ethical and moral precepts of Judeo-Christian teaching mirrored in the world's other major religions. In the investigative reporting tradition, in the news industry's watchdog role over powerful institutions, in journalists' antipathy to excessive power and extravagant wealth, in their impulse to correct social inequities and to represent the interests of the downtrodden, in their carrying out of the public service mission and the role of the socially responsible journalist—in all these time-honored functions, journalists manifest aspects of a religious ethic that has been deeply ingrained in the American journalistic consciousness and surfaces in ways that few journalists even associate with a religious tradition.

Yet journalists have seen the most sacred aspect of their professional mission come under assault in recent years by the growing power of media conglomerates, the pressure of bottom-line dictates, and marketing and management systems designed to ensure that economic goals become predominant in the newsroom. I have described this environment as creating a "spiritual crisis," at least in the figurative sense, for journalists, many of whom have become alienated from an enterprise they see forsaking its higher mission and purpose. They now face the prospect of high-technology figures like Gates, in many respects the antithesis of the journalistic personality, and his ruthlessly conquering new technology moving into and transforming their field.[2]

Gates, of course, would like to fulfill a prophetic role, but most journalists are not likely to be comfortable with it. As the modern American symbol of grandly conspicuous wealth and business success at any cost, Gates stands for many of the very things that journalists—at least journalists functioning in their most honored and noblest role—would oppose. Such prophetic journalists as Lincoln Steffens, Ida Tarbell, Upton Sinclair, and Will Irwin crusaded against the very values of power accumulation and marketplace dominance that Gates epitomizes. The media critic George Seldes's description of the "Lords of the Press" certainly applies to Gates and his fellow computer entrepreneurs, who envision the media business converging into theirs and being transformed by the developments of modern electronic communications.

Gates, with his book, his regular newspaper column, and his company's move into mass media, has clearly come to enjoy his new journalistic role as a new technology commentator touting the wonders of the unfolding information age. But one wonders how well the journalistic ethic will survive as it becomes blended with the culture of the computer industry and the ethics of a business that is unrelentingly driven by technological innovations, gyrating stock prices, and accelerating marketplace change. Journalists, to be sure, have always served capitalistic, highly commercialized enterprises—what, after all, were the newspapers of Hearst or Pulitzer if not extravagant marketing and money-making machines? But Gates's on-line journalistic operations and the Web sites and interactive services that are now challenging traditional media companies to keep pace with new media developments promise to push journalism ever more forcefully into the vortex of marketplace jockeying, e-commerce, exhausting technological change, and investors fixated on profits and earnings.

Even if Gates's company does not end up as a major player in tomorrow's news business, his stature as the prototype of the modern version of the Horatio Alger success story will continue to influence young people, particularly those young entrepreneurs who are massing in the field of interactive communications and promising to transform the world of news and entertainment with their Internet ventures. There are some indications that as Microsoft purchases other software companies and jockeys to position itself in the synergistic world of multimedia and digital broadcasting, it may decide to step out of the media content business (such as happened when it sold off Sidewalk, its interactive restaurant and entertainment review service). But Gates's story—the Harvard drop-out who has made a vast fortune by challenging the computer establishment and unstintingly pushing the frontiers of computer software development—exercises a powerful hold over a generation that, in many respects, has come to see the news business as just another place in cyberspace, as a field that must transform itself or die, and as an element in a gold-rush environment where the goal is to get rich young and damn the consequences. The Gates mystique and the mythology surrounding the creation of his megabillion-dollar computer empire promise to set the tone for an age that is only slightly interested in what Bill Gates might have to say about God but even less so in what God might have to say about the priorities of Bill Gates.

Where religion and the coverage of religion will fit into this world of perpetual media transformation is anyone's guess. If religion itself and the nature of worship are being transformed by the media environment, as some have suggested, then speculating about the press's future treatment of religion may not be worthwhile. But if religion requires a grasp of the traditions of the past and a focus on what is eternal—as opposed to a fixation on a fleeting present—then journalism's situation at the turn of the twenty-first century is a precarious one. Journalism's drift away from any acknowledgment or knowledge of the moral grounding of journalistic ethics and morals, combined with the grinding commercial, economic, and technological pressures that are reshaping editorial values, has left the profession on a fragile footing. Journalists do not need to know anything about religion to recognize that their highest and most honored values are connected to a tradition that transcends the task of getting and spending. Still, journalism's tie to the Judeo-Christian tradition is an important one, and, as journalists lose sight of it, one cannot simply presume that secularized ethical and moral values will serve the same purpose. Journalists have traveled some distance from the days when Benjamin Franklin argued that only a religious people can maintain the nation's moral fiber and make a success of democracy. But as time goes by and the profession's connection to the nation's religious heritage grows more distant and tenuous, it is risky to assume that journalists' moral disposition and their ethical outlook may not change, too. Without a clear sense of moral purpose and ethical rootedness—and without some sense of where those values come from—it may only be a matter of time before the evangelists of the marketplace convince journalists to place their allegiance with the commercial mission of their news organization and to judge their role solely through the measurements of the economic calculus.

One can count on the fact that—given the history of religious revivalism in America and the current trends of religious participation—religion will not go away just because the media do not comprehend it fully or cover it in all its dimensions. Few in the religious community, it is fair to say, are holding their breath waiting for news organizations to engage in more thoughtful treatment of religion. Journalists, of course, must always take with a grain of salt what the subjects of their coverage say about them. But there appears to be a consensus across religious groups that journalists often do not "get it" when it comes to the portrayal of people of faith and the way they express the spiritual underpinning of their lives. The culture of journalism, in the eyes of many religious people, both conservative and liberal, is inimical to the culture of faith, and no amount of handwringing (or surveying the tastes and preferences of their audience) by media executives is likely to change that impression.

I have argued throughout this book that this view is not necessarily true— that one needs to have a clearer understanding of how journalists work to see the way religion influences the operations of the profession. Although journalists do themselves and their audience a disservice when they do not recognize the role that religion plays in their professional value system, the religious public often slights journalism by not recognizing how much the profession is animated by powerful religious impulses. A profession committed to balance and the reiteration of both sides of a story is never going to treat religion in ways that will fully satisfy true believers. It is also true that journalists, with their cynical postures and their commitment to getting the story at all costs, do not work in an environment in which spirituality is openly acknowledged or accepted, and they cannot be expected to be overtly religious in their professional attitudes and activities. But the prophetic side of the religious tradition and the moral principles grounded in the country's religious heritage still provide the ethical moorings of the profession, as our survey of journalists demonstrated. Regardless of whether journalists are self-proclaimed believers (and more of them are than their critics think), they respond positively to the moral and ethical values that grow out of biblical teachings and the other great religious traditions.

Journalists are highly attuned to hypocrisy, and their disgust at the discrepancy between what is preached and what is practiced among religious folk can run quite high. Journalists' response to the travails of the sanctimonious, the tripped-up moralizers, and the scandal-ridden judgers-of-others may not always sound as if it originates in the prophet's contempt for cant and pretense (journalists have had to come to grips with some pretty large questions of hypocrisy in their own ranks), but that is where their moral kinship with the religious tradition runs strongly.

The spiritual side of religion is clearly where many journalists have to stretch the most to understand and cover the experience of the faithful. The most emotional aspects of religious faith grow, at core, out of personal, spiritual experience, yet few people would find the newsroom, with its practical routines and its commitment to efficiently putting out a news product, a conducive environment to confront such issues as conversion, revelation, and mystical insight. Journalists like to see themselves as perfectly capable of understanding matters they have not personally experienced, but, like most everyone else, they often do not rise to the task. Religious belief that grows out of the acceptance of rigid doctrinal teachings or dogmatic commitment to a religious system may offend the independent-minded tradition of the journalism profession, but the claim of those who have had a profound religious experience may agitate the typical newsroom denizen the most. The journalistic impulse to detach, to be an observer, to watch the world from the safety of the outsider's stance is endemic to the profession, and the challenge to this position by those who claim that religious experience should be trusted can be a deeply disturbing proposition for the journalistic personality. Journalists, after all, do not like to believe they have been excluded from any life experience, and they certainly do not like being told about it by people who think their experience gives them greater insights into life's truths.

In my thirteen years in the journalism business, I found my colleagues open-minded when it came to dealing with those who maintained a tolerant outlook on the world but hostile when they felt they were being preached at, condescended to, or treated as if they were morally deficient. Journalists have been highly suspicious of religious absolutists who claim, for example, that correct religious belief leads to salvation and that salvation can be treated as a possession to be acquired and shared only with one's fellow believers. The culture wars that have defined the battle lines between conservative Christians and the liberal political community (including many journalists, if one believes the polls on journalists' political beliefs) are not something that can be wished away by marketing-minded editors hoping to please their audience by simply tapping into the faith interests of readers and viewers. Journalists must learn to treat religion with greater sympathy, understanding, and sensitivity, but not by letting their brains fall out or proclaiming readers' beliefs should somehow set the tone of coverage. Within their own version of a belief system, journalists have an obligation to stay faithful to their own eternal verities—demanding sound evidence, stripping away fraud and deceit, correcting injustices, and rooting out corruption—which should never be altered simply because certain members of their audience are willing to assert their own beliefs as the final measure of truth. The adversarial relationship between journalists and the subjects of their coverage is not going to go away and should not. That certainly holds true for the religious community where, as James Gordon Bennett discovered, there is much false piety and where journalism should not be afraid to tread just because some claim divine authority for their actions.

In the course of this book, I hope I have not left the impression that the task of reconciling modern journalism to the world of faith and religion is going to be easy. The tension between the religious community and a profession committed to hard facts, tangible evidence, and the exposure of hypocrisy—if journalists are true to their professional obligations—cannot be made to disappear simply by declaring good will on both sides. The antipathy many journalists feel toward organized religion is legitimate in many instances, and Christians, if they are honest, know, as Voltaire, Mark Twain, and Upton Sinclair recognized, that members of the faith community often do not live up to the demanding moral precepts that Jesus called for among his followers. Christians can hardly enjoy hearing this criticism from people they consider irreverent, iconoclastic, and even blasphemous, but a good case can be made that many of the journalists who have thought the most about Christianity have been, despite their often heterodox views, some of the most trenchant commentators about the Christian community's failure to follow the principles of its founder.

At the same time, members of the faith community are on target when they complain about the incapacity or the unwillingness of journalists to take seriously the importance of the spiritual dimension in the lives of so many people. Some journalists buck this trend, but because there are so few of them, it makes the point even more strongly. Bill Moyers has built a small but enthusiastic following by interviewing for public television a wide range of intellectuals, philosophers, and religious figures about their beliefs and their perspectives on faith. The ABC television news anchor Peter Jennings, in his efforts to make commercial television news more sensitive to issues of faith, has been a notable exception to the rule, too. But, beyond that, one is hard-pressed to find a commentator in the national press who tackles the subject of religion in a way that demonstrates an understanding of the topic beyond its political implications (which is about as far as most journalists like to explore the subject). One can take heart, of course, from the studies that indicate news organizations are treating issues of faith, spirituality, and personal values more seriously. But with so little motivation to improve coverage beyond marketing concerns, mainstream news organizations will probably never really convince the public—let alone the religious community—that they have a genuine interest in covering the religious element of stories in a knowledgeable and in-depth fashion.

Perhaps I have stretched the conventional definition by characterizing the angst felt by so many news workers as a "spiritual crisis" and linking it to the religious traditions out of which news values were formed. But journalists, uncomfortable as they may be in the face of strong religious experience, are often people of powerful passions, ideals, and visions of how the world should be. The missionary mind-set of the committed journalist—and the way it can be thwarted in the typical corporate news environment—does not have to be tied to religion by analogy only. Many journalists believe they are serving a cause higher than the commercial goals of their news organization, and they feel much heartache at seeing their professional values refashioned around the imperatives of market-oriented corporate management systems. Whether one wants to compare the pain of this adjustment with the sufferings of the faithful is, of course, open to question. But the expression *calling*, defined as a vocational commitment to a higher and greater duty than one's own or one's company's narrow self-interest, has religious significance even in the journalistic context.

It has been an eye-opening experience to discover just how rich the connections are between the profession I once practiced and my religious heritage. Like George Fox, who described his moments of religious insight as "openings," I have had glimpses of divine activity in the world, and I have experienced the presence of a force larger than my own ego. Even though I would not call myself a religious convert or even a highly religious person, I have become comfortable around religious people and the language they use, and I have come to value the role of religion in building community, providing the human-to-human connections that give life its warmth and its richness, and demonstrating the important daily lessons of worship and humility. Still, the journalist stirs strongly in me—even as my sympathy for the world of religion has grown. I have never lost my doubt, my skepticism, or my instinct to question—and I hope that I never will. My faith has become even stronger when my doubt has been greatest. In accepting there is a power in the universe that may be beyond my capacity for comprehension or understanding, I have learned to let go—if only a little bit—of my need to control, to explain, and to be in full intellectual charge of my life. I do not pretend I have begun to penetrate to the depths of the insights of the truly spiritually transformed, but I do have a sense of how little I understood as a journalist about the ultimate dimensions of human experience—and how profound was my pride in thinking that I knew all I needed to know then to do my job.

Journalism, of course, is a proud profession, and much of what happens in the business is fueled by individuals' determination to master their circumstances and to bring the world into line with their professional objectives. Journalism also is a macho profession; its practitioners think of themselves as being above human weakness and not needing forgiveness for their sins (or the capacity to forgive others their sins, for that matter). For the most part, journalists have their eye on the material matters of the world, and they have little time and usually little imagination for looking into dimensions that go beyond the real, the tangible, the here-and-now. To take on the challenge of improving coverage of religion will be no small task given the crusty, hard-edged, often self-righteous nature of the journalistic personality. Covering the controversies that come with religion will never be a problem—journalists love controversy, particularly if there is some element of hypocrisy attached to it. But getting inside the softer aspects of religious experience—the parts of religion that speak to the human need for love, fellowship, forgiveness, consolation, and spiritual connection—can take them well outside their comfort zone. Still, if they do this with insight, sympathy, and sensitivity, the religious in the audience may come to recognize that the job is sometimes done right.

I remember soon after I left journalism, a close friend of mine—a deeply religious person—excitedly told me about a story she had read in the *Seattle Times* about a young peace activist who was arrested in El Salvador for supposedly supplying arms to rebel groups and then later released from prison. In the story, the young woman described how she sat in a cell listening to the screams of those being beaten nearby; how she prayed and repeated a vow to herself to be a sign of what it truly means to love; and how, at that moment, the guards in charge of her interrogation ended the beating next door and later shared with her stories of their childhood poverty. "For a moment in my life, I'd done what God asks us to do—which is to surrender ourselves totally to a greater love," she was quoted by the *Times* reporter. "This experience set me free. I finally realized my life belongs to God, not to me."[3]

I, too, had been moved by the story, but not nearly as much as I was moved by my friend's excitement at finding something in the newspaper that seemed to speak so directly to her religious condition. It is hard to think of a mainstream commercial media organization's providing the possibility for spiritual insight or spiritual transformation, but it can happen. Journalism is seldom thought of as a pipeline for the transcendent or the spiritual—or journalists as the source for the transmission of the experience of the divine. But journalism—with its witnessing to the shared human experience, with its commitment to values and principles that hold community together, with its roots in the moral and ethical principles of the greatest religious teachings—has the potential, when practiced right, to present life as it is lived in the richest depths of the human core and at the highest peaks of transcendent experience. It is in doing this kind of journalism that news organizations can demonstrate that the sacred life of the universe does flow through all things, even the news media.

Notes

Preface

1. Michael R. Fancher, "We're Sending Our Reporters to Church to Learn about Politics," *Seattle Times,* May 29, 1994, A2. The project was an "awkward thing" that was "executed clumsily and sounded bad," said Jim Simon, a veteran *Times* political writer, at a 1996 conference on media and religion. "A lot of us resisted it. . . . There was a lot of cynicism about it," he added. After an initial flurry of activity, the project was dropped.

2. Alicia C. Shepherd, "The Media Get Religion," *American Journalism Review,* December 1995, 19–20.

3. Doug Underwood, *When MBAs Rule the Newsroom: How the Marketers and Managers Are Reshaping Today's Media* (New York: Columbia University Press, 1993).

4. For an Internet discussion, use search words "Yahoo!" and "Filo" and "Yang" on the Yahoo! search engine and then click on "Yahoo Interview: Part 1 of 2." See also Gary DeMar, "Yahoo! Hermeneutics," <www.prophecy.books.com>; and Zola Levitt, "Notes on Revelation—Y2K/Yahoo," <www.mv.com>. Both can also be accessed by using search words "yahweh" and "yahoo!" on Yahoo! For an academic discussion of the matter, see Richard Crider, "Yahoo (Yahu): Notes on the Name of Swift's Yahoos," *Names* 41 (June 1993): 103–9; and Laura B. Kennelly, "Swift's Yahoo and King Jehu: Genesis of an Allusion," *English Language Notes* 26 (March 1989): 37–45. Crider noted, for example that Swift's library contained a Bible with Hebrew scriptures in Hebrew, and Kennelly speculates that Swift's term may have been a satiric allusion to Jehu, the Israelite commander of 2 Kings who was famous as a furious charioteer and a destroyer of wicked kings. However, it also has been speculated that the Irish-born Swift fashioned his satiric language from the Irish he heard spoken around him and that *yahoo* spoken phonetically comes from "Ye who" (as in the sense of "Ye who behave thus"). Victoria Glendinning, *Jonathan Swift* (London: Hutchinson, 1998), 164; Marjorie W. Buckley, "Key to the Language of the Houyhnhnms in *Gulliver's Travels,*" in *Fair Liberty Was All His Cry: A Tercentenary Tribute to Jonathan Swift, 1667–1745,* ed. A. Norman Jeffares (London: Macmillan, 1967), 270. Finally, it has been suggested that Swift, the mocker of humankind, hoped to lure interpreters into finding false meanings in his words and to trap them into erroneous readings of *Gulliver's Travels.* Deborah Baker Wyrick, *Jonathan Swift and the Vested Word* (Chapel Hill: University of North Carolina Press, 1988), 180.

Introduction

1. Richard Reeves, *What the People Know: Freedom and the Press* (Cambridge, Mass.: Harvard University Press, 1998), 103.

2. Quoted in John C. Merrill, *Existential Journalism* (Ames: Iowa State University Press, 1996), 39.

3. Ibid., 51.

4. Gregor T. Goethals, *The TV Ritual: Worship at the Video Altar* (Boston: Beacon, 1981), 137.

5. George Gallup Jr. and D. Michael Lindsay, *Surveying the Religious Landscape: Trends in U.S. Beliefs* (Harrisburg, Pa.: Morehouse, 1999), 13, 15, 25.

6. George Gallup Jr. and Jim Castelli, *The People's Religion: American Faith in the 90's* (New York: Macmillan, 1989), 47.

7. William F. Fore, *Mythmakers: Gospel, Culture, and the Media* (New York: Friendship, 1990), 137.

8. Quoted in "The Erosion of Values," *Columbia Journalism Review,* March–April 1998, 45.

9. Stephen J. Whitfield, "The Jewish Contribution to American Journalism," in *Media and Religion in American History,* ed. William David Sloan (Northport, Ala.: Vision, 2000), 166–85.

10. Although the term *Old Testament* has fallen out of favor in some circles, one most be careful that, in abandoning it, important historical and theological context is not lost. When I refer to the Hebrew scriptures, I mean the material taken from Jewish tradition that is incorporated into the Bible by Christians (recognizing that the inclusion is disputed by Catholics, Protestants, and Jews). At the same time, I also refer throughout the book to the New Testament of the Bible. One can, of course, decide to refer to Christian scriptures instead of the New Testament, but the term *Christian scriptures* would, in effect, need to refer to both sections of the Bible since they are linked in such an important fashion and are both central to Christian belief. However, since Christians use the term *New Testament,* but Jews do not refer to the *Old Testament,* it makes some sense to retain the former while dropping the latter.

11. The term *Judeo-Christian* is a tricky one because there is nothing that can be called "Judeo-Christianity" in the historical or theological sense. Christians draw on the Hebrew scriptures as an important basis of their beliefs, but not in the same ways that the followers of Judaism do. Jews recognize the shared elements of their faith and their moral teachings with Christianity, but most do not accept the Christian notion of Jesus as the messiah, and the New Testament is not a part of Jewish worship. The concept of Judeo-Christian is valuable, however, because it acknowledges in the broadest cultural sense the ways that Jewish tradition—both separately and in the way it has influenced Christianity—has helped shape American life, as well as providing a more inclusive basis for describing the socioreligious heritage of a nation that is portrayed too often in narrowly Christian terms.

12. Harold Innis, *Empire and Communications* (1950; reprint, Toronto: University of Toronto Press, 1972); Harold Innis, *The Bias of Communication* (1951; reprint, Toronto: University of Toronto Press, 1991).

13. Daniel J. Czitrom, *Media and the American Mind: From Morse to McLuhan* (1982; reprint, Chapel Hill: University of North Carolina Press, 1983), 174–75. See also W. Terrence Gordon, *Marshall McLuhan: Escape into Understanding* (New York: Basic, 1997), 27, 55, 75, 132; Donald Creighton, *Harold Adams Innis: Portrait of a Scholar* (Toronto: University of Toronto Press, 1957), 39–40, 72; and Derrick de Kerckhove, "The New Psychotechnologies," in *Com-*

munication in History: Technology, Culture, Society, ed. David Crowley and Paul Heyer (1991; reprint, White Plains, N.Y.: Longman, 1995), 329–34.

14. Thomas E. Boomershine, "Jesus of Nazareth and the Watershed of Ancient Orality and Literacy," in *Semeia 65: Orality and Textuality in Early Christian Literature,* ed. Joanna Dewey (Atlanta: Scholars Press, 1995), 7–36.

15. Joanna Dewey, "Textuality in an Oral Culture: A Survey of the Pauline Traditions," in *Semeia,* ed. Dewey, 37–65.

16. Walter J. Ong, *The Presence of the Word: Some Prolegomena for Cultural and Religious History* (1967; reprint, Minneapolis: University of Minnesota Press, 1986).

17. Jürgen Habermas, *The Structural Transformation of the Public Sphere,* trans. Thomas Burger, with the assistance of Frederick Lawrence (1989; reprint, Cambridge, Mass.: MIT Press, 1999).

18. James W. Carey, *Communication as Culture: Essays on Media and Society* (Boston: Unwin Hyman, 1989), 165.

19. One reason that I favor Innis over Habermas is that I contend religious impulses and spiritual factors play a major role in the operation of the mass media, whether journalists recognize it or not. However, it is doubtful Habermas would see religion or religious discussion as having a large role in his idealization of the public sphere, given the fading role he sees religious institutions playing in eighteenth-century Europe. Habermas contended that religion has become a largely "private matter" since the Protestant Reformation broke the Catholic church's hold on European learning (Habermas, *The Structural Transformation of the Public Sphere,* 11). Habermas tended to view religion as part of the authoritarian structure that the members of the eighteenth-century "public sphere" were gathering to oppose or supplant in their coffeehouse get-togethers and early newspaper publications. Although his references were oblique, he discussed religion mostly in negative terms (Ibid., 8). Also Habermas, as one might expect of a neo-Marxist, was most interested in the clash of politics, economics, and broader social forces and consigned religion to a backdrop role (Ibid., 68).

20. Rudolf Bultmann, *Jesus and the Word* (1934; reprint, New York: Scribner's, 1958); William E. Hordern, *A Layman's Guide to Protestant Theology* (1955; reprint, New York: Collier, 1986), 191–209.

21. There are signs that the gap between the religiosity of Americans and other Western journalists holds true for Canadian versus American journalists, but the gap is much narrower. For example, in our study, a key measure of journalists' religious orientation (with 1 the lowest and 5 the highest) showed American journalists at 4.0 compared with Canadian journalists at 3.5. In addition, 60 percent of the American journalists who responded to our survey were members of a church, compared with 46 percent of Canadian journalists.

Chapter 1: Prophetic Journalism

1. Mitchell Stephens, *A History of News: From the Drum to the Satellite* (New York: Viking, 1988), 86–90, 133.

2. John Milton, *Areopagitica* (1644; reprint, Santa Barbara, Calif.: Bandanna, 1992).

3. Cecil W. Sharman, *George Fox and the Quakers* (London: Quaker Home Service, 1991), 49.

4. William C. Braithwaite, *The Beginnings of Quakerism to 1660* (1912; reprint, York, England: William Sessions, 1981), 181; George Fox, *Journal of George Fox,* ed. John L. Nickalls (London: Religious Society of Friends, 1986), 201 (quote).

5. Braithwaite, *The Beginnings of Quakerism,* 107–9, 172, 281, 444–45.

6. H. Larry Ingle, *First among Friends: George Fox and the Creation of Quakerism* (New York: Oxford University Press, 1994), 121.

7. Quoted in Sharman, *George Fox and the Quakers,* 123.

8. Douglas Gwyn, *Apocalypse of the Word: The Life and Message of George Fox, 1624–1691* (1986; reprint, Richmond, Ind.: Friends United, 1991), 126–35. One can view Jesus and his ministry in the tradition of the Hebrew prophets, but when I use the term *prophet,* I am referring to the prophets (Isaiah, Jeremiah, Ezekiel, Amos, etc.) whose names give title to the chapters of Hebrew scripture incorporated into the Bible.

9. Ingle, *First among Friends,* 69, 107. See also George Fox, *The Works of George Fox,* ed. T. H. S. Wallace (1831; reprint, State College, Pa.: New Foundation Publications, 1990).

10. Fox, *Journal,* 11.

11. Jeremiah 31:31–34, in the Hebrew scriptures of *The Holy Bible,* New Revised Standard Version (Iowa Falls, Iowa: World Bible Publishers, 1989), 755.

12. Horace Greeley, *Recollections of a Busy Life* (New York: J. B. Ford, 1869), 523.

13. Quoted in Leonard Downie Jr., *The New Muckrakers* (New York: Mentor, 1976), 201.

14. Ibid., 58.

15. Lincoln Steffens, *The Autobiography of Lincoln Steffens* (New York: Harcourt, Brace, 1931), 357. James S. Ettema and Theodore L. Glasser have also noted the connection between investigative reporting and the prophetic tradition—they call it "the voice of Jeremiah"—in urging modern journalists to acknowledge more openly the moral mission in their work. James S. Ettema and Theodore L. Glasser, *Custodians of Conscience: Investigative Journalism and Public Virtue* (New York: Columbia University Press, 1998), 126 (quote), 201.

16. Finley Peter Dunne, *Observations by Mr. Dooley* (New York: Harper, 1906), 239.

17. Quoted in Downie, *The New Muckrakers,* 197 ("cheerfully angry" quote), 204 ("permanent sense of outrage" quote), 204–5 ("black and whites" quote).

18. Quoted in Judith M. Buddenbaum, "'Judge . . . What Their Acts Will Justify': The Religious Journalism of James Gordon Bennett," *Journalism History* 14 (Summer–Autumn 1987): 61.

19. Quoted in Frank Luther Mott, *American Journalism: A History of Newspapers in the United States through 260 Years, 1690 to 1950* (New York: Macmillan, 1950), 232–33.

20. Herbert J. Gans, *Deciding What's News: A Study of CBS Evening News, NBC Nightly News, Newsweek, and Time* (New York: Vintage, 1980), 204.

21. Richard Hofstadter, *The Age of Reform: From Bryan to F.D.R.* (New York: Vintage, 1955), 186.

22. Downie, *The New Muckrakers,* 8.

23. Jack Anderson with James Boyd, *Confessions of a Muckraker: The Inside Story of Life in Washington during the Truman, Eisenhower, Kennedy, and Johnson Years* (New York: Ballantine, 1980), 13.

24. Maxwell Geismar, ed., *Mark Twain and the Three R's: Race, Religion, Revolution—and Related Matters* (New York: Bobbs-Merrill, 1973), 155.

25. Quoted in Buddenbaum, "'Judge . . . What Their Acts Will Justify,'" 60.

26. Quoted in W. A. Swanberg, *Pulitzer* (New York: Scribner's, 1967), 139 ("renegade Jew" quote), 140 ("Judas Pulitzer" quote), 141 ("His face" quote).

27. See the chapter "Mystics, Prophets, Rhetorics: Religion and Psychoanalysis," in David Tracy, *Dialogue with the Other: The Inter-Religious Dialogue* (Grand Rapids, Mich.: Eerdmans, 1990), 9–26; and Kay Redfield Jamison, *Touched with Fire: Manic-Depressive Illness and the Artistic Temperament* (New York: Free Press, 1994), 18, 109, 113, appendix B. The list of jour-

nalist-literary figures who battled depression or nervous disorders includes not only Twain, Whitman, and Dreiser but also Samuel Johnson, James Boswell, William Dean Howells, Stephen Crane, Jack London, Ring Lardner, Sherwood Anderson, Ernest Hemingway, Sinclair Lewis, James Agee, Graham Greene, and Truman Capote, among others. To bring this analysis full circle, it should be noted that Fox, early journalist and religious proselytizer, also suffered from debilitating depressions and evidenced a manic-depressive personality; religious enthusiasm provided the counterbalance to his regular bouts of despair. Ingle, *First among Friends*, 48, 175, 229–31. See also Anthony Storr, *Solitude: A Return to the Self* (New York: Ballantine, 1988).

28. Theodore Dreiser, *A Book about Myself* (New York: Boni and Liveright, 1922), 468 ("attacked" quote), 470 ("undoubtedly semi-neurasthenic" and "immense" quotes).

29. S. Robert Lichter, Stanley Rothman, and Linda S. Lichter, *The Media Elite: America's New Powerbrokers* (Bethesda, Md.: Adler and Adler, 1986), 20–53, 71–92, 104, 114, 119–20, 127, 131.

30. Justin Kaplan, *Lincoln Steffens: A Biography* (New York: Simon and Schuster, 1974), 278–79 ("muckraking himself" quote), 280 ("black moods" and "hopelessness" quotes).

31. Quoted in Downie, *The New Muckrakers*, 83.

32. Quoted in Elizabeth L. Eisenstein, *The Printing Revolution in Early Modern Europe* (1983; reprint, Cambridge: Cambridge University Press, 1992), 148 (Foxe quote), 154 (Defoe quote).

33. Quoted in George Perkins, Barbara Perkins, and Phillip Leininger, *Benét's Reader's Encyclopedia of American Literature* (New York: HarperCollins, 1987), 822.

34. Quoted in J. Herbert Altschull, *From Milton to McLuhan: The Ideas behind American Journalism* (New York: Longman, 1990), 107.

35. Michael Schudson, *Discovering the News: A Social History of American Newspapers* (New York: Basic, 1978), 98.

36. Mott, *American Journalism*, 382–84.

37. Quoted in Kaplan, *Lincoln Steffens*, 119–20.

38. James Woodress, *Willa Cather: A Literary Life* (1987; reprint, Lincoln: University of Nebraska Press, 1989), 185–86.

39. Kaplan, *Lincoln Steffens*, 119.

40. Marshall McLuhan, *Understanding Media: The Extensions of Man* (New York: Mentor, 1964), 36–45.

41. Although the new breed of television "shout" shows featuring round-table political discussions and audience participation has featured "hot" personalities with intense, aggressive styles, these shows—most of which appear on cable—have relatively small followings. It is not possible to name a "hot" personality on television who has achieved widespread fame and following among the general television viewing audience.

42. Joshua Meyrowitz, *No Sense of Place: The Impact of Electronic Media on Social Behavior* (1985; reprint, New York: Oxford University Press, 1986), 268–304, 307–13.

43. McLuhan, *Understanding Media*, 70 ("message of cultural and technological challenge" quote), 71 ("artists," "prophetic," "next technology," and "counter-irritant" quotes), 72 ("numb us" quote), 75 ("endless power" and "hypnotize themselves" quotes).

Chapter 2: The Profits of Reform

1. Eisenstein, *The Printing Revolution*, 149. It is estimated that between 1517 and 1519, Luther's thirty publications sold well over 300,000 copies, making Lutheranism "the first child of the printed book." Quoted in ibid, 145.

2. Quoted in ibid., 148.

3. Quoted in Kemper Fullerton, "Calvinism and Capitalism: An Explanation of the Weber Thesis," in *Protestantism and Capitalism: The Weber Thesis and Its Critics*, ed. Robert W. Green (1959; reprint, Boston: Heath, 1965), 7.

4. David Freeman Hawke, *Franklin* (New York: Harper and Row, 1976), 41, 81.

5. Eisenstein, *The Printing Revolution*, 18–19 (quotes on Fust), 150 ("concern about salvation" quote), 167 ("spiritual aspirations" quote).

6. Quoted in ibid., 147.

7. R. H. Tawney, *Religion and the Rise of Capitalism* (1926; reprint, New York: Mentor, 1954), 80.

8. Quoted in Eisenstein, *The Printing Revolution*, 167.

9. Ibid., 153; Tawney, *Religion and the Rise of Capitalism*, 34, 38–39.

10. Quoted in Tawney, *Religion and the Rise of Capitalism*, 89.

11. Ibid., 235.

12. Quoted in Mott, *American Journalism*, 233.

13. Ibid.

14. Quoted in Swanberg, *Pulitzer*, 99.

15. Mott, *American Journalism*, 269–71.

16. Dreiser, *A Book about Myself*, 469 ("veritable hell" and "vaulting ambition" quotes), 478–79 ("elevating discourses" and "pecksniffery" quotes).

17. Will Irwin's series, published in *Collier's* in 1911, is reprinted in *The American Newspaper*, ed. Clifford F. Weigle and David G. Clark (Ames: Iowa State University Press, 1969).

18. W. A. Swanberg, *Citizen Hearst* (1961; reprint, New York: Macmillan, 1986), 625.

19. See Twain quote about this period in Geismar, *Mark Twain and the Three R's*, 103.

20. Alexis de Tocqueville, *Democracy in America*, 2 vols., trans. Henry Reeve (1840; reprint, New York: Knopf, 1960), 1:111–14.

21. Mott, *American Journalism*, 395.

22. Schudson, *Discovering the News*, 31–35.

23. Al Neuharth, *Confessions of an S.O.B.* (New York: Doubleday, 1989), 71–83, 154–68, 183–93.

24. Peter Prichard, *The Making of McPaper: The Inside Story of USA Today* (Kansas City, Mo.: Andrews, McMeel, and Parker, 1987), 287–89.

25. Quoted in Shepherd, "The Media Get Religion," 19–20.

26. Quoted in Leonard Grossman, *The Electronic Republic: Reshaping American Democracy in the Information Age* (New York: Viking, 1995), 147.

27. Daniel J. Boorstin, *Democracy and Its Discontents: Reflections on Everyday America* (New York: Random House, 1974), 12–21.

28. George Seldes, *Lords of the Press* (New York: Julian Messner, 1938).

29. Altschull, *From Milton to McLuhan*, 215.

30. Eisenstein, *The Printing Revolution*, 93.

31. Gans, *Deciding What's News*, 246–47. This does not mean that corporations do not support socially worthwhile programs and engage in charitable activities. Most corporations subscribe to the ethic of serving as "good corporate citizens," and this is certainly true of many major media organizations. However, one would be hard-pressed to find an American media company or a corporate media executive (with the possible exception of Ted Turner) identified with putting worthy causes above the bottom-line goals of the company.

32. Fore, *Mythmakers*, 19, 21, 41–43, 55, 81 (quotes), 85–89.

33. Doug Underwood, "It's Not Just in L.A.," *Columbia Journalism Review,* January–February 1998, 24–26; Charles Rappleye, "Cracking the Church State Wall," ibid., January–February 1998, 20–23; William Woo, "Why Willes Is Wrong," ibid., January–February, 1988, 27.

34. Michael Fancher, "The Metamorphosis of the Newspaper Editor," *Gannett Center Journal* 1 (Spring 1987): 73, 80.

35. Les Brown, *Television: The Business behind the Box* (New York: Harvest, 1971), 15–16.

36. Jack Miles, "Prime Time's Search for God," *TV Guide,* March 29–April 4, 1997, 26.

Chapter 3: *Skeptics of Faith or Faith in Skepticism?*

1. Quoted in James Boswell, *The Life of Samuel Johnson,* ed. Frank Brady (1791; reprint, New York: Signet, 1968), 169.

2. W. Jackson Bate, *Samuel Johnson* (1975; reprint, New York: Harcourt Brace Jovanovich, 1979), 316; John Wain, *Samuel Johnson* (New York: Viking, 1974), 198–99.

3. Quoted in Boswell, *The Life of Samuel Johnson,* 7.

4. Altschull, *From Milton to McLuhan,* 77.

5. Boswell, *The Life of Samuel Johnson,* 132, 156.

6. Clifford G. Christians, John P. Ferré, and P. Mark Fackler, *Good News: Social Ethics and the Press* (New York: Oxford University Press, 1993), 18–48.

7. This, they say, has left journalists with a "bankrupt" epistemology and an "empty handed . . . intellectual treasury" in our "postliberal age." Ibid., 44.

8. See, for example, Altschull, *From Milton to McLuhan;* Calhoun Winton, *Sir Richard Steele, M.P.: The Later Career* (Baltimore: Johns Hopkins University Press, 1970), 13–14; and Robert M. Otten, *Joseph Addison* (Boston: Twayne, 1982), 109.

9. Altschull, *From Milton to McLuhan,* 36–37.

10. Quoted in ibid., 40–41.

11. Quoted in ibid., 82.

12. It is often assumed that the separation clause in the U.S. Constitution grew out of a fundamental Enlightenment principle about the separation of church and state, but the clause actually had a more pragmatic origin: colonies that had tried to maintain a version of a state church (most notably Massachusetts and Virginia) found it impossible to maintain such an institution because of the diversity of religious groups migrating to their territory. By the time the First Amendment was drafted, this circumstance—combined with a general Enlightenment antipathy toward religious authority and many colonists' negative experiences with religious persecution in Europe—led to the practical solution of allowing people of all religious beliefs to worship without having to deal with a state church.

13. Habermas, *The Structural Transformation of the Public Sphere,* 59–61.

14. Ibid., 141–235.

15. This may not be what Habermas had in mind when he viewed this period as the loftiest expression of the "public sphere," nor can we assume that he would want modern journalists to be impressed by the way their counterparts of that era mixed their editorial writing with their personal ambition, their social climbing, their involvement in government service, and their promotion of religious and political policy. Jonathan Swift, for example, was at the center of a press management campaign by Tory leaders, and his journalism has been described as propaganda that, while it pretended to be dispassionate and nonpartisan, always was designed to convince the public of the Tory cause. Richard Steele, coeditor of the *Spectator* and the *Tatler,* lived off party patronage, serving as commissioner of the Stamp

Office and in a series of other government posts; his colleague Joseph Addison interspersed journalism with a number of political jobs. Johnson, while working as a newspaper editor, also took on the responsibility of "recording" the debates of Parliament, even though he was almost never in the gallery of the House of Commons and composed them from information provided by assistants. For twenty years, the speeches were universally regarded as authentic until Johnson took credit for a famous speech by William Pitt, which Johnson told friends that he had penned on his own. Habermas, *The Structural Transformation of the Public Sphere,* 8–9, 11–12, 68; Richard West, *Daniel Defoe: The Life and Strange, Surprising Adventures* (1998; reprint, New York: Carroll and Graf, 2000), 66–117, 140–51, 165, 195–97, 202–3, 214, 219; Bate, *Samuel Johnson,* 203–5; Glendinning, *Jonathan Swift,* 79, 101–2, 105, 111.

16. Quoted in Chester F. Chapin, *The Religious Thought of Samuel Johnson* (Ann Arbor: University of Michigan Press, 1968), 98.

17. Altschull, *From Milton to McLuhan,* 59.

18. Quoted in Chapin, *The Religious Thought of Samuel Johnson,* 86–87.

19. Ernest Campbell Mossner, *The Life of David Hume* (1954; reprint, Oxford: Oxford University Press, 1980), 393–94; Boswell, *The Life of Samuel Johnson,* 156, 216, 397–98 (quote).

20. Quoted in Chapin, *The Religious Thought of Samuel Johnson,* 21–22.

21. Mossner, *The Life of David Hume,* 306; Carl L. Becker, *The Heavenly City of the Eighteenth-Century Philosophers* (1932; reprint, New Haven, Conn.: Yale University Press, 1966), 38–39.

22. Boswell, *The Life of Samuel Johnson,* 132, 136–37 (quote), 156.

23. Chapin, *The Religious Thought of Samuel Johnson,* 82.

24. Quoted in Boswell, *The Life of Samuel Johnson,* 156.

25. Peter Smithers, *The Life of Joseph Addison* (1954; reprint, Oxford: Oxford University Press, 1968), 439–40; Otten, *Joseph Addison,* 9 (quote).

26. Quoted in Smithers, *The Life of Joseph Addison,* 440–41.

27. Quoted in Mott, *American Journalism,* 17 (first quote), 19 (second quote).

28. Benjamin Franklin, "The Runaway Apprentice" (from Franklin's *Autobiography*), in *The Harper American Literature,* ed. Donald McQuade, Robert Atwan, Martha Banta, Justin Kaplan, David Minter, Cecelia Tichi, and Helen Vendler (New York: Harper and Row, 1987), 166.

29. Altschull, *From Milton to McLuhan,* 107.

30. Alfred Owen Aldridge, *Benjamin Franklin and Nature's God* (Durham, N.C.: Duke University Press, 1967), 8.

31. Ibid., 8–10, 45 (quote), 83–89, 252, 269.

32. Quoted in Edwin S. Gaustad, *Sworn on the Altar of God: A Religious Biography of Thomas Jefferson* (Grand Rapids, Mich.: Eerdmans, 1996), 131.

33. Richard E. Amacher, *Benjamin Franklin* (New York: Twayne, 1962), 154–55.

34. W. E. Woodward, *Tom Paine: America's Godfather, 1737–1809* (New York: Dutton, 1945), 336–40; Howard Fast, *Citizen Tom Paine* (1943; reprint, New York: Bantam, 1964), 244–45; Peter Brock, *Pioneers of the Peaceable Kingdom* (1968; reprint, Princeton, N.J.: Princeton University Press, 1970), 148.

35. Voltaire was a deeply searching individual who, like many religious skeptics, was consumed with the questions of religion and believed that Christianity's shortcomings came about because it did not live up to its own ideals. That Voltaire was unpredictable in the expression of his religious sentiments is hardly a surprise; his confounding statements often were thrown out with a mischievous disregard for intellectual consistency and a deep pleasure in baffling both his critics and his admirers. But Voltaire's love of natural religion was a

serious business to him, and he seldom joked about his fundamental religiosity. "We condemn atheism, we detest barbarous superstition, we love God and the human race: that is our dogma," he once wrote. Quoted in Kathleen O'Flaherty, *Voltaire: Myth and Reality* (Cork, Ireland: Cork University Press, 1945), 97–148 (quote on 100).

36. Becker, *The Heavenly City*, 30–31.

37. Altschull, *From Milton to McLuhan*, 79–80.

38. Becker, *The Heavenly City*, 36–37.

Chapter 4: Mystics, Idealists, and Utopians

1. Quoted in Altschull, *From Milton to McLuhan*, 194.

2. William F. Thrall, Addison Hibbard, and C. Hugh Holman, *A Handbook to Literature* (1936; reprint, New York: Odyssey, 1960), 425–27.

3. Mott, *American Journalism*, 372.

4. Perkins, Perkins, and Leininger, *Benét's Reader's Encyclopedia*, 305–6.

5. Greeley, *Recollections of a Busy Life*, 68–74 (quote on 71).

6. Glyndon G. Van Deusen, *Horace Greeley: Nineteenth-Century Crusader* (Philadelphia: University of Pennsylvania Press, 1953), 412 ("defamation" quote), 416 ("New Dawn," "New Departure," "dream" quotes), 420–24.

7. Quoted in Henry Luther Stoddard, *Horace Greeley: Printer, Editor, Crusader* (New York: Putnam's, 1946), 325.

8. Van Deusen, *Horace Greeley*, 27.

9. Quoted in John Tebbel and Sarah Miles Watts, *The Press and the Presidency: From George Washington to Ronald Reagan* (New York: Oxford University Press, 1985), 149.

10. Altschull, *From Milton to McLuhan*, 194.

11. Philip Callow, *Walt Whitman: From Noon to Starry Night* (London: Allison and Busby, 1992), 5 (quote), 17, 103, 110; Walt Whitman, *Leaves of Grass* (1892; New York: Bantam, 1990); Justin Kaplan, *Walt Whitman: A Life* (New York: Simon and Schuster, 1980); Shelley Fisher Fishkin, *From Fact to Fiction: Journalism and Imaginative Writing in America* (Baltimore: Johns Hopkins University Press, 1985).

12. Quoted in John A. Pollard, *John Greenleaf Whittier: Friend of Man* (1949; reprint, [Hamden, Conn.]: Archon, 1969), 470; Jessamyn West, ed., *The Quaker Reader* (1962; reprint, Wallingford, Pa.: Pendle Hill, 1992), 332–43.

13. Charles H. Brown, *William Cullen Bryant* (New York: Scribner's, 1971), 398.

14. Quoted in Callow, *Walt Whitman*, 187.

15. Pollard, *John Greenleaf Whittier*, 78, 119, 166, 318–20 (quotes on 320).

16. Robert B. Sargent, "Anglo-American Encounter: William Cullen Bryant, Dickens, and Others," in *William Cullen Bryant and His America: Centennial Conference Proceedings, 1878–1978*, ed. Stanley Brodwin and Michael D'Innocenzo (New York: AMS, 1983), 180.

17. Quoted in Michael D'Innocenzo, "William Cullen Bryant and the Newspapers of New York," in *William Cullen Bryant*, ed. Brodwin and D'Innocenzo, 40 ("bellyful" quote), 41 ("daily drag" quote), 44–45.

18. R. Rio-Jelliffe, "'Thanatopsis' and the Development of American Literature," in *William Cullen Bryant*, ed. Brodwin and D'Innocenzo, 144–45.

19. Thomas L. Brasher, *Whitman as Editor of the Brooklyn Daily Eagle* (Detroit: Wayne State University Press, 1970), 21–22.

20. Quoted in C. Brown, *William Cullen Bryant*, 325–26.

21. Quoted in Pollard, *John Greenleaf Whittier*, 385.

22. Quoted in Mott, *American Journalism*, 278.

23. Quoted in C. Brown, *William Cullen Bryant*, 4.

24. James Thurber, "The Secret Life of Walter Mitty," in *Vintage Thurber: A Collection in Two Volumes of the Best Writings and Drawings of James Thurber* (London: Hamish Hamilton, 1963), 27–30.

25. Quoted in Gerald Langford, *The Richard Harding Davis Years: A Biography of a Mother and Son* (New York: Holt, Rinehart and Winston, 1961), 101.

26. Mark Twain, *Life on the Mississippi*, in *The Unabridged Mark Twain*, 2 vols., ed. Lawrence Teacher, (Philadelphia: Running, 1979), 2:422.

27. Mark Twain, "Fenimore Cooper's Literary Offenses," in ibid., 1:1250.

28. For one of the wonderful satires in literature on the "dishonest" nature of journalism in the nineteenth century, see the opening chapter in William Dean Howells, *The Rise of Silas Lapham* (1885; reprint, New York: Penguin, 1986), 3–23. The mixture of cynicism, insincerity, and sycophancy of the reporter Bartley Hubbard as he interviews the paint merchant Lapham for his "Solid Men of Boston" series captures all the scorn that such authors as Howells and his friend Twain felt for the journalism they were forced to practice in their time.

29. Mark Twain, *The Adventures of Huckleberry Finn* (1884–85; reprint, New York: Laurel, 1971).

30. Jean Jacques Rousseau, *Jean Jacques Rousseau: His Educational Theories Selected from Émile, Julie and Other Writings*, ed. R. L. Archer (Woodbury, N.Y.: Barron's Educational Series, 1964); William Wordsworth, "Ode: Intimations of Immortality from Recollections of Early Childhood," in *The Prelude: Selected Poems and Sonnets*, ed. Carlos Baker (1800; reprint, New York: Holt, Rinehart and Winston, 1966), 152–58.

31. Richard Crowder, *Carl Sandburg* (New York: Twayne, 1964), 94.

32. Joseph Haas and Gene Lovitz, *Carl Sandburg: A Pictorial Biography* (New York: Putnam's, 1967), 85, 90, 93 (quote).

33. Hazel Durnell, *The America of Carl Sandburg* (Washington, D.C.: University Press of Washington, D.C., 1965), 67 ("spiritual essence" and "faith and hope" quotes), 68 (Peale quote and "mighty carillons" quote).

34. Quoted in Haas and Lovitz, *Carl Sandburg*, 92.

35. Ernest Hemingway, *The Sun Also Rises* (1926; reprint, New York: Collier, 1986), 245.

36. Geneviève Moreau, *The Restless Journey of James Agee* (New York: Morrow, 1977), 39–41, 49–51, 226–27.

37. Edward Wagenknecht, *John Greenleaf Whittier: A Portrait in Paradox* (New York: Oxford University Press, 1967), 101–2; Pollard, *John Greenleaf Whittier*, 77.

38. Gans, *Deciding What's News*, 42–52.

39. Greeley, *Recollections of a Busy Life*, 479 (first quote), 481 (second quote).

40. Ibid., 525–26.

41. Quoted in Downie, *The New Muckrakers*, 150.

Chapter 5: Muckraking the Nation's Conscience

1. Kaplan, *Lincoln Steffens*, 146.

2. Upton Sinclair, *The Autobiography of Upton Sinclair* (New York: Harcourt, Brace and World, 1962), 70.

3. Kaplan, *Lincoln Steffens*, 23.

4. The muckrakers saw the New Testament as filled with examples of Jesus or the apostles

"muckraking" the social, political, and religious institutions of their time: Jesus angry and upset at the money changers in the Temple (Mark 11:15–19, Matthew 21:12–13, Luke 19:45–48, John 2:13–22); Jesus warning of the difficulties of the rich in gaining eternal life (Luke 18:18–30, Matthew 19:16–30); Jesus weeping at the evil and corrupt condition of Jerusalem (Luke 19:41–44); Jesus exhorting his followers to be generous to the poor, the crippled, and the lame (Luke 14:12–14). "New Testament" or "New Covenant" of *The Holy Bible,* New Revised Standard Version, 20–22, 45, 73, 77–79, 88.

5. Leon Harris, *Upton Sinclair: American Rebel* (New York: Crowell, 1975), 170–71.

6. Quoted in Kaplan, *Lincoln Steffens,* 175.

7. Steffens, *Autobiography,* 526.

8. Quoted in Patrick F. Palermo, *Lincoln Steffens* (Boston: Twayne, 1978), 74. Many other muckrakers specifically mention Jesus as the model for their professional work and the source of their moral inspiration. During his editing career, S. S. McClure in letters marveled that "God was here as a man, and I can't get away from that" and declared, "God approves of our work." Ida Tarbell said she believed Christianity was simply the "best system" because it was based on "the brotherhood of man." Ray Stannard Baker felt that Christ had obtained a "unity with God" that he sought in his own life, and he believed that what the church needed were "Elijahs" willing to "imitate the life of Christ." Quoted in Bruce J. Evensen, "The Evangelical Origins of Muckraking," in *Media and Religion,* ed. Sloan, 190 (McClure quote), 192 (Tarbell quote), 195–96 (Baker quote).

9. Steffens, *Autobiography,* 525. The avowed purpose of muckraking, Kaplan wrote, was to "awaken [the] Christian conscience" and to "bring Israel out of the house of bondage and to cast out moneychangers and devils." The muckrakers, Kaplan continued, "yearned to find Christian solutions to social problems and believed in the practical utility of the Golden Rule," adding, "They and their political counterparts spoke with fine theological inexactitude of sin, guilt, redemption, conversion, adopted revivalist techniques and were often grossly overoptimistic." Kaplan, *Lincoln Steffens,* 118 (first three quotes), 119 ("They and their political counterparts" quote).

10. Kaplan, *Lincoln Steffens,* 118.

11. Steffens, *Autobiography,* 526 ("preached to Christians" quote), 688 ("recognize Christianity" quote).

12. Quoted in Harris, *Upton Sinclair,* 168–69. Sinclair went on to cite examples of priestly exploitation, fear, and ignorance among the Babylonians, Hebrews, Buddhists, Aztecs, and Christians, and he accused the churches of supporting slavery, subjugating women, and resisting all advances of science—all themes that have become popular critiques with those who would judge Christianity by the worst aspects of its history. Ibid., 169.

13. Kaplan, *Lincoln Steffens,* 22.

14. Sinclair, *Autobiography,* 31 (quote); Harris, *Upton Sinclair,* 11–12; Upton Sinclair, *The Profits of Religion: An Essay in Economic Interpretation* (New York: Vanguard, 1918), 92.

15. Peter Lyon, *Success Story: The Life and Times of S. S. McClure* (New York: Scribner's, 1963), 5. The sect in which McClure was reared was different from the denomination known today as the Church of the Brethren.

16. Kaplan, *Lincoln Steffens,* 118.

17. William Allen White, *The Autobiography of William Allen White* (Lawrence: University Press of Kansas, 1990), 54.

18. Ida M. Tarbell, *All in the Day's Work: An Autobiography* (1939; reprint, Boston: G. K. Hall, 1985), 16.

19. Kaplan, *Lincoln Steffens,* 117.

20. Evensen, "The Evangelical Origins of Muckracking," 188.

21. For an example of the evangelical Christian who mixed biblical conservatism with political progressivism, see Garry Wills's description of the "Great Commoner," William Jennings Bryan, in Garry Wills, *Under God: Religion and American Politics* (New York: Simon and Schuster, 1990), 99.

22. Jon Butler, *Awash in a Sea of Faith: Christianizing the American People* (Cambridge, Mass.: Harvard University Press, 1990), 165, 177, 221.

23. Quoted in Kaplan, *Lincoln Steffens*, 119.

24. White, *Autobiography*, 216.

25. Mary E. Tomkins, *Ida M. Tarbell* (New York: Twayne, 1974), 17 ("Puritan fist" quote), 23 ("Davidian slingshot" quote), 62 ("Joan of Arc" quote).

26. Palermo, *Lincoln Steffens*, 114; Will Irwin, *The Making of a Reporter* (New York: Putnam's, 1942), 152; Lincoln Steffens, *Moses in Red* (Philadelphia: Dorrance, 1926).

27. Tarbell, *All in the Day's Work*, 298.

28. White, *Autobiography*, 45–46, 216 ("have-nots" quote).

29. Ray Stannard Baker, *American Chronicle: The Autobiography of Ray Stannard Baker* (New York: Scribner's, 1945), 26–33; William T. Stead, *If Christ Came to Chicago* (Chicago: Laird and Lee, 1894).

30. Sinclair, *Autobiography*, 31.

31. Quoted in Harris, *Upton Sinclair*, 27. Mystical experiences were to recur throughout Sinclair's life, coming in "unexpected places, and at unpredictable times," he said. "You may call this force your own subconscious mind, or God, or the Cosmic Consciousness, I care not what fancy name you give; the point is that it is there, and always there." Quoted in ibid., 28; W. A. Swanberg, *Dreiser* (New York: Scribner's, 1965), 460.

32. Quoted in Harris, *Upton Sinclair*, 28 ("force" quote), 225 ("dogmatic" and "universe" quotes).

33. Kaplan, *Lincoln Steffens*, 25.

34. Tomkins, *Ida M. Tarbell*, 20 (quote); Kathleen Brady, *Ida Tarbell: Portrait of a Muckraker* (New York: Seaview/Putman, 1984), 19–20.

35. Baker, *American Chronicle*, 57.

36. White, *Autobiography*, xvi, 167 (quote).

37. Quoted in Harris, *Upton Sinclair*, 106.

38. Baker, *American Chronicle*, 57 ("deep down," "essential truth," and "serpent" quotes), 58 ("safe harbor," "insidious temptation," and "ready to unite" quotes). Baker's interest in the "new" religions of his time can be found in his book *The Spiritual Unrest* (New York: Frederick A. Stokes, 1910).

39. James 2:17 and Romans 3:28, "New Testament," 146, 220.

40. Sinclair, *Autobiography*, 31 ("fairy tale" quote), 32 ("agnostic" quote).

41. Quoted in Irwin, *The Making of a Reporter*, 151–52.

42. Baker, *American Chronicle*, 32.

43. Ibid., 366–67.

44. Tarbell, *All in the Day's Work*, 346, 358 (quote).

45. Quoted in Harris, *Upton Sinclair*, 158.

46. Quoted in Lyon, *Success Story*, 389.

47. Ibid.

48. Ibid., 390 ("magazine" quote), 400–401 ("Bowled over," "civilization," and "problem of democracy" quotes).

Chapter 6: Mencken, Monkeys, and Modernity

1. Dreiser, *A Book about Myself*, 69 ("hard, gallant adventurers," "finally liberated," "moralistic and religionistic qualms," and "fixed moral order" quotes), 70 ("life as fierce" quote).

2. Theodore Dreiser, *Sister Carrie* (1900; reprint, New York: Signet, 1961).

3. Dreiser, *A Book about Myself*, 457 ("lingering filaments" quote); Swanberg, *Dreiser*, 60 ("Spencer" quote).

4. Theodore Dreiser, *The Bulwark* (New York: Doubleday, 1946); Swanberg, *Dreiser*, 459–60 (quote on 460).

5. Swanberg, *Dreiser*, 460, 493, 502, 518.

6. Ibid., 459–60 ("quest" quote), 460 (Mencken quote).

7. Richard O'Connor, *Bret Harte: A Biography* (Boston: Little, Brown, 1966), 13–14.

8. H. L. Mencken, *A Mencken Chrestomathy* (1949; reprint, New York: Vintage, 1982), 493.

9. Justin Kaplan, *Mr. Clemens and Mark Twain: A Biography* (New York: Simon and Schuster, 1966), 14 ("stock in trade" quote), 39–56 ("vagabonds," "Christ walked," "withering," and "Second Advent" quotes on 54), 70 ("son of the devil" quote), 119 ("Noah's Ark" quote), 377–78 ("burned at the stake" quote).

10. Twain, *Huckleberry Finn*; Mark Twain, *The Mysterious Stranger* (1916; reprint, Berkeley: University of California Press, 1982); Mark Twain, *Letters from the Earth*, ed. Bernard DeVoto (1962; reprint, New York: Perennial, 1974). Twain's dark musings in *Letters from the Earth* were not published until more than fifty years after his death, when the death of his daughter removed the last obstacle to their publication.

11. Edwin H. Cady, *The Road to Realism: The Early Years, 1837–1885, of William Dean Howells* (Syracuse, N.Y.: Syracuse University Press, 1956), 57, 148–51 ("soft" quote on 149 and "often trust" quote on 151).

12. Andrew Sinclair, *Jack: A Biography of Jack London* (1977; reprint, New York: Pocket, 1979), 32–33, 84, 98, 113, 134, 170, 177.

13. Franklin Walker, *Frank Norris: A Biography* (1932; reprint, New York: Russell and Russell, 1963), 15, 37–40, 84–85, 262–63.

14. Quoted in R. W. Stallman, *Stephen Crane: A Biography* (New York: Braziller, 1968), 5.

15. Stephen Crane, "The Open Boat," in *The Harper American Literature*, ed. McQuade et al., 1439–55 ("throw bricks" quote on 1450 and "indifferent" quote on 1452).

16. Wills, *Under God*, 109.

17. Mencken, *A Mencken Chrestomathy*, 67.

18. Wills, *Under God*, 99–107.

19. Walter Lippmann, *Public Opinion* (1922; reprint, New York: Free Press, 1965), 53–100.

20. Quoted in Edward J. Larson, *Summer for the Gods: The Scopes Trial and America's Continuing Debate over Science and Religion* (New York: Basic Books, 1997), 94 ("serio-comedy," "humiliating proceeding," and "shame" quotes), 125, 256–57 ("glorious explosion" quote). It is worth noting that the slant of the movie is consistent with what conservative Christians claim was the press's tendency to stereotype fundamentalism—and its chief advocate, William Jennings Bryan—during the Scopes trial. Marvin Olasky cited numerous press accounts in many of the country's major newspapers that ridiculed biblical literalists and made fun of the anti-evolutionists at the Scopes trial. In particular, he claimed the portrayal of Bryan as "losing" the debate to Darrow was more a function of the press's bias than of Bryan's actual performance. "Most major newspaper reporters produced so much unobservant cover-

age that it often seemed as if they were watching the pictures in their head rather than the trial in front of them," Olasky wrote. Marvin Olasky, "Journalists and the Great Monkey Trial," in *Media and Religion*, ed. Sloan, 217–29 (quote on 226).

21. Mencken, *A Mencken Chrestomathy*, 79.

22. Ibid., 84–85.

23. Luke Timothy Johnson, *The Real Jesus: The Misguided Quest for the Historical Jesus and the Truth of the Traditional Gospels* (San Francisco: Harper Collins, 1996), 9–10.

24. Merrill, *Existential Journalism*, 8–9.

25. Albert Camus, *The Stranger*, trans. Stuart Gilbert (New York: Vintage, 1942), 153–54; Albert Camus, *The Plague*, trans. Stuart Gilbert (1948; reprint, New York: Vintage, 1991), 217–19.

26. Alba Amoia, *Albert Camus* (New York: Continuum, 1998), 28–31 (quote on 31).

27. Camus, *The Plague*, 292. Some modern journalists—with their conscious (or more often unconscious) embrace of existentialist life attitudes—might be surprised to learn that even existentialism is anchored in religious tradition. Existentialism's earliest propounder, Søren Kierkegaard, agonized over his commitment to Christianity and his quest to work out a relationship with God, and Christian existentialists, such as the theologians Paul Tillich and Dietrich Bonhoeffer, labored to reconcile the alienating conditions of the twentieth century with the embrace of a higher, if less precisely orthodox, level of spiritual faith. William Barrett, *Irrational Man: A Study in Existential Philosophy* (1958; reprint, Garden City, N.Y.: Doubleday Anchor, 1962), 149–76; Hordern, *A Layman's Guide to Protestant Theology*, 170–90, 210–29.

28. Carlos Baker, *Ernest Hemingway: A Life Story* (New York: Scribner's, 1969), 449.

29. Hemingway, *The Sun Also Rises*.

30. Ernest Hemingway, *The Old Man and the Sea* (New York: Scribner's, 1952); Ernest Hemingway, *For Whom the Bell Tolls* (New York: Scribner's, 1940).

31. A. Sinclair, *Jack*, 227–28.

32. James Agee, *A Death in the Family* (1957; reprint, New York: Bantam, 1969).

33. Willa Cather, *O Pioneers!* (1913; reprint, New York: Signet, 1989).

34. Graham Greene, *The Power and the Glory* (1940; reprint, New York: Bantam, 1954); Graham Greene, *The Heart of the Matter* (1948; reprint, New York: Viking, 1963); Graham Greene, *The End of the Affair* (1951; reprint, New York: Penguin, 1977); Michael Shelden, *Graham Greene: The Man Within* (London: Heinemann, 1994), 6 ("doubting convert" quote), 342–43 ("religion" and "religious" quotes).

35. Woodress, *Willa Cather*, 75, 242 (quote), 335, 337–38, 384, 406; Willa Cather, *Death Comes for the Archbishop* (1927; reprint, New York: Vintage, 1971).

36. Ronald Steel, *Walter Lippmann and the American Century* (Boston: Little, Brown, 1980), 5, 7, 589 (quote).

37. Walter Lippmann, *A Preface to Morals* (New York: Macmillan, 1929), 8 ("acids of modernity" quote), 12 ("irreligion of the modern world" quote), 320 ("simple customs" and "obediently follow" quotes), 326 ("dead notions" and "human personality" quotes).

38. Ibid., 31.

Chapter 7: Pragmatism and the "Facts" of Religious Experience

1. Quoted in Steel, *Walter Lippmann and the American Century*, 17–18 (quote on 18).

2. William James, *The Varieties of Religious Experience: A Study in Human Nature*, ed. Martin E. Marty (1902; reprint, New York: Penguin, 1987), 423–24.

3. Altschull, *From Milton to McLuhan*, 2.

4. Ibid., 225–26; William James, *Essays in Pragmatism*, ed. Alburey Castell (1948; reprint, New York: Hafner, 1966).

5. R. W. B. Lewis, *The Jameses: A Family Narrative* (1991, reprint, New York: Anchor, 1993), 441–43 (quote on 441). Hemingway's exposure to James is discussed in Michael Reynolds, *The Young Hemingway* (Oxford, England: Blackwell, 1986), 121–22.

6. Quoted in Henry Samuel Levinson, *The Religious Investigations of William James* (Chapel Hill: University of North Carolina Press, 1981), 9–10.

7. Sinclair, *Autobiography*, 132–33.

8. Steel, *Walter Lippmann and the American Century*, 18.

9. Lewis, *The Jameses*, 203.

10. James, *The Varieties of Religious Experience*, 472.

11. Quoted in Levinson, *The Religious Investigations*, 25.

12. James, *The Varieties of Religious Experience*, 19.

13. Quoted in Don C. Seitz, *The James Gordon Bennetts, Father and Son: Proprietors of the New York Herald* (Indianapolis: Bobbs-Merrill, 1928), 85.

14. James, *The Varieties of Religious Experience*, 20.

15. In our nationwide survey of journalists' religious attitudes, 87 percent agreed or strongly agreed with the passage from James 2:17: "Faith, by itself, if it is not accompanied by action is dead. . . . Show me your faith without deeds, and I will show you my faith by what I do." Only 4 percent disagreed or strongly disagreed with the passage, and 9 percent had no opinion.

16. James, *The Varieties of Religious Experience*, 454–55 ("perceptions of fact" quote), 457 ("religious sphere" quote).

17. Gerald E. Myers, *William James: His Life and Thought* (New Haven, Conn.: Yale University Press, 1986), 455.

18. James, *The Varieties of Religious Experience*, 516.

19. Ibid., 507 ("Does God really exist" quote), 517 ("God is real" quote), 519 ("divine facts" quote).

20. Quoted in Myers, *William James*, 452.

21. Ibid., 454. Or as another biographer put it, James never attempted to "define religion, but rather the life of religion." Gay Allen Wilson, *William James: A Biography* (New York: Viking, 1967), 432.

22. James, *The Varieties of Religious Experience*, 519.

23. Myers, *William James*, 462.

24. Ibid., 479.

Chapter 8: *Trusting Their Guts*

1. E. W. Scripps, *I Protest: Selected Disquisitions of E. W. Scripps*, ed. Oliver Knight (Madison: University of Wisconsin Press, 1966), 178.

2. Ibid., 186 ("teaching department" quote), 377 ("outside the pale" and "These men" quotes), 434 ("Christ taught" and "Christ's teachings" quotes), 731–32.

3. Robert N. Bellah, "Civil Religion in America," in *Religion in America*, ed. William G. McLoughlin and Robert N. Bellah (Boston: Houghton Mifflin, 1968), 3–23. See also the discussion of this issue by the *Los Angeles Times* journalist Stephen Burgard in his book *Hallowed Ground: Rediscovering Our Spiritual Roots* (New York: Insight, 1997), 52–53, 63–65.

4. Edmund B. Lambeth, *Committed Journalism: An Ethic for the Profession* (Bloomington: Indiana University Press, 1986), 27.

5. Jay Newman, *The Journalist in Plato's Cave* (London: Associated University Presses, 1989), 183 ("religious awakening" quote), 185 ("vaguely Christian world view" and "observer" quotes).

6. Warren Breed, "Social Control in the Newsroom: A Functional Analysis," *Social Forces* 33 (May 1955): 326–35.

7. Ted Curtis Smythe, "The Reporter, 1880–1900: Working Conditions and Their Influence on the News," *Journalism History* 7 (Spring 1980): 6 ("not fully developed" quote), 8 ("Editors praised" quote).

8. Dreiser, *A Book about Myself,* 70.

9. Scripps, *I Protest,* 377.

10. Hazel Dicken-Garcia, *Journalistic Standards in Nineteenth-Century America* (Madison: University of Wisconsin Press, 1989), 184–85.

11. Marion Tuttle Marzolf, *Civilizing Voices: American Press Criticism, 1880–1950* (New York: Longman, 1991), 27, 29, 128.

12. Dicken-Garcia, *Journalistic Standards,* 183–85, 217–19, 235.

13. Ibid., 219.

14. Marzolf, *Civilizing Voices,* 53.

15. Ibid., 50–51; Dicken-Garcia, *Journalistic Standards,* 233.

16. Clifford G. Christians and Catherine L. Covert, *Teaching Ethics in Journalism Education* (Hastings-on-Hudson, N.Y.: Hastings Center, 1980), 2.

17. Marzolf, *Civilizing Voices,* 64–70, 81, 113–14; Lippmann, *Public Opinion,* 226–30, 239–49.

18. Quoted in Altschull, *From Milton to McLuhan,* 283.

19. Marzolf, *Civilizing Voices,* 140–42. See also Seldes, *Lords of the Press.*

20. Carl Bernstein and Bob Woodward, *All the President's Men* (1974; reprint, New York: Touchstone, 1987), 15, 35–36, 120–22, 210; Katharine Graham, *Personal History* (New York: Knopf, 1997), 462; Ben Bradlee, *A Good Life: Newspapering and Other Adventures* (New York: Simon and Schuster, 1995), 326, 346.

21. James Boylan, "Newspeople," *Wilson Quarterly,* special issue (1982): 85.

22. Quoted in Tom Goldstein, *The News at Any Cost: How Journalists Compromise Their Ethics to Shape the News* (1985; reprint, New York: Touchstone, 1986), 132.

23. Quoted in Lambeth, *Committed Journalism,* 175–76.

24. Quoted in A. James Reichley, *Religion in American Public Life* (Washington, D.C.: Brookings Institution, 1985), 101.

25. Quoted in Aldridge, *Benjamin Franklin and Nature's God,* 129.

Chapter 9: "I Will Show You My Faith by What I Do"

1. Quoted in Alicia Shepherd, "Out of Control," *American Journalism Review,* October 1998, 22.

2. Quoted in John Dart and Jimmy Allen, *A First Amendment Guide to Religion and the News Media* (New York: Freedom Forum First Amendment Center, 1993), chap. 6:8.

3. Marvin Olasky, *Prodigal Press: The Anti-Christian Bias of the American News Media* (Wheaton, Ill.: Crossway Books, 1988), 71. Jay Rosen, the academic public journalism proponent, observed that it is "hard to deny" newsrooms are "citadels of secularism"—a commonly held view both within journalism and outside of it. Jay Rosen, *What Are Journalists For?* (New Haven, Conn.: Yale University Press, 1999), 27.

4. Lichter, Rothman, and Lichter, *The Media Elite,* 21–53. It should be noted that the 1986

study by Lichter, Rothman, and Lichter, which focused on journalists in the New York City and Washington, D.C., areas, has been criticized for drawing too broad conclusions from too narrow a sample of journalists. While some have speculated that journalists in those major media markets may be less religiously inclined, critics of Lichter, Rothman, and Lichter have noted that other surveys of journalists across the country indicate they do consider themselves to be religious. However, it is only fair to point out that conservatives, who often focus their criticism on the major media outlets in the East, have argued that the religious attitudes of those journalists are most important because they control the agenda of the organizations that distribute the news nationally.

While our study did not single out major East Coast news organizations, our data did indicate that journalists at large newspapers (over 100,000 circulation) tend to report slightly lower religious orientations than those at smaller newspapers, thus reinforcing the criticism that a study of only large news organizations could be expected to underestimate journalists' religiosity. Our survey showed journalists at large newspapers reported religion was less important to them than did those at smaller newspapers (3.68 compared with 3.95 on a scale of 5.00); fewer were church members (57 percent compared with 62 percent); and they reported slightly lower levels of church attendance.

5. Stewart M. Hoover, *Religion in the News: Faith and Journalism in American Public Discourse* (Thousands Oaks, Calif.: Sage, 1998), 56.

6. Dart and Allen, *A First Amendment Guide,* chap. 6:1–2.

7. David H. Weaver and G. Cleveland Wilhoit, *The American Journalist in the 1990s: U.S. News People at the End of an Era* (Mahwah, N.J.: Erlbaum, 1996), 13–15. Weaver and Wilhoit also found that 72 percent of the journalists surveyed said religion is very important or somewhat important to them.

8. Rothman surveys, cited in S. Robert Lichter, Linda S. Lichter, and David R. Amundson, *Media Coverage of Religion in America, 1969–1998* (Washington, D.C.: Center for Media and Public Affairs, 2000); April 18, 2001, press release on Pew Charitable Trust Website (<www.pewtrusts.com>). Search in religion program area/key words "Lichter" and "Amundson." The Rothman study was part of a Pew Charitable Trust–funded report that found, among other things, that religion news had doubled from the 1980s to the 1990s (with the greatest increases coming in coverage of "non-traditional" religions); that most religion news deals with political issues rather than matters of faith or spirituality; that churches and denominations made news most often when they were involved in public policy debates or authority conflicts; and that coverage of scandals involving churches and clerics tripled from the 1970s to the 1990s.

9. There also have been some nonquantitative, in-depth studies of journalists' faith. Two notable ones—both of which relied largely on personal and testimonial statements of religiously oriented journalists—were published by the Nieman Foundation at Harvard University and included examinations of the audience for religious news and summaries of studies on journalists' religiosity. See "God in the Newsroom," *Nieman Reports* 47 (Summer 1993): 3–54; and "The Faith of Journalists," ibid., 51 (Fall 1997): 5–49.

10. Ernest C. Hynds, "Large Daily Newspapers Have Improved Coverage of Religion," *Journalism Quarterly* 64 (Summer–Autumn 1987): 444–48; Hoover, *Religion in the News,* 55, 85. Although Hoover saw improvements, he listed some additional factors to explain the continued media resistance to better religion coverage, including the dominance of an irreligious and politically liberal "media elite"; the historic secularism of American education; the concern about the separation of religion from other constitutionally protected freedoms (such

as freedom of the press); the growing view of religion as a private activity; the press's traditional suspicion of established institutions (such as organized religion); and fear of controversy, complexity, and what cannot be empirically proved. For other analyses of changes and
improvements in religion coverage, see Judith Buddenbaum, *Reporting News about Religion:
An Introduction for Journalists* (Ames: Iowa State University Press, 1998); Judith Buddenbaum
and Stewart M. Hoover, "The Role of Religion in Public Attitudes toward Religion News,"
in *Religion and Mass Media: Audiences and Adaptations,* ed. Daniel A. Stout and Judith Buddenbaum (Thousand Oaks, Calif.: Sage, 1996), 136–37; and Eric Kevin Gormly, "The Study
of Religion and the Education of Journalists," *Journalism and Mass Communication Educator* 54 (Summer 1999): 24–39.

11. Mark Silk, *Unsecular Media: Making News of Religion in America* (Urbana: University
of Illinois Press, 1995), xi–xii, 141–51.

12. Bennett quoted in Buddenbaum, "'Judge . . . What Their Acts Will Justify,'" 61; E. W.
Scripps to Judge Ben B. Lindsey, Juvenile Court, Denver, Colo., January 4, 1912, Series 1, Sub-
series 1.2, box 14, folder 2, E. W. Scripps Correspondence, Ohio University Library.

13. The questionnaire was mailed to Canadian journalists for two reasons. First, Canadian journalists make up a portion of the membership of both the Investigative Reporters and
Editors organization and the Religion Newswriters Association. Second, the inclusion of journalists in Canada, which shares important elements of its press tradition and religious history with the United States, was seen as adding depth and breadth to the study by expanding
the focus to North American journalism in general.

14. A variety of factors may have held down the number of respondents: journalists may
consider the subject of their religious beliefs to be too personal; they may consider it unprofessional to reveal their beliefs; and they may be sensitive to the criticism they have received
from religious groups and do not want to reinforce impressions already held about them.
Because of the high response rate from the Religion Newswriters Association (48 percent),
we also speculated that journalists with an interest in religion were more prone to return
the questionnaire than those with less interest. To test this, as well as the potential bias in
the self-selection process among respondents, we telephoned a number of the nonrespond-
ing journalists to whom we had mailed questionnaires and asked if they would be willing
to answer a few questions. Among the 37 who agreed, we were able to deduce that they were
likely to say religion or spirituality was less important in their lives (a mean score of 2.75)
than were our survey respondents (a mean score of 3.96). From this, one might conclude
that the journalists who chose to return the questionnaire tended to be more religiously
oriented than those who did not and that this should be taken into account in drawing
any conclusions about journalists as a whole from those who responded to our survey. In
addition, 24 of the 27 initial nonresponders who answered the question indicated that they
did not consider it unprofessional to reveal publicly their religious beliefs, and 14 of the
initial nonrespondents said that they were simply too busy to fill out the questionnaire or
did not remember receiving it.

15. Hynds found that 78 percent of religion specialists at newspapers with at least 100,000
circulation indicated membership in a church; Buddenbaum reported in a survey of religion
reporters at both large and small newspapers that only 10 percent indicated no religious affiliation. Hynds, "Large Daily Newspapers Have Improved Coverage of Religion," 445; Judith
M. Buddenbaum, "The Religion Beat at Daily Newspapers," *Newspaper Research Journal* 9
(Summer 1988): 57–69.

16. Don Ranly, "How Religion Editors of Newspapers View Their Jobs and Religion," *Journalism Quarterly* 56 (Winter 1979): 844–49. We chose to do a factor analysis as the best method for grouping our respondents by sets of answers that gave us meaningful patterns for classifying their religious beliefs beyond what our initial conceptual framework would have anticipated. Our analysis identified thirty items that were used to place journalists into categories of religious views. Indexes were constructed from each of the factors by summing each respondent's scores over all the items loading on each factor and dividing by the number of items loading on that factor. Items with negative loadings were reverse scored. In the data analysis, the findings about investigative reporters, religion reporters, and other journalists were compared, and there were some statistically significant differences. For example, religion reporters were more "Christian" and "compassionate," while investigative and religion reporters were more "reform" oriented (see table 14). However, we concluded that the differences were not so great that they outweighed the benefits of using the broadest representation of journalists' religious values that our data provided. We therefore included items from all respondents when we performed a factor analysis. Still, it is important to keep in mind these small discrepancies, as well as the fact that the sample is not a scientific sampling of journalists in the United States and Canada, in part because the focus on investigative and religion reporters may have skewed the findings in their direction somewhat. For more details, see Doug Underwood and Keith Stamm, "Are Journalists Really Irreligious? A Multidimensional Analysis," *Journalism and Mass Communication Quarterly* (forthcoming).

17. A factor analysis also was conducted on these items using principal components extraction followed by varimax rotation. Thirteen items were identified as measures of journalists' support for "putting faith into action." The three types of journalists-in-action that we had anticipated in our conceptual framework—"faithful," "ambivalent," and "reform"—were identified in the factor analysis, plus a fourth dimension that we labeled "independent." In three of the four items (ambivalent, reform, and independent), the dimensions were statistically weak (i.e., low reliability, low number of factors). However, since the results of the factor analysis fit so closely with our conceptual model, we decided to keep all four factors for purposes of our analysis. In particular, we kept the "reform" category, even though it contained only two factors, because it was so central to our hypothesis and because the two quotes (Dunne and Pearson) so strongly reflect the journalistic reform mind-set. In retrospect, we wish we had included more reform-oriented questions in the survey to strengthen the validity of the findings.

18. Sixteen groups could potentially be distinguished by our cross-tabulation, but the low frequency of overlap of the Christian and compassionate dimensions with the secular and eclectic dimensions forced us to collapse them into two mixed types—Christian/secular/eclectic and compassionate/secular/eclectic. This left us with ten classes of religious values for our analysis: none; secular; eclectic; secular/eclectic; Christian/secular/eclectic; compassionate/secular/eclectic; Christian/compassionate; Christian/compassionate/secular; Christian/compassionate/eclectic; and Christian/compassionate/secular/eclectic. In reducing these ten dimensions to three, our analysis showed some similarities with Ranly's, which identified three types of religious editors ("ambivalent," "humanistic," and "believer"). Ranly, "How Religion Editors of Newspapers View Their Jobs and Religion," 846–49.

19. Again, a factor analysis was performed on these items using principal components extraction followed by varimax rotation. We kept dimensions with low reliability and only two factors in our analysis because of their consistency with our conceptual framework.

20. To keep this finding in perspective, one must remember that journalists are still less religiously oriented than the American public. While 72 percent of our respondents said religion or spirituality was important to them, 87 percent of Americans say religion is important to them. Gallup and Lindsay, *Surveying the Religious Landscape,* 10.

Chapter 10: Religion, Morality, and Professional Values

1. Mark Silk, "A Civil Religious Affair," *Religion in the News,* Spring 1999, 3–5, 22.

2. Lippmann, *A Preface to Morals,* 321 ("old rules" quote), 323 ("sages" quote), 324 ("old symbols" quote).

3. The *Minneapolis Star Tribune,* claiming that perhaps 40 million Americans with no religious affiliation "are capable of being moral citizens, good neighbors and law-abiding voters who live under the graceful canopy of the U.S. Constitution and the Bill of Rights," editorialized that "the argument that religion is essential to moral behavior is insulting and dangerous." Quoted in Mark Silk, "Preacher Joe," *Religion in the News,* Fall 2000, 6.

4. Silk, for example, cited a number of values of the modern mass media that must be seen as "establishmentarian" in the religious sense of the word: applause for good works, embrace of tolerance, contempt for hypocrisy, rejection of false prophets, denunciation of scandal, and concern about religious decline. Silk argued that the religion the mass media prefer is "domestic and generous and friendly" and does not threaten good order or represent views hostile to the culture at large. Silk, *Unsecular Media,* 142–43.

5. For discussions of how journalistic ethics work in cultural and religious contexts broader than just the Judeo-Christian, see Clifford Christians and Michael Traber, eds., *Communication Ethics and Universal Values* (Thousand Oaks, Calif.: Sage, 1997).

6. I use here the same data base from our survey of the religious views of American and Canadian journalists used in the previous chapter. For more details, see Doug Underwood, "Secularists or Modern Day Prophets: A Study of Journalists' Ethics and Their Connection to the Judeo-Christian Tradition," *Journal of Mass Media Ethics* 16, no. 1 (2001): 33–47.

7. The analysis focused on whether subjects' responses to the independent variable (i.e., the importance of religion or spirituality in their lives) influenced their responses to the journalistic quotations and biblical passages. Subjects were broken into low, moderate, and high categories based on the degree to which religion or spirituality was important to them. These categories then were used in one-way analyses of variance in which the twenty journalistic quotations and the ten biblical passages served as the dependent variables.

8. Despite their positive response to "prophetic" calls for reform, many American journalists have come to see themselves as morally neutral in their approach to the news. Many journalists have taken the stance of noninvolvement to the degree that they do not join community organizations, publicly acknowledge their position on political issues, or—like Len Downie, the editor of the *Washington Post*—even register to vote.

9. A similar pattern was found in subjects' responses to the Drew Pearson quote and a parallel passage from 1 Timothy. Again, journalists who responded similarly to the Pearson quote, regardless of their religious orientation, responded in ways more reflective of their religious views when asked to endorse the Timothy quote.

10. In addition, of the 60 percent of respondents who said they were members of a congregation, 96 percent belonged to Christian churches, and 3 percent were members of Jewish congregations.

Chapter 11: *The Cult of Science and the Scientifically Challenged Press*

1. John Noble Wilford, "New Findings Help Balance the Cosmological Books," *New York Times,* February 9, 1999, F1. The early Christian theologian St. Augustine presaged modern science—and must have equally baffled many of his contemporaries—with this comment: "The world was made, not in time, but simultaneously with time." Augustine's explanation was purely metaphysical; he was purporting to show that an omnipotent God was the creator of time and was of such grandeur that he existed outside of temporal matters. But, as Milic Capek put it, "if we disregard his theological language, we can hardly deny that [Augustine's] thought anticipated" the view of modern physicists. Milic Capek, *The Philosophical Impact of Contemporary Physics* (Princeton, N.J.: D. Van Nostrand, 1961), 353–54.

2. Some scientists are not quite so enthusiastic about Hawking's celebrity status. Robert Park, a University of Maryland physicist, complained in a *New York Times* op-ed piece that Hawking's writings and the documentaries about him have become something for people who see the old myths of creation as "quaint and "unsatisfying" and seek to find a new "glimpse of God in the laws of physics." Park lamented the comments of scientists whose eagerness to "see" God in scientific advances holds such appeal for "pop" cosmologists. Scientists must "learn to be careful with that sort of talk," he added. "It panders to reincarnationists, crop-circle devotees and other fans of Great Unsolved Mysteries." Robert L. Park, "A Cosmology of Your Very Own," *New York Times,* October 9, 1992, A33.

3. Analysis based on Nexis general news search (keyword: "Hawking, Stephen") from May 1990 to May 2000. In one story alone, there were references to science as a new religion, the "high priests" of physics, and Hawking as a "martyred genius." Another story demonstrated the fascination the press has for Hawking, who has lived for more than thirty years with a degenerative disease that was supposed to kill him years ago, by describing his condition as "one of God's grimmer jokes." Gerard Seenan, "Mind over Matter; Stephen Hawking," *Glasgow Herald,* February 28, 1998, 13; Hal Hinson, "'History of Time': Cosmic Complexities," *Washington Post,* September 25, 1992, B7. See Einstein quote in Jeremy Bernstein, *Einstein* (New York: Viking, 1973), 221; Hawking's play on Einstein's quote is quoted in Frederic Golden, "One Step beyond Black Holes," *San Francisco Chronicle,* September 12, 1993, "Sunday Review" section, 1.

4. Hinson, "'History of Time,'" B7. Interestingly, the stories do little to illuminate Hawking's stances on traditional religion. One story described him as a "resolute atheist," but another reported how he planned a church blessing for his second marriage. Seenan, "Mind over Matter," 13; Nadine Brozan, "Chronicle," *New York Times,* September 16, 1995, 20.

5. Abraham Pais, *Einstein Lived Here* (New York: Oxford University Press, 1994), 138–39 (quotes), 252.

6. James Reston Jr., *Galileo: A Life* (New York: HarperCollins, 1994), 55.

7. Altschull, *From Milton to McLuhan,* 45, 50, 60–62, 77–84, 138, 161–72, 223–28.

8. Lippmann, *Public Opinion,* 53–100.

9. Quoted in Roger Highfield and Paul Carter, *The Private Lives of Albert Einstein* (New York: St. Martin's, 1993), 189; Pais, *Einstein Lived Here,* 147.

10. Quoted in Pais, *Einstein Lived Here,* 179–80.

11. Quoted in Peter Michelmore, *Einstein, Profile of the Man* (New York: Dodd, Mead, 1962), 166.

12. Highfield and Carter, *The Private Lives of Albert Einstein,* 189.

13. Stephen W. Hawking, *A Brief History of Time: From the Big Bang to Black Holes* (1988; reprint New York: Bantam, 1990), 23, 28; Pais, *Einstein Lived Here,* 15–34.

14. Bertrand Russell, *The ABC of Relativity* (1925; reprint, New York: Mentor, 1969), 16.

15. Capek, *The Philosophical Impact of Contemporary Physics,* xiv (Reichenbach quote), xv ("Newtonian-Euclidian subconscious" quote).

16. Stephens, *A History of News,* 133, 175.

17. Pais, *Einstein Lived Here,* 148.

18. Ted Anton and Rick McCourt, introduction to *The New Science Journalists,* ed. Ted Anton and Rick McCourt (New York: Ballantine, 1995), 7.

19. Sharon M. Friedman, "The Journalist's World," in *Scientists and Journalists: Reporting Science as News,* ed. Sharon Friedman, Sharon Dunwoody, and Carol L. Rogers (New York: Free Press, 1986), 3–41.

20. Anton and Court, introduction to *The New Science Journalists,* 12.

21. Louis Trenchard More, *Isaac Newton: A Biography* (New York: Scribner's, 1934), 44–45; Gale E. Christianson, *In the Presence of the Creator: Isaac Newton and His Times* (New York: Free Press, 1984), 78.

22. Christianson, *In the Presence of the Creator,* 77–79; More, *Isaac Newton,* 44.

23. For example, Voltaire titillated his readers by writing that Newton died chaste and that he owed his appointment to the Royal Mint not to his great merit but to the fact that his "very charming" niece had won the favor of the chancellor of the Exchequer. Christianson, *In the Presence of the Creator,* 349, 423; Frank E. Manuel, *A Portrait of Isaac Newton* (Cambridge, Mass.: Harvard University Press, 1968), 191, 229–30.

24. A. Rupert Hall, *Isaac Newton: Adventurer in Thought* (Oxford, England: Blackwell, 1992), 217.

25. Quoted in John Fauvel, Raymond Flood, Michael Shortland, and Robin Wilson, introduction to *Let Newton Be!* ed. John Fauvel, Raymond Flood, Michael Shortland, and Robin Wilson (Oxford: Oxford University Press, 1988), 3.

26. Charles Coulston Gillispie, *The Edge of Objectivity: An Essay in the History of Scientific Ideas* (1960; reprint, Princeton, N.J.: Princeton University Press, 1990), 145–46, 157–58.

27. Basil Willey, *The Seventeenth Century Background: Studies in the Thought of the Age in Relation to Poetry and Religion* (1935; reprint, New York: Doubleday Anchor, 1953), 20–21, 277.

28. Quoted in Gillispie, *The Edge of Objectivity,* 147.

29. Frank E. Manuel, *The Religion of Isaac Newton* (Oxford: Oxford University Press, 1974), 28, 64; Jan Golinski, "The Secret Life of an Alchemist," and John Brooke, "The God of Isaac Newton," in *Let Newton Be!* ed. Fauvel et al., 147–83; More, *Isaac Newton,* 25, 158–59; Gillispie, *The Edge of Objectivity,* 147–49.

30. Quoted in Becker, *The Heavenly City,* 52.

31. Quoted in Manuel, *A Portrait of Isaac Newton,* 124.

32. In contrast, reporters and cartoonists, obviously less reverent and more relishing of controversy than were their editorial superiors, often tended to see the dispute as great fun. Ronald W. Clark, *The Survival of Charles Darwin: A Biography of a Man and an Idea* (New York: Random House, 1984), 127–28; Peter Brent, *Charles Darwin* (New York: Harper and Row, 1981), 344, 461.

33. Clark, *The Survival of Charles Darwin,* 180. Darwin's theory maintains that all species of plants and animals developed from earlier forms by adapting and transmitting the hereditary traits necessary for survival in their environment. However, as so often happens when

the press is involved, the symbol of the dispute became its caricature—in this case, cartoons involving Darwin and the monkey, which appeared in dozens of nineteenth-century publications and were based on Darwin's belief that humankind shared its ancestry with the monkey world.

34. Ibid., 180–81.

35. Adrian Desmond and James Moore, *Darwin* (New York: Warner, 1991), 671.

36. Ibid., 670–71 (quote); Brent, *Charles Darwin*, 517–18; Gertrude Himmelfarb, *Darwin and the Darwinian Revolution* (New York: Norton, 1968), 441–42. It should be remembered, too, that Darwin's attitude toward religion was a highly complex one, deeply painful in its oscillation between belief, agnosticism, and despair. Throughout his life, Darwin struggled with "the Victorian dilemma," as his biographers Desmond and Moore wrote, "destitute of faith, yet terrified at skepticism." Darwin was not a contentious man, and he refused to be pulled publicly into the feuds of the intelligentsia over issues of faith and science (although it is clear that he cheered on his defenders from the background). In his autobiography, however, he finally came clean, and, while acknowledging that one could be a theist and an evolutionist, he still confessed he felt profoundly uncertain about the existence of God. "I am sorry to have to inform you that I do not believe in the Bible as a divine revelation, and therefore not in Jesus Christ as the son of God," he wrote to one correspondent during the "Delphic Oracle phase" of his later career, as biographers Desmond and Moore described it, when Darwin was asked to comment on all sorts of matters, but particularly about science and religion. Desmond and Moore, *Darwin*, 268 ("Victorian dilemma" and "destitute of faith" quotes), 634 ("do not believe" and "Delphic Oracle" quotes).

37. Quoted in Brent, *Charles Darwin*, 519.

38. Paul Davies, *About Time: Einstein's Unfinished Revolution* (London: Penguin, 1995), 91, 164, 277; Pais, *Einstein Lived Here*, 129.

39. Bernstein, *Einstein*, 221; Pais, *Einstein Lived Here*, 129; Davies, *About Time*, 277.

40. Edward MacKinnon, "Bohr and the Realism Debates," in *Niels Bohr and Contemporary Philosophy*, ed. Jan Faye and Henry J. Folse (Dordrecht, The Netherlands: Kluwer, 1994), 284; Abraham Pais, *Niels Bohr's Times: In Physics, Philosophy, and Polity* (Oxford: Oxford University Press, 1991), 431.

41. Pais, *Einstein Lived Here*, 37.

42. Albert Einstein, *The Quotable Einstein*, comp. and ed. Alice Calaprice (Princeton, N.J.: Princeton University Press, 1996), 148 ("noblest motive" quote), 149 ("rewards and punishes" and "finer speculations" quotes), 151 ("universal causation" and "religious feeling" quotes).

43. John Polkinghorne, *The Faith of a Physicist: Reflections of a Bottom-Up Thinker* (1994; reprint, Minneapolis: Fortress, 1996), 63, 65.

44. Einstein, *The Quotable Einstein*, 158.

45. Davies, *About Time*, 277.

46. Ben H. Bagdikian, *The Information Machines: Their Impact on Men and Media* (New York: Harper Colophon, 1971), 263.

Chapter 12: *The Mind of the Inquiring Reporter*

1. Quoted in Peter Gay, *Freud: A Life for Our Times* (New York: Norton, 1988), 535–36 (Freud quote on 535).

2. Ibid., 450 ("facile judgments" and "Herr Professor" quotes); Giovanni Costigan, *Sigmund Freud: A Short Biography* (New York: Macmillan, 1965), 261 (*London Times* demands); Sig-

mund Freud, *The Future of an Illusion,* trans. and ed. James Strachey (1961; reprint, New York: Norton, 1989).

3. Quoted in Gay, *Freud,* 453.

4. Costigan, *Sigmund Freud,* 256.

5. Quoted in Steel, *Walter Lippmann and the American Century,* 46.

6. Quoted in Gay, *Freud,* 458.

7. Quoted in ibid., 527.

8. Ibid.

9. Quoted in Gerhard Wehr, *Jung: A Biography* (Boston: Shambhala, 1987), 107.

10. Quoted in Vincent Brome, *Jung* (London: Macmillan, 1978), 151.

11. Quoted in Costigan, *Sigmund Freud,* 155.

12. Ibid., 152.

13. Philip Rieff, *Freud: The Mind of the Moralist* (New York: Viking, 1959), 293.

14. Ibid., 257 ("substitute doctrine" quote), 290 ("original disease" quote).

15. Ibid., 299.

16. David Foster, "Lust for Heroism Can Warp, and Boomerang in Disaster," Associated Press, July 31, 1996; Michael Hedges, "FBI Says 'Hero' Is Sometimes the Killer," Scripps Howard News Service, July 30, 1996; David Kindred, "Strange Turn of Events: A Hero Becomes a Fool," *Atlanta Journal–Constitution,* July 31, 1996, A10.

17. Rieff, *Freud,* 24, 35 ("hidden god" quote), 90, 93–94, 182. Freud, Rieff maintained, kept his "humanistic literacy under wraps" and only privately admitted his intellectual debt to such figures as Kant, Voltaire, Feuerbach, Empedocles, and Plato (he also apparently avoided reading Nietzsche for fear of being less original). Ibid., 254 (quote); Gay, *Freud,* 45–46.

18. Quoted in Wehr, *Jung,* 302.

19. Quoted in ibid., 108.

20. Ibid., 392.

21. Brome, *Jung,* 159 (quote), 167.

22. Carl Jung, "A Communication," *New Republic,* February 21, 1955, 30–31 ("better," "something nice," "ancient absurdities," and "Virgin birth" quotes); Carl Jung, "The Challenge of the Christian Enigma," *New Republic,* April 27, 1953, 18 ("do not fit," "portrait of Jesus," and "loyalty" quotes). Sinclair's letter to Jung is in *New Republic,* February 21, 1955, 30.

23. Quoted in Wehr, *Jung,* 388. While working journalists have not shown much interest in Jung, one ex-journalist turned academic has. Jack Lule argued that Jung's theories of archetypes should be seen as central to interpreting the mythical role that news stories play in modern life. Jack Lule, *Daily News, Eternal Stories: The Mythological Role of Journalism* (New York: Guilford, 2001), 200–201.

24. Quoted in Wehr, *Jung,* 324.

25. Chris Argyris, *Behind the Front Page: Organizational Self-Renewal in a Metropolitan Newspaper* (San Francisco: Jossey-Bass, 1974), 1–64, 267–68.

26. See Sigmund Freud, *Civilization and Its Discontents,* trans. and ed. James Strachey (New York: Norton, 1961).

Chapter 13: The Press, Politics, and Religion in the Public Square

1. Roger Morris, *Richard Milhous Nixon: The Rise of an American Politician* (New York: Henry Holt, 1990), 626; Richard Nixon, *RN: The Memoirs of Richard Nixon* (New York: Grosset and Dunlap, 1978), 138–39. The quote is from Morris's account. Nixon's account has him saying, "Let a good Quaker stop this fight."

2. Quoted in Morris, *Richard Milhous Nixon*, 627.

3. Nixon himself used the Greek tragedy analogy in describing his political fall from grace. Nixon, *RN*, 1072.

4. Wills, *Under God*, 61.

5. Morris, *Richard Milhous Nixon*, 115–16, 236, 242–43; Fawn M. Brodie, *Richard Nixon: The Shaping of His Character* (New York: Norton, 1981), 163–64.

6. H. Larry Ingle, *Quakers in Conflict: The Hicksite Reformation* (Knoxville: University of Tennessee Press, 1986); Thomas D. Hamm, *The Transformation of American Quakerism: Orthodox Friends, 1800–1907* (1988; reprint, Bloomington: Indiana University Press, 1992); John Punshon, *Portrait in Grey: A Short History of the Quakers* (1984; reprint, London: Quaker Home Service, 1991), 153–205; Rufus M. Jones, *The Later Periods of Quakerism*, 2 vols. (1921; reprint, Westport, Conn.: Greenwood, 1970), 1:435–540.

7. Quoted in Morris, *Richard Milhous Nixon*, 280.

8. Charles P. Henderson Jr., *The Nixon Theology* (New York: Harper and Row, 1972), 32–33.

9. Oliver Pilat, *Drew Pearson: An Unauthorized Biography* (New York: Harper's Magazine Press, 1973), 205.

10. Ibid., 5 ("personally peaceful" and "professionally warlike" quotes); Morris, *Richard Milhous Nixon*, 446 ("running battle" quote).

11. Wills, *Under God*, 18. See also Benjamin J. Hubbard, "The Importance of the Religion Angle in Reporting on Current Events," in *Reporting Religion: Facts and Faith*, ed. Benjamin J. Hubbard (Sonoma, Calif.: Polebridge, 1990), 3–19. It is interesting that in the 2000 presidential contest between George W. Bush and Al Gore, both candidates were presented as "born-again" politicians with a strong religious commitment (Bush as a Methodist, Gore as a Baptist). This perceived similarity in background served to minimize the coverage about the role of religion in their political visions, however, instead of increasing the scrutiny or the depth of analysis. A typical example is a Scripps Howard News Service campaign piece that indicated the next president would believe in God and family life, claim to have received his values from his loving parents, and have had his life transformed by Jesus: "You can plug in the name after Nov. 7." Bush's comment that Christ was the "political philosopher" who influenced him the most received some press attention, as did Gore's comment that, when faced with important political questions, he asks what Jesus would do. Gore's selection of Senator Joseph Lieberman, an orthodox Jew, also stirred up a good deal of press coverage about the role of religion in politics, though some criticized the press for focusing too much on the political implications of Lieberman's orthodox Jewish beliefs and not enough on the political impact of the orthodox Christian beliefs of Gore and Bush. Reed Branson, "Religion Still Has Its Place in Politics," Scripps Howard News Service report in the *Seattle Post-Intelligencer*, October 10, 2000, A9; Richard N. Ostling and Julia Lieblich, "The Candidates' Spiritual Side," Associated Press report in the *Seattle Times/Seattle Post-Intelligencer*, July 16, 2000, A3.

12. The press's aversion to religion is so strong that I found only one article in the mainstream press during the period of the scandal and the impeachment hearings that examined how the beliefs of Baptists of Bill Clinton's generation about sexual rules might have influenced Clinton's claims that he did not have "sex" with Lewinsky during their tryst in the White House. Asked whether what Clinton did is considered "adultery" or even "sex" in the Baptist understanding of the term, Steve Marini, a Wellesley College religion professor who is Clinton's age, told *Newsweek* magazine, "Our basic rule growing up Baptist was that anything short of penetration didn't count." Foy Valentine, the head of the Southern Baptists' Christian Life Commission for twenty-seven years, added, "What he [Clinton] did is

disgusting, but not what I would consider adultery. And I think that most Baptists would agree." Quoted in Kenneth Woodward, "Sex, Sin and Salvation," *Newsweek,* November 2, 1998, 37.

13. Stephen Carter, *The Culture of Disbelief: How American Law and Politics Trivialize Religious Devotion* (New York: Anchor, 1994), 105–35.

14. Wills, *Under God,* 19.

15. It is ironic that a press corps that had grown jaded and surly during the Nixon and Johnson administrations decided to pillory Jimmy Carter, one of the most deeply religious presidents, whose major fault seemed to be that he looked on Washington, D.C., politics with the scorn of a moralistic outsider. It is even more ironic when one considers Carter was defeated by Ronald Reagan, who seldom attended church but was embraced by the religious Right. As political commentators seldom note, rhetoric and political stances often go further in wooing the religious vote than do the credentials of genuine belief.

16. Carter, *The Culture of Disbelief,* 77–78.

17. Silk, *Unsecular Media,* 141 ("gives no offense" and "religion news" quotes), 149 ("religion is dynamite" and "moral packaging" quotes).

18. Quoted in Reichley, *Religion in American Public Life,* 99.

19. Quoted in ibid., 104 ("patriot" quote), 105 ("government" and "constitution" quotes).

20. Quoted in ibid., 195 (Lincoln quote), 214 (Roosevelt quote).

21. Quoted in Kaplan, *Walt Whitman,* 128 (*Brooklyn Eagle* quotes), 130 ("our arms" quote).

22. Carter, *The Culture of Disbelief,* 51 (Gedicks quote), 67 ("American habit" and "political preaching" quotes), 70 ("one's theology" quote), 97.

23. Henderson, *The Nixon Theology,* 177–78, 184–85 (quote on 185).

24. Quoted in Morris, *Richard Milhous Nixon,* 103.

25. Henderson, *The Nixon Theology,* xi ("patriotism and piety" quote), 193 ("patriotism his religion" quote). Ironically, Nixon's actual theology was more liberal than his followers probably realized. In a college paper Nixon wrote at Whittier College, he discussed the fundamentalism of his early religious indoctrination and his drift away from his parents' belief in the infallible and literal interpretation of the Bible. In the paper, Nixon said he had come to see Jesus' life in more symbolic terms—terms that appear to make him a liberal Christian rather than an orthodox believer in Jesus' divinity and physical resurrection. The important thing, Nixon wrote, is that "Jesus lived and taught a life so perfect that he continued to live and grow after his death—in the hearts of men. It may be true that the resurrection story is a myth, but symbolically it teaches the great lesson that men who achieve the highest values in their lives may gain immortality." In the autobiographical writings of his retirement years, Nixon was still quoting his college paper as his best expression of his religious faith—a sign, one suspects, of how much his faith had ossified and how little it was a dynamic force in his life. Richard Nixon, *In the Arena: A Memoir of Victory, Defeat, and Renewal* (New York: Simon and Schuster, 1990), 88–89; Morris, *Richard Milhous Nixon,* 127–29; Nixon, *RN,* 16 (portions of the quoted paper appear in both Nixon autobiographies, but a fuller version appears in the Morris biography).

26. Sidney E. Ahlstrom, *A Religious History of the American People* (New Haven, Conn.: Yale University Press, 1972), 147. This quote comes from John Winthrop, the governor of the Massachusetts Bay colony. For a further discussion of the "revivalist" style of politics, see Richard John Niehaus, *The Naked Public Square* (Grand Rapids, Mich.: Eerdmans, 1984), 104–6.

27. Gans, *Deciding What's News,* 264.

28. Pilat, *Drew Pearson,* 302–3, 305 (quote).

29. Anderson, *Confessions of a Muckraker*, 35, 122, 170, 320, 388.

30. Niehaus, *The Naked Public Square*, 203.

31. Anderson, *Confessions of a Muckraker*, 394.

Chapter 14: Foundations of Sand

1. Aaron Zitner, "Render unto Bill That Which Is Bill's; False Rumor of Purchase of Church by Microsoft Shows Internet Power," *Boston Globe*, December 17, 1994, 77.

2. See James Wallace's *Overdrive: Bill Gates and the Race to Control Cyberspace* (New York: Wiley, 1997), 175, 183–84, for an account of these events, which included a Microsoft staff-attended retreat at a mansion near Kirkland, Washington, and Gates's continued ruminations at his second home on the Hood Canal, from which emerged a memo by Gates outlining the company's new commitment to the Internet as the communications medium of the future.

3. Bill Gates, with Nathan Myhrvold and Peter Rinearson, *The Road Ahead* (1995; reprint, New York, Penguin, 1996), xiii–xiv.

4. Joshua Cooper Ramo Chama, "Finding God on the Web," *Time*, December 16, 1996, 62.

5. John Durham Peters, *Speaking into the Air: A History of the Idea of Communication* (Chicago: University of Chicago Press, 1999), 29 ("dream of communication" quote), 179 ("heart-shaped box" quote), 185 (Cooley quote).

6. Chama, "Finding God on the Web," 67. For those who find signing onto the Net a near religious experience, Chama postulated, the Web is "a vast cathedral of the mind, a place where ideas about God and religion can resonate, where faith can be shaped and defined by a collective spirit. . . . Interconnected, we may begin to find God in places we never imagined." Ibid.

7. Marshall McLuhan, *The Gutenberg Galaxy: The Making of Typographic Man* (1962; reprint, New York: Signet, 1969), 42–43; McLuhan, *Understanding Media*, 36–45; Marshall McLuhan and Bruce R. Powers, *The Global Village: Transformations in World Life and Media in the Twenty-First Century* (1989; reprint, New York: Oxford University Press, 1992), 62, 136–37.

8. Quoted in Chama, "Finding God on the Web," 67.

9. McLuhan, *Understanding Media*, 67.

10. Altschull, *From Milton to McLuhan*, 341.

11. Jennifer J. Cobb, *Cybergrace: The Search for God in the Digital World* (New York: Crown, 1998), 44 ("soul of cyberspace" quote) 45 ("sacred mechanisms," "medium of grace," and "fundamental role" quotes), 52 ("theology of cyberspace" quote).

12. McLuhan, *Understanding Media*, 84.

13. I am not saying that process theologians have not shown an interest in ethics or questions of democracy—they have. But the highly intellectualized and generalized nature of their speculation and the often obscure nature of their prose make it doubtful whether one could find in their abstractions any meaningful basis for interpreting human impulses or taking action in the world. For example, here is what Whitehead said of morality: "Morality is always the aim at that union of harmony, intensity, and vividness, which involves the perfection of importance for that occasion" and "Morality consists in the control of process so as to maximize importance. It is the aim of greatness of experience in the various dimensions belonging to it." On democracy, he wrote, "The basis of democracy is the common fact of value-experience as constituting the essential value of each pulsation of actuality. Everything has some value for itself, for others, and for the whole. . . . We have no right to deface the

value-experience which is the very essence of the universe." Quoted in Randall C. Morris, *Process Philosophy and Political Ideology: The Social and Political Thought of Alfred North Whitehead and Charles Hartshorne* (Albany: State University of New York Press, 1991), 86 (first quote), 87 (second quote), 129–30 (third quote). Whitehead's view of religion, Walter Lippmann once said, is "incomprehensible to all who are not highly trained logicians," adding, "For while this God may satisfy a metaphysical need in the thinker, he does not satisfy the passion of the believer." Lippmann, *A Preface to Morals,* 26.

14. Stephens, *A History of News,* 274.

15. Czitrom, *Media and the American Mind,* 6 (Morse quote), 10 ("secret of Nature" quote); Carolyn Marvin, *When Old Technologies Were New* (New York: Oxford University Press, 1988), 65 (*Scientific American* quote), 66 (telephone counsel quote), 126 ("religious revelation" quote); Erik Barnouw, *Tube of Plenty: The Evolution of American Television,* rev. ed. (New York: Oxford University Press, 1982), 15 (De Forest quote); Jerry Mander, *Four Arguments for the Elimination of Television* (New York: Quill, 1978), 29–30.

16. Henry David Thoreau, *Walden and Civil Disobedience,* ed. Owen Thomas (1854; reprint, New York: Norton, 1966), 35; Chesterton quoted in Gordon, *Marshall McLuhan,* 48.

17. McLuhan, *Understanding Media,* 30 ("bars of a melody" quote), 33 ("spell" quote), 34 ("magic of media" quote).

18. Pierre Teilhard de Chardin, *The Phenomenon of Man,* trans. Bernard Wall (1959; reprint, New York: Harper, 1965).

19. Ong, *The Presence of the Word,* 290 ("Christian living" quote), 309 ("inwardness" and "interiority" quotes), 313 ("entry for the divine" quote).

20. Gordon, *Marshall McLuhan,* 27, 54–56 ("character of every society" quote on 56), 239 ("deliberately keep Christianity" quote). In 1973, McLuhan's private correspondence contained this comment: "At one time, when I was first becoming interested in the Catholic Church, I studied the entire work of G. K. Chesterton and the entire group from the pre-Raphaelites and Cardinal Newman through to Christopher Dawson and Eric Gill. All of this really is involved in my media study, but doesn't appear at all." Ibid., 75.

21. See Matthew 7:24–27, "New Testament," 7. Even the title of this book is a reminder of how fleeting and fragile the fortunes of the modern new media company can be. Yahoo! has been seen as a symbol of both the soaring economic success of the Internet and its plummeting back to earth. In January 2001, Yahoo! stock, following the trend of other Internet stocks that crashed after a huge ballooning in value while the Internet was first being commercialized, traded for $26.50, almost one-tenth its $250 peak. Bruce Meyerson, "Yahoo!'s Grim Fortunes Stir Weird Updates," Associated Press dispatch in *Seattle Post-Intelligencer,* January 15, 2001, C4.

22. McLuhan, *Understanding Media,* 55. Although McLuhan is widely seen as one of the world's foremost techno-mystics and techno-enthusiasts, he did, in fact, spend a good amount of time warning about the price humans pay for celebrating and making themselves "numb" to the effects of modern technology. "As long as we adopt the Narcissus attitude of regarding extensions of our own bodies as really out there and really independent of us, we will meet all technological challenges with the same sort of banana-skin pirouette and collapse." Ibid., 73.

23. Innis, who is Ong's philosophical father so to speak, never forgot this, and, although dying before the impact of television had spread throughout the culture, he looked with great concern at the damaging social effects of developments in electronic communications.

24. Theodore Roszak, *The Cult of Information: The Folklore of Computers and the True Art of Thinking* (New York: Pantheon, 1986), 208.

Chapter 15: *The Gospel of Public Journalism*

1. Quoted in Jay Rosen, "The Action of the Idea: Public Journalism in Built Form," in *The Idea of Public Journalism*, ed. Theodore L. Glasser (New York: Guilford, 1999), 24.

2. Alicia Shepherd, "The Gospel of Public Journalism," *American Journalism Review*, September 1994, 29.

3. Rosen, "The Action of the Idea," 25; Rosen, *What Are Journalists For?* 194 (Armao quote).

4. Rosen, *What Are Journalists For?* 194. Rosen rebutted this criticism by noting that "true believers entertain no doubts" and that public journalism—which operates by trial and error, not indoctrination—cannot fit the definition of a "cult built on the certainty that it is right." He went on to claim that their critics have a vested interest in portraying public journalists as zealots. "If the reformers were dizzy revivalists preaching sin and salvation, then the remainder of the craft looked secular and rationalist, almost scientific by comparison," he wrote. "The apparent conflict was not between one press philosophy and another; it pitted religious zeal against sober skepticism, a rising cult against cooler heads, a confused and confusing band of reformers against those who were clear in their purpose and needed no movement to give them direction." Ibid., 194–95.

5. Jay Rosen, *Getting the Connections Right* (New York: Twentieth Century Fund, 1996), 24 ("relentless cynicism," "something inspiring," and "corrosion of their souls" quotes), 25 ("hardened realism" and "ethos of disgruntlement" quotes).

6. Christians, Ferré, and Fackler, *Good News*, 53–54, 98–99, 112–13, 118, 153 ("humanized workplace" and "servant leadership" quotes), 190 ("root metaphors" quote).

7. The solutions, of course, often need to be political, but public journalism advocates tend to steer away from real political involvement and are suspicious of political institutions. Many public journalism campaigns operate on the assumption that citizens working on their own outside the political and governmental establishment can accomplish more. There are, however, few examples of real world "solutions" that have resulted from public journalism campaigns. This is discussed in Michael Schudson, "The Public Journalism Movement and Its Problems," in *The Politics of News/The News of Politics*, ed. Doris Graber, Denis McQuail, and Pippa Norris (Washington, D.C.: Congressional Quarterly Press, 1998), 132–49.

8. The Pew Center for Civic Journalism provides a good catalogue of the kind of issues taken up by advocates of public journalism. This summary was taken from Pew's *Civic Catalyst* and other foundation publications from 1998–99, which listed many of the major public journalism projects that were being tackled at news organizations around the United States.

9. John McManus outlined what in the public journalism movement he considers to be complementary and in conflict with the move toward market-oriented journalism at today's news organizations. For him, public journalism serves a role similar to that of market-oriented journalism in that civic stories often are cheap to discover and report; most civic stories do not embarrass the local power structure; the focus groups and audience surveys that underpin civic journalism can also serve the marketing goals of news organizations; and organizing town meetings may help build audience. However, civic stories may drive away entertainment-oriented consumers; may require that the interests of all citizens be served rather than just the demographic audience attractive to advertisers; often take more time and

talent to produce than quick-hit, "neutral" stories; and may take sides on issues that risk alienating portions of the audience. McManus concluded that public journalism has been practiced only "episodically and partially" at news organizations, and then only "following the least expensive precepts." "Civic journalism is afloat, but it's a dinghy bobbing in the wake of a titanic freighter headed in a nearly opposite direction—the USS Profit-Maximizer," McManus declared. John McManus, "Can Media Firms Do Well by Doing Good (Civic Journalism)?" (Talk to panel of Association for Education in Journalism and Mass Communication Convention, New Orleans, La., August 4, 1999). See also John H. McManus, *Market-Driven Journalism: Let the Citizen Beware?* (Thousand Oaks, Calif.: Sage, 1994).

10. Quoted in Shepherd, "The Gospel of Public Journalism," 34.

11. Rosen, "The Action of the Idea," 24.

12. Quoted in Jean B. Quandt, *From the Small Town to the Great Community: The Social Thought of Progressive Intellectuals* (New Brunswick, N.J.: Rutgers University Press, 1970), 70.

13. Quoted in Fred H. Matthews, *Quest for an American Sociology: Robert E. Park and the Chicago School* (Montreal: McGill-Queen's University Press, 1977), 23 (quote), 29.

14. Davis Merritt, *Public Journalism and Public Life: Why Telling the News Is Not Enough* (Hillsdale, N.J.: Erlbaum, 1995), 4–5 ("decline in journalism" and "codependent" quotes), 6 ("communitarian movement" quote), 87 ("frustration," "malaise," and "boiling over" quotes).

15. Quoted in Quandt, *From the Small Town to the Great Community,* 34.

16. Quoted in Altschull, *From Milton to McLuhan,* 191 (Whitman quote); Perkins, Perkins, and Leininger, *Benét's Reader's Encyclopedia,* 822 (Paine quote).

17. Matthews, *Quest for an American Sociology,* 25 ("liberal utopia" quote); Steven C. Rockefeller, *John Dewey: Religious Faith and Democratic Humanism* (New York: Columbia University Press, 1991), 175 ("moral commitment" quote).

18. Quoted in Matthews, *Quest for an American Sociology,* 29.

19. Ibid., 20 ("touching naivete" quote), 26 ("secularized deity" quote). Matthews applied the term "secularized deity" to Herbert Spencer's view of the natural world but implied it is also applicable to Dewey's and Park's view of social science, and I agree.

20. Quoted in Quandt, *From the Small Town to the Great Community,* 31.

21. Quoted in Rockefeller, *John Dewey,* 188–89.

22. Quoted in ibid., 191. "In the thought of the communitarians, the spiritual freight carried by the means of communication was considerable," said Jean Quandt. Dewey, she said, regarded communication as "an instrument of the coming kingdom," and she quoted him as saying that "it is in democracy, the community of ideas and interest through community of action, that the incarnation of 'God' in man . . . becomes a living, present thing." Quandt, *From the Small Town to the Great Community,* 73.

23. Quoted in Rockefeller, *John Dewey,* 193.

24. Matthews, *Quest for an American Sociology,* 20 ("agnostic moralist" quote); Winifred Raushenbush, *Robert E. Park: Biography of a Sociologist* (Durham, N.C.: Duke University Press, 1979), 169 ("nominal" quote).

25. Quoted in Raushenbush, *Robert E. Park,* 170.

26. Quandt, *From the Small Town to the Great Community,* 145–46, 152–54.

27. Quoted in ibid., 59.

28. Raushenbush, *Robert E. Park,* 15–16.

29. Quoted in Matthews, *Quest for an American Sociology,* 9–10. See also Park's description of his writing life in Raushenbush, *Robert E. Park,* 15–17.

30. Quandt, *From the Small Town to the Great Community,* 68.

31. Matthews, *Quest for an American Sociology,* 11, 28; Raushenbush, *Robert E. Park,* 21.

32. Quandt, *From the Small Town to the Great Community,* 68–71.

33. Quoted in Everett M. Rogers, *A History of Communications Study: A Biographical Approach* (New York: Free Press, 1997), 189.

34. Carey, *Communication as Culture,* 15 ("transmission" quote and definition of the concept), 16 ("redemptive" quote), 18 ("ritual" quote, with further definition of the concept on 18–20), 21 ("religious rituals" and "cultural form" quotes); quoted in Lule, *Daily News, Eternal Stories,* 210–11 ("mass" quote).

35. Analysis developed from search of *Seattle Times* electronic data base, Suzallo Library, University of Washington from 1994 to May 2000, with the keywords "Front Page Forum."

36. Habermas, *The Structural Transformation of the Public Sphere,* 27–88, 141–235. For thoughtful critiques of Habermas, see David Trend, *Cultural Democracy: Politics, Media, New Technology* (Albany: State University of New York Press, 1997), 13–14; and John B. Thompson, *The Media and Modernity: A Social Theory of the Media* (Stanford, Calif.: Stanford University Press, 1995), 69–75.

37. Keith R. Stamm, *Newspaper Use and Community Ties: Toward a Dynamic Theory* (Norwood, N.J.: Ablex, 1985), xi; Philip Meyer, "A Struggle with the News Research Puzzle," *Presstime,* February 1982, 4–5. The media researcher Leo Bogart has noted this phenomenon, too, and he warns that much readership research is suspect because the public tends to say it wants or reads more in the newspaper than it actually does and to expect newspapers to meet a higher standard of coverage than what readers personally use in the newspaper. Leo Bogart, *Press and Public: Who Reads What, When, Where, and Why in American Newspapers* (Hillsdale, N.J.: Erlbaum, 1981), 250.

38. Stamm, *Newspaper Use and Community Ties,* 3–12. For an important analysis of the research about public journalism's failings and successes, see Keith Stamm, "Of What Use Civic Journalism: Do Newspapers Really Make a Difference in Community Participation?" in *Communication and Community,* ed. Gregory J. Shepherd and Eric W. Rothenbuhler (Mahwah, N.J.: Erlbaum, 2001), 217–34. Stamm concluded that his research and that of others suggest civic or public journalism has made a contribution to community involvement but that the contribution is not large. Stamm suggested that the town meetings and public forums traditionally used in public journalism may not be the most effective means for expanding citizen participation. He contended news organizations should be more concerned with involving citizens at the early stages of their settling in communities, when they are just building community ties.

Chapter 16: Jesus without Journalists

1. Elaine Pagels, *The Gnostic Gospels* (New York: Vintage, 1981), xi–xii, 13. The "Gospel of Mary" was one of the few Gnostic texts discovered before the 1945 find, but both extant copies are extremely fragmentary, with key sections missing. Karen L. King, introduction to "The Gospel of Mary," in *The Nag Hammadi Library in English,* 3d rev. ed., ed. James M. Robinson (San Francisco: Harper and Row, 1988), 524.

2. Pagels, *The Gnostic Gospels,* 16; "The Gospel of Mary," trans. George W. MacRae and R. McL. Wilson, ed. Douglas M. Parrott, in *The Nag Hammadi Library,* ed. Robinson, 524–27.

3. David Friedrich Strauss, *The Life of Jesus Critically Examined,* trans. George Eliot (1835; reprint, London: Swan Sonnenschein, 1906). See also Albert Schweitzer, *The Quest of the Historical Jesus,* trans. W. Montgomery (1910; reprint, New York: Macmillan, 1950), 68–120.

4. Robert W. Funk, Roy W. Hoover, and the Jesus Seminar, *The Five Gospels: The Search for the Authentic Words of Jesus* (New York: Macmillan, 1993).

5. The Bible does not indicate what Jesus wrote. John 8:6–8, "New Testament," 95.

6. Boomershine, "Jesus of Nazareth and the Watershed of Ancient Orality and Literacy," 7–36. Some evangelical scholars dispute that there was such a time lag in the production of the Bible's account of Jesus' life and argue that a portion of the gospels was written by his contemporaries closer to Jesus' death (most notably the book of John, which they contend was written by the Apostle John). But this viewpoint is widely disputed in mainstream biblical scholarly circles.

7. Ong, *The Presence of the Word*, 185–91.

8. Meyrowitz, *No Sense of Place*, 268–304.

9. Ong, *The Presence of the Word*, 190–91.

10. It must be pointed out that in other journalistic traditions, particularly in many European countries, the emphasis on "balance," "impartiality," and "telling both sides of the story" is less pronounced than in the United States, where journalists tend to consider this the measure of "objectivity." For many European journalists, "objectivity" is seen less as a mirror to be held up to society and more about "getting to the hard facts of a political dispute," which can include a high degree of interpretation, research analysis, and opinion. Thomas E. Patterson, "Political Roles of the Journalist," in *The Politics of News*, ed. Graber, McQuail, and Norris, 17–32.

11. Johnson, *The Real Jesus*, 112–17.

12. Burton L. Mack, *Who Wrote the New Testament? The Making of the Christian Myth* (San Francisco: Harper Collins, 1995), 6–7. It is important to remember that ancient writers—living in a much more community-based culture—had an entirely different view of what was meant by authority and put little stock in our modern notions of individual authorship. In living so close to the practices of oral tradition, where much common wisdom was attributed to mythical or legendary heroes of the culture, ancient authors often wrote under the name of important cultural figures whose authority was widely trusted, incorporated legend and widely held oral beliefs into their "factual" accounts of events, and attributed general wisdom to great cultural heroes.

13. Pagels, *The Gnostic Gospels*, xiv, 58, 77–78.

14. On the public's trust of television news, see Frank Newport and Lydia Saad, "A Matter of Trust," *American Journalism Review*, July–August 1998, 32.

15. Edward Jay Epstein, *News from Nowhere: Television and the News* (1973; reprint, New York: Vintage, 1974), 3–43; Gladys Engel Lang and Kurt Lang, *Politics and Television Re-viewed* (Beverly Hills, Calif.: Sage, 1984), 29–57.

16. Bultmann, *Jesus and the Word*, 20–22.

17. Johnson, *The Real Jesus*, 77.

18. Ibid., 143.

Chapter 17: Visions of Mary and the Less Than Visionary Press

1. For book-length treatments of the phenomenon, see Sandra Zimdars-Swartz, *Encountering Mary* (Princeton, N.J.: Princeton University Press, 1991); Mark Garvey, *Searching for Mary: An Exploration of Marian Apparitions across the U.S.* (New York: Plume, 1998); and Elliott Miller and Kenneth R. Samples , *The Cult of the Virgin: Catholic Mariology and the Apparitions of Mary* (1992; reprint, Grand Rapids, Mich.: Baker Book House, 1994).

2. Mike Harden, "Official Web List of Spiritual Visions Has Missed a Few," *Columbus Dispatch*, May 4, 1998, 1B.

3. James Anderson, "Virgin's Devotees Building Miracle," *Ottawa Citizen*, July 24, 1999, E10; Peter Smith, "Miraculous Growth: Vision of Virgin Has Turned Bosnian Shrine into Boomtown," Religion News Service article in *Arizona Republic*, February 27, 1999, D6; Nicole Veash, "Visions of Mary and Mammon," *London Independent*, July 16, 1998, 9; Richard Boudreaux, "Last Secret of Fatima Foretold Attack on Pope, Vatican Says," *Los Angeles Times*, May 14, 2000, A1.

4. The analysis included seventy-five stories found in a Nexis search for the keywords "Mary" and "Visions," in the general news section of major newspapers between April 1997 and May 2000.

5. Byron Crawford, "Many Hold Washington County Spot Sacred—Visitors to Virgin Mary Shrine Report 'All Kinds of Miracles,'" *Louisville Courier-Journal*, December 12, 1997, 1B.

6. Martin Merzer, "True Believers Still Flock to See Vision of Mary," Knight-Ridder story in *New Orleans Times-Picayune*, December 21, 1997, A36.

7. John Bacon, Traci Watson, and Richard Wolf, "Woman Tells of Vision of Mary to Georgia Crowd," *USA Today*, October 14, 1998, 3A.

8. Alfonso Chardy, "Family Reveals Religious Image," *Miami Herald*, May 28, 2000, 10A.

9. Sofka Zinovieff, "Visionaries Spread the Virgin's Cult," *Financial Times* (London), April 24, 1999, 24.

10. Journalists' commentary is seldom added to the stories in U.S. newspapers either unless it is in columns, and only there do journalists express skepticism. Among the 75 stories analyzed, only 4 were columns, 3 in U.S. newspapers. All three expressed strong skepticism about the Marian visions phenomena or ridiculed it in some form or another. Perhaps not surprisingly, given some non-American journalists' latitude in adding personal and historical perspective to their news reporting, the 12 news stories that included analysis, commentary, or sociological perspective were all in newspapers from England, Canada, and New Zealand; the only U.S. exceptions were an analysis of a Marian vision on a local highway sign in the *Seattle Times* and a Religion News Service article about the Bosnian site reported in the *Arizona Republic*. Smith, "Miraculous Growth"; Sally MacDonald, "Signs of Hope on Highway—Some Find Direction in Visions of Virgin," *Seattle Times*, April 11, 1997, A1.

11. When the Vatican puts its official approval on a Marian vision, the story tends to get much better play than stories that do not have Vatican approval. For example, note the front-page play the Vatican publication of the secret of Fatima received on May 14, 2000, in such august publications as the *Los Angeles Times*, the *New York Times*, the *London Telegraph*, and the *Montreal Gazette*.

12. Anyone who expects to see more in-depth coverage of Marian visions on local television might be disappointed. For example, a sighting of a Mary vision on a highway sign near Yakima, Washington, which received some coverage in the Seattle newspapers, also was mentioned on local TV news. However, note the minimal attention in the newscasts: KIRO-TV, April 6, 1997 (62 words); KOMO-TV, April 7, 1997 (33 words); KOMO TV, April 7, 1997 (20 words); KIRO TV, April 7, 1997 (35 words); KIRO TV, April 7, 1997 (29 words); KOMO TV, April 8, 1997 (15 words); KIRO TV, April 10, 1997 (18 words). Nexis search, keywords "Mary" and "Visions" in general news index.

13. The high-water point for the coverage of the resurgence of interest in Mary may have come with *Time* magazine's 1991 story that declared, "A grass-roots revival of faith in the Virgin is taking place wordwide. Millions of worshipers are flocking to her shrines, many of

them young people. . . . The late twentieth century has become the age of the Marian pilgrimage." Quoted in Miller and Samples, *The Cult of the Virgin,* 15 (quote), 115.

14. For a critical Protestant critique, see ibid., 11–12, 19–76, 126–35.

15. Mark Garvey described Mary's appeal this way: "In many ways she's easier to warm up to than her inscrutable son. And by virtue of her having once been one of us, she is generally thought to be more sympathetic, more understanding of human weakness and suffering. In the messages received by many modern-day visionaries, hers is the voice of tenderness." Garvey, *Searching for Mary,* 231–32.

16. Ibid., 232.

Chapter 18: *Proselytizing and Profits*

1. Quoted in David Neff, "Outsiders No More," *Christianity Today,* April 28, 1997, 22.

2. Ann Wroe, "The Fires of Faith," *Media Studies Journal,* Fall 1995, 50.

3. Dart and Allen, *A First Amendment Guide,* chap. 1:1 ("chasm" and "alien cultures" quotes); chap. 2:1 ("Red Sea" quote).

4. Quoted in ibid., chap. 4:5.

5. Quoted in ibid., chap. 4:19.

6. Quoted in ibid., chap. 4:23.

7. The search was conducted in the general news section of Nexis from January 2, 2000, to June 20, 2000, using the keywords "Christian" and "Conservative" (447 stories); "Christian" and "Liberal" (110 stories); "Christian Coalition" (221 stories); and "National Council of Churches" (143 stories). The search was conducted in June 2000. A similar search today would turn up slightly more stories in some categories and slightly fewer stories in others.

8. Of the stories that were identified in the general key word search, only regular news accounts and those articles in which the organization played a key role were selected. Fifty-two out of 142 Christian Coalition stories that fit the analytical framework contained negative commentary (such words as "fanatical," "extreme," or "devious"), while the rest were positive (with such favorable words as "principled" or "underappreciated") or neutral (with no positive or pejorative language or quotes).

9. Twelve out of 95 National Council of Churches stories that fit the analytical framework (see the previous note) contained negative commentary ("too liberal"), while the rest did not. It is difficult to find a liberal religious organization that parallels the Christian Coalition in its avowed intention to influence public policy. Another liberal group, People for the American Way, is not religiously affiliated, but it involves itself in religious controversies, such as the contest between the teaching of creationism, evolution, and prayer in public schools. In the period analyzed, People for the American Way was more positively treated in the press than was the Christian Coalition, although with far less coverage. Only two of 29 stories about the organization could be considered negative.

10. Much of the controversy surrounding the Christian Right during the period examined was generated by the attacks on Pat Robertson and Jerry Falwell by the Republican presidential aspirant John McCain, who called them "agents of intolerance" and complained of their "evil influence." Quoted in David Barstow, "The 2000 Campaign: The Arizona Senator; McCain in Further Attack, Calls Leaders of the Christian Right 'Evil,'" *New York Times,* March 1, 2000, A18.

11. The council's high political profile in this case (it funded the legal case of Elian Gonzales's family and relatives in Cuba) was somewhat rare and led to more news coverage for the

organization than usual—although critical stories in the mainstream media (which editorially supported, for the most part, the return of the boy to his relatives in Cuba) were minimal. Beyond that, most of the other controversial coverage of the council involved a financial crisis at the organization and its support of victims of American atrocities in the Korean War and protesters of a U.S. naval bombing site in Puerto Rico.

12. Eighteen out of 33 analytical pieces about the Christian Coalition were respectful but negative, meaning that the pieces took the Christian Coalition and its political agenda seriously but criticized the organization in balanced fashion for its loss of influence or its tactical errors. The nonrespectful stories, columns, or editorials contained sarcasm or ridicule. Positive stories (often by conservative columnists or editorials in more conservative publications) tended to stress that the Christian Coalition was misunderstood and underappreciated.

13. While the council's financial problems and its support of Elian Gonzales's relatives in Cuba drew most of the negative coverage, there were a number of positive profiles of the organization's leadership during the Elian Gonzales controversy, as well as a number of very glowing pieces about the organization's work in supporting efforts to help the poor and the homeless.

14. Some of the coverage of the National Council of Churches involved stories about denominations that maintained their membership even though they felt the council was too liberal and too active politically.

15. Quoted in Czitrom, *Media and the American Mind,* 188.

16. Quoted in David Paul Nord, "Systematic Benevolence: Religious Publishing and the Marketplace in Early Nineteenth-Century America," in *Communication and Change in American Religious History,* ed. Leonard I. Sweet (Grand Rapids, Mich.: Eerdmans, 1993), 246.

17. Quoted in Quentin J. Schultze, "Evangelicals' Uneasy Alliance with the Media," in *Religion and Mass Media,* ed. Stout and Buddenbaum, 69.

18. Quoted in ibid., 65–66.

19. Ibid., 70.

20. Jeffrey K. Hadden, "The Rise and Fall of American Televangelism," *Annals of the American Academy of Political and Social Science* 527 (May 1993): 125; Stewart Hoover and Douglas K. Wagner, "History and Policy in American Broadcast Treatment of Religion," *Media, Culture and Society* 19 (January 1997): 18–19.

21. Quoted in Hoover and Wagner, "History and Policy in Broadcast Treatment of Religion," 16.

22. Ibid., 17–19 (National Association of Broadcasters quotes on 18–19); Jack Kuney, "'Dat Ole' Time Religion': Broadcasting and the Pulpit," *Television Quarterly,* Winter 1994, 70.

23. Hadden, "The Rise and Fall of American Televangelism," 125.

24. Quoted in Dart and Allen, *A First Amendment Guide,* chap. 4:20.

25. Hadden, "The Rise and Fall of American Televangelism," 118; Andrew S. Buckser, "Sacred Airtime: American Church Structures and the Rise of Televangelism," *Human Organization* 48 (Winter 1989): 371.

26. Kuney, "'Dat Ole' Time Religion,'" 71–72; Buckser, "Sacred Airtime," 371.

27. Hoover and Wagner, "History and Policy in Broadcast Treatment of Religion," 10; Buckser, "Sacred Airtime," 371; Tim Stafford, "When Evangelicals Look in the Mirror, Do We See the Host of the 700 Club Staring Back?" *Christianity Today,* August 12, 1996, 30; Peter G. Horsfield, *Religious Television: The American Experience* (New York: Longman, 1984), 88–100.

28. Hadden, "The Rise and Fall of American Televangelism," 117.

29. Nord, "Systematic Benevolence," 240 ("frightening and exhilarating" and "marketplace" quotes), 241 ("fighting fire" quote).

30. Ibid., 243 ("foul and exciting," "satanic press," and "morally corrosive power" quotes), 244 ("intoxicating" quote), 247 ("devil works fast" quote).

31. John W. Kennedy, "Redeeming the Wasteland," *Christianity Today,* October 2, 1995, 92.

32. Steve Bruce, *Pray TV: Televangelism in America* (London: Routledge, 1990), 149–54 (definition and discussion of "health and wealth" gospel), 154 ("opportunity structure" and "Christian message flattered" quotes).

33. Fore, *Mythmakers,* 81. Robert Fortner extended this critique by asking why the Christian church community did not object when the federal government and the commercial broadcasters developed the commercial model of broadcasting in the 1930s instead of a public service model. Fortner contended this was because the churches, like much of the rest of the public, were caught up in the romance of broadcasting and the "giddiness' of their own involvement in what James Carey has called the "mythos" of technology. Fortner quoted William Hiram Foulkes, "There is something so uncanny and so far-reaching in the persuasiveness of the radio waves that to the Christian it might well become another Pentecost—a potential Pentecost at least," and Walter A. Maier, the *Lutheran Hour*'s first radio preacher, "God grant that this is only the beginning, that someday many other spires of steel may radiate Christ even as structurally they point to heaven." Robert S. Fortner, "The Church and the Debate over Radio/1919–1949," in *Media and Religion,* ed. Sloan, 233 (Carey quote), 234 ("giddiness" and "Pentecost" quotes), 235 ("radiate Christ" quote).

34. Quoted in Kennedy, "Redeeming the Wasteland," 93.

35. Hadden, "The Rise and Fall of Televangelism," 116–17.

Chapter 19: *Pluralism and the Press's Blind Spots*

1. Jack Sullivan, "Flight 990 Tragedy: Terror Suspects Abound if Sabotage Discovered," *Boston Herald,* November 1, 1999, 8.

2. Sixteen stories were found using "EgyptAir," "crash," and "terrorist" as keywords in Nexis, general news category, October 31, 1999, to November 30, 1999; 29 stories using "EgyptAir," "crash," and "terrorism"; and 46 stories using "EgyptAir," "crash," and "mechanical."

3. Seventy-two stories were found in Nexis, general news, between October 31, 1999, and November 30, 1999, using "EgyptAir," "crash," and "suicide" as keywords.

4. The study, which examined the content of seven Canadian daily newspapers for a year, said the coverage led to negative stereotypes and helped perpetuate hate crimes against Muslims. "Media Biased against Islam, Report Finds," *Toronto Star,* September 29, 1999.

5. Teresa Watanabe, "Dalai Lama: Humble Man Inspires Awe," *Los Angeles Times,* October 11, 1999, B1. Compare this headline to, for example, "'Death-Prayer' Label Hurtful to Muslims," *Toronto Star,* November 27, 1999.

6. Edward W. Said, *Covering Islam: How the Media and the Experts Determine How We See the Rest of the World* (1981; reprint, New York: Vintage, 1997), xi–xii. M. H. H. Adnan, another media scholar, listed additional reasons for biased coverage of Islam in the Western press: Muslim leadership of nationalist and anticolonial movements, the Arab-Israeli conflict, the energy crisis in the West, an overplaying of conflict and violence in the Middle East, and a misrepresentation of Muslim concepts, such as the role of women. M. H. H. Adnan, "Mass Media and Reporting Islamic Affairs," *Media Asia* 16 (1989): 63–70.

7. Neil A. Lewis and Philip Shenon, "The Crash of EgyptAir: The Overview: Egyptians See U.S. as Rushing to Find Reason for Crash," *New York Times,* November 18, 1999, A1.

8. Teresa Watanabe, "L.A. Muslims Consider Crash Accusations Inflammatory," *Los Angeles Times,* November 18, 1999, A24.

9. Muhammad I. Ayish and Haydar Badawi Sadig, "The Arab-Islamic Heritage in Communication Ethics," in *Communication Ethics and Universal Values*, ed. Christians and Traber, 121–23; Said Amir Arjomand, "Islam, Politics, and Iran in Particular," and Robert W. Hefner, "Profiles in Pluralism: Religion and Politics in Indonesia," in *Religion on the International News Agenda*, ed. Mark Silk (Hartford, Conn.: Greenberg Center, 2000), 60–101.

10. Said, *Covering Islam*, 10.

11. John Daniszewski, "Cultural Chasm in EgyptAir Inquiry," *Los Angeles Times*, November 22, 1999, A1.

12. William K. Piotrowski, "Tibet II: Monastic Spinmeister," *Religion in the News*, Fall 2000, 21–22.

13. Gans, *Deciding What's News*, 48–50; Jamake Highwater, *The Primal Mind: Vision and Reality in Indian America* (1981; reprint, New York: New American Library, 1982).

14. For discussions of the Western influence on news values by scholars of Islam, Hinduism, Buddhism, and African and Native American religions, see Christians and Traber, eds., *Communication Ethics and Universal Values;* and Silk, ed., *Religion on the International Agenda.* See also Anthony Smith, *The Geopolitics of Information: How Western Culture Dominates the World* (New York: Oxford University Press, 1981). A keyword search of Nexis shows how this phenomenon works in terms of the loaded adjectives and formulaic concepts that are most commonly applied to non-Christian religions by the Western media. For example, in a search of articles (mostly from American, Canadian, and British daily newspapers) in the Nexis news index for the last ten years (from May 1991 to May 2001), the word "intolerance" is most commonly linked with Islam (96 articles), followed by Hinduism (16), Christians (14), Buddhism (12), and cults (1). The term "mind control" is most commonly linked with cults (62 articles), Christians (9), Buddhism (1), and none for Islam and Hinduism. "Terrorism" is linked with Islam (over 1,000 articles), cults (33), Buddhism (21), Christians (14), and Hinduism (12). In contrast, in a search of Nexis articles going back ten years, the word "harmony" is linked with Buddhism (41), Christians (29), Islam (8), cults (2), and Hinduism (1); the word "Enlightenment" with Christians (179), Buddhism (137), cults (66), Islam (40), and Hinduism (10); and "Inner Peace" with Christians (26), Buddhism (18), cults (6), Islam (4), and none for Hinduism. This admittedly crude measurement does not even capture the full picture of how often world religions are presented in the Western press through the lens of commonly held preconceptions about what those religions represent. For example, a search of Nexis for the same ten-year period turns up 15 articles about Sufism, the mystical branch of Islam that has grown popular in the West, that contain such words as "beauty," "brotherhood," "unity," "tolerance," "selflessness," and "universalism," while only 1 article discusses the bitter dispute between certain Sufi leaders, who charge that elements of Islam are extremist and condone terrorism, and more traditional Muslim leaders, who contend the sect is cultic, corrupt, blasphemous, and idolatrous. Other measurements, such as the linkage of Buddhism with terrorism, are most often articles about Buddhist shrines and temples that have been the object of terrorism—meaning that Buddhism seldom shows up in the Western media except in the most positive terms.

15. In our nationwide survey of journalists' religious beliefs, reporters and editors responded more positively to the statement, "Journalistic values should draw upon the ethical and moral traditions of all great religions" (a mean of 3.28 on a scale where 1 = strongly disagree and 5 = strongly agree) than to the statement, "Christian values should underpin journalistic values" (a mean of 2.07).

16. Clifford Christians, "The Ethics of Being in a Communications Context," in *Communication Ethics and Universal Values*, ed. Christians and Traber, 12–15.

17. Quoted in "Murdoch's Comments Anger Tibetans," *Chicago Sun-Times*, September 7, 1999, 21. Murdoch's comments garnered this response from a Tibetan exile, who said Murdoch should stop making "moral judgments, particularly about someone like the Dalai Lama. He should stick to making money." Quoted in ibid.

Afterword

1. Some believe this may have happened with Microsoft's antitrust battles with the federal and state governments, but that remains to be seen.

2. In fairness to Gates, his image has improved in recent years, particularly as he and his wife have given generously to causes combating global and national problems of education, hunger, health, and social deprivation. In this sense, Gates is fulfilling the reform aspect of the journalistic personality (as well as the noblesse-oblige progressivism of wealthy media moguls of the past). However, as we have seen, this would not have impressed the muckrakers or other critics of America's media barons, who used ruthless business practices to amass their fortunes and then turned philanthropic in their later years.

3. Carol M. Ostrom, "A True Believer: Faith was Jennifer Casolo's Saving Grace," *Seattle Times*, January 16, 1990, A1.

Selected Bibliography

Agee, James. *A Death in the Family.* 1957. Reprint, New York: Bantam, 1969.

Ahlstrom, Sidney E. *A Religious History of the American People.* New Haven, Conn.: Yale University Press, 1972.

Aldridge, Alfred Owen. *Benjamin Franklin and Nature's God.* Durham, N.C.: Duke University Press, 1967.

Altschull, J. Herbert. *From Milton to McLuhan: The Ideas behind American Journalism.* New York: Longman, 1990.

Amacher, Richard E. *Benjamin Franklin.* New York: Twayne, 1962.

Amoia, Alba. *Albert Camus.* New York: Continuum, 1998.

Anderson, Jack, with James Boyd. *Confessions of a Muckraker: The Inside Story of Life in Washington during the Truman, Eisenhower, Kennedy, and Johnson Years.* New York: Ballantine, 1980.

Anton, Ted, and Rick McCourt, eds. *The New Science Journalists.* New York: Ballantine, 1995.

Argyris, Chris. *Behind the Front Page: Organizational Self-Renewal in a Metropolitan Newspaper.* San Francisco: Jossey-Bass, 1974.

Bagdikian, Ben H. *The Information Machines: Their Impact on Men and Media.* New York: Harper Colophon, 1971.

Baker, Carlos. *Ernest Hemingway: A Life Story.* New York: Scribner's, 1969.

Baker, Ray Stannard. *American Chronicle: The Autobiography of Ray Stannard Baker.* New York: Scribner's, 1945.

———. *The Spiritual Unrest.* New York: Frederick A. Stokes, 1910.

Barnouw, Erik. *Tube of Plenty: The Evolution of American Television.* Rev. ed. New York: Oxford University Press, 1982.

Barrett, William. *Irrational Man: A Study in Existential Philosophy.* 1958. Reprint, Garden City, N.Y.: Doubleday Anchor, 1962.

Bate, W. Jackson. *Samuel Johnson.* 1975. Reprint, New York: Harcourt Brace Jovanovich, 1979.

Becker, Carl L. *The Heavenly City of the Eighteenth-Century Philosophers.* 1932. Reprint, New Haven, Conn.: Yale University Press, 1966.

Bernstein, Carl, and Bob Woodward. *All the President's Men.* 1974. Reprint, New York: Touchstone, 1987.

Bernstein, Jeremy. *Einstein.* New York: Penguin, 1976.

Bogart, Leo. *Press and Public: Who Reads What, When, Where, and Why in American News-papers.* Hillsdale, N.J.: Erlbaum, 1981.

Boorstin, Daniel J. *Democracy and Its Discontents: Reflections on Everyday America.* New York: Random House, 1974.

Boswell, James. *The Life of Samuel Johnson.* Edited by Frank Brady. 1791. Reprint, New York: Signet, 1968.

Bradlee, Ben. *A Good Life: Newspapering and Other Adventures.* New York: Simon and Schuster, 1995.

Brady, Kathleen. *Ida Tarbell: Portrait of a Muckraker.* New York: Seaview/Putman, 1984.

Braithwaite, William C. *The Beginnings of Quakerism to 1660.* 1912. Reprint, York, England: William Sessions, 1981.

Brasher, Thomas L. *Whitman as Editor of the Brooklyn Daily Eagle.* Detroit: Wayne State University Press, 1970.

Brent, Peter. *Charles Darwin.* New York: Harper and Row, 1981.

Brock, Peter. *Pioneers of the Peaceable Kingdom.* 1968. Reprint, Princeton, N.J.: Princeton University Press, 1970.

Brodie, Fawn M. *Richard Nixon: The Shaping of His Character.* New York: Norton, 1981.

Brodwin, Stanley, and Michael D'Innocenzo, eds. *William Cullen Bryant and His America: Centennial Conference Proceedings, 1878–1978.* New York: AMS, 1983.

Brome, Vincent. *Jung.* London: Macmillan, 1978.

Brown, Charles H. *William Cullen Bryant.* New York: Scribner's, 1971.

Brown, Les. *Television: The Business behind the Box.* New York: Harvest, 1971.

Bruce, Steve. *Pray TV: Televangelism in America.* London: Routledge, 1990.

Buddenbaum, Judith. *Reporting News about Religion: An Introduction for Journalists.* Ames: Iowa State University Press, 1998.

Bultmann, Rudolf. *Jesus and the Word.* 1934. Reprint, New York: Scribner's, 1958.

Burgard, Stephen. *Hallowed Ground: Rediscovering Our Spiritual Roots.* New York: Insight, 1997.

Butler, Jon. *Awash in a Sea of Faith: Christianizing the American People.* Cambridge, Mass.: Harvard University Press, 1990.

Cady, Edwin H. *The Road to Realism: The Early Years, 1837–1885, of William Dean Howells.* Syracuse, N.Y.: Syracuse University Press, 1956.

Callow, Philip. *Walt Whitman: From Noon to Starry Night.* London: Allison and Busby, 1992.

Camus, Albert. *The Plague.* Translated by Stuart Gilbert. 1948. Reprint, New York: Vintage, 1991.

———. *The Stranger.* Translated by Stuart Gilbert. New York: Vintage, 1942.

Capek, Milic. *The Philosophical Impact of Contemporary Physics.* Princeton, N.J.: D. Van Nostrand, 1961.

Carey, James W. *Communication as Culture: Essays on Media and Society.* Boston: Unwin Hyman, 1989.

Carter, Stephen. *The Culture of Disbelief: How American Law and Politics Trivialize Religious Devotion.* New York: Anchor, 1994.

Cather, Willa. *Death Comes for the Archbishop.* 1927. Reprint, New York: Vintage, 1971.

———. *O Pioneers!* 1913. Reprint, New York: Signet, 1989.

Chapin, Chester F. *The Religious Thought of Samuel Johnson.* Ann Arbor: University of Michigan Press, 1968.

Christians, Clifford G., and Catherine L. Covert. *Teaching Ethics in Journalism Education.* Hastings-on-Hudson, N.Y.: Hastings Center, 1980.

Christians, Clifford G., John P. Ferré, and P. Mark Fackler. *Good News: Social Ethics and the Press.* New York: Oxford University Press, 1993.

Christians, Clifford, and Michael Traber, eds. *Communication Ethics and Universal Values.* Thousand Oaks, Calif.: Sage, 1997.

Christianson, Gale E. *In the Presence of the Creator: Isaac Newton and His Times.* New York: Free Press, 1984.

Clark, Ronald W. *The Survival of Charles Darwin: A Biography of a Man and an Idea.* New York: Random House, 1984.

Cobb, Jennifer J. *Cybergrace: The Search for God in the Digital World.* New York: Crown, 1998.

Costigan, Giovanni. *Sigmund Freud: A Short Biography.* New York: Macmillan, 1965.

Creighton, Donald. *Harold Adams Innis: Portrait of a Scholar.* Toronto: University of Toronto Press, 1957.

Crowder, Richard. *Carl Sandburg.* New York: Twayne, 1964.

Crowley, David, and Paul Heyer, eds. *Communication in History: Technology, Culture, Society.* 1991. Reprint, White Plains, N.Y.: Longman, 1995.

Czitrom, Daniel J. *Media and the American Mind: From Morse to McLuhan.* 1982. Reprint, Chapel Hill: University of North Carolina Press, 1983.

Dart, John, and Jimmy Allen. *A First Amendment Guide to Religion and the News Media.* New York: Freedom Forum First Amendment Center, 1993.

Davies, Paul. *About Time: Einstein's Unfinished Revolution.* London: Penguin, 1995.

Desmond, Adrian, and James Moore. *Darwin.* New York: Warner, 1991.

Dicken-Garcia, Hazel. *Journalistic Standards in Nineteenth-Century America.* Madison: University of Wisconsin Press, 1989.

Downie, Leonard, Jr. *The New Muckrakers.* New York: Mentor, 1976.

Dreiser, Theodore. *A Book about Myself.* New York: Boni and Liveright, 1922.

———. *The Bulwark.* New York: Doubleday, 1946.

———. *Sister Carrie.* 1900. Reprint, New York: Signet, 1961.

Dunne, Finley Peter. *Observations by Mr. Dooley.* New York: Harper, 1906.

Durnell, Hazel. *The America of Carl Sandburg.* Washington, D.C.: University Press of Washington, D.C., 1965.

Einstein, Albert. *The Quotable Einstein.* Compiled and edited by Alice Calaprice. Princeton, N.J.: Princeton University Press, 1996.

Eisenstein, Elizabeth L. *The Printing Revolution in Early Modern Europe.* 1983. Reprint, Cambridge: Cambridge University Press, 1992.

Epstein, Edward Jay. *News from Nowhere: Television and the News.* 1973. Reprint, New York: Vintage, 1974.

Ettema, James S., and Theodore L. Glasser. *Custodians of Conscience: Investigative Reporting and Public Virtue.* New York: Columbia University Press, 1998.

Fast, Howard. *Citizen Tom Paine.* 1943. Reprint, New York: Bantam, 1964.

Fauvel, John, Raymond Flood, Michael Shortland, and Robin Wilson, eds. *Let Newton Be!* Oxford: Oxford University Press, 1988.

Fishkin, Shelley Fisher. *From Fact to Fiction: Journalism and Imaginative Writing in America.* Baltimore: Johns Hopkins University Press, 1985.

Fore, William F. *Mythmakers: Gospel, Culture, and the Media.* New York: Friendship, 1980.

Fox, George. *Journal of George Fox.* Edited by John L. Nickalls. London: Religious Society of Friends, 1986.

———. *The Works of George Fox.* Edited by T. H. S. Wallace. 1831. Reprint, State College, Pa.: New Foundation Publications, 1990.

Freud, Sigmund. *Civilization and Its Discontents.* Translated and edited by James Strachey. New York: Norton, 1961.

———. *The Future of an Illusion.* Translated and edited by James Strachey. 1961. Reprint, New York: Norton, 1989.

Friedman, Sharon, Sharon Dunwoody, and Carol L. Rogers, eds. *Scientists and Journalists: Reporting Science as News.* New York: Free Press, 1986.

Funk, Robert W., Roy W. Hoover, and the Jesus Seminar. *The Five Gospels: The Search for the Authentic Words of Jesus.* New York: Macmillan, 1993.

Gallup, George, Jr., and Jim Castelli. *The People's Religion: American Faith in the 90's.* New York: Macmillan, 1989.

Gallup, George, Jr., and D. Michael Lindsay. *Surveying the Religious Landscape: Trends in U.S. Beliefs.* Harrisburg, Pa.: Morehouse, 1999.

Gans, Herbert J. *Deciding What's News: A Study of CBS Evening News, NBC Nightly News, Newsweek, and Time.* New York: Vintage, 1980.

Garvey, Mark. *Searching for Mary: An Exploration of Marian Apparitions across the U.S.* New York: Plume, 1998.

Gates, Bill, with Nathan Myhrvold and Peter Rinearson. *The Road Ahead.* 1995. Reprint, New York, Penguin, 1996.

Gaustad, Edwin S. *Sworn on the Altar of God: A Religious Biography of Thomas Jefferson.* Grand Rapids, Mich.: Eerdmans, 1996.

Gay, Peter. *Freud: A Life for Our Times.* New York: Norton, 1988.

Geismar, Maxwell, ed. *Mark Twain and the Three R's: Race, Religion, Revolution—and Related Matters.* New York: Bobbs-Merrill, 1973.

Gillispie, Charles Coulston. *The Edge of Objectivity: An Essay in the History of Scientific Ideas.* 1960. Reprint, Princeton, N.J.: Princeton University Press, 1990.

Glasser, Theodore, ed. *The Idea of Public Journalism.* New York: Guilford, 1999.

Glendinning, Victoria. *Jonathan Swift.* London: Hutchinson, 1998.

Goethals, Gregor T. *The TV Ritual: Worship at the Video Altar.* Boston: Beacon, 1981.

Goldstein, Tom. *The News at Any Cost: How Journalists Compromise Their Ethics to Shape the News.* 1985. Reprint, New York: Touchstone, 1986.

Gordon, W. Terrence. *Marshall McLuhan: Escape into Understanding.* New York: Basic, 1997.

Graber, Doris, Denis McQuail, and Pippa Norris, eds. *The Politics of News/The News of Politics.* Washington, D.C.: Congressional Quarterly Press, 1998.

Graham, Katharine. *Personal History.* New York: Knopf, 1997.

Greeley, Horace. *Recollections of a Busy Life.* New York: J. B. Ford, 1869.

Green, Robert W., ed. *Protestantism and Capitalism: The Weber Thesis and Its Critics.* 1959. Reprint, Boston: Heath, 1965.

Greene, Graham. *The End of the Affair.* 1951. Reprint, New York: Penguin, 1977.

———. *The Heart of the Matter.* 1948. Reprint, New York: Viking, 1963.

———. *The Power and the Glory.* 1940. Reprint, New York: Bantam, 1954.

Grossman, Lawrence K. *The Electronic Republic: Reshaping American Democracy in the Information Age.* New York: Viking, 1995.

Gwyn, Douglas. *Apocalypse of the Word: The Life and Message of George Fox, 1624–1691.* 1986. Reprint, Richmond, Ind.: Friends United, 1991.

Haas, Joseph, and Gene Lovitz. *Carl Sandburg: A Pictorial Biography.* New York: Putnam's, 1967.

Habermas, Jürgen. *The Structural Transformation of the Public Sphere.* Translated by Thomas Burger, with the assistance of Frederick Lawrence. 1989. Reprint, Cambridge, Mass.: MIT Press, 1999.

Hall, A. Rupert. *Isaac Newton: Adventurer in Thought.* Oxford: Blackwell, 1992.

Hamm, Thomas D. *The Transformation of American Quakerism: Orthodox Friends, 1800–1907.* 1988. Reprint, Bloomington: Indiana University Press, 1992.

Harris, Leon. *Upton Sinclair: American Rebel.* New York: Crowell, 1975.

Hawke, David Freeman. *Franklin.* New York: Harper and Row, 1976.

Hawking, Stephen W. *A Brief History of Time: From the Big Bang to Black Holes.* 1988. Reprint, New York: Bantam, 1990.

Hemingway, Ernest. *For Whom the Bell Tolls.* New York: Scribner's, 1940.

———. *The Old Man and the Sea.* New York: Scribner's, 1952.

———. *The Sun Also Rises.* 1926. Reprint, New York: Collier, 1986.

Henderson, Charles P., Jr. *The Nixon Theology.* New York: Harper and Row, 1972.

Highfield, Roger, and Paul Carter. *The Private Lives of Albert Einstein.* New York: St. Martin's, 1993.

Highwater, Jamake. *The Primal Mind: Vision and Reality in Indian America.* 1981. Reprint, New York: New American Library, 1982.

Himmelfarb, Gertrude. *Darwin and the Darwinian Revolution.* New York: Norton, 1968.

Hofstadter, Richard. *The Age of Reform: From Bryan to F.D.R.* New York: Vintage, 1955.

The Holy Bible, New Revised Standard Version. Iowa Falls, Iowa: World Bible Publishers, 1989.

Hoover, Stewart M. *Religion in the News: Faith and Journalism in American Public Discourse.* Thousand Oaks, Calif.: Sage, 1998.

Hordern, William E. *A Layman's Guide to Protestant Theology.* 1955. Reprint, New York: Collier, 1986.

Horsfield, Peter G. *Religious Television: The American Experience.* New York: Longman, 1984.

Howells, William Dean. *The Rise of Silas Lapham.* 1885. Reprint, New York: Penguin, 1986.

Hubbard, Benjamin J., ed. *Reporting Religion: Facts and Faith.* Sonoma, Calif.: Polebridge, 1990.

Ingle, H. Larry. *First among Friends: George Fox and the Creation of Quakerism.* New York: Oxford University Press, 1994.

———. *Quakers in Conflict: The Hicksite Reformation.* Knoxville: University of Tennessee Press, 1986.

Innis, Harold. *The Bias of Communications.* 1951. Reprint, Toronto: University of Toronto Press, 1991.

———. *Empire and Communications.* 1950. Reprint, Toronto: University of Toronto Press, 1972.

Irwin, Will. *The American Newspaper.* Edited by Clifford F. Weigle and David G. Clark. Ames: Iowa State University Press, 1969.

———. *The Making of a Reporter.* New York: Putnam's, 1942.

James, William. *Essays in Pragmatism.* Edited by Alburey Castell. 1948. Reprint, New York: Hafner, 1966.

———. *The Varieties of Religious Experience: A Study in Human Nature.* Edited by Martin E. Marty. 1902. Reprint, New York: Penguin, 1987.

Jamison, Kay Redfield. *Touched with Fire: Manic-Depressive Illness and the Artistic Tempera-ment.* New York: Free Press, 1994.

Jeffares, A. Norman, ed. *Fair Liberty Was All His Cry: A Tercentenary Tribute to Jonathan Swift, 1667–1745.* London: Macmillan, 1967.

Johnson, Luke Timothy. *The Real Jesus: The Misguided Quest for the Historical Jesus and the Truth of the Traditional Gospels.* San Francisco: Harper Collins, 1996.

Jones, Rufus M. *The Later Periods of Quakerism.* 2 vols. 1921. Reprint, Westport, Conn.: Green-wood, 1970.

Kaplan, Justin. *Lincoln Steffens: A Biography.* New York: Simon and Schuster, 1974.

———. *Mr. Clemens and Mark Twain: A Biography.* New York: Simon and Schuster, 1966.

———. *Walt Whitman: A Life.* New York: Simon and Schuster, 1980.

Lambeth, Edmund B. *Committed Journalism: An Ethic for the Profession.* Bloomington: Indi-ana University Press, 1986.

Lang, Gladys Engel, and Kurt Lang. *Politics and Television Re-viewed.* Beverly Hills, Calif.: Sage, 1984.

Langford, Gerald. *The Richard Harding Davis Years: A Biography of a Mother and Son.* New York: Holt, Rinehart and Winston, 1961.

Larson, Edward. *Summer for the Gods: The Scopes Trial and America's Continuing Debate over Science and Religion.* New York: Basic Books, 1997.

Levinson, Henry Samuel. *The Religious Investigations of William James.* Chapel Hill: Univer-sity of North Carolina Press, 1981.

Lewis, R. W. B. *The Jameses: A Family Narrative.* 1991. Reprint, New York: Anchor, 1993.

Lichter, S. Robert, Linda S. Lichter, and David R. Amundson, *Media Coverage of Religion in America, 1969–1998.* Washington, D.C.: Center for Media and Public Affairs, 2000.

Lichter, S. Robert, Stanley Rothman, and Linda S. Lichter. *The Media Elite: America's New Powerbrokers.* Bethesda, Md.: Adler and Adler, 1986.

Lippmann, Walter. *A Preface to Morals.* New York: Macmillan, 1929.

———. *Public Opinion.* 1922. Reprint, New York: Free Press, 1965.

Lule, Jack. *Daily News, Eternal Stories: The Mythological Role of Journalism.* New York: Guil-ford, 2001.

Lyon, Peter. *Success Story: The Life and Times of S. S. McClure.* New York: Scribner's, 1963.

Mack, Burton L. *Who Wrote the New Testament? The Making of the Christian Myth.* San Fran-cisco: Harper Collins, 1995.

Mander, Jerry. *Four Arguments for the Elimination of Television.* New York: Quill, 1978.

Manuel, Frank E. *A Portrait of Isaac Newton.* Cambridge, Mass.: Harvard University Press, 1968.

———. *The Religion of Isaac Newton.* Oxford: Oxford University Press, 1974.

Marvin, Carolyn. *When Old Technologies Were New.* New York: Oxford University Press, 1988.

Marzolf, Marion Tuttle. *Civilizing Voices: American Press Criticism, 1880–1950.* New York: Longman, 1991.

Matthews, Fred H. *Quest for an American Sociology: Robert E. Park and the Chicago School.* Montreal: McGill-Queen's University Press, 1977.

McLoughlin, William G., and Robert N. Bellah, eds. *Religion in America.* Boston: Houghton Mifflin, 1968.

McLuhan, Marshall. *The Gutenberg Galaxy: The Making of Typographic Man.* 1962. Reprint, New York: Signet, 1969.

————. *Understanding Media: The Extensions of Man.* New York: Mentor, 1964.

McLuhan, Marshall, and Bruce R. Powers. *The Global Village: Transformations in World Life and Media in the Twenty-First Century.* 1989. Reprint, New York: Oxford University Press, 1992.

McManus, John H. *Market-Driven Journalism: Let the Citizen Beware?* Thousand Oaks, Calif.: Sage, 1994.

McQuade, Donald, Robert Atwan, Martha Banta, Justin Kaplan, David Minter, Cecelia Tichi, and Helen Vendler, eds. *The Harper American Literature.* New York: Harper and Row, 1987.

Mencken, H. L. *A Mencken Chrestomathy.* 1949. Reprint, New York: Vintage, 1982.

Merrill, John C. *Existential Journalism.* Ames: Iowa State University Press, 1996.

Merritt, Davis. *Public Journalism and Public Life: Why Telling the News Is Not Enough.* Hillsdale, N.J.: Erlbaum, 1995.

Meyrowitz, Joshua. *No Sense of Place: The Impact of Electronic Media on Social Behavior.* 1985. Reprint, New York: Oxford University Press, 1986.

Michelmore, Peter. *Einstein, Profile of the Man.* New York: Dodd, Mead, 1962.

Miller, Elliott, and Kenneth R. Samples. *The Cult of the Virgin: Catholic Mariology and the Apparitions of Mary.* 1992. Reprint, Grand Rapids, Mich.: Baker Book House, 1994.

Milton, John. *Areopagitica.* 1644. Reprint, Santa Barbara, Calif.: Bandanna, 1992.

More, Louis Trenchard. *Isaac Newton: A Biography.* New York: Scribner's, 1934.

Moreau, Geneviève. *The Restless Journey of James Agee.* New York: Morrow, 1977.

Morris, Randall C. *Process Philosophy and Political Ideology: The Social and Political Thought of Alfred North Whitehead and Charles Hartshorne.* Albany: State University of New York Press, 1991.

Morris, Roger. *Richard Milhous Nixon: The Rise of an American Politician.* New York: Henry Holt, 1990.

Mossner, Ernest Campbell. *The Life of David Hume.* 1954. Reprint, Oxford: Oxford University Press, 1980.

Mott, Frank Luther. *American Journalism: A History of Newspapers in the United States through 260 Years, 1690 to 1950.* New York: Macmillan, 1950.

Myers, Gerald E. *William James: His Life and Thought.* New Haven, Conn.: Yale University Press, 1986.

Neuharth, Al. *Confessions of an S.O.B.* New York: Doubleday, 1989.

Newman, Jay. *The Journalist in Plato's Cave.* London: Associated University Presses, 1989.

Niehaus, Richard John. *The Naked Public Square.* Grand Rapids, Mich.: Eerdmans, 1984.

Nixon, Richard. *In the Arena: A Memoir of Victory, Defeat, and Renewal.* New York: Simon and Schuster, 1990.

————. *RN: The Memoirs of Richard Nixon.* New York: Grosset and Dunlap, 1978.

O'Connor, Richard. *Bret Harte: A Biography.* Boston: Little, Brown, 1966.

O'Flaherty, Kathleen. *Voltaire: Myth and Reality.* Cork, Ireland: Cork University Press, 1945.

Olasky, Marvin. *Prodigal Press: The Anti-Christian Bias of the American News Media.* Wheaton, Ill.: Crossway Books, 1988.

Ong, Walter J. *The Presence of the Word: Some Prolegomena for Cultural and Religious History.* 1967. Reprint, Minneapolis: University of Minnesota Press, 1986.

Otten, Robert M. *Joseph Addison.* Boston: Twayne, 1982.

Pagels, Elaine. *The Gnostic Gospels.* New York: Vintage, 1981.

Pais, Abraham. *Einstein Lived Here.* New York: Oxford University Press, 1994.

———. *Niels Bohr's Times: In Physics, Philosophy, and Polity.* Oxford: Oxford University Press, 1991.

Palermo, Patrick F. *Lincoln Steffens.* Boston: Twayne, 1978.

Perkins, George, Barbara Perkins, and Phillip Leininger, eds. *Benét's Reader's Encyclopedia of American Literature.* New York: HarperCollins, 1987.

Peters, John Durham. *Speaking into the Air: A History of the Idea of Communication.* Chicago: University of Chicago Press, 1999.

Pilat, Oliver. *Drew Pearson: An Unauthorized Biography.* New York: Harper's Magazine Press, 1973.

Polkinghorne, John. *The Faith of a Physicist: Reflections of a Bottom-Up Thinker.* 1994. Reprint, Minneapolis: Fortress, 1996.

Pollard, John A. *John Greenleaf Whittier: Friend of Man.* 1949. Reprint, [Hamden, Conn.]: Archon, 1969.

Prichard, Peter. *The Making of McPaper: The Inside Story of USA Today.* Kansas City, Mo.: Andrews, McMeel, and Parker, 1987.

Punshon, John. *Portrait in Grey: A Short History of the Quakers.* 1984. Reprint, London: Quaker Home Service, 1991.

Quandt, Jean B. *From the Small Town to the Great Community: The Social Thought of Progressive Intellectuals.* New Brunswick, N.J.: Rutgers University Press, 1970.

Raushenbush, Winifred. *Robert E. Park: Biography of a Sociologist.* Durham, N.C.: Duke University Press, 1979.

Reeves, Richard. *What the People Know: Freedom and the Press.* Cambridge, Mass.: Harvard University Press, 1998.

Reichley, A. James. *Religion in American Public Life.* Washington, D.C.: Brookings Institution, 1985.

Reston, James, Jr. *Galileo: A Life.* New York: HarperCollins, 1994.

Reynolds, Michael. *The Young Hemingway.* Oxford, England: Blackwell, 1986.

Rieff, Philip. *Freud: The Mind of the Moralist.* New York: Viking, 1959.

Robinson, James M., ed. *The Nag Hammadi Library in English.* 3d rev. ed. San Francisco: Harper and Row, 1988.

Rockefeller, Steven C. *John Dewey: Religious Faith and Democratic Humanism.* New York: Columbia University Press, 1991.

Rogers, Everett M. *A History of Communications Study: A Biographical Approach.* New York: Free Press, 1997.

Rosen, Jay. *Getting the Connections Right.* New York: Twentieth Century Fund, 1996.

———. *What Are Journalists For?* New Haven, Conn.: Yale University Press, 1999.

Roszak, Theodore. *The Cult of Information: The Folklore of Computers and the True Art of Thinking.* New York: Pantheon, 1986.

Rousseau, Jean Jacques. *Jean Jacques Rousseau: His Educational Theories Selected from Émile, Julie and Other Writings.* Edited by R. L. Archer. Woodbury, N.Y.: Barron's Educational Series, 1964.

Russell, Bertrand. *The ABC of Relativity.* 1925. Reprint, New York: Mentor, 1969.

Said, Edward W. *Covering Islam: How the Media and the Experts Determine How We See the Rest of the World.* 1981. Reprint, New York: Vintage, 1997.

Schudson, Michael. *Discovering the News: A Social History of American Newspapers.* New York: Basic, 1978.

Schweitzer, Albert. *The Quest of the Historical Jesus.* Translated by W. Montgomery. 1910. Reprint, New York: Macmillan, 1950.

Scripps, E. W. *I Protest: Selected Disquisitions of E. W. Scripps.* Edited by Oliver Knight. Madison: University of Wisconsin Press, 1966.

Seitz, Don C. *The James Gordon Bennetts, Father and Son: Proprietors of the New York Herald.* Indianapolis: Bobbs-Merrill, 1928.

Seldes, George. *Lords of the Press.* New York: Julian Messner, 1938.

Sharman, Cecil W. *George Fox and the Quakers.* London: Quaker Home Service, 1991.

Shelden, Michael. *Graham Greene: The Man Within.* London: Heinemann, 1994.

Shepherd, Gregory J., and Eric W. Rothenbuhler, eds. *Communication and Community.* Mahwah, N.J.: Erlbaum, 2001.

Silk, Mark. *Unsecular Media: Making News of Religion in America.* Urbana: University of Illinois Press, 1995.

———, ed. *Religion on the International News Agenda.* Hartford, Conn.: Greenberg Center, 2000.

Sinclair, Andrew. *Jack: A Biography of Jack London.* 1977. Reprint, New York: Pocket, 1979.

Sinclair, Upton. *The Autobiography of Upton Sinclair.* New York: Harcourt, Brace and World, 1962.

———. *The Profits of Religion: An Essay in Economic Interpretation.* New York: Vanguard, 1918.

Sloan, William David, ed., *Media and Religion in American History.* Northport, Ala.: Vision, 2000.

Smith, Anthony. *The Geopolitics of Information: How Western Culture Dominates the World.* New York: Oxford University Press, 1981.

Smithers, Peter. *The Life of Joseph Addison.* 1954. Reprint, Oxford: Oxford University Press, 1968.

Stallman, R. W. *Stephen Crane: A Biography.* New York: Braziller, 1968.

Stamm, Keith R. *Newspaper Use and Community Ties: Toward a Dynamic Theory.* Norwood, N.J.: Ablex, 1985.

Stead, William T. *If Christ Came to Chicago.* Chicago: Laird and Lee, 1894.

Steel, Ronald. *Walter Lippmann and the American Century.* Boston: Little, Brown, 1980.

Steffens, Lincoln. *The Autobiography of Lincoln Steffens.* New York: Harcourt, Brace, 1931.

———. *Moses in Red.* Philadelphia: Dorrance, 1926.

Stephens, Mitchell. *A History of News: From the Drum to the Satellite.* New York: Viking, 1988.

Stoddard, Henry Luther. *Horace Greeley: Printer, Editor, Crusader.* New York: Putnam's, 1946.

Storr, Anthony. *Solitude: A Return to the Self.* New York: Ballantine, 1988.

Stout, Daniel A., and Judith Buddenbaum, eds. *Religion and Mass Media: Audiences and Adaptations.* Thousand Oaks, Calif.: Sage, 1996.

Strauss, David Friedrich. *The Life of Jesus Critically Examined.* Translated by George Eliot. 1835. Reprint, London: Swan Sonnenschein, 1906.

Swanberg, W. A. *Citizen Hearst.* 1961. Reprint, New York: Macmillan, 1986.

———. *Dreiser.* New York: Scribner's, 1965.

———. *Pulitzer.* New York: Scribner's, 1967.

Sweet, Leonard I., ed. *Communication and Change in American Religious History.* Grand Rapids, Mich.: Eerdmans, 1993.

Tarbell, Ida M. *All in the Day's Work: An Autobiography.* 1939. Reprint, Boston: G. K. Hall, 1985.

Tawney, R. H. *Religion and the Rise of Capitalism.* 1926. Reprint, New York: Mentor, 1954.

Tebbel, John, and Sarah Miles Watts. *The Press and the Presidency: From George Washington to Ronald Reagan.* New York: Oxford University Press, 1985.

Teilhard de Chardin, Pierre. *The Phenomenon of Man.* Translated by Bernard Wall. 1959. Reprint, New York: Harper, 1965.

Thompson, John B. *The Media and Modernity: A Social Theory of the Media.* Stanford, Calif.: Stanford University Press, 1995.

Thoreau, Henry David. *Walden and Civil Disobedience.* Edited by Owen Thomas. 1854. Reprint. New York: Norton, 1966.

Thrall, William F., Addison Hibbard, and C. Hugh Holman. *A Handbook to Literature.* 1936. Reprint, New York: Odyssey, 1960.

Thurber, James. *Vintage Thurber: A Collection in Two Volumes of the Best Writings and Drawings of James Thurber.* London: Hamish Hamilton, 1963.

Tocqueville, Alexis de. *Democracy in America.* 2 vols. Translated by Henry Reeve. 1840. Reprint, New York: Knopf, 1960.

Tomkins, Mary E. *Ida M. Tarbell.* New York: Twayne, 1974.

Tracy, David. *Dialogue with the Other: The Inter-Religious Dialogue.* Grand Rapids, Mich.: Eerdmans, 1990.

Trend, David. *Cultural Democracy: Politics, Media, New Technology.* Albany: State University of New York Press, 1997.

Twain, Mark. *The Adventures of Huckleberry Finn.* 1884–85. Reprint, New York: Laurel, 1971.

———. *Letters from the Earth.* Edited by Bernard DeVoto. 1962. Reprint, New York: Perennial, 1974.

———. *The Mysterious Stranger.* 1916. Reprint, Berkeley: University of California Press, 1982.

———. *The Unabridged Mark Twain.* 2 vols. Edited by Lawrence Teacher. Philadelphia: Running, 1979.

Underwood, Doug. *When MBAs Rule the Newsroom: How the Marketers and Managers Are Reshaping Today's Media.* New York: Columbia University Press, 1993.

Van Deusen, Glyndon G. *Horace Greeley: Nineteenth-Century Crusader.* Philadelphia: University of Pennsylvania Press, 1953.

Wagenknecht, Edward. *John Greenleaf Whittier: A Portrait in Paradox.* New York: Oxford University Press, 1967.

Walker, Franklin. *Frank Norris: A Biography.* 1932. Reprint, New York: Russell and Russell, 1963.

Wallace, James. *Overdrive: Bill Gates and the Race to Control Cyberspace.* New York: Wiley, 1997.

Wehr, Gerhard. *Jung: A Biography.* Boston: Shambhala, 1987.

West, Jessamyn, ed. *The Quaker Reader.* 1962. Reprint, Wallingford, Pa.: Pendle Hill, 1992.

West, Richard. *Daniel Defoe: The Life and Strange, Surprising Adventures.* 1998. Reprint, New York: Carroll and Graf, 2000.

White, William Allen. *The Autobiography of William Allen White.* Lawrence: University Press of Kansas, 1990.

Whitman, Walt. *Leaves of Grass.* 1892. Reprint, New York: Bantam, 1990.

Willey, Basil. *The Seventeenth Century Background: Studies in the Thought of the Age in Relation to Poetry and Religion.* 1935. Reprint, New York: Doubleday Anchor, 1953.

Wills, Garry. *Under God: Religion and American Politics.* New York: Simon and Schuster, 1990.

Wilson, Gay Allen. *William James: A Biography.* New York: Viking, 1967.

Winton, Calhoun. *Sir Richard Steele, M.P.: The Later Career.* Baltimore: Johns Hopkins University Press, 1970.

Woodress, James. *Willa Cather: A Literary Life.* 1987. Reprint, Lincoln: University of Nebraska Press, 1989.

Woodward, W. E. *Tom Paine: America's Godfather, 1737–1809*. New York: Dutton, 1945.

Wordsworth, William. *The Prelude: Selected Poems and Sonnets*. Edited by Carlos Baker. 1800. Reprint, New York: Holt, Rinehart and Winston, 1966.

Wyrick, Deborah Baker. *Jonathan Swift and the Vested Word*. Chapel Hill: University of North Carolina Press, 1988.

Zimdars-Swartz, Sandra. *Encountering Mary*. Princeton, N.J.: Princeton University Press, 1991.

Index

DOUG UNDERWOOD is an associate professor of communication at the University of Washington in Seattle and the author of *When MBAs Rule the Newsroom*. A former political and legislative reporter for the *Seattle Times* and a congressional correspondent for the Gannett News Service, he has written for media reviews and academic publications on such topics as journalism ethics, journalism economics, the role of technology in the newsroom, and the influence of profit pressures on journalists. He began researching the relationship between journalism and religion while on leave at the Earlham School of Religion, a Quaker seminary in Indiana.

The History of Communication

The University of Illinois Press
is a founding member of the
Association of American University Presses.

Composed in 10.5/12.5 Minion
with Fenice Bold display
by Jim Proefrock
at the University of Illinois Press
Manufactured by Thomson-Shore, Inc.

University of Illinois Press
1325 South Oak Street
Champaign, IL 61820-6903
www.press.uillinois.edu